A Crooked River

A Crooked River

Rustlers, Rangers, and Regulars on the Lower Rio Grande, 1861–1877

Michael L. Collins

University of Oklahoma Press : Norman

This book is published with the generous assistance of the Kerr Foundation, Inc.

Library of Congress Cataloging-in-Publication Data

Names: Collins, Michael L., 1950– author.
Title: A crooked river : rustlers, rangers, and regulars on the lower Rio Grande, 1861–1877 / Michael L. Collins.
Description: Norman : University of Oklahoma Press, 2018. | Includes bibliographical references and index.
Identifiers: LCCN 2017041392 | ISBN 978-0-8061-6008-5 (hardcover : alk. paper)
Subjects: LCSH: Lower Rio Grande Valley (Tex.)—History—19th century. | Texas—History—Civil War, 1861–1865. | Reconstruction (U.S. history, 1865–1877)—Texas. | Frontier and pioneer life—Texas, South. | Frontier and pioneer life—Texas—Lower Rio Grande Valley. | Culture conflict—Texas— Lower Rio Grande Valley—History—19th century. | Texas, South— Relations—Mexico. | Mexico—Relations—Texas, South.
Classification: LCC F392.R5 C649 2018 | DDC 976.4/05—dc23
LC record available at https://lccn.loc.gov/2017041392

For Adrian, Lincoln, and Gwen

The crookedness of the Rio Grande cannot be exaggerated. It is extremely muddy, the banks low, and utterly without interest. . . . Passing up this stream the question arises: For what are we here? For such a country as this why expend such blood and treasure?

Helen Chapman, 1848

Contents

Illustrations

Figures

Maps

Acknowledgments

Without the abiding support of many individuals, this study would not have been possible. First, I am especially grateful for the able assistance and guidance of numerous professionals who always kept me on the right trail. A special note of thanks is due to Donaly Brice, now retired, and the rest of the staff of the Texas State Library and Archives. Donaly's wealth of knowledge regarding the maze of manuscript collections in the state archives in Austin, his willingness to share his time, his thoughts, and his love for the Lone Star State were critically important in identifying so many primary sources that formed the body of this work. He has truly been a selfless trailblazer for so many serious researchers who have combed through the official records of the state of Texas.

To Patrick Cox, formerly associate director of the Dolph Briscoe Center for American History at the University of Texas in Austin, I owe a tremendous debt for his encouragement, his counsel, and his faith in this project. I am also most thankful for the help offered by the staff at the Briscoe Center. Without these dedicated men and women, who were always there to lead me toward and then through the treasure trove buried in finding aids and files, I might still be there sifting through endless stacks of materials.

Any serious scholar needs a home base for their research. In my case, for many years it was the Moffett Library at Midwestern State University in Wichita Falls, Texas. I am greatly appreciative of the able assistance of Dr. Clara Latham and her dedicated staff. Always collegial and eager to help, they all demonstrated extraordinary patience in navigating me through the bold but sometimes bewildering new world of the internet and online digital resources. I would also like to acknowledge my longtime colleague Harry Hewitt for always being there, sharing his vast knowledge of the history of the U.S.-Mexico border, and especially for his willingness to translate letters and documents written in Spanish that provided a more balanced perspective than I otherwise might have had. For Carol Zuber-Mallison, I am especially thankful for her time and talent in creating the historical maps that enhance the reader's understanding and, I hope, enjoyment of the following narrative. To my late mentor and friend, Professor Ben H. Procter, goes all the credit for teaching me most everything I learned about practicing the craft of history.

Last, to my loving wife, Carol, who was nothing less than my full partner in this project, I am forever indebted. Her unfailing support, her kind understanding, and her sustaining patience through it all were nothing less than an inspiration for me.

A Crooked River

Introduction

The southern tip of Texas points to Mexico like a dagger. Flat, dry, mostly treeless, the sandy plain cuts 150 miles and more below the Nueces River, slicing across a semiarid prairie choked with gnarled mesquite, knotted shrubs, and clumps of creosote and chaparral. Thickets of thorny brush are so entangled and intertwined that a man on horseback—or even an entire herd of cattle—could disappear for days at a time. Little separates heaven and earth in this country besides barbed wire fences and stunted vegetation. Except for an occasional windmill, hardly anything rises higher than the head of a horse. On a typical day, the sun blazes overhead, knifing through scattered clouds that drift in from the Gulf of Mexico. Nothing else defines the blue sky that stretches from one horizon to the other. At night, the pale glow of the moon and the infinity of stars flicker above, distant reminders that the grasslands of South Texas seem so isolated. The drought-scarred land of the lower Rio Grande is so remote, so far away from the heavens, so far from everything—except a jagged border with Mexico.

It has often been said that civilization began along the banks of great rivers. In the case of the Lone Star State, however, it should be said that civilization—at least by Texas standards—devolved into savagery along a crooked river that flows between two North American nations. Even before the U.S.-Mexican War (1846–48) the Rio Grande represented the front lines of a larger racial and cultural war destined to leave a bitter legacy for future generations. For Anglos and Tejanos alike, that legacy lives on. After the signing of the Treaty of Guadalupe Hidalgo in 1848, which formally recognized the Rio Grande as the international border, it was as if some of the worst elements of the United States drained into southernmost Texas while some of the most dangerous criminals in Mexico crept up from northern border states and splashed across the Rio Grande into what Texans have long misnamed "the Valley." And that ongoing conflict—including the campaigns of Anglo-Texans who, despite their allegiance to the Confederacy, still styled themselves "Rangers"—only intensified during the turbulent years of the American Civil War.

The contours of history, like the currents of a meandering river, move along a winding path toward an uncertain future. But through the course of time and human events one force seems almost certain, at least as much as anything can be certain. Each generation inherits the burdens of the past—for better and for worse—and each leaves a bequest to the future. The truth is timeless, much like a shifting river. As if being carried on rapids that began at some distant source in the headwaters of history, every generation navigates and explores, seeking a better path that will lead beyond the tributaries of its tribal beginnings toward an uncharted, though hopefully better, place.

Conflict is a constant of history. One can even argue that the experience of peoples and nations is the story of ongoing wars interrupted only by sporadic periods of peace. If that standard is applied, the lower Rio Grande during the mid-nineteenth century offers a classic case in point. Tragically, the legacy of the Rio Grande Valley is one of cultural and racial conflict. More specifically, it is the chronicle of clashing claims to this storied land so rich in resources. None of those competing claims to the wealth of the region remains rife with greater controversy than the epic saga of the range cattle industry, which had its primitive beginnings in the brush country of northern Mexico and South Texas. Central also to the divisive debate stands the iconic institution of the Texas Rangers, or "Los Rinches" as people of Mexican heritage often called mounted troops and later law enforcement officers of the Lone Star State.

And through the center of that story courses a crooked river, a current of slow-moving waters that, through time, has shifted in course, forming an international boundary that remains a troubled border. That river symbolizes all that separates—and all that connects—two peoples and two nations. Never a fixed boundary, never a border that simply divides the lawful from the lawless, or the good from the bad, the Rio Grande remains today a shifting line not merely on a map but also in the mind and the imagination.

Following the American Civil War the tinderbox of violence that was the borderlands of South Texas erupted as the continuing conflict along the Rio Grande again set one race and nationality against the other. Confederate deserters, refugees from Reconstruction, desperadoes of every shade and description who had learned little in life but the bloody business of war now mixed with Mexican *bandidos* and *insurrectos* (or Juaristas) fleeing the rebellion against Maximilian, the French-imposed emperor of Mexico. From their enclaves along both banks of the Rio Grande, bandits raided with impunity, robbing and killing before disappearing into their sanctuaries of chaparral and mesquite thickets. Few on either side of the border or the racial divide were spared the consequences. After all, cruelty and barbarism recognize no boundary, whether racial or geographic.

After 1865 another squall of the violence swept across the lower Rio Grande. Border banditry, and specifically cattle rustling, reached epidemic proportions. The contagion of cattle theft and lawlessness concerned both Texas state authorities and federal officials so much that in 1872 President Ulysses S. Grant appointed a three-member commission, headed by Thomas P. Robb of Georgia, to tour the river frontier. Grant instructed the commissioners to investigate the troubles and then to report their findings and recommendations to the commander in chief and Congress. Returning to Washington in January 1873, the Robb Commission published a formal report cataloging the crimes of Mexican bandits and rustlers, most allegedly directed by the old jefe and longtime nemesis of the Texas Rangers, Juan Nepomuceno Cortina. In sum, the American commissioners blamed the disorder on the negligence and complicity of Mexican officials, and of course on the so-called Red Robber of the Rio Grande, General Juan Cortina (even though it was a myth perpetuated by Texans that he sported a red beard).[1]

Not to be outdone, the Federal Republic of Mexico answered with its own version of events: La Comision Pesquisadora de la Frontera del Norte, or the Commission of Investigation of the Northern Frontier. Predictably, this inquest countered, alleging that the troubles along the border were attributed to the insolence of ambitious gringo filibusters, thieving Anglo stockmen, and landgrabbers aided by leaders in Texas and Washington, D.C.[2]

By the spring of 1875, Texas governor Richard Coke believed the situation so dire that he dispatched state adjutant general William Steele and state senator Joseph E. Dwyer into the border region to gather evidence of ongoing crimes and atrocities. The report of Dwyer and Steele blamed much of the recent lawlessness on Texan volunteer militia and vigilantes who were engaged in "private killing." The inspectors confirmed that the Texans' frustrations and fierce determination to punish those who plundered their rangelands spurred them to administer frontier "justice" at the end of a rope, and to do so in the name of "the law." Notably, the official report to Governor Coke claimed that most of the victims of vigilante violence were Tejanos, or Texans of Mexican heritage, farming and ranching on the Texas side of the Rio Grande.[3]

Almost in desperation, Governor Coke then ordered Ranger Captain Leander H. McNelly's Special Force of Washington County volunteers south of the Nueces River. More like a motley lot of farm boys and east-ern "dandies" than a company of law enforcement officers, these Rangers wore no uniforms, no insignia, no evidence of rank. And to a man, they reflected their captain's grim determination to rid the region of rustlers and thieves—no matter by what means. The story of the subsequent cam-paign by McNelly's Rangers has been told and retold, with historians from Walter Prescott Webb to Chuck Parsons and Marianne Hall Little con-tending that McNelly's Rangers' operations all but succeeded in ending cattle rustling on the river frontier, at least in the short term. Moreover, these historians and others have argued that Cortina himself was largely responsible for the contagion of cattle rustling and murder, and that local magistrates in northern Mexico were likewise just as culpable.[4]

In fact, the historical record supports the argument that the border wars of the 1860s and 1870s were but another chapter in the ongoing racial and cultural conflict for supremacy over the Rio Grande Valley. Moreover, these wars neither began with the rise of Cortina in 1859 nor ended in 1877 with his forced removal from the frontier by the newly ascended president of Mexico, Porfirio Díaz. The evidence likewise reinforces that McNelly's campaign in the Nueces Strip and lower Rio Grande may have succeeded in terrifying Mexicans and Tejanos but failed to bring cattle rustling to an end, as many of the captain's admirers would like to believe. Simply put, historical evidence, some of it unavailable to Professor Webb eight decades ago, reveals a more complex mosaic of events than previ-ously presented.

Early in 1963, just seven weeks before he died in a single-car accident on Interstate Highway 35 south of Austin, Webb admitted that his classic 1935 study *The Texas Rangers: A Century of Frontier Defense* remained in need of revision. In response to a letter from South Texas resident Enrique Mendiola, who expressed skepticism about the historian's objectivity in treating the Mexican side of the story, Webb confessed that his vantage point and views had changed over the decades. He conceded, "I under-stand that you, or any citizen of Mexican descent, would be impatient of my account." Then Webb shared that along the nineteenth-century bor-der cattle theft had always been the stock and trade of Anglos and Latinos alike. "If the Kings and Kenedys and Armstrongs did not put their brands on other people's stock, they . . . [were] the only cow people of that age who failed to do so. These Texans even stole from one another," Webb admitted. "The unfortunate fact is that the Mexicans were not as good at keeping records as were the people on this side."[5]

Such a stunning admission from one of the most celebrated scholars Texas has ever produced might have shocked many Anglo-Texans. But the confession would not have surprised anyone of Mexican heritage—past or present—living on either side of the Rio Grande. Their *corridos*, or border ballads, still speak of the day when danger was a constant companion and death was as common as dirt in the brush country of South Texas. The haunting lyrics of these ballads still echo lamentations of a lawless land and of a time not that long ago when livestock was stolen with impunity and lives cut short in a barbaric conflict called the "Skinning Wars."[6]

As for the role of the Texas Rangers in these events, people of Mexican heritage unsurprisingly recount a different version of events than their Anglo counterparts. Understandably, while Anglo-Texans exhibit great pride in the Ranger tradition, going even so far as to depict the storied frontier fighters as incapable of wrongdoing, Tejanos remember Los Rinches (the phonetic pronunciation of "Rangers" in Spanish) as mounted demons to be feared, men who terrorized people of Mexican heritage while riding through their history like the dreaded horsemen of the apocalypse. They termed them Los Diablos Tejanos, or "Texas Devils"—and for good reason.

Perhaps no Tejano ever stated it more forcefully than Texas state senator Joe Bernal of San Antonio. In 1967 he boldly charged that the world-famous Texas Rangers were "the Mexican Americans' Ku Klux Klan. All they need is a white hood with *Rinches* written across it." Using the derisive term for Rangers, or any Anglo law enforcement authority, Bernal thus echoed the cry that leaders of the Lone Star State, and notably their enforcers on the borderlands, had long treated those of Mexican descent as subjects, not citizens. To understand such an indictment, Anglo-Texans and Tejanos alike must begin by viewing—with honesty and objectivity—the prism of events that transpired along the lower Rio Grande in the mid-nineteenth century. For the mutual mistrust and antipathy long held by Anglo-Texans and people of Mexican heritage alike remain deeply rooted in the turbulent years that followed the signing of the Treaty of Guadalupe Hidalgo in 1848.[7]

To argue that the war with Mexico ended with the settlement of 1848 would be to ignore the full weight of historical evidence. With that in mind, the following narrative is intended to serve as a companion to the author's earlier study *Texas Devils: Rangers and Regulars on the Lower Rio Grande, 1846–1861*. Together, these two volumes may provide a reappraisal of events for those who search for greater understanding and perhaps even a reconciliation with the past—no matter how uncomfortable the truth.

In his seminal study of the Texas Rangers, Webb sought to uncover the truth as he saw it. In so doing, he admitted that he began weaving together an account of the storied frontier institution that was held together by the only common "thread of unity" he could find—that of the "great leaders, the captains," as he described the likes of John Coffee "Jack" Hays, Ben McCulloch, John Salmon "Rip" Ford, Leander H. McNelly, John B. Jones, and later lawmen like Bill McDonald and Frank Hamer who followed in the "Ranger tradition." It is true that, as with any military, paramilitary, or law enforcement organization, the Rangers were always as good—and only as good—as their leaders. But to view the history of the Texas Rangers only from the top down is to fail to see the full picture of their deeds and, sometimes, misdeeds.[8]

Professor Webb only came to acknowledge that fact near the end of his life. In 1962 he mused to a younger colleague about practicing the craft of history. "This is more than just a job of work," he confided, "and we shouldn't hang a 'Men at Work' detour sign on it." In other words, no topics or controversies are off-limits, and no subject is the exclusive territory of any investigator or group of scholars. No stop signs, no caution signs, no red lights or barricades should impede the high road to historical truth. That includes the road of discovery leading to the much-revered Texas Rangers, whose legend in the Lone Star State rivals that of the martyrs of the Alamo. Near the end of his days, Webb offered a bit of wisdom and professional advice to those who would follow his trail. "Historians are supposed to *reflect* on the past . . . [not merely] record it."[9]

"Reflection" was what Webb did, and what he taught his students to do. Webb understood that each generation should revisit and reconsider the past in the light of its own experiences. During his last years, Webb grew to realize that other scholars would someday follow his tracks and that they would surely scout the historical landscape, scour the record, and discover new and different evidence—evidence either unavailable to him or that he had overlooked, neglected, or even ignored. He also knew that in so doing future historians would inevitably arrive at conclusions different from those that he had reached.

If only Webb had reflected more on the fact that the Texas Rangers of the nineteenth century bore little if any resemblance to the elite modern law enforcement agency that served Texas in his own day and continues to serve the public today. Maybe then his fellow Texans—and other Americans—would better understand that a balanced and honest presentation of the Rangers' role in the border wars of the nineteenth century does not amount to heresy or sacrilege. It is simply history as it happened, not history as it should have been.

Before following the trail of Webb's pioneering work, therefore, the investigator should first acknowledge that the historical definition of Texas Ranger has been blurred by fiction writers, Hollywood filmmakers, and the popular folktales of Texans who have every reason to be proud of their rich and colorful history. Popular myths aside, before the modern era the Ranger was less a professional lawman than a citizen soldier, a volunteer mustered into the state militia by officers appointed under the authority of either the governor of Texas or the state adjutant general. More than a few of these young recruits had themselves been on the "wrong side" of the law. Many were running from a past they wanted to leave behind.

As for one of Webb's principal protagonists, Ranger Captain Leander H. McNelly, succeeding generations of scholars have continued to lionize the laconic Texas lawman as a bona fide "badass" who administered gunpowder "justice" in taming the borderlands of South Texas. While grudgingly acknowledging that McNelly's methods—which included the torture and execution of prisoners—were "terribly brutal and cruel," they insist that he and his Rangers were "nevertheless effective" in suppressing cattle rustling and banditry. In blunter terms, it was a violent time and place, and extraordinary measures were understandable and, by inference, even warranted. The ends justified the means, or so these scholars imply.[10]

While tracking down the truth about Captain McNelly and the facts surrounding his campaign against cattle rustlers and border bandits, Professor Webb traveled in the autumn of 1930 to the actual scene of the events that had transpired over five decades earlier. He had toured the border in 1924 and was now returning to follow the trail of McNelly's Rangers. Driving a Model T Ford down the bumpy back roads crossing the scrubby plains of the Rio Grande Valley, he was accompanied by a promising young historian and protégé named J. Evetts Haley, who had just published his sweeping history of the XIT Ranch, the great cattle kingdom that sprawled across most of the Texas Panhandle. Together they traversed the lower Rio Grande country, searching for eyewitnesses who could shed light on the storied Rangers and their legendary captain who had dared to cross into Mexico in November 1875, presumably just to recover a herd of stolen Texas cattle. They first interviewed two aging veterans of McNelly's Rangers, George Durham and William Callicott. Both had grown old and gray, but they still had stories to tell, plenty of them. Driving through the brush country that had given birth to the United States' range cattle industry, from the Santa Gertrudis headquarters of the King Ranch to Port Isabel, they made their way to Brownsville. There they met up with Webb's friend Harbert Davenport, a local attorney and civic leader who reportedly knew as much border history as any man alive, at least on the Texas side of the river. Early the next morning the three men drove out to the Palo Alto Prairie, then steered farther up the Texas side to Rio Grande City, then to Los Ebanos where they crossed by ferry into Mexico to Camargo.[11]

The entire experience was like traveling back in time. "Here we ran a gauntlet of . . . Mexican customs and immigration men," Webb recalled. As soon as they set foot on Mexican soil, a "young and officious immigration officer" approached them. As Webb related, the official seemed to be in a "bad humor" and "was at no pains to conceal that fact." Puffing on his cigarette, the young customs agent looked over the three gringos and then asked in English, "Where are you going?" "To Las Cuevas," Webb offered. "How long will you be over there?" the officer pressed. "Three or four hours," Webb estimated.[12]

At that awkward moment, Davenport intervened. Like a persuasive lawyer arguing a difficult case, he explained that he had to attend to some legal business at Las Cuevas and that he was representing a Mexican client who held a disputed land claim in Texas and wanted to regain his rightful legal title. At that point the young Mexican official stared across the river and at last nodded his approval—but not before warning the three Texans that the ferry closed at 4:30 P.M., and it was noon already.

Driving some twenty miles along a sandy road that seemed as rough as an old washboard, Webb and company wound their way to the town of San Miguel, once known as the Rancho Las Cuevas. The simple, rustic ranching community looked much like it had in 1875. Lining the dusty streets were a few stone houses, but most dwellings were mere hovels of wood, wattle work, and baked clay—*jacales*, as they are called. A cluster of horse and cattle corrals still stood in the clearings outside town. Not far beyond the rail fences, a rambling adobe house sat alone. In almost any other place it would have been considered a humble home, but in San Miguel the modest structure dominated the village.[13]

So did the family that lived there. "We found the town full of blue-eyed Mexicans," Webb remembered, "apparently most of them named Flores." They were all descendants of the late Juan Flores Salinas, the much-revered ranchero who had founded the settlement. Even those families of different names were somehow related, by blood or by loyalty. After meeting with Davenport's friend and client, a Señor Longoria, the party of Texans walked the short distance to a monument that rose fifteen feet above the dusty town street. Made of baked brick and crowned by a cross, the memorial bore an inscription in Spanish. Loosely translated into English, the epitaph read, "To Citizen Juan Flores Salinas who died fighting for his country on November 19, 1875." Juan Flores—the same person whose name Webb recognized from official Texas documents as the leader of the ring of cattle thieves that once ran the largest rustling operation on the lower Rio Grande—was still much respected here, a local hero of the first order.

Next Longoria led Webb and his party to an adobe dwelling just outside the village where they found the subject of their search. Leonardo Flores had been only a boy when Captain McNelly led the raid on Las Cuevas. Longoria explained that Leonardo had survived the Rangers' attack. But Webb was warned that the wizened and wrinkled old man might be reluctant to talk about it—at least to tell his story to a gringo. At first, when asked about McNelly's raid on the compound all those years ago, the aging vaquero raised his hand, waving it in refusal. Finally, he asked, "Is it the truth you want?" Webb immediately answered, "Yes." "Ah," the old Mexican offered, nodding his head and gesturing that he would tell all he remembered, and what he had learned from his elders. It was so long ago, he began.[14]

Webb and the others listened intently as the aging vaquero recounted the events. He told Webb how a company of mounted Texans—"Los Rinches," he called them—had crossed the river and attacked the ranch that morning without any warning or apparent provocation. There were many women and children there. He was among them. Admitting that he ran for his life as soon as he heard the roar of gunfire, old Leonardo spoke of the terror of seeing friends and family gunned down by the strangers with long guns and six-shooters. The bloodshed, the bullets flying, and later the burials were all ingrained in his memory. His skin may have been cracked and weather beaten like old leather, his face and hands hardened by years of working under the sun, but his mind remained clear, his recollections remarkably vivid.

But "the story he told did not tally with the one told by McNelly," Webb recorded. The details were faded, but the fear that the old man expressed seemed as real as if the Rangers' raid had happened only yesterday. Admiringly, old Leonardo spoke of his people's bravery in the face of the equally fearless Texas Rangers, of their great sacrifice in defense of their families and their homes. Hearing Leonardo's account of Captain McNelly's legendary raid on Las Cuevas and of the death of Juan Flores, who was revered on the Mexican bank but reviled on the Texas side of the border, Webb could only muse, "A man's character may be the same on both sides of the Rio Grande, but his reputations bear little resemblance to each other."[15]

It was a most valuable lesson that Webb should have learned from old Leonardo: on the other side of the river there was another side of the story. And that story also needed and deserved to be told. The following narrative of events was undertaken and written in that spirit—not for the sake of political correctness but for the sake of historical accuracy. Relying mostly on personal memoirs, previously unmined manuscript collections, and government documents in repositories in Austin, Texas, Washington, D.C., and elsewhere, this record of events is intended to shed new light on the border troubles along the lower Rio Grande between 1861 and 1877. In so doing, this study proposes some new perspectives, among them a corrective lens for the Texas Rangers' role in that struggle, and that of the U.S. military.

Even today, people of the Rio Grande Valley live in the long shadow of the U.S.-Mexican War and the continuing strife that defined the border-lands of South Texas. In a sense, they remain captives of that struggle and the bitter legacy it left behind. What follows here is an attempt to provide historical context for the conflict on the lower Texas-Mexico border. This study, therefore, is largely the story that Walter Prescott Webb never told.

Prologue
Thieves of Bagdad

The sleepy blue waters of the Laguna Madre are typically calm and peaceful. Splashed with a brilliant sun on most days, illumined at night by a pale moonlight, the inland saltwater channel is a sanctuary from the constant winds and churning surf that lash the Gulf side of South Padre Island. Protected from the weathering forces of an uncertain sea, the intercoastal waterway, with its secluded coves and hidden estuaries, is shielded by the beaches of that elongated sandbar known as South Padre. Below its southern tip a smaller island stretches out, providing a windswept refuge for seagulls and sand cranes. As the name suggests, Brazos Santiago reaches out from South Bay like the arms of a saint, welcoming seafaring men from many nations to the mouth of the Rio Grande. Just below this sprawling desolate island, Boca Chica Bay, barely two miles long, forms a narrow inlet that suits its Spanish name (in English, "little mouth"). By all appearances, it is a peaceful enclave overlooking the ocean.

For generations, this yawning entrance to the Rio Grande has welcomed mariners from distant ports of call. Ahead in the channel and two miles to the northwest of Brazos Island rises the historic lighthouse at Port Isabel, a landmark known to sailors the world over. Its beacon symbolizes the meeting place of the Rio Grande and the Gulf of Mexico. The landmark also represents the nexus of two North American nations. The solitude of a surrounding tropical setting belies the fact that, for a brief but bloody time during the American Civil War, this serene bay was the confluence of *three* North American nations and the meeting place of more than half a dozen major European countries, some at war with one another, all in competition for the coveted riches of the region. And these rivals no longer measured the wealth of the bountiful land by treasures of silver and gold but by marketable commodities such as cotton and other cash crops, then by cattle grazing on the open ranges.

Today the serenity of such a scene belies the fact that in another time, a time not that long ago, the border along the lower Rio Grande was something less than a peaceful paradise. It was a time when the pride and innocence of Texan youth inspired the cruel illusion of a bloodless struggle for Southern independence, a time when Mexican insurrectionists were fighting to rid their homeland of foreign imperialism, a desperate time when the Gulf Plains of South Texas became a strategic focal point of a titanic struggle to determine the future and fate of three nations. To understand the squall of violence and lawlessness that swept over the Rio Grande delta region during the turbulent decade that followed the American Civil War, it is first important to view the war years as an important tributary in time connecting the border's violent past to the tumultuous events of the postwar Reconstruction era. Almost as significant, it is necessary to recognize that the so-called Ranger tradition in Texas did not vanish during the war years, as Walter Prescott Webb implied by his omission of the period, but merely took on a different appearance, that of the gray cloth of the Confederate States of America.

The makeup of Texan military forces along the border with Mexico changed little after the opening months of 1861, but the strategic significance of the lower Rio Grande grew greatly during the next four years. Still a volatile and violent frontier, a border bristling with bandits, bad men, renegades, and cattle rustlers, the Rio Grande Valley remained a breeding ground for some of the worst elements in the Lone Star State as well as northern Mexico. All things considered, it is little wonder that between 1861 and 1865 the region assumed even greater importance as a strategic military objective. From the outset of the American Civil War, the Lincoln administration established a grand strategy to blockade the entire length of the Confederate coastline, from the waters of the Chesapeake to the mouth of the Rio Grande. To achieve this goal, Union gunboats, schooners, sloops, and ships of the line regularly patrolled the entrances to all major ports, U.S. naval vessels hovering near the coastline of every Confederate port from Virginia to Texas. While the first of these ships did not appear off the coast of South Texas until months after the stunning news of the fall of Fort Sumter, officials in Texas nevertheless justly feared that trade along the Gulf Coast—commerce so vitally important to the survival of the fledgling Confederacy—might soon be choked off. For the people of the Rio Grande delta, the stakes were thus raised with the outbreak of the war as control of the great river became a military objective of the highest strategic importance to the Confederacy, to the United States, and to a troubled Mexico.

Despite the early difficulties that an ill-prepared U.S. Navy experienced in implementing the blockade, Texan leaders readied themselves for the worst. So did merchants engaged in the profitable cotton trade that was the lifeblood of the newly born Confederacy. While New Orleans, Galveston, and Indianola first came under the aim of Federal gunboats, an increasing number of wagons laden with cotton rumbled overland and funneled southward into the Rio Grande Valley, the freight caravans making their way to Brownsville and across river by ferry to the markets of Matamoros or by steamboat to Bagdad. From there, these stores could be sold then hauled hundreds of miles to the south by teamsters to the Mexican coast for shipment overseas.[1]

So critically important was this thriving commerce in cotton that by the autumn of 1861 all roads leading to the border became crowded with long lines of mule- or ox-drawn wagons from as far away as Louisiana and Mississippi. Indeed, it was as if the mouth of the Rio Grande suddenly became the only conduit for commerce within a thousand miles. Teamster John Warren Hunter remembered that "a never ending stream of cotton" clogged the streets of Brownsville even before the Union quarantine took effect. With mule trains carrying immense shipments of the precious commerce, Brownsville soon became, in his words, "the greatest shipping point in the South." Just across the river, the population of Matamoros more than doubled during the first year of the American Civil War. The sprawling warehouses of the Mexican border town quickly filled with bales of cotton, which were typically stacked to the ceilings of every storage facility in the city. No wonder the people of the border long remembered this period as Los Algodones—the "time of cotton."[2]

British blockade runner William Watson of the schooner *Rob Roy* recalled that, as the wartime quarantine produced a "cotton famine" in England and all across Europe, a "mania" overtook speculators who were willing to pay any price and accept any risk to profit from the trade. If the cotton business had been lucrative before the war, it now promised unimaginable riches for those who could brave the blockade and deliver the goods to European markets. The equation was simple. The Confederate economy rested largely upon the sale of cotton to overseas manufacturers. At the same time, the success of the entire Confederate war effort depended heavily upon the exchange of cotton for arms and military stores. On the other side of the Atlantic, a cotton-starved Europe awaited every shipment that could navigate around the Union blockade. The textile factories of England and the looms of France would stand idle unless the all-important contraband could be transported through the dense timbers of East Texas and across the coastal plains of South Texas, then loaded onto ships at the mouth of the Rio Grande to be smuggled through the Gulf of Mexico, into the Caribbean, and across the Atlantic.[3]

Not surprisingly, merchant ships of many nations collected near the mouth of the Rio Bravo where they dropped anchor below Brazos Santiago, on the leeward side of the island. There each vessel unloaded manufactured articles on skiffs before filling their cargo holds with bales of cotton to be sold in Havana and other foreign ports. Because only light draft riverboats could negotiate the shallow waters of the Rio Grande, few of these vessels could navigate upriver to the docks at Matamoros. Necessity, and the inducements of a lucrative trade, thus dictated that a new place of commercial deposit and exchange would grow near the mouth of the great river. The site of the settlement would be a mere mile downcoast from Brazos Island and strategically located on the Mexican side of the river. Peculiarly enough, the port would be called Bagdad.[4]

"From what cause it got its name," Watson recorded, "I do not know, unless from the likeness to a port on a river flowing through a sandy desert." At first only a small and squalid village, then a thriving sprawl of ramshackle shanties, clapboard shacks, thatched *palapas*, and tents, the upstart settlement looked more like a modern-day Sodom and Gomorrah than a major hub of commerce. Protected from the surf of the Gulf, ships—literally dozens at a time—anchored in the inlet below Bagdad. Both sailing vessels and modern steamers crowded together near the beaches, the tangle of masts and canvas sails mixing with metal smokestacks to create an odd but grandiose spectacle. On the sandy banks of the river, hundreds of dockworkers could be seen on any day loading and unloading cargoes, the bales of cotton piling up and stretching almost as far as the eye could see. Nearby, the brawling village of Bagdad, called by one contemporary a "miserable" place, spread out along the desolate beach, its many businesses offering every imaginable form of entertainment and profession, from the oldest to the newest. Barrooms, brothels, and gambling dens were the most plentiful. In the narrow paths and alleys that separated the drab huts, an unwashed mass milled about amid a stream of peddlers and paupers. The human scenery included the most seamy and sordid elements on this barbaric frontier. Drifters, deserters, saddle tramps, desperadoes of every type and description, depraved men, most with a loathsome past, they were the dregs of the border. All of them mingled with the horde of extortion artists, highwaymen, thieves, and land pirates who had descended upon the region. Sailors, surly and adventuresome men of the sea, unrepentant rogues and ruffians who were the refuse of many nations, they were an assorted human spectacle, truly a combustible mixture of remorseless characters. And then there were the unmentionables, the prostitutes or "soiled doves," who came by the score to relieve the rogues of their wages. Even children, called "street Arabs" by one contemporary, prowled the back alleys of Bagdad, the sad-faced little beggars looking to pick the pocket of any unsuspecting stranger or to steal his horse and belongings.[5]

As the bustling port of Bagdad (also called Boca del Rio) rose from the beaches, it was apparent that the bawdy shantytown would serve as the principal commercial outlet for the people of South Texas, and even as the backdoor for the entire beleaguered Confederacy. Clippers, cutters, and tall ships of all descriptions began to sail into Brazos Pass in the fall of 1861, anchoring at Bagdad alongside steamers and barges that moved downriver from Matamoros.[6]

With the arrival of these vessels came cool autumn breezes, winds that blew in from the Gulf of Mexico, reminding everyone of the changing of the seasons. Before long, however, chilling gales from the North would forewarn the people of the Valley not only of winter's impending siege but also of the ever-present threat of a Union invasion.

The Hanging of Captain Montgomery

For people on both sides of the river the danger posed by an imminent Union invasion seemed so far away compared to the threats closer to home. The growing lawlessness that had characterized the lower Rio Grande during the antebellum years only intensified with the coming of the American Civil War. By the opening months of 1862, cattle rustling and horse theft, already commonplace along both sides of the border, had become the livelihood of many a marauding band. After all, during what Mexicans termed the "Confederate War," entire droves of drifting cattle and roaming herds of mustangs had been abandoned on the South Texas plains. At the same time, bandits infested the brush country of the Nueces Strip, gunmen prowling seemingly at every turn, lurking and waiting to fall upon any unsuspecting traveler with a fine horse, a full purse, or a wagon loaded with cotton. Worse yet, attempting to apprehend these criminal elements, local law enforcement officials were soon forced to rely upon Confederate Partisan Rangers who were as apt to apply their own standards of justice with six-shooters, rifle carbines, or twelve feet of rope. Summary executions on the prairies thus became the accepted norm, and almost no one dared to question the disappearance of any accused desperado who allegedly deserved to die. As English adventurer Robert Williams stated the case, "It was the rule to take a man's life, if any kind of pretext could be found for so doing. I never heard of anything like it, except perhaps in the French revolution." In sum, during the war years "Judge Lynch" ruled this river frontier.[7]

This terrifying reality soon became apparent to Union officials seeking to recruit men in arms on the Mexican side of the river. While Octaviano Zapata's Union-inspired marauders continued their raids into Texas, wreaking havoc with Confederate supply trains and disrupting commerce along the river, agents of Colonel Edmund Jackson Davis worked feverishly to recruit expatriate Texans, Unionists who had fled the noose and now sought the safety of Mexican soil. With the aid of U.S. consul Leonard Pierce in Matamoros, Colonel Davis (a former South Texas judge) enlisted Union sympathizers, despite the threat of Colonel James Duff's Confederate partisans who vowed to hang every Yankee officer north and south of the border. Operating out of Matamoros, Davis's accomplices moved up and down the Texas side of the river late that winter, inspiring fellow loyalists to join them in the Union ranks of the newly formed First Texas Cavalry, U.S. (first organized in New Orleans). They had little trouble bringing to their side a ragged collection of mercenaries—German Unionists, Anglo exiles, Confederate deserters and Mexican *renegados*. In so doing, they also established a valuable network of spies who would willingly operate north of the river, even in the shadow of Fort Brown, to help prepare the way for a Union invasion force.[8]

Brigadier General Hamilton P. Bee, commanding the Confederate garrison at Brownsville, was equally determined to defeat any such Union invasion of the lower Rio Grande. In the predawn hours of March 6, 1863, General Bee learned that the Federal steamer *Honduras* was anchored in Mexican waters off the shores of Boca Chica near the mouth of the Rio Grande. Bee's spies also informed him that 180 Yankee soldiers were aboard the troop transport and that their commander was none other than the tall, lithe Florida native who had become an adopted son of South Texas—thirty-five-year-old Colonel Edmund J. Davis. Bee reported to Confederate authorities that, as his spies south of the river observed, Davis had come ashore four days later, ostensibly to collect his wife, Anne Elizabeth ("Lizzie"), and their two young sons, Britton and Waters, who were living in exile in Matamoros. For General Bee, the most disturbing news of all was that Davis, the man he had termed the "Texas renegade who was the proved originator of all the troubles on this frontier," was beyond his reach, just across the "narrow river dividing us from those who had brought so much disgrace on Texas."[9]

The fact that their enemies were just across the river had never stopped the "Texas Devils" in the past. And it would not deter General Bee's Partisan Rangers now. In the early morning darkness of March 15, what Bee characterized as "a party of citizens and soldiers off duty," but made up mostly of men of Duff's Thirty-Third Texas Cavalry, threaded their way through the thickets along the river and then boarded two flatboats and crossed into Mexico. Before dawn more than one hundred Confederate raiders under the command of Major George W. Chilton and Captain William H. Brewin captured—without even firing a shot—a garrison of thirty Mexican soldiers who had been left guarding a temporary customs house just upriver from Bagdad. As Confederate guerrilla Robert Williams remembered the startled prisoners, "Never did I see men so scared . . . for they seemed to think they would be murdered, and many fell on their knees and begged for their lives."[10]

After the Texan raiders assured their captives that they had no intention of harming them but would soon release them if they remained quiet, they marched the prisoners in two columns abreast some two miles upriver, through the maze of mesquite and chaparral. Williams recalled that "it was not altogether a pleasant stroll along the black path, where you could scarcely see your hand before you." At approximately 4:30 A.M. the Confederate raiders came upon a campsite on the river bank; they suspected that Unionist leaders were in hiding there. Not even a single picket stood guard around the perimeter of tents. Such was the confidence of the commanding officer, Colonel Edmund J. Davis. On Chilton's command the Texan irregulars shattered the morning stillness with a volley of rifle shots and blood-curdling rebel yells.

It was all over in less than five minutes. While several of Davis's partisans scattered into the brush, a few others were gunned down as they attempted to escape. Williams recorded that although the enemy "showed but little fight," most offering no resistance, one Union officer "fought like a wildcat." Before being overpowered and disarmed, forty-nine-year-old Captain William Montgomery slashed his way through the camp with a bowie knife, wounding two of the Confederates. As for Colonel Davis and three other staff officers, termed "renegades" by General Bee's raiders, they surrendered with less of a fight. By the time the brief exchange of gunfire had ended, the first gray of dawn appeared in the east. Soon after sunrise the Texan irregulars secured their prisoners and tended to their own wounded. Then they crossed back to the north bank of the Rio Grande and sent a dispatch upriver to Brownsville to inform General Bee of their success.[11]

What they failed to report during the next twenty-four hours was that they threatened the Union officers with execution if they refused to reveal all they knew about Federal operations on the border. They also hushed the grisly truth: to prove their resolve, the Texans hanged Captain Montgomery from a small tree alongside the trail that paralleled the river. "Davis was spared, and taken into camp under strong escort," Williams remembered. "There the desire to hang him was very strong," Williams added. If not for the intercession of General Bee and Colonel Duff, who feared Union reprisal if Colonel Davis were lynched, another "private and amateur hanging" would surely have been carried out. "When the war was over, I met Davis again in Indianola at the house of my friend and partner Dr. Hughes," Williams later recalled. "He told me that during that night's march . . . he fully expected to be strung up on every tree we came to."[12]

Based on Williams's account it seems likely that the Texan irregulars who seized the Union partisans and executed Montgomery were members of "Duff's Regiment," or "Duff's Rangers" as troops of the Thirty-Third Texas Cavalry proudly styled themselves. They even wore the floppy black felt hats with the Lone Star emblazoned upon each of them, both trademarks of the mounted Rangers who fifteen years earlier had ridden into Mexico alongside the likes of Jack Hays, Ben McCulloch, and Samuel H. Walker. Little wonder that, with their presence, word quickly spread along the south bank that the hated Texas Devils had again violated Mexican sovereignty, as they had so many times during the past two decades. Even more certain, the "incident," as Bee termed it, caused a serious rift in Confederate-Mexican relations. Understandably too, future Texas governor Edmund J. Davis never forgot his narrow escape from Duff's Confederate Partisan Rangers.[13]

General Bee predictably denied any knowledge of the raid across the river. Moreover, he stubbornly insisted that the action had been carried out against his explicit standing orders to respect the border and thus the territorial sovereignty of Mexico. "I shall promptly disown the act as authorized or connived . . . in any way by me," he assured his Confederate military superiors. General Bee probably understated the case when he also wrote later that day, "This affair has created great excitement in Matamoros." General Albino Lopez, commander of Mexican Federal

forces in the state of Tamaulipas, vehemently protested the border crossing, demanding that Bee order his troops to return the prisoners and "set
them at liberty" on Mexican soil. He also implored General Bee to censure
and even punish those responsible for the attack, and finally to do all in his
power to prevent any such outrages in the future. Calling the seizure of
Davis and company "one of the most serious crimes against international
law," Lopez further insisted, "Mexico is a neutral territory, in which for-
eigners enjoy equal guarantees, regardless of political parties." In polite
though threatening terms, he persisted that the military forces of Mexico
would defend their sovereign soil from any invasion, even what the Texans
might consider a minor one. Not to miss the opportunity to lodge grievances regarding other violations of Mexican neutrality, Lopez also bitterly complained about the arrest of an American citizen named Maddox,
who was apparently snatched from his rowboat on the Mexican side near
Bagdad. He also objected to other recent river crossings, most notably a
raid conducted by members of Captain Santos Benavides's Confederate
irregulars who allegedly "created disturbances" in the village of Nuevo
Laredo weeks earlier.[14]

General Bee quickly responded. But his answer was not what General
Lopez and other Mexican officials wanted to hear. First, Bee admitted that
he had been present at the arrest of Maddox but that the "boat was a few
feet off the left bank of the river" and well within what he determined to
be the "jurisdiction of Texas." Second, while he promised to investigate
the affair at Nuevo Laredo, he expressed regret at the precipitous conduct
of his troops in crossing into Mexico to capture Union agents. Still, he
claimed that the raid was the "legitimate result of the scandalous conduct" of U.S. consul Leonard Pierce, who was allegedly "openly enlist-
ing soldiers" for the Union "in the streets of Matamoros." Bee therefore
blamed existing border tensions on U.S. government officials, who, he
charged, held only "defiance and contempt for the neutrality of Mexico."
Finally, he informed Lopez that the Union prisoners in question were not
in his custody, and he even confessed that he knew nothing of their whereabouts, or even if they were still alive.[15]

Duff's Partisan Rangers

As winter began to lift across the lower Rio Grande, protests regarding the
Texan Partisan Rangers' brazen and sometimes brutish behavior would
be heard as far away as the Confederate capital of Richmond, Virginia.

Despite such complaints, Confederate officials offered no apologies to Union "renegades" staging on the south banks of the Rio Bravo. From his headquarters at Monterrey on March 21, José A. Quintero, diplomatic agent for the Confederate States of America, expressed his regrets to Confederate secretary of state Judah P. Benjamin. Quintero assured Benjamin that he as well as Santiago Vidaurri, governor of the state of Nuevo León, were "not surprised" to learn of the arrest of Davis and company, and even considered the action a "natural consequence of the favors shown by Mexican authorities to the United States Consul at Matamoros, and the vagabonds he has recruited to join the United States Army." Furthermore, Quintero and Vidaurri firmly believed that the Confederate foray across the river was justified as "a good offset to the Zapata raid on Texas." They even admitted that Pierce's consulate had been allowed to become "a recruiting office for our enemies." Then Quintero reassured Benjamin that the crossing of the Texan troops had been warranted, and that Captain Montgomery would "not commit treason again in this world" because he was now "permanently located in the soil of . . . [your] country." Finally, while confessing that the entire affair was regrettable, Quintero insisted that Montgomery was still "deserving of . . . [his] fate."[16]

Meanwhile, Bee and Lopez exchanged several courteous notes. But beneath the proper protocol and solicitous wording of these dispatches, a defiant tone prevailed. After three days of hurling carefully crafted but disguised insults back and forth, the two leaders tried to put the matter to rest. On March 18 Bee notified Lopez that, as requested, he had ordered the release of Davis and two of his fellow captives. He notified his counterpart that the Union officers had been held in a camp below Brownsville and that he had already dispatched a column of his cavalry with orders to return them to the south bank. Then an indignant Bee added, "Were I to consider the many instances in which the dignity of my country has been outraged, and the lives and property of my fellow citizens sacrificed, by persons operating under the advice and control of this same E. J. Davis, while harbored on the neutral soil of Mexico, I might perhaps be justly led to a different determination." Finally, Bee cautioned Lopez that "the affair, otherwise so much to be regretted, may serve to warn the residents of both sides of the river against the repetition of acts" that might lead to "such unhappy occurrences." Of course, in keeping with custom he concluded, "I have the honor to be, very respectfully, your obedient servant."[17]

The word "obedient," however, was not in the Texan vocabulary. Not when it came to respecting the authority and sovereignty of the neighboring nation to the south, nor for that matter even the orders of their own commanding officers. An English adventurer visiting the Rio Grande Valley just two weeks later learned that hard truth. Colonel Arthur James Lyon Fremantle, recently a cavalry officer in Her Majesty's Coldstream Guards, arrived at the mouth of the Rio Grande on April 1 aboard the HMS *Immortalité*. The following morning, he disembarked with a Texan merchant named McCarthy. Making their way aboard a cutter the short distance to Bagdad, the British traveler and his companion observed more than seventy vessels docked near the squalid little port, where bales of cotton extended along the beach as far as they could see. Shortly before noon Colonel Fremantle received permission to cross to the Texas side, where he was introduced to several Confederate officers who were sitting around a campfire, their enlisted men in bivouac nearby. Among the officers sat Colonel James Duff, commander of the ragtag, route-step regiment of horsemen who proudly called themselves Partisan Rangers.[18]

During the conversation, the proper English gentleman learned firsthand of the feared reputation of the Thirty-Third Texas Cavalry and of the stunning absence of discipline within their ranks. Duff, a handsome and well-spoken Scotsman, explained to Fremantle that he "couldn't cross the river . . . as he with some of his men had made a raid over there three weeks ago and carried away some *renegados*, one of whom named Montgomery they had *left* on the road to Brownsville. By the smiles of the officers, I could easily guess that something very disagreeable must have happened to Montgomery," Fremantle wrote. He understood they meant that the Union officer had been "*left for all eternity*" in the ground near the Rio Grande. Before leaving camp, the well-attired Englishman could not help but notice that the unwashed Texans, dressed in their loose flannel shirts, baggy trousers, and trademark broad-brimmed black hats, looked at him with both curiosity and suspicion.[19]

What happened next during his trip to Brownsville that afternoon only confirmed Fremantle's own suspicions about the brutal methods of these unrepentant Texans who styled themselves "Rangers." A Mexican guide identified as "Ituria" (more likely Yturria) drove him on the uneven road that ran beside the Rio Grande, and as their buggy bumped along the mesquite-covered plain Fremantle encountered several surly-looking characters passing downriver. "Every person we met carried a six-shooter," he recalled. After a few miles on the trail, Fremantle crossed paths with General Hamilton P. Bee, who invited him to share beef and beer at his camp on the roadside. "We talked politics and fraternized very amicably for more than an hour," Fremantle remembered. "He said the Montgomery affair was against his sanction, and he was very sorry for it." Then Bee's tone became resentful when he admitted that Colonel Davis "would also have been put to death had it not been for the intervention of his [Davis's] wife."[20]

What Fremantle did not know, or he neglected to mention, was the fact that "poor Montgomery," called by Williams a "thorough-paced scoundrel," had a criminal background almost equal to that of his executioners. In fact, before the war he had been charged with murder in both Caldwell and Nueces counties. Nevertheless, Montgomery would long remain a martyr to the Union cause. On the border, Fremantle learned, it was more important what side of the war you were on than what side of the river you were on.[21]

Not long after bidding Bee farewell and continuing upriver, Fremantle came upon a macabre scene that shocked even the battle-seasoned veteran of the Crimean War. Off to the right of the road he observed the site where Montgomery had been *left*. "He had been slightly buried, but his head and arms were above the ground, his arms tied together, the rope still around his neck, but part of it still dangling from quite a small mesquite tree," Fremantle remembered. "Dogs or wolves had probably scraped the earth from the body, and there was no flesh on the bones." In summary, the British officer wrote, "I obtained . . . my first experience of lynch law within three hours of landing in America."[22]

One week later Fremantle again met up with members of Duff's command. Nothing that he observed that day at their encampment below Brownsville changed his initial impression that they were an unruly and disheveled rabble. "Duff's Regiment is called the Partisan Rangers," he again recorded in his diary, noting the Texans' identification with earlier frontier martial traditions. "Although a fine lot of men, they don't look well at a foot parade, on account of the small amount of drill they have undergone, and the extreme disorder of their clothing." Then the British observer noted that their stock of weapons included everything from rifle carbines to Colt revolvers and bowie knives, also known as "Texas toothpicks."[23]

Fremantle observed that Duff's troops not only carried their own personal arsenals but they also possessed more prejudices than pride in the practice of traditional military arts. "They told me they were usually in the habit of scalping an Indian when they caught him, and that they never spared one, as they were such an untamable and ferocious race." He also commented that the boys from Texas boasted openly of how they had quelled the "counterrevolution of Unionists" in the Hill Country. "Nothing could exceed the rancor with which they spoke of these *rene-gados*, as they called them, who were principally Germans." An amused but disgusted Fremantle listened to their seemingly endless braggadocio and their simple faith in their own superiority over Mexican "Greasers" as well as "savage" Indians and black slaves. Finally, he shuddered at their suggestion that all enemies of Texas deserved the same fate as Captain Montgomery and the German Unionists they had shot and hanged in the Hill Country. "When I suggested to some of the Texans that they might as well bury the body of Montgomery a little better, they did not at all agree with me, but said it ought not to have been buried at all, but left hanging as a warning to other evildoers."[24]

As it turned out, some of these very same horsemen of Duff's command were among the Confederate guerrillas who had tracked down and massacred thirty-six German Unionists the previous August near the waters of the upper Nueces. Many of their victims were young German farmers who were captured and then shot execution-style. The victims had been guilty of nothing more than attempting to flee to Mexico to escape the Confederate Conscription Act of 1862. Their fate at the hands of Duff's "Rangers" would be misnamed the "Battle of the Nueces" by many Southern sympathizers and some future historians. But German Unionists of the Texas Hill Country would rightfully remember the event as an atrocity, and only one more war crime during a year of terror they justly called Die Hangerzeit, or the "Hanging Time," because of the number of young men lynched by rebel forces who dignified themselves with names such as "Rangers" and "Cavalry."[25]

Fremantle learned well that the indignation of these zealous Texans was righteous in an almost religious sense. He also learned that their judgment of enemies was both swift and final. After they had regaled him that evening with songs and campfire talk of Texan crusades against the Comanche, Mexican outlaws, and Union loyalists, Colonel Fremantle retired for the night, perhaps wondering if these young Texans and not the Indians and Mexican bandits were the real barbarians of this border country.

The following morning Colonel Duff and his men treated the Englishman to a display of Texan horsemanship and cattle wrangling that almost defied description. Riding at full speed, then tilting and dropping to the sides of their saddles while holding to the pommel with one hand and gripping their horses' ribs with clenched knees, they reached to the ground to pick up their hats with the other hand. And as they raced through the camp releasing a rebel yell that would have terrified even the bravest warrior, they proudly waved their black felt hats in the air as if the articles were symbolic of their identity as Rangers. "I saw them lasso cattle," Fremantle added, "and catch them by the tail at full gallop, and throw them by slewing them around. This is called tailing." But when Fremantle inquired of Duff whether his gallant horsemen could remain in the saddle while vaulting a fence, the Scotsman chuckled and informed him that they were more adept at chasing Comanche warriors and border bandits than at steeplechase.[26]

When the demonstration concluded, several Texans surrounded a smiling Colonel Fremantle. "They were all extremely anxious to hear what I thought of the performance," the British cavalryman recalled, "and their thorough good opinion of themselves was most amusing." Nervously, Fremantle admitted to them that he had never seen a pageant quite like theirs. Robert Williams, who rode with these border ruffians of Duff's regiment, thought little better of the Confederate commanders than Fremantle did of their rank-and-file volunteers. As for the ruthless Duff, Williams wrote, "I never thought him fit for even 4th Corporal." Even harsher words he reserved for Major George W. White, the commissary agent for the Rio Grande district, who allegedly worked to make his own fortune in the cotton trade while procuring arms and munitions for Confederate forces. According to Williams, White was a "habitual drunkard" who "neither knew nor cared anything about soldiering." He accused a "Captain Kaupmann" of being "a heavy, besotted-looking lager beer-drinking Dutchman" who was "rarely sober." Yet another officer named only as "Captain Turner" (most likely Richard Taylor) was identified as a "windy, gassy fellow" who liked to boast that he could single handedly "whip a whole regiment of Yankees." Of Colonel Philip N. Luckett, Rip Ford's old comrade-in-arms, he noted that the longtime physician and former Ranger was "a very pleasant fellow, though a thirsty one . . . [and] entirely ignorant of military matters." Only Colonel Augustus Buchel, the old Prussian drill sergeant, was identified by Williams as an "efficient officer" who was always dependable. Even at that, Williams alleged, Buchel was said to be "reformed"—in other words, having found his lord and salvation only at the bottom of an empty liquor bottle. Still, Williams characterized the lot of these Texan commanders as "incompetent rascals" who were "unfitted [*sic*] for command." And all of them, he charged, were more concerned with amassing and protecting their personal wealth than with defending the borders of Texas.[27]

Like Colonel Fremantle, Williams was a "cultured" Englishman who held others to a higher standard of conduct. Unsurprisingly, U.S. consul Leonard Pierce agreed with Williams's assessment. Writing from his office in Matamoros that the Texas troops and their leaders across the river were "demoralized and disorderly in the extreme," Pierce alleged that these self-styled "Rangers" bragged that, given the opportunity, they would "burn and destroy everything of both friend and foe." The growing number of desertions from the ranks of the Texan troops provided further evidence of the lack of discipline that generally characterized state troops in South Texas. Of the many months of inactivity, and the problem with boredom for the Confederate partisans serving on the river frontier, Williams recalled, "There was no real soldiering to be done, and I spent my time, when not actually on duty, in hunting and fishing, or visiting friends in Brownsville and Matamoros." The fact that these irregulars serving under the Confederate flag were "so long quartered so close to the Mexican border" explained why "we lost a very large number of men by desertion. It was so easy for those who were sick of soldiering to slip across the river that they couldn't resist the temptation." Consequently, Williams remembered, he spent as much time patrolling the river for deserters as he did scouting for Mexican bandits and Union spies.[28]

Colonel John S. Ford, head of Confederate conscription office in Austin and later commander of the Second Texas Cavalry (CSA) stationed along the line of the lower Rio Grande, also admitted that a "great number" of these deserters had "gotten into trouble in their respective commands, and saw no means to escape punishment, except by leaving." He further noted that, by many reports, some recruits were guilty of drunkenness, thievery, insubordination, and even violent conduct. Several of their officers were even worse, a few commanders behaving like "tyrants" and driving away volunteers and conscripts alike. "An officer when prejudiced against a private can give him a lively foretaste of hell," Ford summarized the climate of repression and fear that often prevailed among Confederate units on the border.[29]

After receiving his own foretaste of hell at the hands of Duff's Partisan Rangers, Colonel Edmund J. Davis understood such characterizations of the Texan troops serving on the Rio Grande. Although he gained his release from General Bee's Confederate irregulars, who remanded him to the custody of U.S. consul Pierce in Matamoros, he never forgot the experience. One fellow Unionist living in exile on the south bank of the Rio Bravo recalled that sometime in late May Colonel Davis received a hero's welcome in Matamoros. His reception in the city's military plaza was complete with military honors, speeches of tribute and a Mexican band playing mariachi music as well as the stirring refrains of "Hail, Columbia," "Yankee Doodle," "The Star-Spangled Banner," and "Hail to the Chief." As the observer described, however, "It was a sad solemn mingling of patriotic sentiments—cheers for the Great American Republic mingled with the gloomy, sorrowful, vengeful sympathy for Montgomery and his family." The ceremony and celebration of Colonel Davis's return to freedom then ended with every Union sympathizer present swearing an oath to avenge the murder of the martyred Captain William Montgomery. No one really cared about Montgomery's crimes or his reputation before the war. He was a hero now, at least in the collective memories of his fellow Unionists.[30]

As for Edmund Jackson Davis, the future Republican governor of Texas during Reconstruction, he had lived to fight another day. But so had the Texas Devils who had strung up Captain Montgomery and nearly hanged Colonel Davis as well.

1
The Devil's Horsemen

As the sun dropped below the western horizon on the evening of August 9, 1862, a brilliant array of colors burst over the rugged landscape of Southwest Texas. Spectacular hues of gold, orange, and red erupted across the rocky cedar-clad hills overlooking the headwaters of the Nueces. It was an awe-inspiring scene that twenty-eight-year-old John W. Sansom would never forget. Unrolling his blanket and tossing his saddle on the ground, he probably hoped for nothing more than some peace and rest. But the camp around him was alive with the festive sounds of laughter, song, and revelry. Voices in English and German filled the evening air, as did the smell of venison cooked over a campfire. Sansom covered himself and stared into the stars. It had been a long day on the trail, a difficult fifteen-mile horseback ride over some of the roughest terrain in Texas. His body ached.[1]

Not since Sansom had ridden with James H. Callahan's Rangers seven years earlier had he passed through this harsh country. But it was different then. In 1855 he had been chasing renegade Indian marauders. But on this trip, he was no mere private. This time his Unionist friends and neighbors had elected him captain of their company.

Even so, just as before, he was running for his life. But this time he was not being chased by a thousand determined Mexican *federales*. Nor was he fleeing Mexico with the flames of Piedras Negras at his back. Instead, he was now riding *toward* the Rio Grande and the *safety* of Mexican soil. And the border lay less than two days' ride ahead. Just two more days, his commanding officer assured him, and he and more than sixty of his fellow Unionists would reach freedom. Just two more days and they would stand beyond the reach of the Confederate conscription law and the long arm of the Lone Star State. Since leaving the banks of the Pedernales, Sansom and his friends had forded the Medina and the Frio, and now they were just a couple of hard days on saddle to the Rio Bravo. All that separated them now from the protection promised by the Mexican border was fewer than forty miles of broken prairie. Just two more days and Sansom and his comrades could escape the horrors of the fratricidal war that had divided the nation. Just one more sunset remained, maybe two, and only one more river to cross.

But Sansom must have wondered if this sunset might be his last. Something seemed wrong, terribly wrong, to the young seven-year veteran of the ranging service. Just before sundown he had tried desperately to persuade his commander, Major Gustav "Fritz" Tegener, to push on to the border without delay. Strangers had been reported observing their slow-moving column from a distance. At least two different hunting parties had seen them. Why would Tegener not believe him when he had pleaded that the men should strike camp and move out quickly? Why would the major not believe his own scouts who had told him that they were being followed? Why had Tegener not listened? There was a full moon rising, and it would be the perfect time to press ahead, Sansom had urged Tegener. Danger was following closely behind, he warned. Yet an aloof Tegener remained confident in his plan, and his pace toward the border. The major was a fool, Sansom must have thought to himself when he heard the order to bed down and settle in for the night.[2]

Why was Major Tegener placing only two sentries in the nearby cedar breaks lining the banks of the West Fork of the Nueces? And why did he instruct his men to camp in an open meadow where they could be easily seen in the light of a full moon? It was a perfect spot for an ambush. Could Tegener not see that too? Should they at least douse their campfires, and maintain silence in the dark?

But it was too late to worry about that now. There was nothing left to do but rest. Dawn would come soon enough, and if all went well, in less than forty-eight hours the company of Unionists should reach their sanctuary on the other side of the Rio Grande. Once across, Sansom reassured himself, no one could force him to fight for an unjust cause. He would rather die a free man than raise arms against the United States. He would rather die in defense of freedom, he had explained to his family and friends, than in defense of slavery.

To Sansom and his fellow Union loyalists the German hamlets of Kerrville, Comfort, and Fredericksburg—all nestled in the scenic Texas Hill Country—seemed so far away now, and the promised asylum of Mexico so close they could almost reach out and touch it. It had been eight days since more than sixty young men—most of them German, all members of an organization called the Union Loyal League—had set out from Turtle Creek in southwestern Kerr County. Four days since Captain John Sansom of Kendall County, a Mexican guide named Pablo Díaz, and several Anglo-Texans had joined the flight to the border. To be sure, progress toward their intended destination, the confluence of the Devil's River and the Rio

Grande, had been slow and difficult. But as a restless Sansom reclined and closed his eyes, and the campfire beside him flickered faintly, none of that seemed to matter. All the other men had finally hushed their chatter and called off their playful wrestling games. All the patriotic speeches about loyalty to the Union and love of liberty had also subsided.[3]

Now it was quiet, finally. Even the evening breeze seemed to have died down. And when the embers of the campfire at last burned out, one could hardly hear a sound. Only a mournful songbird, a few chattering crickets, the faint trickling of waters running over the rocks that covered the narrow bed of the nearby Nueces. A deathly stillness settled over the scene as Sansom drifted to sleep, both rifle and revolver at his side. It was almost as if he could hear forever, and hear nothing.

But his better instincts told him the enemy was out there. Somewhere in the darkness they were watching and waiting. Then it happened. Shortly after 3:00 A.M. fellow Unionist Leopold Bauer shook Sansom and motioned for him to remain quiet. Now awake, Sansom scrambled to his feet, grabbed his weapons, and followed Bauer into the cedar breaks. He was unprepared for what happened next. "When we had gone about sixty yards . . . [Bauer] in front, and I about twenty feet behind him," without warning a single shot rang out, and Bauer fell dead. Seeing his friend drop to the ground, Sansom instinctively raised his rifle and returned fire.[4]

But it was no use. Dozens of Confederate partisans rose up from the brush, their silhouettes plainly visible in the moonlight as they rushed toward him. Knowing that the gunfire had alerted his comrades, Sansom raced back toward Tegener's camp, and within seconds he found himself exposed in an open plain, stumbling and scrambling toward the safety of the closest timberline. He was caught in the middle of a murderous cross fire between the Confederate irregulars and a furious countercharge and fusillade of fire from the Unionist camp. Not far from Sansom, Ernst Besler, a second German sentry who was posted in the cedar, also fell fatally wounded. Robert Williams, who rode with the Confederate partisans, recalled that the German boys appeared like a "swarm of bees," and "confusion reigned supreme" in his own ranks during the opening moments of the fight. "No one knew what to do," he remembered.[5]

Then came the command to charge, and all hell broke loose. The company of Texas mounted volunteers who had been trailing Tegener's party for nearly a week suddenly hurled themselves headlong toward the enemy camp. From the south and east they surged to within fifty meters of Tegener's position, all the while pouring a steady fire into the startled

Unionists. The initial exchange claimed several injured on both sides, among them Major Tegener, who sustained two serious wounds. Williams remembered vividly the terrifying sounds of battle, "The bullets were whistling pretty thickly over our heads." Then when the firing subsided, cries and moans could be heard as the wounded called out for help, but no one dared even to carry water to them for fear of becoming a target himself.

Then a lull in the fighting followed. For more than an hour, and what must have seemed like an eternity, a surreal silence fell over the scene. But the quiet belied the impending danger. With both sides reluctant to advance again into a hail of rifle fire, Sansom crawled through the tall weeds to a place of safety. "It occurred to me at once," he recalled, "that I could do the greatest good . . . by making a careful reconnaissance of the Confederate forces, and this I did effectively by creeping around to their rear, and so near to them, as to fully satisfy myself concerning their numbers and their location." Having scouted the strength and disposition of the rebel force, he began to work his way back toward his friends, crouching over and keeping his head low to avoid detection.

Soon after Sansom located the enemy, they almost found him. In making his way back to camp Sansom failed to move far enough to the west to avoid the partisans' pickets. "I walked right up to a squad of Confederates," he recollected, "concealed in a thick standing grove of cedars, some sixty yards southwest of the Unionist camp. Before I knew it I was so close to the party that I could easily have put my hand on one of them. Noticing that they wore no hats but had handkerchiefs tied around their heads, I immediately took off my hat, and carrying it in my hand, backed away." Then he added, "They saw me plainly, but, I reckon supposed me to be a Confederate. At any rate they . . . let me go." Now snaking his way on his belly, Sansom inched back toward camp. It had been a close call.[6]

Minutes later, however, Sansom again came face to face with death. Only this time it was his own comrades who first mistook him for the enemy. "When about twenty feet from the camp," he recorded, "I heard the click of the locks of guns about to be aimed at me." Fearing the worst, he ducked his head and called out, "Don't shoot, [it's] Sansom." Hearing nothing, he repeated his cry until Captain Kramer returned, "Come on, come on captain. I came near shooting you."[7]

Little wonder that Sansom urged Kramer and his fellow officers to retreat at once. Outnumbered at least two to one, they were almost surrounded and soon would be cut off from any hope of escape. Their enemy was well positioned, commanding the rugged cliffs that towered some sixty feet above the north bank of the Nueces. The Unionists were also outgunned as their muzzle-loaders were no match for the Confederates' breechloaders. Major Tegener lay badly wounded on his pallet, bleeding profusely, yet he still refused to relinquish command, even though his men were stunned and confused. Worse still, the sun would soon come up, leaving them exposed in the tall grasses with nothing but their saddles as cover. They must move out, and move out immediately, Sansom pleaded with Tegener, while some of their horses were tethered together nearby. Otherwise, their mounts would be scattered and they would all be killed.[8]

But Sansom's appeals again went unheeded. What Sansom and the others had no way of knowing at that time was just how determined and even brutal an enemy they were up against. The Confederate raiders who had been following them—numbering as many as a hundred heavily armed horsemen—comprised two companies attached to the Second Texas Mounted Rifles and one company of state partisans under the command of Captain James Duff, the same volatile and irascible Scotsman who had recently declared martial law in the Texas Hill Country and conducted a sweep of several German communities known to be enclaves for Union loyalists. Recognized widely as a man whose antipathy for abolitionists and German immigrants equaled his enmity for Mexican "greasers" loyal to the Union, this freighter and teamster turned militia commander possessed more prejudices than martial prowess or political acumen. Like the men he led, Duff had no compunction about ransacking and burning the cabins of German Unionists, destroying their crops in the field, stealing their horses, and shooting their livestock. Neither did his "Partisan Rangers," as they were called. Duff had no intention of bringing in prisoners for interrogation. Neither did his young "Rangers."[9]

When daylight broke over the battlefield, the Confederate force under the immediate command of Lieutenant Colin McRae moved toward the Unionist camp again. This time they formed a single file and moved in a "steady and slow advance," as McRae reported, approaching to within thirty paces as they poured round after round into a demoralized enemy. Although faced with the shock effect of such a close-quarters barrage, Tegener's command returned fire, but many soon broke and ran into the thickets. As August Hoffman recalled of that bloody Sunday morning, their cumbersome muzzle-loaders were no match for the revolvers and breech-loading rifles of Duff's Rangers and the boys of the Second Texas Mounted. McRae matter-of-factly reported of the Unionists' retreat, "From the many signs of blood I infer many of those escaping were seriously wounded."[10]

Following the fight, a heavy smell of gunpowder hung in the air. So did the stench of death. As the sun rose over the South Texas landscape and Duff's Partisan Rangers surveyed the scene of carnage, which Williams described as a "ghastly one," many could not help but be sickened by the sight. At least thirty-two German Unionists lay dead, their corpses littering the field alongside the carcasses of some of their horses. In the confusion of Tegener's hurried retreat, the Unionist militia had also left at least seventeen seriously wounded men to the mercy of their captors. As for the Confederate force, which included not only Duff's partisans but also one detachment from Captain John Donelson's Rangers and another assigned from Captain Clay Davis's state troops, at least two volunteers had been shot dead during the pitched battle, and eighteen others wounded.[11]

In the aftermath, Lieutenant McCrae tried to take charge of the situation, despite being confined to a litter with a serious gunshot wound. Described by Williams as a "brave and kindly man," McCrae ordered his troops to remove the enemy wounded and place them in the shade of a nearby grove of trees. Then he instructed them to begin the grim task of burying their own dead and dispatching couriers to arrange for ambulances to transport their injured. The sun burned overhead as the bloated and bloodied bodies of the German dead were left where they fell, their swollen corpses mere food for the buzzards and coyotes that scavenged this rocky brush country. The stifling humidity rose that morning, as did the cries of the wounded, who pleaded for cool water from the nearby Nueces. Meanwhile, some of the Confederate officers directed their irregulars to round up nearly two hundred horses that the fleeing Germans had abandoned. As for the wounded animals, at least those that had sustained serious injuries, The Texan partisans put them out of their misery with well-placed pistol shots. By midafternoon, therefore, the smell of human remains and horse flesh filled the nostrils of every survivor.[12]

But the worst was yet to come. Duff may not have even been on the scene that Sunday afternoon when the unthinkable command was given, though it mattered little. His men understood well his standing order that no quarter would be given to German "abolitionists" and "bushwhackers." Despite his awareness of that dreaded directive, Robert Williams never actually believed that his comrades were capable of carrying out such a horrific deed as a mass execution. But he would never forget his astonishment upon first hearing the chilling sounds of pistol reports piercing the afternoon stillness. He soon learned that the gunshots coming from a nearby thicket were not those of a military honor guard saluting the dead, nor the announcement of another attack, but something far more terrible. Williams vividly remembered grabbing his rifle and running toward the gunfire, then being stopped by one of his fellow Rangers. "You needn't be in a hurry," the Texan announced, reaching out to grab his comrade, "it's all done; they've shot the poor devils and finished them off." Stopping in his tracks, a stunned private Williams shuddered, then shook his head in disbelief. "Oh yes, they're all dead, sure enough," the soldier repeated to him, "and a good job too."[13]

Williams recalled his deep sense of outrage and shame upon realizing that every last German prisoner had been executed, shot in the head at point-blank range. He recorded in his memoir that the senseless massacre of unarmed wounded men was the work of a "Lieutenant Luck," whom he described as a "remorseless, treacherous villain." And he left little doubt that the atrocity committed along the banks of the Nueces was but the worst in a series of wrongs that state volunteers committed against German Unionists during the Civil War. As for Lieutenant McRae, he simply recounted to his superiors that the enemy "offered determined resistance and fought with desperation, asking no quarter whatever." Then the remorseless McRae added one last haunting sentence: "Hence I have no prisoners to report."[14]

The following morning the Texan irregulars transported their own wounded in wagons over twenty miles to Fort Clark, near the town of Brackettville. In the coming days squads of Duff's Rangers tracked down several German survivors and shot them as if they were wild dogs, several of the victims reportedly being gunned down while trying to cross the Rio Grande. Meanwhile, in the Hill Country north and west of San Antonio other state volunteer companies descended upon isolated German homesteads, torching the farms and fields of suspected members of the Union Loyal League, even lynching a few of those believed to be Yankee spies, Northern incendiaries, and agents of abolitionism.[15]

All for the Union

The following year another squall of violence swept over the Nueces Strip. The source of this latest storm, however, was not the long-standing sanguinary racial war between Texan and Mexican but rather continued resistance to the Confederate Conscription Act and, in turn, the fear of an impending Union invasion. Understandably, the Mexican border country became a refuge to German immigrants who populated the cedar-covered hills of Texas. And that river frontier became a dumping ground for every deserter, draft dodger, and desperate Unionist seeking safety from the mounted demons known as Duff's Partisan Rangers. No wonder that most would come to know these Texan irregulars, by early 1863 stationed at Ringgold Barracks near Rio Grande City, as the "Devil's Horsemen."[16]

According to at least one contemporary account, Henry Schwethelm and two other survivors of the fight on the Nueces escaped to the Mexican side of the river and made their way to Monterrey, then on to Vera Cruz. Months later they sailed to New Orleans, which was occupied by Union forces under the command of the controversial General Benjamin F. Butler. Along with other exiled Texan Unionists they joined the First Texas Cavalry Regiment (U.S.), organized by Colonel Edmund J. Davis.[17]

Longtime attorney, Laredo city councilman, former district attorney, and judge of the sprawling Twelfth Judicial District of the state of Texas, which stretched downcoast from Corpus Christi to Brownsville and upriver to Eagle Pass, Edmund J. Davis seemed like an atypical Texan Unionist. A southerner by birth and experience, he had also been a faithful member of the Democratic Party, though he had aligned for a time with the Whig Party until the mid-1850s. Like Texas governor Sam Houston, whom he greatly admired, Davis broke ranks with the secessionists in his own party. At the same time, however, he held little sympathy for the most militant of abolitionists, seeing the incendiary elements of the antislavery movement as just as dangerous as the most combustible of Southern fire-eaters. Moreover, his father-in-law, state senator Forbes Britton of Corpus Christi, who had openly supported secession, stood among the most influential politicians and wealthiest landowners in all of South Texas.[18]

While German Texans were preparing to flee the state in May 1862, Davis crossed to Matamoros and, with the help of U.S. consul Leonard Pierce, boarded a steamer bound for New Orleans. There Davis joined two prominent fellow Texans, state representative John L. Haynes of Rio Grande City and friend and fellow attorney William Alexander of Austin. From New Orleans the three Unionist leaders sailed for Washington, D.C., where they apparently pressed the highest officials in the U.S. government with their bold plan to arm Union loyalists along the border, then to reoccupy Brownsville. On August 4, 1862—coincidentally, the day after Tegener's column struck out from Kerr County for the Rio Grande—President Lincoln met briefly with these three men at the White House, then scribbled a brief note urging Secretary of War Edwin M. Stanton to grant Davis and his companions an audience. "Please see these Texas gentlemen, and talk with them," the president wrote. "They think if we could send 2500 or 3000 arms, indeed a vessel, to the vicinity of the Rio Grande, that they can find the men there who will re-inaugurate the National Authority on the Rio Grande first, and probably on the Nuesces [*sic*] also." Then President Lincoln closed his note by asking Stanton to solicit the opinion of General Henry W. Halleck, general-in-chief of the army, regarding the feasibility of such a plan. During their brief stay in Washington, the three Texan Unionists also attempted to meet with none other than Major Samuel Peter Heintzelman, who was no stranger to the lower Rio Grande and its people. Only three years earlier Heintzelman had commanded an expeditionary force of the Second U.S. Infantry and Texas Volunteer Rangers in pursuit of the elusive border chieftain Juan N. Cortina. He was one of the few men in Washington who knew anything about the Rio Grande Valley and its recent conflicts. Thus began the first high-level discussions regarding a Federal strategy to arm Union support-ers along the Texas border.[19]

Before long, E. J. Davis, now a commissioned colonel in the U.S. Army, became the chief instrument of this plan to restore Federal authority on the Rio Grande frontier. Still, Haynes seemed to be in the best position to recruit Tejano and Mexican volunteers for the Union cause. Never a Cortina sympathizer, former state representative Haynes nevertheless had remained resistant to the most strident anti-Mexican sentiments in the Texas state legislature. Empathetic with the plight of both landless peones and dispossessed rancheros, he stood tall in the eyes of Hispanic peoples of the border, and almost alone as an Anglo-Texan who could be trusted. Likewise defiant in his opposition to the secessionist cause, and more spe-cifically the local Brownsville and Cameron County Anglo power elite so closely identified with it, he could rally friends on both sides the river to fight the rebels and the Lone Star flag that flew over them. Although he once called President Lincoln an "obnoxious man," Haynes still despised the landholding, slave-owning aristocracy of Texas and the South even more. And he was quick to remind any Union loyalist who would listen— whether Latino, Anglo, or otherwise—that he shared their love for liberty, as well the misery that they suffered at the hands of the Texan Confeder-ate government. As he summarized his reasons for leaving his family and fleeing into Mexico the previous spring, "I left Texas from a sense of duty to my country, to my conscience and I wish to do my whole duty in the restoration of the authority [of the United States]."[20]

Perhaps Colonel Davis best summarized the plight of Haynes. A "true Union man," Haynes had been "run out of Texas" because of his loyalty to the United States. Even in victory, Davis lamented that his friend and fellow Unionist "suffered and lost more in conflict than any of us."[21]

But Haynes was not alone. Throughout 1862 a steady stream of American refugees crossed the border into Mexico, literally hundreds of them seeking sanctuary in Matamoros. Leaving behind everything they owned, sometimes even their families, they sought political asylum and protection. Federal troopers, former prisoners of war who had escaped and eluded the grasp of Confederate authorities, deserters from both the Northern and Southern armies, desperate young Texans fleeing the draft law, Union men looking for the opportunity to join U.S. forces, or for the chance simply to catch a steamer bound for New York, Philadelphia, or Boston, all crowded into the Mexican border city. Most presented themselves to U.S. consul Leonard Pierce, who described the lot of them as "destitute of funds" and without any means of support.[22]

"The town is fast filling up with them," a despairing Pierce had informed Secretary of State William Seward in the spring of 1862. After news spread of the passage of the Confederate Conscription Act that April, Pierce had reported that the situation along the lower Rio Grande had grown even worse. Confederate officers and dozens of men identifying themselves as Texas "Partisan Rangers" had stormed into the streets of Matamoros, busting down doors and, with "pistols presented," arrested accused "spies" and "traitors." According to Pierce, the angry Texans "went about the streets boasting that they would take . . . every man who claimed to be a Union man." Then he had concluded, "It was a most outrageous affair."[23]

Pierce had likewise reported to Seward that the rebels then transported an unspecified number of these prisoners across the river to Fort Brown, where all were interrogated, some incarcerated, others pressed into military service, and a few allegedly hanged without benefit of formal arraignment or trial. The reign of terror continued for months as Texas state partisans frequented Matamoros, in defiance of Mexican authorities, and rounded up anyone who, in Pierce's words, they "considered obnoxious." Even on Mexican soil, therefore, Union loyalists were not safe, at least not when Partisan Rangers stood poised to conduct punitive raids across the river.[24]

The wave of indiscriminate violence continued. Pierce's dispatches throughout the remainder of the year contained multiple references to shootings and stabbings in the cantinas, boarding houses, brothels, and even in the crowded streets of Matamoros. Typically, the victims were American citizens stranded with just enough money to encourage bandits, though not enough to purchase passage on an eastbound steamer. The influx of dozens of cotton brokers, arms dealers, and other war profiteers into the bustling city that swelled to more than eight thousand inhabitants caused it to outgrow its capacity to provide housing, food, and medical care. Worse still, these miscreants, malcontents, and murderers looking for an easy way to make a living turned Matamoros into a place of daily danger and combustion.[25]

To compound matters for local authorities, the entire Republic of Mexico, which had been caught in the whirlwind of civil war since 1858, was fast falling into the clutches of opportunistic French imperialists. Ravaged by economic blight, a staggering public debt, military repression, and a grasping Roman Catholic clergy still desperately trying to hold on to political influence and church lands, the ailing Mexican nation seemed ready for foreign conquest, just as Sam Houston had prophesied a few years earlier. With Napoleon III of France and his scheming royal relatives installing Archduke Ferdinand Maximilian of Austria upon a makeshift Mexican throne, and with a French expeditionary force of more than one hundred thousand in occupation of Mexico City, the troubled country trembled in the convulsions of war and revolutionary change. Understandably, the human refuse of that conflict as well as the "Confederate War" north of the Rio Grande threatened to turn the border into a killing field. Texans, especially those along the border, thus had good reason for concern.

By December 1862 the coming winter promised the people of the Rio Grande Valley little but uncertainty. As the blustery north winds blew across the South Texas plains, again announcing the changing of seasons, yet another chilling gale of violence swept the region. The flash point occurred in Starr County during the first week in December when Octaviano Zapata, a thirty-two-year-old ranchero known to share Juan Cortina's hatred for the Texans, led an attack against a Confederate courier and escort near Roma. Zapata's raiders killed three of Refugio Benavides's dispatch riders and left their bodies for the carrion-eating animals. Reportedly, one of Zapata's men carried a guidon bearing the standard of the Stars and Stripes of the United States. Then, on December 26, Zapata's raiders, probably numbering more than fifty, again rode under the U.S.

flag as they fell upon a military supply train near Rancho Soledad, located some fifteen miles downriver from Ringgold Barracks. Before retiring into the brush, they plundered several wagons and killed all but one of the teamsters. Apparently, the lone survivor of the raid stumbled into Rio Grande City the following day to recount his harrowing escape.[26]

That same week an even larger raiding party of border bandits splashed across the Rio Grande near Clareño and rode up to the rancho of Zapata County judge Ysidro Vela, an avowed enemy of Juan Cortina. Dragging the venerable magistrate from his home, the raiders hanged him from the nearest tree while they forced his wife and children to watch. As Vela's lifeless body dangled between the heavens and the earth, swinging and twisting in the wind, Zapata's assassins pinned a note to the corpse warning that the "death penalty would be inflicted on any person who dared to take the body down for burial." In retaliation for this barbaric act, a platoon of Captain Benavides's Confederate partisans departed Ringgold Barracks the following day and descended upon Rancho Soledad, where they reportedly found a cache of stolen property, said to be left from the attack upon the supply train three weeks earlier. In their rage and in revenge for the lynching of Judge Vela they burned more than a dozen jacales and *ranchitos* along the river that reportedly belonged to Zapata supporters.[27]

The killing and destruction did not end there, nor did the increased lawlessness that characterized the lower Rio Grande during the war years. Neither did the unrelenting challenges of nature. After a drought had crept over South Texas for the past two years, one traveler could describe the land in stark terms, "You cannot imagine how desolate, barren, and desertlike this country is; not a spear of grass, not a green shrub, with nothing but moving clouds of sand to be seen on these once green prairies."[28]

Colonel John S. Ford, "Old Rip," described conditions in equally graphic language, "Around water holes, then dry, could be seen hundreds of domestic animals, dead, their flesh seemingly dried upon their bones." For many miles, from the Nueces to the lower Rio Grande, the land was parched and cracked open by the searing sun. When promising thunderheads appeared in the distance they simply seemed to disappear as fast as they had formed. Only occasional water wells provided the traveler relief—if the wells were not jealously guarded by heavily armed vaqueros. And some of those wells had already gone dry. Ford recalled the time as resembling "scenes described in the Bible." It was as if the plagues of ancient Egypt were descending upon the lower Rio Grande.[29]

The cloudless skies that long summer provided as little hope as the news from the distant eastern war front. At a time when a drop of rain was as precious as life itself, every river town experienced an outbreak of the dreaded yellow fever—the second during the past four years. Still more misery spread across the land as more cases of typhoid and dysentery were reported in the camps of the Texan troops. Spreading too were the terrifying rumors that smallpox had revisited the border, but those reports proved false. Amid these events what had been a mere trickle, then a steady stream, of refugees crossing the Rio Grande into Mexico was fast becoming a flood of immigrants that resembled the exodus from Pharaoh's Egypt. Only in this case there was no Red Sea to cross, just the shallows of the Rio Grande.[30]

The Fall of Brownsville

The impartial heat of July brought even more misery and distress compounded by the stunning news of General Ulysses S. Grant's siege and capture of the strategic river fortress at Vicksburg, Mississippi, and of General Robert E. Lee's defeat at an obscure Pennsylvania crossroads village called Gettysburg. For supporters of the Confederate cause, it almost seemed as if the uncertain elements and unpredictable forces of nature had conspired with the unforgiving fates of war. Yet it was not the news of distant battles but reports of mutiny among state troops that caused a panic on the border.

At the center of this fear, and the resulting alarm that spread rapidly along the Rio Grande, was an enigmatic nineteen-year-old adventurer named Adrian Vidal. Described by Robert Williams as "a vain, trifling fellow without any experience who cared for nothing except gambling and drinking," Vidal was brash and ambitious. With a fair complexion and hazel eyes, a fiery temperament and unequaled skill as an equestrian, he had been given a captain's commission in Duff's command. Little wonder that some Confederate troops questioned openly whether wealth, class, privilege, and family influence rather than merit might have accounted for his appointment. After all, Vidal's stepfather was the storied South Texas steamboat entrepreneur, landowner, and cattle raiser Mifflin Kenedy. A native of Monterrey, a recent resident of Mier, and now a Texan of Mexican heritage—and one whose mother had married into the wealthy Anglo elite—Vidal was a man whose loyalties were divided between peoples on both sides of the river.

Judging by his actions in the autumn of 1863, Vidal's loyalties were apparently divided in another respect. During the last week of October, he turned deserter and led an entire company in rebellion against local Confederate military authorities. The result was a ruthless two-day killing spree reminiscent of Zapata's recent raids and Cortina's earlier depredations in Brownsville. With as many as sixty disgruntled "Rangers" riding alongside him, Vidal struck several ranchos downriver from Brownsville, plundering and ransacking homesteads, rustling livestock, rounding up horses, and stealing as much cotton as he could carry off in wagons. Leaving behind a trail of death and destruction, Vidal and his renegades gunned down anyone who got in their way.[31]

Not even their former comrades were spared, as an incident on the afternoon of October 26 proved. Two of General Bee's couriers, privates Dashiell and Litteral of Company A, Duff's Thirty-Third Regiment, rode into Vidal's camp some fourteen miles below Brownsville. After dismounting and announcing that they carried an express from General Hamilton Bee, the two weary horsemen accepted an invitation to rest and share a drink with their fellow Rangers. The unsuspecting dispatchers tied up their horses and enjoyed libations with Vidal's men, then mounted up again and continued some two miles back toward Brownsville, where they encountered Captain Vidal and his scouts. No sooner had they greeted the captain, however, than Vidal and several of his raiders pulled pistols and began firing on them. Dashiell, the son of state adjutant general Jeremiah Y. Dashiell, was mortally wounded, while Litteral received a gunshot wound to the mouth as he fled on horseback.[32]

Soon after sunset Litteral rode his heavily lathered horse into Fort Brown and staggered up to General Bee's headquarters. Unable to speak, and still bleeding from the mouth, he motioned for a pencil and paper and then began frantically writing down an account of his terrifying escape. Bee was stunned. Although warned by spies that Union-inspired renegades planned to attack Brownsville that night, he never believed that Vidal might be behind the treachery. Quickly, word spread of the alarm as Bee, who had only nineteen Confederate troops remaining at post, sent ten of his regular cavalry under Lieutenant Jack Vinton on a reconnaissance toward the mouth of the river. "I then called on the citizens of Brownsville to rally to my aid," Bee reported, "but before anything like an approximation to organization or order could be made, the pickets under Vinton were driven to within 1 mile of the town." Bee, who ordered that his men wheel two artillery pieces out of Fort Brown toward the road to

Boca del Rio, had good reason to fear that the city might fall to mutineers and murderers.

"Fully satisfied then that Vidal and his whole company were traitors," Bee wrote two days later, "I, with the able assistance of Brigadier General [James] Slaughter, Colonel Duff, Major [George] Magruder, Jr., . . . and Captain Winston, was enabled, with the cordial assistance of the citizens, to get the two heavy guns into a favorable position, and [establish] something like order and organization among the men." Realizing now that Vidal's intention was to overrun the small Confederate garrison at Fort Brown and seize the town's warehouses that were brimming with cotton, General Bee dispatched couriers toward the Palo Alto Prairie to retrieve the three companies of Duff's cavalry encamped in the thickets. "The night passed with every available man I could arm standing in line of battle," he recorded.[33]

But the anticipated raid on Brownsville never came. On October 28 Bee could write confidently that he was at last satisfied that "the enemy was Vidal's company alone, increased by a few *rancheros* from either side" of the river. So he concluded, while the danger may still have been present, "The excitement has quieted down, although the citizens are all on duty." Little did Bee know that Vidal's raiders had merely bypassed Brownsville, then attacked the Rancho Ramereño on the next bend of the river upstream, the murderous band shooting to death three men and hanging two others before slipping across the river. Bee did not yet fully understand that a much greater danger awaited him, nor that the peril would appear on the eastern horizon—and sooner than he had anticipated.[34]

While the indecisive General Bee waited and fretted at Fort Brown, storm clouds were gathering off the Gulf Coast of South Texas. As fate would have it, this tempest brought not only ominous skies but also the changing tides of war. After failing to launch a combined land and sea operation in the coastal waters off Sabine Pass on September 8, 1863, Major General Nathaniel Banks of the Union Army and U.S. Navy Admiral David Farragut had shifted their attack four hundred miles downcoast to the mouth of the Rio Grande. Now their plan changed. They would strangle the Confederacy by choking off the cotton trade on the Mexican border. In other words, the strategic ports located upcoast, including Galveston, could wait.

On the afternoon of November 1, a violent gale blew in from the north. High winds and swelling waves lashed the shores of South Padre Island and Brazos Santiago. These angry gusts from the Gulf brought not only curling white caps of sea and threatening walls of black clouds but also a small flotilla of Federal gunboats. At the lead of this formation was the USS *McClellan*, the flagship of the fleet, and several escort vessels that were merely the advanced guard of a large Union armada of twenty-six transports that carried some seven thousand Union regulars. Through the mists of that gray afternoon the *McClellan* appeared, and on its bridge stood a confident and determined General Banks, the newly appointed commander of the U.S. Gulf theater.[35]

Former Speaker of the U.S. House of Representatives and, more recently, the governor of Massachusetts, the forty-seven-year-old General Banks may have been more a political than a military appointment. He was certainly not a career soldier, nor was he much of a sailor. As the events of the past week had proved, the seasick troops that he commanded were no better. Faced with the specter of inclement weather, Banks had nevertheless pushed his fleet through a violent Gulf storm that threatened the destruction of his ships and his entire command. Two days before his arrival on the South Texas coast, while caught in a furious squall of strong winds that tossed his ships around like strands of straw, he had panicked when his creaking vessel began taking on water. As cresting waves crashed over the decks of his flagship and his bilge pumps failed, he frantically tried to lighten the ship's load by ordering his men to pitch first baggage, then in desperation dozens of terrified horses and mules, into the ocean.[36]

Apparently, the tactic worked. Despite emerging from the tempest safely, and without losing so much as a single ship, Banks's transports were separated, and his forlorn fleet was scattered at sea. Even so, just the rumor of Union regulars off the shores of Brazos Santiago would be enough to cause General Hamilton Bee to prepare his tiny garrison to evacuate Brownsville and withdraw inland. On November 2 Bee dispatched Captain Dick Taylor's scouts to Point Isabel to determine the disposition and strength of enemy forces that had begun coming ashore the previous night. The next morning, when notified by Confederate couriers that several companies of Federal cavalry were encamped at Boca Chica beach and that Taylor had begun to fall back along the road to Brownsville, Bee instructed ten of his troops to escort a number of teamsters northward toward the Nueces, their train of wagons laden with his own personal cache of cotton. Like other Confederate officials during the war, Bee had profited mightily from the cotton trade—and he stood to lose much if that commerce was interrupted.[37]

By most accounts the forty-three-year-old General Hamilton P. Bee carried all the credentials of an experienced leader. In 1839 President Mirabeau B. Lamar had handpicked the native South Carolinian to survey the newly established boundary between the Republic of Texas and the United States. Four years later, President Sam Houston had appointed him commissioner to convene a peace council with the Penateka band of Comanche. During the war with Mexico, Bee had served under the legendary Ranger commander Benjamin McCulloch. Like all his contemporaries who fought in that defining campaign, he had learned skirmish tactics and the lightning-quick charge in battle from none other than *el diablo* himself, Colonel "Jack" Hays of the First Regiment of Texas Volunteers. Later in that war he had ridden with Lamar's company of Colonel Peter H. Bell's Texas Volunteers. Following the conflict, he had moved to Laredo, where he was elected to a seat in the Texas legislature, a post he held for five terms. Between 1855 and 1857 he had even swung the coveted gavel as Speaker of the state house.[38]

But it was not prior military prowess that prompted his appointment as brigadier general in the Confederate States Army in March 1862. Like so many commissions issued during the war, his was pure politics, plain and simple. As with many others with political connections and powerful contacts, Bee had finally risen to his level of incompetence. Now, faced with a crisis, that lack of leadership ability would at last show.

Before he fled Brownsville on the afternoon of November 3, 1863, Bee also ordered his tattered little command, many recovering from a drunken spree the night before, to burn Fort Brown. Determined that nothing of value would fall into the hands of the enemy, Bee supervised his troops as they torched the post. Then he instructed them to push several artillery pieces into the mud of the Rio Grande and to slide into the river any remaining bales of cotton that had not already been ferried across to Matamoros. It was a chaotic scene, "a disgraceful orgy," as Williams recalled. While many panic-stricken citizens escaped to the Mexican side of the river that day, the blaze at Fort Brown raged out of control, spreading to nearby warehouses and docks along Levee Street. As a few frantic residents of Brownsville worked feverishly to prevent the blaze from engulfing the surrounding commercial district, one depot filled with eight thousand pounds of condemned gunpowder caught fire. Several men ran for their lives, and within seconds of the flames rising to the rooftop a massive explosion shattered the building and showered cinder and burning debris over much of the city. For miles around, the dancing flames and black cloud of billowing smoke could be seen rising over Brownsville.[39]

Although Confederate authorities had ordered General Bee to hold Fort Brown at all costs and to "use every effort to repulse" the enemy, he now evacuated his post and abandoned the town, leaving much of it smoldering and in ruins. Thus, he effectively surrendered his station without offering any resistance. Personally escorting his wagons that spilled over with cotton as they bumped across the South Texas prairies, he hurried from the border with as much cotton as he could carry.

As for his vaunted state volunteers, including elements of the Thirty-Third Texas Cavalry of Colonel Duff, they too resolved that retreat was better than certain defeat and capture—or even death. Reacting to the rumors of a Union invasion, they turned tail and rode across the Arroyo Hondo and over the windswept wastes of the Wild Horse Desert. Like their commanding general, they did not stop running until they had reached the safety of Captain Richard King's Santa Gertrudis Ranch five days later.[40]

From his camp at King's ranch on November 8, 1863, Bee commended Duff's command for their "good conduct" and sense of order and discipline during the hasty withdrawal. What he failed to report, however, was that before leaving the border his rowdy irregulars had purportedly looted stores in Brownsville and plundered abandoned ranches en route to the Santa Gertrudis. He also neglected to record that along the way his volunteers had helped themselves to the livestock that wandered freely over the ranges of the Nueces Strip. Even in retreat, therefore, Bee's Confederate partisans—among them elements of Duff's Partisan "Rangers"—continued to claim by force of arms this vast country and the wealth that it represented. In that respect, little separated some of them from the common thieves and bandits that still infested the southernmost border with Mexico.[41]

Indeed, the events along the lower Rio Grande between 1861 and 1865 revealed that the deeply rooted traditions of the Texas Mounted Rangers—both the best and the worst of those abiding traditions—continued uninterrupted during the American Civil War.

2
Old Rip Returns

Mr. Lincoln's army returned to the lower Rio Grande much as it had left at the outset of the war two and a half years earlier—disorganized and in disarray. The Gulf tempest that tossed General Nathaniel Banks's fleet throughout the night of October 30, 1863, created pandemonium aboard the Federal troop transports approaching the South Texas coast. Captain Chester Barney of the Twentieth Iowa Volunteer Infantry recalled the terrifying scene at sea: "All for a time was confusion on board, and the shouting of the ship's officers, howling of the wind, snapping of ropes and rigging, and roaring of waves . . . told plainly enough that we had encountered a great storm." While the crews scrambled aboard the decks of the Union gunboats in a frantic attempt to maintain control of their vessels, troopers below were pitched about in their hammocks, most seasick in the swaying and rolling of the ocean. The timbers of the ships moaned and the beams above their heads sighed in the strong winds. Private Benjamin F. McIntyre of the Nineteenth Iowa Infantry scribbled in his diary, "It seems as if every plank would spring from their places." He noted in haste, "The mad caps dash over us. . . . Our boat plunges fearfully . . . threatening to heave far into the deep its human cargo." No wonder that Barney and McIntyre, like many of their fellow Union soldiers, would never forget their welcome to Texas.[1]

By sunrise the next morning, the high winds and heavy swells had blown most of the Union ships off course, leaving the fleet scattered off Port Aransas. Two schooners and their entire crews were reported lost at sea, while another ship was so badly damaged by the storm that its sailors and soldiers had to be rescued shortly before the listing wooden hull was abandoned and left to sink beneath the waves. The following day, November 1, the weather broke, and by noon the tattered fleet—or what was left of it—appeared off Brazos Santiago, within sight of the entrance to the Rio Grande. Unfortunately, for General Banks and his men, the clear skies that morning failed to portend a successful landing.[2]

Indeed, almost nothing went as planned. That morning from his position on the bridge of the USS *McClellan*, General Banks ordered his gunboats to open fire on Bagdad, believing the squalid port to be a Confederate stronghold. What Banks failed to realize, however, was that the

Stars and Bars of the Confederacy did not fly over the town. Nor did the red, white, and green banner of the Republic of Mexico. Instead, Banks was later embarrassed to learn, the flag of France now waved over the beaches at Bagdad. He had fired upon a friendly nation. Several companies of French troops, loyal to Emperor Maximilian, had recently occupied the port, previously unknown to U.S. War Department officials, and these forces now stood determined to prevent this hub of the cotton trade from falling into the hands of Mexican forces loyal to the deposed President Benito Juárez.

It was Banks's first embarrassing mistake—but it would not be his last. Ordering his gunboats to reverse course and his flagship's captain to signal his most sincere apology, Banks turned his fleet back toward the windward shore of Brazos Santiago, but not before shelling the tiny fishing village of Clarksville on the Texas side of the river. Laying anchor in sight of the desolate sandbar island guarding the gateway to the Rio Grande, Banks awaited the next sunrise to go ashore.[3]

Captain Chester Barney recalled the chaotic scene that November 2 when he observed the soldiers of the Nineteenth Iowa Infantry attempting to disembark and conduct an amphibious landing in small surfboats. During the first wave, several small landing boats capsized in the choppy waters. A few Union soldiers drowned, other troopers were pulled alive from the foaming surf, and a handful of horses and pack mules were reportedly lost. Fortunately for those waiting on the decks of the Union schooners, Banks suspended the operation until a small steamboat, the *William Bagley*, could be brought forward to load troops for safe transport to Point Isabel on the mainland.[4]

The Union troops who landed and moved upriver included mostly young recruits from Iowa and Illinois. But among these Federal troops also marched units bound to receive the special attention of General Hamilton Bee's scouts watching the entire scene from a distance through spy glasses. The "Corps d'Afrique," black troopers of the Sixteenth Infantry and the Ninety-Fifth U.S. Colored Infantry, were laboring in support of the First U.S. Colored Engineers constructing pontoon bridges and loading docks to assist in the amphibious landing. Until now, Texan spies and their commanders had only heard rumors that the Union army was deploying units made up exclusively of black soldiers, many of them former slaves who had rushed to the Union standard following the announcement of President Lincoln's Emancipation Proclamation. Word raced upriver to the Anglo and Tejano populace, therefore, that "Old Abe's Negroes" were armed and would soon advance up the Rio Grande.[5]

News of Banks's landing and his subsequent attack on Bagdad touched off a whirlwind of chaos and violence. People along both banks of the Rio Grande braced themselves amid rumors of arrests, executions, and wanton acts of banditry. As Captain Barney recorded, "All these commotions, revolutions, and excitements in great measure sprung from the mistake made by [General Banks and] the commander of our vessel in . . . [shelling] the town of Bagdad, then in possession of the French, which the Mexicans at Matamoros interpreted as a demonstration in favor of the Liberals [Juaristas], and forthwith proceeded to adopt '*revolutionizing*' as a means best calculated" to achieving their ends.[6]

The dusty town of Brownsville, at the extreme southern tip of Texas, seemed so far away from the war in the East. But with General Hamilton P. Bee's hurried evacuation and the landing of a Union expeditionary force, the stark realities of war returned to the Rio Grande Valley that had known so much sorrow and suffering. It was as if the howling storm that had battered the Gulf Coast earlier in the week was but a prelude to the whirlwind that was soon to sweep the entire river frontier. Looters and lawless rogues of the worst type ruled the streets and alleys of Brownsville, which seemed otherwise deserted, first burned then abandoned to border ruffians from both sides of the river. Pistol-wielding robbers now held the lone ferry that carried people and commerce to Matamoros, closing traffic to all but those holding hard currency. So desperate was Cameron County judge Israel Bigelow that he even sent word across the river to his old hated enemy, General Juan Nepomucino Cortina, pleading for him to intervene with an armed force to spare Brownsville from further disorder and bloodshed. No doubt amused at the irony, Cortina, who had captured the city in the autumn of 1859 and ignited a brief but bloody border war, refused. He had other important business to attend, or so he said.

Cortina may have persuaded a forty-five-year-old former strong arm of the Mexican Army, General José María Cobos, to respond to Bigelow's appeal. Cobos, the brash rebel chieftain, dispatched some two hundred armed supporters across the Rio Grande for the ostensible purpose of arresting common thieves. But Cobos was less than altruistic in his purpose and actions. He had only aligned himself with Cortina to overthrow Manuel Ruiz, the governor of Tamaulipas who favored the return of President Benito Juárez, the besieged champion of Mexican nationalism.[7]

Meanwhile, as Union troops reappeared on the coast and advanced overland from Brazos Santiago and Boca Chica, tensions rose among rival factions on the opposite bank. Another upheaval swept Matamoros, the city that had long been a welter of conflict owing to the strategic importance of the cotton trade and, more recently, the arrival of the French Imperialistas loyal to Maximilian. In the early morning darkness of November 6, just hours before his spies reported that U.S. troops would begin occupying Brownsville, General Cobos seized Matamoros by force. He even ordered the arrest of Ruiz and proclaimed himself Governor of Tamaulipas. This coup d'état was accomplished with the express support of General Cortina.[8]

Not until midmorning did the Stars and Stripes again float above the charred remains and fallen ramparts of Fort Brown. After several days of anarchy and terror, some semblance of order returned as Union blue-coats now patrolled the streets and protected shops and markets. Elements of the Thirteenth Maine Volunteers and First Missouri Light Artillery entered the town to the cheers of local Unionists, some who wrongly believed that the war was now over. The following afternoon, a quiet Sunday, church bells pealed announcing the arrival of the Nineteenth Iowa Volunteers. Private Benjamin McIntyre recalled that the trail from Point Isabel to Brownsville had been marked with "a singular white flaky substance," the obvious reference being to the recent exodus of hundreds of wagons laden with cotton. He also noted in his diary that the fortifications dignified with the name Fort Brown had been destroyed by fire. A sense of calm had settled over the still-smoldering town, and merchants were already preparing to reopen businesses undamaged by the fires. Despite it all, everything seemed to be returning to normal.[9]

The same could not be said for the sister city across the river. On November 7, 1863, an emboldened Cobos instructed his loyal lieutenant governor, Romulo Vila, to carry out the prompt execution of the ousted and imprisoned Governor Ruiz. At first, a scheming General Cortina watched and waited as the drama played out. Then, without any warning, Cortina sent his supporters to arrest Cobos and Vila. With a swiftness characteristic of such local "revolutions," the Cortinistas held a summary court-martial under the false pretext that Cobos and Vila were Imperialistas. Cortina's supporters promptly convicted both prisoners of treason and stood them before a firing squad. So stunning were the day's events that U.S. consul Leonard Pierce informed General Banks that he feared his consulate might be attacked, whereupon Banks vowed to send Union regulars across the border "if the American flag or your person is threatened."[10]

But no such action would be necessary. After orchestrating the executions of his former compatriots, the guileful Cortina released Ruiz, who promptly issued two pronunciamientos hailing Cortina as a liberator. Not known for an abiding sense of loyalty, Cortina responded immediately by removing Ruiz from power again; then he dispatched a twenty-five-man armed escort to the Brownsville ferry to hasten Ruiz's "retreat from the city." Days later Cortina recalled former governor Jesús de la Serna, a leader more to his personal liking.[11]

But the shrewd Cortina had not heard the last of Ruiz. A mere six weeks later, Ruiz, determined to retake Matamoros and the governor's seat, returned to the lower Rio Grande with an armed force of six hundred Mexican loyalists. As Cortina and Serna entrenched themselves behind barricades of Texas cotton and readied for an assault, the newly arrived commander of Union expeditionary forces at Fort Brown, General Napoleon Jackson Tecumseh Dana, expressed concern about the "great panic and confusion" across the river and fear that an attack was "hourly expected."[12]

Not until the first week in January 1864 did Ruiz arrive at the gates of Matamoros. Fortunately, while a pitched battle seemed imminent, forces of compromise were at work. Faced now with an enemy superior in strength, Cortina consented to negotiations that resulted in an agreement that Governor de la Serna would relinquish to Ruiz the office of governor. In turn, Cortina agreed to join forces with Ruiz to allow his rival to place General José Macedonio Capistrán in command of the army, and to accept the post of second in command. Still, relations between the rival factions in Matamoros remained strained at best.[13]

Then all hell broke loose. On the afternoon of January 12, 1864, Cortina insisted that his loyalists had not been paid for their services as promised. Amid the growing tension the commander of Cortina's infantry, Colonel Octavio Cárdenas, stormed into the headquarters of the governor and confronted Ruiz with demands for compensation. In a matter of minutes the governor's personal guards dragged Cárdenas outside into the courtyard and shot him. Before sundown, an enraged Cortina ordered a reprisal, positioning a battery of twelve pounders at the Plaza de Hidalgo, and a terrifying artillery duel ensued. The battle of shot and shell continued through the night.[14]

Understandably, Consul Pierce wrote to General Frances Herron, who had just arrived on the scene to take command from Dana, "My person and family are in great danger, as the road between here and the ferry is said to be infested with robbers." Reporting that he held one million dollars in specie and "a large amount of other property in my charge at the consulate," Pierce concluded that the city would soon be plundered and that he feared being a target of Cortina and his partisans. Ruiz likewise scribbled a note to General Herron, admitting that he was powerless to protect Pierce and his mission. The situation seemed untenable, all agreed.[15]

General Herron did not hesitate to act. He ordered four companies of the Twentieth Wisconsin under the command of Major Henry Bertram across the river to relieve the U.S. consulate. Herron first forwarded his assurances to Ruiz and Cortina that his troops would "take no part in the fight." In the predawn hours of January 13, Bertram arrived at the U.S. consulate only to find Pierce sitting with angry members of both the Ruiz and Cortina camps, each demanding an explanation of why U.S. armed forces had violated the sovereignty of Mexico.[16]

By sunrise the Cortinistas had turned the battle in their favor, and before noon the matter was decided. Ruiz and his supporters had been routed in a fierce struggle that had claimed the lives of at least three hundred Mexican combatants. With the smell of gunpowder still thick in the air, Cortina proclaimed himself governor of Tamaulipas. In his first official act, Cortina "allowed" Major Bertram and his U.S. troopers to retire across the river unmolested. One of the bloodiest days in the history of the Rio Grande Valley thus ended with the old Red Robber triumphant once again. In the words of historian Jerry Thompson, "In less than five years, through sheer bravado and cunning determination, he had risen from a little-known and illiterate Cameron County *ranchero* to the pinnacle of power in Tamaulipas."[17]

Now only one man stood in Cortina's path—Old Rip Ford. Few on either side of the border doubted that Juan Cortina was behind the coup d'état to rid himself of Ruiz and any other rivals. Fewer still were surprised that, in such a time of violence and chaos along the lower Rio Grande, an ambitious man like Cortina would rise to power. Even fewer were caught off guard by the means and methods of his rapid ascent. Certainly, Ford was not.

Ford even expected to hear that, to curry favor with U.S. officials, Cortina would attempt to deny Texans the benefits of shipping their cotton across the border and on to international markets. He also understood that Texans and Tejanos alike would simply circumvent such a blockade, just as Confederate corsairs had long evaded the Union blockade along the Gulf Coast. As Ford predicted early in 1864, cotton traders simply rerouted their commerce upriver, along more circuitous routes to Roma and Rio Grande City, Laredo, and even as far north as Eagle Pass.

With the electrifying news of a Union invasion of South Texas, Ford began expressing his disdain for the desk job that had confined him to an office in Austin for almost twenty months. Since June 1862 he had served as superintendent of the newly created state Bureau of Conscription. Only reluctantly had he accepted the charge of overseeing an onerous measure he had termed "unfortunate"—the first draft law in U.S. history. Shuffling papers, serving warrants, and tracking down draft dodgers proved less than satisfying.

By the fall of 1863 Ford was firmly restating his gnawing desire to return to a field command. Just days before Christmas, Old Rip got his wish. General John Bankhead Magruder called on the legendary Ranger captain to drive the Federals from Brownsville, just as he had done three years earlier. After the newly commissioned Colonel Ford was officially relieved of his administrative duties in Austin, he issued an impassioned call for Texan volunteers to "rally to the standard" for "the honor of the State, for the sake of the glorious memories of the past, the hopes of the future." In such times of crisis Ford had never been at a loss for inspirational words.[18]

No one was more pleased by the appointment than Ford's old friend, ranchero Richard King. Upon hearing the news, he penned a letter to the longtime Ranger leader, expressing his delight about his "coming out our way after the Yankees." Then he affirmed, "I believe the people [of South Texas] have more confidence in you than anyone else." In closing, Captain King cautioned Ford that there was little forage on the prairies for his horses and livestock, and he even admitted that some of his own cattle were in a "starving condition." But he promised his support and specifically pledged to provide enough beef to feed "all the men you can bring. . . . You can have all of mine you need and anything else I have which may be of service."[19]

Although growing gray, Ford still cast an imposing presence. Standing just over six feet tall, his stooped frame and chiseled features were softened somewhat by a fair, ruddy complexion and piercing blue eyes. Almost every Texan knew the name and the fame associated with the Ranger affectionately called "Old Rip" (so named for his U.S.-Mexican War service as Colonel Jack Hays's adjutant who signed death certificates with the familiar postscript "Rest in Peace," shortened to "RIP"). From the killing fields of Mexico to the campaigns against the feared Comanche to the battles with border bandits along the lower Rio Grande, his reputation as a fighter had preceded him. If any Texan might chase an enemy all the way through the gates of hell, the people of South Texas believed that man would be Rip Ford. One contemporary, W. Jeff Maltby, acknowledged that the legendary Ford held the "very highest respect of all who knew him." Maltby further observed of the flinty old Ranger, "He seemed to . . . [live] a charmed life that was proof against shot, shell, fire, or sword for he passed through a long and eventful career with but little bodily harm." In sum, Maltby even went so far as to liken the iconic Old Rip to no less than George Washington, stating that he was "first in war, first in peace, and first in the heart of [Texas] frontiersmen."[20]

Ford's Rio Grande Campaign

As he waited out the opening weeks of 1864 in San Antonio, Ford received news that some of his former Rangers were raising volunteer companies in South Texas. Word had spread that Old Rip would soon be back in command. Not surprisingly, hundreds of Texans responded to Ford's call and assembled near Alamo Plaza, so many of them that the colonel could not maintain an accurate daily count. Amid the excitement, however, Ford could not help but notice that most of the enlistees were either men beyond the draft age of thirty-five or mere boys as young as sixteen.[21]

Ford's troubles mounted faster than the recruits he could muster. All he had to do now was transform a mob comprising mostly young farmers, frontiersmen, shopkeepers, surveyors, saloon regulars, and city lawyers into a disciplined fighting force. Moreover, without siege artillery at his disposal, with no funds to procure provisions, with good horses as well as tack and saddles in short supply, and reliable firearms being available only through weapons dealers south of the Rio Grande, Ford's leadership would be tested to the limit.

Worse still, Indian depredations were reportedly growing in intensity along the Rio Grande frontier as marauding bands of Lipan Apache and Kickapoo were emboldened by news that the white men and Mexicans alike were fighting each other. Just as troubling, General Cortina seemed more determined than ever to choke off commerce along the river frontier and strangle the Texans' economy by denying them the benefits of trade with the French, the British, or anyone else. Persistent rumors of smallpox and yellow fever along the lower Rio Grande also made their way north-ward, the fear of a great plague spreading even faster than the contagions themselves. To compound the misery, the most severe drought yet known to descend upon South Texas threatened to make 1864 one of the most dreadful years in the annals of the Rio Grande Valley.[22]

After ten weeks of preparation and training, Ford and some 1,300 mounted state troops of the Second Texas Cavalry departed San Antonio on an expedition to the lower Rio Grande. Riding through Alamo Plaza at the front of the formation, a grim-faced Colonel Ford thought to himself that the campaign ahead promised to be anything but quick and easy. The events of the next week only confirmed that belief. Moving southward, then angling eastward and downstream along the dry bed of the Nueces, Ford and his "Cavalry of the West," as he termed his expeditionary force, found few wells and even fewer water holes. Where fresh water would have been expected in most years, nothing could be located but an occa-sional stagnant pool and a trail of rotting carcasses, the bones of hundreds of cattle, goats, deer, and feral hogs littering the countryside. Buzzards swung in the air overhead as the column descended the Nueces. Mile after mile the dry bed was strewn with skeletons and skulls left for the scaveng-ing coyotes and turkey vultures. Ford and his troops must have thought to themselves, or maybe even wondered aloud, that the sandy riverbed appeared to mark the entrance to hell.[23]

After a week on the trail, with little water and even less forage for their animals, Ford's dust-covered column approached the outpost of San Fer-nando, less than a day's ride upriver from Corpus Christi. It had been an ominous beginning to what turned out to be the final campaign of Ford's military career—and the last of the American Civil War.

Still, Colonel Ford, exhausted from seven hard days in the saddle, was overjoyed when he recognized the handsome figure of his longtime pro-tégé, the "boy bugler of the Battle of Cerro Gordo," Major Mat Nolan. Ford and young Nolan, now sporting a full beard, had served together under Jack Hays in Mexico. Surely Old Rip must have swelled with pride at the sight of the still-youthful commander who had also saddled up along-side him during the campaigns against the Comanche and, more recently, during the "Cortina War" of 1859–60. As for Nolan, he could not help but notice that his old mentor was aging, frail and obviously tired, yet still with the same hard features and that familiar look of determination.[24]

Ford gave no indication to Nolan or anyone else that he was already suf-fering from a recurrence of the "fever." He never complained in front of his troops about the chills that caused him to shiver, sometimes uncontrollably, especially at night after the campfires were doused. He never let on about the cold sweats that made it difficult and sometimes impossible for him to rest. But it showed. He looked pale, his once muscular frame now drawn and gaunt, his eyes drooped and sunken, his body visibly weakened by what was most likely malaria.

While encamped on the lower Nueces, Ford received his first reliable intelligence about the military situation in South Texas. Major Nolan informed him of recent Union activities in the region. Specifically, Nolan described a clash with the Mexican bandit–turned-Unionist Captain Cecilio Valerio earlier in the month near Los Patricios (south of present-day Falfurrias), some fifty miles southwest of Banquete. Although Nolan's company of mounted riflemen was outnumbered two to one and while they were "indifferently armed" and facing an enemy equipped with Burnside carbines and Colt revolvers, his irregulars acquitted themselves well. Nolan recalled a "desperate fight" in the mesquite thickets along the road, noting that "the loss of the enemy must have been severe. Five dead bodies were found in the *mesquital,* but from the trails seen, showing that men had been dragged off when wounded, and pools of blood discovered, it is almost certain that at least 12 or 15 were killed or wounded." Nolan likewise informed Ford that many of the enemy's horses were "left on the ground either killed or wounded." He also reported three of his own men had been killed during the action.[25]

Not only was the fight notable for being the last incursion of Union troops into the Nueces Strip, it also loomed large for another reason. After the battle, one Confederate partisan brought Nolan a letter found on the body of Valerio's adjutant. The communication addressed to Valerio from Camargo and dated March 2, 1864, indicated that Union volunteers commanded by Colonel John L. Haynes were advancing northward from the Rio Grande with the intent of intercepting Confederates and driving them back toward San Antonio. Apparently, the dispatch implied, the Yankee cavalry, made up mostly of Mexican Unionists and border marauders, had left the river above Brownsville virtually unguarded.[26]

While encamped near Captain King's Santa Gertrudis Ranch, Ford received a communication from his old friend, Santos Benavides. The letter buoyed his spirits. Colonel Benavides reported that the citizens of Laredo had "rallied gallantly" in defense of their town on March 19 to turn back a Union raid. Erecting barricades in the streets, counterattacking the Union cavalry with six-shooters blazing, they repelled an initial assault and eventually routed the enemy, as Benavides expressed, by keeping up a "persistent fire" until the Yankees decided "to skeedadle [*sic*]." Ford also learned from Benavides another important piece of information that, if true, boded well for his expedition: Union forces downriver at Rio Grande City numbered no more than three hundred infantrymen who were supported only by two twelve-pound rifled cannons.[27]

Meanwhile, before departing San Antonio, Ford had sent his wife and one-year-old daughter, Mary Louise, ahead by wagon to the border, but by a safer though longer route that crossed into Mexico at Eagle Pass. Escorted by family confidant Manuel Treviño, Ford's wife and daughter labored on the trail for more than a month before they finally reached Matamoros early in April.

No sooner had Addie and "baby Lulu" arrived in the border city than they received an unexpected visitor. At the home of a friend and admirer of Colonel Ford, the bearded General Juan Cortina stopped by to pay his respects. Most courteous and even charming, Cortina reminded Addie that several years earlier her husband had extended nothing but kindness to his mother, Señora Cavazos, and to his brother, Sabos. Cortina explained that neither his mother nor he would ever forget Ford's graciousness. He had come to return the favor. Mrs. Ford thanked the general, explaining that she might need assistance in arranging for her sister and mother to cross from Brownsville for a visit. Cortina acknowledged her request; then he left with a handful of letters that Addie had penned to her family across the river.[28]

Ford later expressed gratitude for Cortina's magnanimous gesture. But he was also skeptical, never having lost sight of the fact that his longtime nemesis was merely repaying an old debt and trying to ingratiate himself with Ford for political reasons. That summer Ford summed up his doubts about Cortina's sincerity. In a report to Confederate Adjutant Joseph E. Dwyer, Ford observed of Cortina, "He hates Americans; particularly Texans. He has an old and deep-seated grudge against Brownsville. He knows his career is near closed." Ford even predicted that "if he could force his way through our lines, plunder our people, and get within the Yankee lines, it would [be] a *finale* he would delight in."[29]

Ford had sized up Cortina many times before, on several occasions during the 1850s when Addie and he had visited the home of her sister Lou in Brownsville. Ford even grew to respect his rival during the recent border war that bore Cortina's name. Oddly enough, Ford considered Cortina a worthy adversary to be admired for his guile and, more important, his almost chivalric sense of honor. In turn, Cortina understood that Ford was not like most of the Anglos he had come to loathe, and that such a man of unwavering integrity and steadfast courage was rare among Texans and Mexicans alike. In sum, neither man ever underestimated the other—and for good reason.

Ford later recalled that, despite their legendary rivalry, he and Cortina always remained personally on good terms. In an acrid political climate and amid a border culture that cultivated suspicion and mistrust, each held an abiding respect for the other. As a soldier in the service of the Lone Star State, however, Ford understood that in the larger struggle none of that mattered. His loyalty lay with Texas, and only with Texas, and that was not the case with Cortina.[30]

By the spring of 1864 a far greater problem faced Ford and his cause: desertion. Almost daily, frightened young Texans fled into the mesquite thickets, many crossing the river to what they assumed would be the safety of Mexican soil. A few deserters even made their way downriver, somehow hoping that Union forces would feed and protect them. Ford found that Confederate conscripts and new enlistees proved the most likely to slip away, many as soon as they drew their first pay from the quartermaster. Hungry and homesick, with empty pockets but fully loaded revolvers and rifles, they scattered into the brush, many never to be heard from again. One private serving under Colonel Ford suggested factors that contributed to the lack of discipline when he confided in a letter that he was surrounded by unlearned and unwashed men who were almost all from the "lower classes of society." Moreover, he affirmed, "Drinking among the troops is common. I see examples before me every day. It is true that a young man cannot guard himself too closely in camp, particularly along the Rio Grande." Once again, as in earlier border wars, Texan commanders learned the hard lesson: the mixture of alcohol, firearms, and prejudice was most combustible.[31]

Given the obvious obstacles confronting Ford, during the last phase of the war it was only logical that he would fall back upon his experience as a Ranger, and that he would rely mostly on the men he knew and trusted from past campaigns. In a letter dated March 16, 1864, Ford summarized his strategy to his commander, General James Slaughter. He proposed to "cut up, disperse, or drive . . . [inland], all the mounted troops of the enemy and induce them to believe . . . [our forces] are too weak for anything greater." Deception, disruption, evasion, interdiction, secrecy, and surprise would be the elements of his strategy along the lower Rio Grande.

To carry out his tactical plans for an unconventional campaign designed to harass and frustrate Union forces, Ford would rely on the same guerrilla tactics he had learned from Jack Hays in Mexico and later refined in the Comanche campaigns and more recently during the "Cortina War." Not surprisingly, he also remained determined to depend upon his trusted longtime lieutenants: men like Mat Nolan, John Littleton, Philip Luckett, and Santos Benavides—men who had learned field tactics and military discipline from him.[32]

Confident that the river frontier lay open before him, Ford departed the lower Nueces and struck off for the border on March 26. Leaving a force behind to protect his supply lines in the rear and his exposed left from any prowling Union partisans, he advanced toward Laredo. Four days later, while en route, his column met up with several companies of Confederate volunteers returning from the borders of Arizona. Now with more than six hundred irregulars in his command, Colonel Ford proceeded to the Rio Grande by way of the springs at Los Ojuelos, arriving at Laredo on April 15.

Before he could move downriver toward his objectives—Rio Grande City and Brownsville—Ford needed to attend to the delicate diplomatic negotiations with Mexico. First, while in Laredo at the home of Santos Benavides he met with Santiago Vidaurri, former governor of Nuevo León once rumored to be a Juarista but now an open supporter of Maximilian. The likable Ford seized the opportunity to court the favor of the influential leader who remained long on Liberal credentials, despite his recent break with Juárez. Yet as the year wore on Ford also continued to communicate with representatives of the Juárez government, then in exile at El Paso del Norte.

During his conversation with Vidaurri, Ford learned of vague reports that Union *renegados* from across Texas and northern Mexico were gathering on the Mexican side of the river and preparing an offensive. The last thing Ford needed was interference from Mexican officials across the border. At the least, he must ensure that the warring factions in Mexico remain neutral on the Texas side of the river if his Rio Grande expedition was to succeed. Better yet, by cultivating good relations with all parties, he hoped to position himself to procure from both factions in the Mexican conflict desperately needed arms and munitions for his troops. Of course, he planned to use Texas cotton as leverage and collateral for loans.[33]

Leading his column down the Rio Grande early in May, Ford instructed Benavides to protect the rear by scouting upriver as far as Eagle Pass. As he had done many times before, Ford also ordered spies to fan out in front of him and scout the trails that wound their way through the dense thickets along the river shallows. Torrential spring thunderstorms drenched men and horses alike as Ford's column slogged eastward for a week and more, paralleling the Rio Bravo, which now swelled beyond its banks owing to blinding rains. Still, the weeklong downpour was a welcome break from the drought that had lasted as long as the war. Ford hoped that it was a good sign.

As he had anticipated, the way to Brownsville was now clear of any sign of the enemy. Although his Tejano scouts, under the command of Lieutenant Eugenio Garza, encountered a small band of Mexican raiders above Roma, no major incidents deterred Ford in his march downriver. On May 2 the lead elements of Ford's Cavalry of the West arrived in Rio Grande City. Ringgold Barracks had been abandoned weeks earlier by a small garrison of Union troops that had fallen back to Edinburg. For nearly six weeks Ford's Confederate partisans idled away their time at Ringgold, cleaning their weapons, playing cards, swatting flies and mosquitoes, waiting for an opportunity to tangle with the Yankees. No doubt some recruits may have been just waiting for the day when their short-term enlistment would expire. For a few, however, the proximity to the river and the sanctuary of Mexican soil must have been too tempting. By the time Colonel Ford returned from a trip to Camargo and Matamoros to gather information from spies and procure provisions from border profiteers, he was disgusted to learn of increasing numbers of desertions within his command.[34]

Robert Williams remembered, "[Ford's] force did nothing, nor was capable of doing anything, being composed mainly of deserters and loafers of all sorts. These gentry flocked to the gallant Colonel's standard under the well-founded belief that there would be but little discipline, and no danger. In fact," Williams recalled, "they expected a 'good time,' with plenty of gambling and a sufficiency of plunder." In other words, a disorganized rabble posed as Confederate cavalry on the South Texas border. And not even a stern disciplinarian like Ford could mold them into a regiment worthy of their name. More embarrassing to Ford, many of his men even dignified their service and their unit by calling themselves "Rangers" (Old Rip reserved that term for his lead scouts).[35]

Whatever their sins and shortcomings, the Confederate guerrillas who had remained at Colonel Ford's side through the uncertainties of that spring were soon rewarded. They were itching for a fight with the Yankee troops, and before long they would get one. During his scout down the south bank of the Rio Grande, Ford had quietly scoured the border for any information on the strength of the enemy. By the time he returned to Ringgold Barracks early in June, he could report that Union commanders were fast preparing to evacuate Brownsville. To determine if these reports were true, Ford ordered a reconnaissance in force that would rely on his most seasoned cavalry companies to fan out, patrol, and probe the mesquite thickets between Las Rucias Ranch and the banks of the Rio Bravo, some twenty-five miles above Brownsville. The latest intelligence placed Union pickets there, and Old Rip was determined to test these reports before ordering his entire regiment to advance against the enemy.

Ford dispatched Lieutenant Colonel Dan Showalter and Captain Refugio Benavides forward to assess the situation as far south as the Santa Rosa Ranch of prominent landowner, banker, and stockman Charles Stillman. Following a narrow trail that led past several ranchos, including that of stockman John McAllen, Ford pushed ahead. On June 23, near the creek called Como Se Llama he linked up with Showalter and Benavides who reported that a large Union force was encamped several miles downriver at Rancho Las Rucias. First, Ford allowed his men two days of much-needed rest. They had been living on jerked beef for more than a week, and their horses were desperately in need of forage and water. Apparently undetected by the enemy, Ford moved out toward Las Rucias.[36]

On the afternoon of June 25 Ford's column, now numbering some 250, engaged a small Union force in the chaparral and mesquite thickets not far from the site where the Mexican War had begun eighteen years earlier. Advancing to within a few hundred meters of the Federals, Ford positioned his men for a surprise attack. The Union pickets had been caught with their backs to the river. Ford quickly realized that the enemy position presented the opportunity that he had hoped for. On Ford's command, the Confederate cavalrymen surged forward into the brush, galloping headlong through a hail of gunfire while pouring even more shots into the startled enemy. At the head of Ford's line rode Captain James Dunn, a veteran of the U.S.-Mexican War, who had emerged unscathed from the fiercest battles of that campaign. On this day, however, Dunn's luck would run out. During the initial charge, the brave captain tumbled from his saddle mortally wounded.[37]

In the face of such a relentless assault from a determined foe, several companies of Ford's Confederate cavalry scattered into nearby jacales while the Union volunteers frantically attempted to form a defensive line along fence rows and piles of freshly cut mesquite on each side of a lone brick structure. After twenty minutes, during which both forces exchanged random fire, Ford ordered Captain Refugio Benavides to sweep around the enemy's right flank. For some reason, in the confusion of the fight, Benavides mistakenly led a charge toward the enemy's *left* flank, where his column became stalled in the bog and knee-deep waters of a crescent-shaped lagoon. Despite Benavides's near-fatal tactical error, the Union troops still broke ranks and ran, dozens of them dropping their weapons, a few reportedly tossing them into the river during their desperate attempt to escape to the Mexican side.[38]

In all, Colonel Ford had enjoyed a successful day. He counted more than twenty Union dead and thirty-six enemy prisoners, some of them wounded during the fight. He also learned that his men had captured twenty-eight horses and several wagons loaded with provisions. Although many of the Union soldiers had made it safely to the south bank, where they were last seen fleeing as fast as their tired legs could carry them, Ford confidently reported that the road to Brownsville was now open. Even more significant was the dispatch taken from one of the prisoners. As Ford unfolded the letter handed to him by one of his officers, he must have been pleased when he read that the First Texas Union Cavalry was soon to be shipped out to New Orleans. Just as valuable to Ford was the admission of one Union commander that insubordination was also decimating the ranks of Federal volunteers, particularly those recruited from south of the Rio Grande. It was only a matter of time now, or so Ford hoped.[39]

After several days of probing still farther downriver, Ford's scouts confirmed that Federal pickets could only put up minimal resistance before withdrawing toward Brownsville. Through the sweltering heat of July Ford waited for word that the enemy was retreating to the coast. Again, at Ringgold Barracks he assured his volunteers that their patience would pay off. Still, a sense of restlessness moved among the ranks as the weeks wore on without any word.[40]

In times of crisis Ford was quiet, even solitary, not given to much conversation. He was always reticent and reluctant to reveal his plans to anyone. But when he did speak, no one could mistake his commanding presence, his bellowing voice, or his infectious confidence. At times, however, these spartan qualities only isolated the brooding Colonel Ford from even his most trusted officers and enlisted men.

Even so, virtually all who served with Ford held a genuine respect for his strength of character and rare leadership ability. After all, Ford knew the country, the Indians, the Mexicans, and the men he commanded. Years of duty and service might have left him thin and weakened, but he was still every bit a fighting man, a soldier of the first order.

In sum, most who served under Old Rip admired him. But their admiration was tempered by the understanding that he was a warrior, not a saint. Captain Robert Williams remembered the fabled Texan as the "most inveterate gambler and the hardest swearer I ever met, even out West, indeed his power of 'language,' especially when the luck went against him, was almost grotesque in its resourcefulness." Williams recalled that Ford, whether raising a glass of whiskey in a formal toast, or just striking a blow for liberty in a saloon while playing three-card monte, was not only the proverbial hail-fellow-well-met but also an earthy character, always "free with his money, and equally free with his six-shooter," not to mention his strongly held opinions.[41]

While leading men in the field, the legendary old Ranger was all business. His deliberate stare, his icy demeanor in time of peril, his unflinching courage in the face of the enemy, his steely determination, no matter the odds, all inspired confidence. Whatever defines charisma, Ford had it. Williams's assessment notwithstanding, even most of Ford's detractors acknowledged that he was a natural-born leader.

The Execution of Private Garcia

Old Rip's correspondence during the last year of the American Civil War was replete with references to desertions, disobedience, and disciplinary problems among the Texas state troops, some of whom were conscripts serving against their will. Not surprisingly, therefore, dissension, disobedience and "absenteeism" were all too common in the ranks of the Partisan "Rangers" serving on the South Texas border. So was drunkenness, which too often inspired brazen acts of insubordination. The dispatches to and from Ford's company commanders likewise referenced occasional acts of theft, assault, and rape. Court-martial proceedings also consumed the attention of Ford's subordinates, as charges against accused enlisted men ranged from hog stealing to murder. Ford and his superiors regularly documented outbreaks of violence and bloodshed in Confederate camps along the river, with disputes that sometimes ended in eye-gouging, ear-biting brawls.[42]

Earlier in 1864 one Mexican official in Matamoros had complained bitterly about the dregs of the Lone Star State infesting the lower Rio Grande and spilling across the border into his city. "There is a class here . . . who merit the appellation of Ruffians," he reported of the heavily armed Texan refugees congregating in Matamoros, "not good enough for officers and a little too good for the private soldier." Many of these rowdies were no more than mercenaries and soldiers of fortune engaged in the whiskey trade, gunrunning, or both. A few of the more respectable "merchants" smuggled cotton by the barge or wagonload. And all considered the free-ranging cattle to belong to any man with the courage and stealth to steal them. After all, the prospect for profits surely outweighed the risks for those engaged in wartime commerce along the border.[43]

While one Union officer understandably labeled the Confederate partisans operating along the border the "hangmen of Texas," many of the Federal volunteers were little better than their rebel counterparts. Both the First U.S. Texas Cavalry and the Second U.S. Texas Cavalry, the latter being made up mostly of Tejanos and Mexicanos, including a company of marauders known as Vidal's Independent Partisan Rangers, were recruited from the south side of the river. Indeed, such "independent" Federal units—like their Confederate counterparts who often operated independently of higher command—were continually plagued by a general lack of discipline as well as low morale. By most accounts these troubles crossed all lines of color, culture, cause, and nationality.[44]

In fairness to Union recruits in the Rio Grande Valley, they suffered from poor logistical support and were thus most often left with inadequate food, clothing, and medical supplies. Many in the field, with empty bellies though full cartridge belts, understandably resorted to rustling cattle and stealing hogs from farms on both sides of the river. Crimes of violence committed by enlistees against fellow recruits as well as the civilian populace they were sworn to protect likewise alarmed Union commanders. Expressing the racist attitudes of most Anglos who viewed Mexicans with skepticism, if not utter contempt, Private Benjamin F. McIntyre recorded that the Hispanic volunteers who rode in the service of the United States were "dishonest, cowardly, treacherous, and only bide their time to make good their escape." By most accounts, his fellow Union soldiers reflected the same racial prejudice.[45]

While McIntyre's characterization of Tejanos and Mexicanos revealed a most unfortunate prejudice against an entire people, that prejudice was too common among Union as well as Confederate troops. Common too among these volunteers was desertion on a scale not typical of regular units. By the summer of 1864, as preparations were being made to withdraw Union forces from the lower Rio Grande for transport to Louisiana, desertion had reached near-epidemic proportions. So determined were Union commanders to halt the stampede of runaway recruits that, following one court-martial, a board of officers ordered the public execution of a deserter.[46]

Late on the afternoon of June 22, 1864, a solemn drama played out in the streets of Brownsville. It was a somber scene that served to remind volunteers and regulars alike that the most severe consequences awaited anyone who left ranks without official leave. On a still, sun-spangled summer day Union officers carried out the death sentence at Washington Square, near the east end of Elizabeth Street. The day's spectacle focused on a convicted deserter who spoke little English, Private Pedro Garcia of Company E of the Second Texas Union Cavalry. Only days earlier Garcia had confessed to leaving his post for the sole purpose of hunting wild turkey. During his court-martial he had pledged never to desert his post again, and he had begged for mercy, not for himself but for his wife and children. Without him, he had pleaded, they would go hungry.

But Garcia's plea for leniency went unheeded. Private Benjamin McIntyre would never forget the eerie, almost surreal, scene that unfolded shortly after 4:00 that sweltering afternoon. He recorded in his diary, "The Dead March fell upon our ears and soon a squad of soldiers was observed slowly approaching followed by a band of music. Behind them was a coffin carried by four men and immediately followed the dead cart with its victim, near whom walked a priest who had been the constant companion of the doomed man since his execution had been made known."[47]

As the cart carrying the condemned prisoner passed through the ranks of regulars, the band ceased its morbid dirge and the line halted beside an open grave, where the empty wooden coffin was placed. "I must acknowledge for my own part my Spirits were depressed with a sadness to which I was a Stranger. The doomed man stepped from his cart and approached his grave. He was scarce middle aged—in the very prime of life, stout, rugged, and in the enjoyment of health," McIntyre recalled. "He manifested but little feeling in view of his final end and aside from an occasional glance at his grave which displayed a kind of nervousness I saw little or nothing to denote he experienced any feeling regarding the matter." McIntyre then recorded, "He had no word for anyone except the priest who still kept him company and administered the last rites of his religion to him while on his knees before him. After this," McIntyre continued, "he pulled off his shoes, placed the extremities of his pants in his socks, then approaching his coffin kneeled upon it. A bandage was placed over his eyes . . . but he pushed it . . . [aside] and gazed around with seeming indifference upon the armed squad."

A hush then fell over the crowd. A few moments of stillness followed as Father P. F. Parisot administered the last rites, which the condemned man received with "perfect resignation." McIntyre vividly described the drama that happened next: "The word was given *Make ready, Aim*—a dozen rifles were pointed at his breast. It was a moment of painful suspense and was felt by the vast throng—a moment & a human life would be ended. . . . Each one who gazed upon the specticle [*sic*] I doubt not felt the cold blood curdling in his veins & would prefer never again to witness an alike exhibition." Then it happened. "I felt relieved when the word *Fire* was given and I saw the stiffened form fall backward, his breast pierced by a ball. I saw no expression of agony, not the movement of a single muscle." An army surgeon approached the limp frame to determine if any sign of life remained. Signaling that the prisoner still had a pulse, and that a last breath was yet left within his lungs, the physician stepped away. Two members of the firing squad were then hastened forward and ordered to finish the grisly task. They stepped "to within a few yards and fired . . . at his head, one ball crashing through his brain."[48]

With that, it was over. The crowd dispersed as the band again played the dead march, the muffled drums and muted trumpets sounding forth a haunting refrain as Garcia's body was placed in the coffin, lowered into the open grave, and dirt shoveled on the pine box. After returning to his barracks at Fort Brown, Private McIntyre scribbled in his journal, "I have but little to say regarding this affair. I doubt not the example was needed and the dead man merited his fate." But "in his fate there was little or no display of feeling." As for the doomed deserter, "there was a lack of everything which denoted a realization of his situation." McIntyre closed his entry with a postscript, noting that the executed man appeared to be "one of that class who lacked enlightenment, who was very superstitious [*sic*] and [a] firm believer in the roman church and . . . the bright promises the priest had represented as awaiting him."[49]

Sadly, the execution and burial of Private Garcia seemed but a normal event in an abnormal time. After all, the sobering scene of Union soldiers and priests carrying a coffin through the streets of Brownsville was an almost daily ritual that summer. Death and disease were the constant companions of haggard and homesick troopers and hungry peones alike. The scorching heat, an outbreak of smallpox, and crop failures combined with the brackish river water, swarms of mosquitoes carrying malaria and yellow

fever, and rows of filthy, overcrowded hovels to ensure that the cemetery
north of town fast filled with corpses, some of the dead being nameless to
all but their Maker.[50]

Another Crisis Averted

While the Federals prepared for a quiet exodus from the lower Rio Grande,
Ford's spies informed him of the desperate state of affairs at Fort Brown.
Hearing reports of disease and disorder among the Yankee troops, Old
Rip believed that it was only a matter of weeks before all Union forces
would be withdrawn from Texas soil. Little did he know just how soon that
would happen. On July 30, 1864, Ford's scouts cautiously approached the
outskirts of Brownsville, scrambling through the brush and marshes north
of town until they made their way to within one hundred meters of Union
picket lines. Still closer they crept, only to find that the town's perimeter defenses had been abandoned. While the mounted Confederates rode
through the deserted city streets, a few wary residents emerged from their
homes and stores to inform them that the last of the Union soldiers had
left Fort Brown and had withdrawn to Brazos Santiago two days earlier.
In the matter of an hour Ford's mounted partisans reoccupied Brownsville
without even firing a shot.[51]

With Confederate authority thus restored and the commerce in cotton
resumed, Southern sympathizers who had taken refuge in Matamoros,
Reynosa, and other border towns on the south bank began to cross back
into Texas. At the same time, however, following the Federal evacuation,
many Unionists fled to Mexico, some hoping to escape what they believed
to be the despotism of an unholy Confederacy. Still others crossed the
Rio Grande to escape the anticipated Southern surrender and subsequent wrath of Northern Reconstruction that would surely follow the
war. During the waning months of the conflict, therefore, a rush of refugees, mostly Unionists, toward the Mexican border only complicated the
miseries that had visited the Rio Grande Valley. Drifters, draft dodgers,
deserters, even entire families with all their earthly belongings loaded into
wagons or carts plodded toward the Rio Grande, the roads to Brownsville
and other border towns becoming cluttered with the human refuse of this
uncivil war.

So many bedraggled Texans took flight across the Rio Grande during
the final year of the war that newly appointed U.S. consul at Matamoros Emanuel Etchison reported often to officials in Washington that the

streets in front of his office teemed with gaunt and destitute men dressed in tatters. With each passing day, it seemed, Matamoros was fast filling with more ragged refugees—Anglo and Mexicano alike—who were so desperate for protection and a square meal that they spilled across the border in even greater numbers than before.[52]

During the coming weeks, a broiling sun burned overhead, reminding all that there was no relief in sight from the heat, and no end in sight to the war or the torrid passions it inspired. While Ford expressed joy at being reunited with his family in Brownsville, his attention was riveted to the three threats that still faced Confederates on the border. Most ominous, more than 1,500 Federal troops remained dug in along the beaches of the leeward side of Brazos Island. Also entrenched among the sand dunes was a battery of siege guns, twenty-pounders capable of reaching the mainland. Further complicating Ford's position at Brownsville, on August 22, 1864, more than four hundred French marines landed at the entrance to the Rio Grande and again captured Bagdad. Despite assurances from the French commandant that his troops would respect the lives and property of all Texans living north of the river, tensions remained elevated between these elite troops and the Confederate irregulars at Fort Brown as well as their pickets encamped downriver near Rancho Palmito and nearby at White's Ranch. Then there was the matter of the menacing and opportunistic Governor Cortina.[53]

While Cortina might not have been the greatest of his concerns, Ford understood that he was probably the most unpredictable. Caught in the throes of one of the greatest upheavals ever to sweep Mexico, Cortina wavered between loyalty to his countryman Benito Juárez and to the imperial regime of the French usurper, Emperor Ferdinand Maximilian Joseph. All the while, late in August General Cortina ordered his supporters to fire on Ford's pickets across the river, perhaps hoping to provoke Old Rip into a border crossing that might trigger an international incident, one that Cortina hoped might mire the Confederates in a war against the French Imperialistas. Or, Cortina hoped, such a fight might at least ensure that Union troops on the Rio Grande would again be reinforced. Tensions increased early in September when Cortinistas rolled several cannons in place downriver on the right bank opposite the Rancho Palmito and fired on Texan state troops stationed there. Then on September 6, after thunderstorms had rumbled across the valley, Ford's spies informed him that through the morning mists they had observed six hundred of

Cortina's men and a battery of artillery poised near the foggy riverbank just upriver from Matamoros. Convinced that an attack upon Brownsville was imminent, Ford gathered Addie and his daughter and led them to the sanctuary of a Catholic convent.[54]

An angry Ford hurriedly scribbled a message to Cortina, writing in a proper but demanding tone, "I would respectfully inquire, if by these acts you intend to indicate that a state of war exists between your government and that of the Confederate States?" Cortina's answer never came. Neither did the anticipated attack.[55]

Still, the threat of another clash between Cortina and the Texans had not ended. Nor would it end anytime soon. Late in September, the swarthy General Tomás Mejía, described by Ford as a man of "rugged features," marched triumphantly into Matamoros, hoisting the French flag and proclaiming the city for the Imperialistas. Cortina simply changed uniform coats and declared his loyalty to Maximilian. With that simple switch of allegiance, the enigmatic "Red Robber" and Old Rip were finally on the same side of one issue, if not the same side of the river. Still, while Confederates applauded the arrival of Mejía, also described by Ford as "a man of character and distinguished bravery," they were not so naive as to think that the jefe named Cortina would ever stand as their ally. At least Ford was not.[56]

Events in the coming months only cast more doubts on Cortina's sincerity and confirmed Ford's suspicions that his old antagonist could no more be relied upon than a wounded bobcat. Despite his better instincts for survival, Cortina could not mask his disdain for the "devil Texans." Quietly, he prevailed upon his supporters to strike a blow against the hated Diablos Tejanos. Consequently, Cortina's *renegados* crossed to the Texas side with such impunity that they easily seized strategic roads, robbed teamsters, burned abandoned farms, and rustled cattle across the river. United States consul Leonard Pierce even went so far as to call on these thieving Mexican irregulars to be mustered into Union service as "beef hunters or . . . as rangers." So sophisticated and well executed were the Cortinistas' operations to steal and transport Texas livestock down the Gulf Coast to Tampico and other ports that, by the war's end, they had perfected the art of rounding up "lost cattle" and driving them to market. Trailing the herds southward and selling the stock to Spanish buyers for shipment to Cuba, they enjoyed handsome profits from the lucrative wartime trade. That irony could not have been lost on Texans like Charles

Stillman and Old Rip Ford, who had long supported filibusters such as Samuel Lockridge in their efforts to conquer the island of Cuba, known as the "pearl of the Antilles."[57]

For the remainder of 1864 military actions along the lower Rio Grande could best be described as a series of skirmishes, none of which proved decisive. The autumn brought not only a stalemate but also cooler breezes from the Gulf and a much-needed break from the summer heat. A long-awaited stillness at last settled over the border region. Ford's home guard droned away the drab months on picket duty along the river frontier. Only on the occasions when they caught a cattle rustler or a horse thief was their social life enlivened by an impromptu hanging. As Captain Robert H. Williams remembered scenes reminiscent of the Reign of Terror in revolutionary France, members of the Second Texas and other Confederate cavalry units delighted in "hooking up" Mexican "spies" to the "nearest convenient tree." Typically, they would toss a rope over the victim's head and then hoist him up slowly until he had told all that he knew. Then they would pull him upward and leave him dangling from a limb, swinging between the heavens and the earth for all to see. As for deserters, whether Anglo-Texan or Mexicano, Williams admitted that those unfortunate enough to be caught met the same grisly fate: torture and almost certain death.[58]

Despite the discomforting truth that Confederate guerrillas, who still styled themselves "Rangers," left their prisoners hanging in trees as a ghoulish reminder of the long reach of Texan "justice," camp life for Confederate volunteers in South Texas was anything but eventful. For the most part, Texas mounted partisans sat around the campfire playing cards, complaining about the food, and waiting for orders to saddle up and move out. Daily drudgery seemed to mark the mundane existence for the volunteers who were designated as "cavalry." To be sure, the reality was something less than the romantic image later portrayed in popular literature, song, and cinema.

Writing home on December 13, 1864, from Rancho Los Indios, located some twenty miles downstream from Brownsville, Private George Lee Robertson admitted the abject boredom that accompanied his duties. Although speculating that victory was at hand, or so his commanders claimed, he still reported that little had happened to disrupt the dull routines of morning, noon, and night. Yet in a letter to his sister, Fanny, he revealed still more, "Colonel Ford is in camp with the men but he evidently does not like the idea of being superseded by [General] Slaughter and sent to the woods. He was over to see us this evening and talked for an hour or two. He seemed to be in a good humor, which is unusual [for] him." Like many of his fellows, Robertson believed that if Old Rip could mount up and lead them into a fight, all was not lost.[59]

The next time Robertson would see the familiar figure of Colonel Ford it would be five months later, on a windswept plain near Palmito Hill, where both men would literally hear the echoes of the last shots of the American Civil War—echoes that reverberate to this day.

3
Escaping Reconstruction

T he passing of winter and the first appearance of spring always bring
signs of nature's renewal. For the people of the lower Rio Grande
Valley, as the season changes, the land reawakens like a new dawn. Blustery
and bone-chilling winds from the Gulf of Mexico give way to cool ocean
breezes that bring gentle showers. Beneath a warming sun the prairies
again yield a cover of lush grasses and rainbows of wildflowers with appropriately unforgiving names. The red and pink blooms of the devil's bou-
quet burst across the terrain, and the purple flower known as the skullcap
enjoys a short life among the blooming cactus. Sand verbena and spears
of Spanish dagger erupt among the thorny chaparral as well. So does the
giant yucca. Even the gnarled mesquite bears beans that sustain livestock
and deer alike. As part of the annual spring ritual, the Rio Grande rises
and rolls slowly toward the sea with waters that owe their origins to the
melting snows of the great Rocky Mountains more than a thousand miles
to the north. All the while, in "the Valley" of South Texas, morning songbirds, among them the hermit thrush and great blue heron, announce the
arrival of planting season. Everywhere across the countryside the stark
landscape awakens to new life.

Early in March 1865 Colonel John S. Ford and General James Slaughter, commander of the Western Sub-District of Texas, realized a new hope
for peace as they prepared for an extraordinary meeting that was as secretive as it was unlikely. Neither the war-weary citizens of South Texas nor
the state Partisan Rangers performing picket duty on the river frontier
knew anything about a startling proposal that Slaughter had received to
end the fighting along the lower Rio Grande—and perhaps the entire
Trans-Mississippi West.

After all, the source of the proposed peace plan was a virtual unknown to
the people of the border, not the sort of emissary who might be expected
to carry a message of such importance—a message from none other than
the president of the United States, Abraham Lincoln. Major General Lew
Wallace recalled the instructions he had received in the White House
not long before the New Year. He remembered how he "suggested to
President Lincoln that it would be comparatively an easy matter for the
Confederates in the Southwest to cross the border, taking advantage of

the disoriented condition of . . . [Mexico], and establish there an independent empire. Once intrenched in Mexican territory," he cautioned the commander in chief, the rebels "could have gone on warring against the United States indefinitely." Lincoln apparently agreed that the flight of Confederates into Mexico would pose grave military and diplomatic danger for the Union—and that the risks were unacceptable.[1]

Already aware of long-standing Texan territorial designs on lands south of the Rio Grande, and of the Texans' penchant for filibustering and fomenting insurrection in the border states of Mexico, General Wallace shared with President Lincoln his plan to induce Confederate leaders in South Texas to come to the peace table. Early in January 1865 Wallace had happened upon evidence that the idea would work. Unexpectedly, he had received a letter from an "old school-mate," identified by the general only as S. S. Brown, "who had been living near Monterrey, Mexico, a refugee from Texas." Upon reading the correspondence, Wallace noted Brown's claim that the residents of northern Mexico were "feeding and clothing the rebellion, arming and equipping, furnishing . . . materials of war and a specie basis of circulation in Texas." Then Wallace grew encouraged with Brown's observation that south of the border both expatriate Anglo and proud Mexican bitterly opposed the French "usurpers." Given the opportunity and the obvious incentive, Brown convinced Wallace that these forces would join together and "rally under the stars and stripes" to depose the Emperor Maximilian.[2]

On January 13, 1865, while working in his Baltimore headquarters, General Wallace met with Brown, his old friend from Indiana who had lived recently in San Antonio. Following pleasantries and reminiscences, Brown expressed his belief that the remnants of rebel forces along the Rio Grande could be easily persuaded to join their Union rivals in fighting against French imperialism, especially if they understood what might be in it for them. Wallace wrote to General Ulysses S. Grant camped at Center Point, Virginia, the following day, "If overtures were now made . . . [Brown] believed the rebels . . . in western Texas, particularly at Brownsville, would gladly unite with us and cross the river under the Juárez flag." It would be a bold, even risky stroke, Wallace admitted, but one worth taking.[3]

Grant concurred, and apparently so did Lincoln. On January 22 General Grant ordered Wallace to undertake a difficult and potentially dangerous mission. In his letter of appointment Grant deliberately understated its significance as simply a tour to "inspect the condition of military affairs

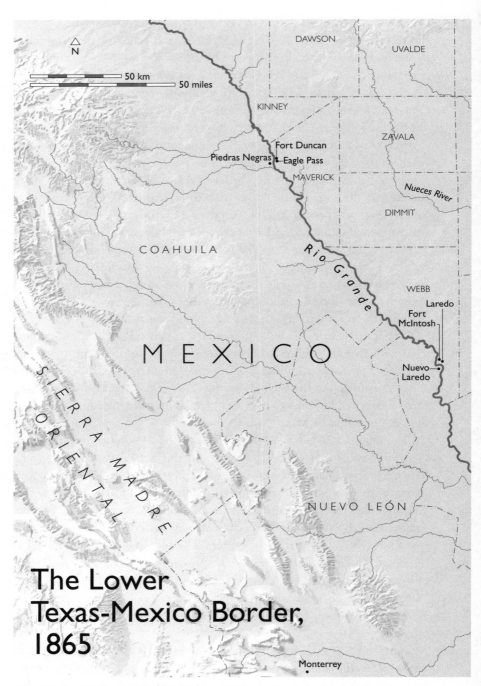

The Lower
Texas-Mexico Border,
1865

Cartography by Carol Zuber-Mallison

. . . on the Rio Grande." By February 22 Wallace could report from New Orleans his intentions to disrupt commerce between the border towns on both banks of the Rio Grande. He also wrote General Grant of his ambitious plan to "initiate the organization of the Territory or new State of Rio Grande," which he proposed could be used as a staging area for the "assemblage of men and materials essential to . . . [military] operations" against Maximilian. Then he proposed to raise "a regiment of Texans now serving in the department." There was no mention of the importance of defending the Monroe Doctrine, and no need for such an obvious reference to broader American foreign policy goals. It was a tacit understanding.[4]

As he paced aboard the USS *Clifton* while it steamed toward the South Texas coast, General Wallace found an intensive study of Spanish to be his daily "refuge." He knew little of the language and was determined to learn quickly. Upon arriving at Brazos Santiago on March 5, however, he found no time for studies. "From the deck of this steamer I can look towards the mouth of the Rio Grande . . . and see more vessels than are to be seen any one day in the harbor of Baltimore, all foreign vessels, loading and unloading cargoes." Already, his spies had informed him that Matamoros was "crowded with goods," mostly cotton, said to be "more in store than in the city of New Orleans."[5]

Although astonished by the bustling border trade that provided "evidence of incompetency on our side," Wallace still found a moment to peer through his field glasses and admire the scenic beauty of a sun-spangled Sunday morning. He reflected back to the days during the war with Mexico when, as a young lieutenant recently out of West Point, he had first set foot on the South Texas coast. "It is now nearly seventeen years since, with the 1st Indiana Volunteers, I landed at this same spot," he penned to his wife, "and now I find the same bleak sand-hills, the same combing billows outside, the same birds, and the same sky." Yet Wallace reflected that he was "not the same boyish soldier dreaming of fame."

Indeed, Wallace now enjoyed little time for daydreaming. Through a series of emissaries, including collector of customs at Brazos Santiago Charles Worthington, Wallace communicated a simple message to his counterpart, General James Slaughter: the war for the Union would soon be over, and the Confederate States would be no more. The real enemy presented along the border to Union forces and Texans alike was now the French invader. So as Wallace prepared to counsel peace, he planned to persuade the Texans to brace themselves again for war. This time he implored the rebels to turn their weapons not on the Union but on Mexico.[6]

General Wallace had good reason to believe that Texans would accept his proposal. Although he knew that they would never take up arms in support of Mr. Lincoln and the Union, they might glory in another chance at conquest south of the Rio Grande. Land, riches, possibly even a presidential pardon could await them. Besides, the former Ranger John S. "Rip" Ford was on his way with General Slaughter. And if Ford could be persuaded, other Texans would surely follow. No one commanded greater loyalty and respect among the rebels in South Texas, Wallace had learned—not Slaughter or anyone else. Only Old Rip was held in such high esteem.

But Wallace had to wait patiently for several days as storms rolled in from the Gulf, bringing howling winds and torrents of rain. On March 11 the skies cleared, allowing Wallace to board a skiff for Point Isabel. His meetings there with Slaughter and Ford, which lasted for the better part of two days, produced conflicting accounts of negotiations that were clearly designed to bring an end to hostilities on the border. Not surprisingly, Wallace's version of the negotiations differed substantially from that of Colonel Ford. The stoic General Wallace recalled that both of his counterparts agreed that the Southern cause appeared doomed and that the rebels were "anxious to find some ground upon which they could honorably get from under what they admitted to be a failing Confederacy." He further reported that the two Texans "entered heartily into the Mexican project. It is understood between us that the pacification of Texas is the preliminary step to a crossing of the Rio Grande."[7]

Ford remembered it differently. He stubbornly recollected that "nothing was decided of a formal nature," although he later confessed that neither Slaughter nor he disagreed with Wallace's conclusion that the Confederate cause was doomed. Still, the opportunistic Ford concluded that not one of his statements could have been construed to be "of a character to cause any Southern man displeasure." In other words, he considered his interest in the Mexico "venture" to constitute neither surrender nor treason. It was simply opportunity.[8]

In the end, however, none of that mattered. Enraged by the apparent willingness of his subordinates to consider defeat, Confederate General John G. Walker, the hotheaded Mississippian headquartered in Houston, rejected Wallace's terms and even intimated that Slaughter and Ford should be punished for what he termed the "blackest treason." Regardless, General Edmund Kirby Smith, commander of the entire Trans-Mississippi Department headquartered in Shreveport, never received Wallace's proposal, and the entire matter ended there.

General Slaughter and Colonel Ford walked away from Wallace believing that a temporary truce had been agreed upon. Although they realized that neither Wallace nor they could speak for higher authorities, they still assumed that no less than General Grant and presumably President Lincoln had signed off on the plan. Until further orders, their state partisans on picket duty along the river could stand down, their horses could forage, and they could await word of their fate.[9]

For the next two months an appearance of calm, not unlike that which precedes a late afternoon squall blowing in from the Gulf, settled over the valley of the lower Rio Grande. Unknown to Colonel Ford and General Slaughter, and to their mounted Confederate partisans encamped on the banks of the Rio Bravo, storm clouds were already gathering along the South Texas coast.

The Battle of Rancho Palmito

Shortly after 8:00 A.M. on May 13, 1865, some eight miles below Brownsville, the plain near Palmito Hill was covered in smoke. A huge black plume rose over the Rancho Palmito and drifted across the South Texas skies. African American troopers of the Sixty-Second Colored U.S. Infantry hurriedly carried out orders issued by their commander, Colonel Theodore H. Barrett, to burn all buildings in the compound. The troopers busily darted about, putting the torch to every log building and clapboard structure, every wagon, every harness, plow, saddle, and stalk of corn that might prove useful to the enemy. They also set the grass ablaze, whether intentionally or by accident. No shelter must be left for the rebels, no food, no forage or grain for their horses.

As the flames engulfed the cabins, corrals, bunkhouses and outbuildings on the perimeter of the compound, advance elements of the Thirty-Fourth Indiana, U.S. Infantry, arrived on the scene. Colonel Barrett ordered them to rest, eat breakfast, and wait. For the next two hours the gathering Union force idled, some troopers perhaps wondering why not even their own officers explained or even understood the nature of their mission. Colonel Barrett had confided his plans to no one. Were they marching on Brownsville? Were they just there to round up horses, mules, and cattle? Or was their task simply to destroy the rebel commissary? Were they conducting a reconnaissance? Perhaps Colonel Barrett had failed to answer these questions because he may not have even known himself.[10]

By 11:00 A.M. troops of the Thirty-Fourth Indiana began to sift through the blackened rubble of the ranch house. Whether for amusement or for military intelligence, several soldiers poked through the smoky, charred ruins of the cabin. What one recovered delighted virtually every Hoosier in camp. Holding aloft a letter from "a lady to her lover in the Confederate service," one trooper read aloud the young woman's request that her gallant young "Reb" bring to her some souvenir from the battlefield, preferably a "Pet Yankee." The Indiana boys roared in approval.[11]

Before the day was out, however, Barrett's troops would have little cause to laugh. Unknown to the Union soldiers, less than seven miles to the west Old Rip Ford was leading his force downriver. The rebel column, made up mostly of raw recruits and the tattered remnants of the Second Texas Mounted Rifles, trudged steadily along the river road that meandered through the marshes and thickets. Ragged though resolute, eager yet weary, and astride mounts that were even more fatigued, Ford's troops looked like mere boys. Unseasoned but brave, they were fiercely determined to drive the "Billy Yanks" into the sea.

George Lee Robertson, who rode with Ford's cavalry that day, summarized their resolve just days earlier when he had written, "There is nothing left for us but to fight. We will show them that we are not subjugated should our armies be disbanded." Nine days later, writing his "Ma" from "Camp John Wilkes Booth" a few miles below Brownsville, he summarized the defiance of his fellow Texans-in-arms, "We are prepared to fight another twenty-five years if necessary."[12]

But Colonel Ford was neither so naive nor unrealistic. As he rode near the front of the column he carried a supreme confidence that his young volunteers were in good spirits. If the looming encounter turned out to be the last battle of the war, he and his fellow Confederates would go out in glory. Either his boys would whip the Yankee bluecoats or they would die trying. Duty, pride, and most important honor dictated that the business of this long war be finished—one way or the other.

As he rode toward his rendezvous with the enemy, Old Rip seethed in anger—and understandably so. The previous evening at his headquarters near Fort Brown he had met with General James Slaughter and discussed reports of Union regulars marching toward Brownsville. Given the imminent threat, Ford had pressed his commander to advance and attack. But the answer he had received was unacceptable. "Retreat," Slaughter had responded. Ford bristled at the suggestion and growled, "You can retreat and go to hell if you wish. These are my men, and I am going to fight." His volunteers had sacrificed too much to run now. Although tired, hungry, and saddle sore, they simply would not admit defeat, and neither would he.[13]

Slaughter apparently acquiesced to Ford's demand to advance on the enemy, perhaps recognizing the reality that—rank notwithstanding—the Texan volunteers serving on the lower Rio Grande considered Ford to be their leader, not Slaughter. They would follow Ford to the ends of the earth. If Old Rip ordered an attack on the Yankee troops, his boys would fight. As Texan John H. Jenkins remembered the situation, "General James E. Slaughter was *called* commander, but John S. Ford in reality led and ordered our force" into battle.

As Ford's disheveled volunteers assembled on the parade grounds of Fort Brown on the evening of May 12 and prepared to march downriver, Slaughter remained in his headquarters. Later that night he issued orders for an attack, though neither Ford nor his subordinates claimed they ever saw them. The following morning, May 13, unaware that Colonel Barrett's bluecoats were burning the abandoned bunkhouses at Rancho Palmito, Ford gathered a battery of artillery and more than two hundred mounted riflemen. Almost every man in Brownsville able to ride joined him, and they waited for General Slaughter to appear at the appointed hour of 11:00 A.M. Slaughter never showed. Ford later learned that his commanding officer was purportedly sitting in his quarters, apparently paralyzed by the unfounded rumor that General Juan Cortina might be in Matamoros planning yet another raid on Brownsville, just as he had in September, 1859.

As if all this were not enough, another problem arose when Confederate artillery captain O. G. Jones approached Ford late on the morning of May 13 and informed him that General Slaughter had given him command of the unit. By now irate, Ford demanded that Jones produce orders to such effect. Seeing none, Ford promptly ordered Jones arrested and placed under armed guard. Hearing that, Captain Jones relented and pleaded with Ford to release him so that he could join his troops in the field. Ford agreed and ordered Jones freed, assuring him that the arrest order was "not personal."[14]

Now, while he prepared for battle, Colonel Ford pondered another equally troublesome issue—the parting pledge General Lew Wallace had offered all those weeks earlier. Wallace had given his word to suspend all Union offensive operations on the lower Rio Grande. But now Union troops were fast advancing on Brownsville. Ford understandably believed that he had been betrayed. All things considered, Old Rip also *believed* that his own personal appointment with destiny awaited. Only one course of action was left to him, he thought, and that was to fight.

All this weighed heavily on Ford as he bellowed out the command to mount up. A three-hour march along familiar trails that paralleled the muddy Rio Grande brought the motley Confederate force to within a mile of Rancho Palmito. There Ford halted his column. From that distance he and his men listened for the faint sounds of intermittent rifle fire. They could little afford to waste time. Ford's scouts, or "Rangers" as Old Rip still insisted on calling them, had reported that Captain William Robinson's company had engaged a larger force of Union troops in the thickets near Rancho Palmito the previous day. Ford had ordered Robinson to maintain contact with the enemy and report their movements. He had since received from Robinson's courier a brief dispatch, informing him of the Union advance and requesting reinforcements. What Ford did not yet fully realize was that Robinson's men had been driven back from the river after a fierce fight that had lasted more than an hour. Now Federal troops occupied the high ground, including a forty-foot ridge rising from the coastal prairie, a modest promontory known as Palmito Hill.[15]

Meanwhile, confusion reigned within the ranks of Colonel Barrett's command. Despite orders to concentrate north of Palmito Hill, the Union troops—numbering more than six hundred—had no further instructions other than to break out rations of hardtack and salt pork. During this critical time Barrett failed to position pickets west of the hill and downriver to guard his rear, or even to deploy defensive lines that used the Rio Grande to his strategic advantage. Had Colonel David Branson of the Sixty-Second Colored Infantry not ordered several sentries to post atop Palmito Hill, no steps would have been taken that day to warn the command of any approaching threat. By midafternoon Barrett had accomplished only two things: he had repelled a smaller force of rebel cavalry the previous day, and he had camped with his back to the hill and the river.

The sun glared overhead as Barrett's bluecoats settled into what little shade was provided by the mesquite and chaparral thickets. Sometime around 3:00 P.M. Colonel Ford arrived at Captain Robinson's position half a mile west of the Palmito plain. After asking Robinson to offer an assessment of the enemy, Ford ordered his troops to dismount and rest

their horses. He then rode alone to a forward position where he could survey the scene firsthand. Dressed in civilian garb, he attracted no particular
attention as he stood in the stirrups and raised his spyglass to scan the field
for any sign of Union troop movements. Seeing a mere handful of sentries
perched atop Palmito Hill, he wheeled his horse around and headed back
to Robinson's camp, convinced that he held the advantage of surprise.[16]

Remarkably, the deployment of Confederate troops so near the Union
command had apparently gone undetected. But Colonel Barrett and his
men would learn of their presence soon enough. Ford gathered his officers
and explained his simple and daring battle plan. With the sun at their backs
they would move forward and attack the enemy. In the heavy thickets to
their front Captain Robinson's company would form the left of a skirmish line, with Captain D. M. Wilson's mounted troops to the right. Two
twelve-pound artillery pieces would remain in the rear. Captain O. G.
Jones would wheel the remaining four cannons into position to Robinson's left. Captain Jesse Vineyard would meanwhile swing his cavalry to
the north to flank the enemy and attack their rear, thus cutting them off
from any retreat to the coast.

Shortly before 4:00 in the afternoon, Ford gave the order to unfurl
the Confederate battle flag. As was his custom, he rode through camp,
encouraging his men to prepare for the fight of their lives. "Ready?" Old
Rip asked his young recruits. An artillery barrage announced the beginning of what was to be the last skirmish of the American Civil War, and the
last act of Old Rip's legendary career as a soldier in the service of Texas.

Just as the Confederate ranks advanced through the tangle of mesquite, Ford's artillerymen, including several French volunteers, sighted an
unexpected threat rounding a sweeping bend in the river. An unidentified
steamboat, with its prominent smokestack rising overhead, was heading
straight toward Ford's position. Unable to determine the identity of the
flag, Ford's artillery fired twice upon the vessel. Fortunately, their aim was
poor, for no sooner had two shots sailed harmlessly into the waters of the
Rio Grande than a ceasefire was called. The vessel was not a ship of the
Union navy but a light steamer belonging to Captain Richard King's and
Mifflin Kenedy's shipping line.[17]

As he had done so many times before as a commander of Texas Rangers,
Colonel Ford issued the command to charge the Union line. The artillery
roared and a bloodcurdling rebel yell spread over the field as some three
hundred mounted Texan irregulars tore through the thickets. Screaming
like Comanche on the warpath, the Texans galloped toward the Union

left. At the same moment, two companies of Captain George Giddings's battalion struck the Union right. The Confederate partisans descended so fast on the unsuspecting bluecoats that many of them broke ranks and raced toward the river. "Barrett and command ran," Ford later recollected, the enemy being "swift of foot . . . like men who had important business at some other place." Amid the confusing scene rifle fire and pistol shots punctuated the desperate cries of Union soldiers as some splashed into the Rio Grande, only to be shot down by their pursuers. Other Federal troops dropped their weapons and ran into the brush.[18]

Sensing the collapse of his defensive lines, Barrett ordered his main body to pull back from the engagement. In his official report, however, he attempted to put the best face on the situation: "Having no artillery to oppose the enemy's six twelve-pounder field pieces our position became untenable. We therefore fell back fighting." Colonel Ford recollected the event differently, insisting that Barrett "seemed to have lost his presence of mind," Old Rip even suggesting that the Union force became unnerved at the sight of the Texans swarming toward their position.

But one indisputable fact remained: a disorderly Union retreat continued until sundown, with Ford's Partisans chasing the Union troops past White's Ranch, some seven miles downriver. Colonel Ford later recalled that the running fight—with the Federal troops doing all the running— proved "how fast demoralized men could get over ground" when motivated by fear. At the end of the day Barrett had lost some thirty killed and wounded, with 113 enlisted men and officers being taken prisoner. Ford counted only five wounded, though the actual number may well have been higher. Still, Ford could hardly have been more pleased with the manner that his mounted troops had routed the enemy and driven them from the field.[19]

Ford's young cavalrymen had delivered a thorough whipping that the Union boys would remember for the rest of their days. By sunset the guns had fallen silent. As the firing ceased, a cheer went up among the Texan ranks. The unmistakable chant could be heard: "Rip! Rip! Rip!" No one could question the decisive outcome, or the leader the young Texan volunteers would long remember and credit for their victory.

"Boys we have done finely," Old Rip announced as darkness settled over the Palmito plain. "We will let well enough alone and retire." After the fighting ceased, General Slaughter appeared on the field. As Colonel Ford remembered, Slaughter rode up and questioned, "You are going to camp here for the night, are you not?" "No sir," Ford snapped. A brief exchange followed, during which Ford informed Slaughter of his intentions. With his camp brimming with prisoners, his horses fatigued, and his mission accomplished, he would withdraw inland to a position where he would be less vulnerable to a possible counterattack or flanking movement.[20]

Night fell and fields of stars shown in the South Texas skies. The faint glow of the moonlight bathed the low-lying coastal plain. All was quiet now. Finally, Ford could stretch out on a blanket, rest his tired body, and consider an uncertain future.

Perhaps it was fitting that in the days following the Battle of Rancho Palmito a sense of tranquility settled over the Rio Grande Valley. Maybe it was also appropriate that the final engagement of the American Civil War was fought on Texas soil less than twenty-five miles from the Palo Alto prairie where the Mexican War began nearly two decades earlier. It was also here—on the lower Rio Grande—that Anglo-American filibusters had gathered to press their ambitious expansionist aims for a Southern, slave-holding nation. Here, overlooking the ramparts of old Fort Brown where Texan volunteers first faced off against Union regulars early in 1861. Here, and not Fort Sumter, where the American Civil War might have begun had it not been for the intercession and negotiations of a savvy old Texas Ranger known as Old Rip.

On to Mexico

While the last shots of the American Civil War still echoed in the Rio Grande Valley, a different kind of war was being fought on another front more than 1,800 miles to the east. With General Robert E. Lee's surrender to General Ulysses S. Grant at Appomattox Court House on April 9, and then the shock of the assassination of President Lincoln just five days later on Good Friday, leaders in Washington had lurched from one crisis to another. The abrasive and controversial Secretary of War Edwin M. Stanton had assumed charge of the investigation into the president's murder, and the subsequent killing of assassin John Wilkes Booth. General Lew Wallace, who had recently returned from the South Texas theater of war, had accepted Stanton's appointment to serve on the military commission that would place on trial and soon convict four of Booth's co-conspirators of plotting to assassinate the president. Already, the newly sworn president Andrew J. Johnson hinted at an impending collision with the so-called Radical Republicans in Congress over the substance and speed of post-war Reconstruction. And now even members of the cabinet, among them

Secretary of War Stanton, joined congressional leaders in openly questioning Johnson's ability to lead a divided nation.[21]

Amid this climate of suspicion and mistrust in Washington a diplomatic
intrigue played out behind the scenes, one as strange as it was ironic.
Matías Romero, the longtime Mexican chargé d'affaires who now also
assumed the title of minister to the United States, worked diligently to
convince American leaders to carry forth with the slain President Lincoln's
secret plans to provide support for the Liberal forces of Benito Juárez in
their struggle against the French-imposed imperial regime.[22]

The Mexican people could not reclaim their nation and rescue their
own future from the clutches of European colonialists without American aid, Romero warned U.S. officials. For many months, the diminutive,
bearded, and well-dressed Romero had insisted that only American intervention could tip the scales toward liberty and justice In Mexico. Now
his private pleas were shifting from demands that the U.S. government
cease its passive policy of allowing France to import weapons and supplies
for the Imperialistas to a more active policy in support of the beleaguered
Juaristas. He requested a U.S. naval blockade of Mexico to prevent the
French from supplying the army of Maximilian. Moreover, monetary support, arms and munitions, and other war materials were needed. He proposed that even mercenaries be allowed to cross the Rio Grande and join
the fight alongside the beleaguered forces of Juárez.

If only Romero could find a sympathetic listener in Washington, one
as committed to the principles of human liberty as the late Mr. Lincoln.
Understandably, an impatient Romero thought that if he failed to obtain
an audience with President Johnson, he must then turn elsewhere. After
all, Secretary of State Seward had been consistent in his position that the
United States must maintain a policy of neutrality and nonintervention
with regard to Mexico. The U.S. government must not emerge from one
civil war triumphant only to become mired in another civil war south of
the Rio Grande, Seward had counseled Lincoln and now Johnson. The
risk of war with France presented too great a risk. Nothing, not even Lincoln's tragic death, had changed Seward's mind.[23]

On April 28, 1865—a mere two weeks after the assassination of President Lincoln—Romero met in Washington, D.C., with several fellow
Mexican patriots to devise a plan to gain American support for the Juaristas. The old *filibustero* General José María Jesús de Carvajal and his
longtime collaborator Don Manuel Zambrano agreed that the time was
right to approach the general-in-chief of the U.S. Army, Ulysses S. Grant,

to confide in him and "seek his counsel." Romero had visited Grant earlier that day and written in his diary that "although he is tired of war, his
major desire is to fight in Mexico against the French." Convinced that former Confederate president Jefferson Davis and other rebel leaders would
soon flee to Mexico to escape Reconstruction, the gruff General Grant
expressed the opinion that Mexico must not become a sanctuary for exiled
rebels who could cause the United States great grief for years to come.
He even hinted to Romero that the war to preserve the American Union
would not truly end until the French regime was ousted from Mexico.
According to Romero, Grant expressed the view that while the U.S. government must not intervene directly in the struggles within Mexico, as
soon as Federal forces were mustered out of service an armed force of as
many as sixty thousand Union veterans might be raised for the purpose of
staging a large mercenary force in South Texas.[24]

"This [proposal] caused the conversation to turn toward the armed
emigration that would soon move toward Mexico," Romero recorded. In
response to concerns about American "soldiers of bad conduct and bad
antecedents" engaging in schemes of conquest, Grant purportedly assured
Romero that, should such a plan come to fruition, any American mercenary force must be led by a man of stature and experience, a respected
commander "of recognized merit and ability" who could prevent the
campaign to liberate Mexico from devolving into plunder by "disorganized parties of filibusters." The name of General William Tecumseh Sherman surfaced during the conversation, though Grant doubted that the
grizzled old warrior would accept the challenge. Such a man as General
Philip Sheridan might actually consider undertaking the mission, Grant
expressed. Much to the pleasure of Romero and the others, Grant apparently even hinted at his own interest in the scheme and agreed that he
would discuss that possibility at a "later date."[25]

On May 9 Romero dined with General Grant and several members of his
staff in Georgetown, but it seemed "not the proper occasion to continue
the conversation." Just four days later a persistent Romero accompanied
Grant by train to Philadelphia, where the Mexican minister remained for
two days as a guest in the Grant residence there. "My principle objective
was to learn if he had decided to go to Mexico," Romero confessed. The
following week, Romero again called on Grant in Georgetown, where the
general informed him that he had ordered General Sheridan to the mouth
of the Rio Grande to command a Union expeditionary force of fifty thousand regulars. Romero's diary entry remained unclear as to whether this

decision might have been a preliminary move pursuant to their earlier discussions, or if the deployment was simply intended to secure the border from the threat of Mexican insurrectionists and, more specifically, to thwart an exodus of Confederate refugees to Mexico. Then Grant revealed his continued complicity in the plot to encourage American "armed emigration" to Mexico for the purpose of aiding the Juaristas. He recommended General John M. Schofield, commander of the Department of North Carolina, as "the most meritorious general" who could be called to lead American soldiers of fortune to the side of Benito Juárez. The forty-three-year-old graduate of West Point had distinguished himself in the Virginia and Carolina campaigns and was known for his loyalty to both Grant and Sherman.[26]

For the next several weeks Romero intensified his efforts to enlist General Schofield in his cause. Schofield later remembered, "In June, 1865, at Raleigh, North Carolina, I received a message from General Grant informing me of my selection and desiring me, if I was willing to consider the proposition to come to Washington . . . [where] I consulted freely with General Grant . . . [and] Señor Romero." As Grant explained to Schofield, the purpose of the mission was to "cause the French army to evacuate Mexico." Schofield recalled that "it was understood by all that force would probably be necessary, and for some time no other means were considered." He was to "have the perfect freedom of action and choice of means" in carrying out the plan. "It was proposed to organize in Mexican territory an army corps under commissions from the government of Mexico, the officers and soldiers to be taken from the Union and Confederate forces who were reported eager to enlist in such an enterprise." At Grant's urging, on June 4 Schofield drafted a request for a leave of absence for thirty days, "with the privilege of applying for an extension."[27]

Meanwhile, Secretary of State Seward had urged President Johnson to call a special cabinet meeting on June 16 to discuss General Grant's plans and actions, especially in view that they were being carried out "without the knowledge of any cabinet member." During this meeting Grant informed the president and his cabinet of the level of troop deployment on the lower Rio Grande. He also explained that he had ordered General Sheridan and his subordinate, General Frederick Steele, to demand that Mexican forces in Matamoros under the command of General Tomás Mejía return cannons as well as small arms and munitions sold to the imperial forces by Confederates crossing the border. Grant seized the opportunity to reiterate his views—which he emphasized were the same as those of the late President

Lincoln—that the American government must never allow any European power to rule a nation neighboring the United States. Apparently, Seward then interjected that negotiations should first be given a chance to succeed and, according to Romero, the secretary of state assured all present that, if proper diplomatic pressure were placed on France, "there would not be a single foreign bayonet in Mexico within six months." Most members of the cabinet concurred. "I greatly fear Seward's efforts," a disappointed Romero scribbled in his diary that evening.[28]

Despite Seward's maneuvering to gain the trust and confidence of President Johnson on the matter of Mexico, General Grant continued to press the issue and even persuaded Secretary of War Edwin M. Stanton to approve of General Schofield's leave of absence, with the understanding that he would at least be allowed to travel to the Rio Grande and northern Mexico to assess the military and political situation there. So on July 15 Grant wrote President Johnson, reaffirming his statements in the cabinet meeting four weeks earlier: "Looking upon the French occupation of Mexico as part and parcel of the late rebellion in the United States, . . . I would respectfully recommend that a leave of absence be given to one of our General officers for going to Mexico to give direction to such emigration [from the United States] as may go to that country."

Ten days later from his headquarters at West Point General Grant issued an order extending Schofield a one-year leave of absence "with authority to leave the United States." The ostensible purpose of this leave was to allow Schofield to join Sheridan on the lower Rio Grande to conduct an unofficial "inspection tour" of the Mexican border. At the same time, Grant communicated to General Sheridan, who had arrived in Brownsville on June 9, that he should extend the same "neutrality" to the French Imperialistas that France had extended to the United States during its own recent rebellion by selling arms to the Confederacy. In other words, Sheridan should do nothing to discourage or hinder the flow of arms and men from the United States to the Juaristas.[29]

In his memoirs, Sheridan recollected that, before his departure for Texas, General Grant had clearly expressed to him that "he looked upon the invasion of Mexico by Maximilian as a part of the rebellion" in the United States and that "our success in putting down secession would not be complete till the French and Austrian invaders were compelled to quit the territory of our sister republic." "On to Mexico," Grant had reportedly joked with aides during this period. Moreover, he even predicted a "long, expensive and bloody war" along the border if the French were not ousted from Mexico. Sheridan also remembered that, once in South Texas, he operated under the constraints imposed by the Johnson administration, and that he was never allowed to confront directly the menace of Maximilian's imperial forces. Supported by Grant, however, that summer Sheridan acted to "prevent, as far as possible, escaping Confederates from joining Maximilian," and he even went so far as to dispatch scouts, some of them irregulars, across the border to "important points in Northern Mexico" to gain information about the movements of imperialist forces and to gather intelligence about Confederates who had crossed the Rio Grande. Sheridan also implied that, were it not for the intercession of Secretary Seward, he might have been allowed to lead U.S. regulars into Mexico to crush the forces of French imperialism and round up every last rebel who had fled there to support the Emperor Maximilian. "It required the patience of Job," Sheridan admitted, "to abide the slow and pokey methods of our State Department, and in truth, it was often difficult to restrain officers and men from crossing the Rio Grande with hostile purpose." In the end Sheridan was only allowed to conduct a "show of force" on the Texas side of the border but was precluded from crossing into Mexico. Frustrated, Sheridan later insisted that "a golden opportunity was lost."[30]

As it turned out, both Sheridan and Grant had reason to fear that thousands of Confederates were preparing for an exodus from Texas. Events that summer proved as well that the Union generals had good reason to suspect that many of these armed rebels, and renegades of all descriptions riding with them, were all too willing to sell their services to the Emperor Maximilian. On May 26, less than two weeks after his victory at Rancho Palmito, Colonel John S. Ford carried his wife "Addie" and little daughter, Mary Louise (or "Lu Lu"), across the river to Matamoros. Anticipating the arrival of Union troops in Brownsville, "Old Rip" sought out General Tomás Mejía, the *comandante* of Maximilian's Imperial forces along the "Line of the Lower Bravo." Of Mejía, Ford recalled, he was "a man of character and of distinguished bravery." Mejía had proved that he was a man to be trusted, one whose reputation for courage and integrity preceded him. No doubt, Ford also listened as Mejía flattered him, explaining how valuable such a distinguished soldier as he would be to the cause of the Imperialistas.[31]

Considering the events of the next several days, Ford had judged Mejía well. One morning late in May, a French lieutenant rode up to the adobe house that Ford had rented for his family in Matamoros. Through an interpreter the officer politely addressed Mrs. Ford, but then in a brusque manner informed her that she must immediately vacate the house, which was needed to quarter French soldiers. Addie explained that her husband was away on business and that neither he nor she were taking any part in the civil war in Mexico; they were merely renting the house, she pleaded. No matter, the officer responded that, if her family were not out of the home in a matter of hours, he would send his soldiers to "throw . . . [their belongings] into the street." After the brash, young officer rode away, Mrs. Ford sent for her husband, who then called on General Mejía and confronted him about the insult and threat. During an angry exchange Ford implied that, if French soldiers evicted his wife and daughter, they would "be lucky to get good sleep" or cross the Rio Grande in the days to come. Mejía attempted to calm Colonel Ford and reassure him that the officious lieutenant had no authority to make such demands, and that he had not authorized the eviction order. At that the matter was settled, and Ford returned to his wife and daughter, explaining that they should unpack their luggage. They were not going anywhere, at least not until Ford had prepared for their safe return to Brownsville. In the coming days all that Colonel Ford could do was watch from the Mexican side of the river as Federal forces again occupied Brownsville.[32]

Shelby's Long March

Elsewhere, in the East Texas town of Marshall, a much larger migration into Mexico was being planned. On the afternoon of May 13, ironically in the hours following Ford's victory at Rancho Palmito several general officers of the Confederacy met at the home of the former secessionist leader and onetime U.S. senator Louis T. Wigfall. General Edmund Kirby Smith, commander of the Department of the Trans-Mississippi West, and General Joseph Shelby, intrepid leader of the famed Iron Brigade from Missouri, called a "consultation" to consider and coordinate a proposed retreat of Confederate forces to Mexico. Missouri governor Thomas Reynolds, the handsome leader who had established a government in exile in Marshall the previous December, also attended. As General Alexander Watkins Terrell of Texas recalled, "We agreed that each of us would address his own command and ask for volunteers to cross the Rio Grande, cooperate with the followers of Juarez, . . . and take the country up to the Sierra Madre mountains. We proposed to stay and establish our own government."[33]

Several in attendance expressed their optimism that the plan would succeed. None were more enthusiastic than General Simon Bolivar Buckner, the fiery Kentuckian with a name befitting a hero; he insisted that as many as five thousand Texans would march with them into Mexico. After all, he argued, the Confederates possessed enough ordnance and stores of provisions to support an entire army. More than four thousand British-made Enfield rifles, still in their crates, provided evidence of that. To entice many fortune seekers, Bolivar and others argued that there remained the allure of land south of the border and even the prospect of mining silver in the mountains of northern Mexico. Others, more idealistic, might see the opportunity to fight alongside an oppressed people seeking freedom from European colonialism and despotism. Some, especially the very young, had known little but fighting and killing for the past four years, so the adventuresome life of a mercenary might appeal to them. Simply put, they stood poised and willing to sell their services to the highest bidder. Maybe, for some who had no home to return to, they could simply find a new beginning. More likely, most of the men merely feared the long arm of federal law and the prospect of punishment. And Mexico promised refuge. Whatever their individual motives, the generals concurred, an entire legion could cross the "Mexican Rubicon" to join in the fight between the Juaristas and Maximilian's imperial forces.[34]

Only the war-weary General Smith expressed doubts. The next forty-eight hours proved him correct. According to Terrell, most of the soldiers camped near Marshall deserted and disappeared into the pine woods. What had been a "forest of Sharps carbines" for several days had now vanished. The lone exception remained Shelby's proud Missourians, numbering no more than two hundred. Through it all they had remained intensely loyal to their leader. If Jo Shelby mounted up and moved out ahead of them toward Mexico, they would follow.[35]

But as preparations were made for a march to the border, Terrell recalled that the reality swiftly settled in on the other commanders. "Our dream of taking a slice from Mexico on the Rio Grande border was now ended," he wrote. "We sought a foreign country with feelings reckless of consequences," he remembered in hindsight. Apparently, when the meetings at Marshall concluded in mid-May, the only thing the Confederate commanders could agree on was that they would go their separate ways, find their own border crossing, then rendezvous in Monterrey. On May 26 General Smith drafted a letter formally surrendering the Confederate Department of the Trans-Mississippi to the Union and ordering his men to go home. But some braced themselves to continue the fight. A few prepared to flee to Mexico.[36]

While Jo Shelby's storied march toward Mexico got underway, a chaotic and tragic scene unfolded in Austin. On June 2 resident Amelia Barr
entered in her diary, "Everything in confusion. Everyone suspicious and
watchful, and there is no law." The streets around the capitol were empty.
Former governor Francis Lubbock and most state officers had already fled
to Mexico. Only a pale and sickly Governor Pendleton Murrah remained
behind, and he was dying of tuberculosis. As one contemporary recollected, Murrah looked like a leader "in ruins." The observer recalled, "All
of those insidious and deceptive approaches of consumption were seen in
his hollow cheeks, the large, mournful eyes, the tall, bent frame that quiv-
ered as it moved." On the afternoon of June 11, Amelia Barr recorded the
sad sight of a tattered column of Confederate soldiers returning from the
Rio Grande campaign. As they rode in front of her house, many slumped
over in their saddles, she "could not help crying as they passed." They had
obviously been through "every deprivation and suffering, through hunger
and thirst." Although "weary, ragged, weather-beaten and battle-scarred,
they had carried aloft their flag with the single star." Through the city
streets they moved slowly toward the capitol as men and women along the
way wept and waved handkerchiefs in tribute.[37]

These bedraggled soldiers joined others who were gathering beneath
the hill on Congress Avenue near the abandoned white limestone capitol. They had come to collect payment for their many months of service,
and they fully expected either gold, silver, or government property in rec-
ompense. During the next three days, more than a thousand embittered
veterans camped on the grounds near the capitol. When their demands
were not met, they turned into an angry mob. Barr recalled how, late
on the afternoon of June 14, the disgruntled soldiers began to loot and
plunder nearby government offices, stores and stables. "They are dividing the mules and horses and saddlery among themselves," she scribbled.
"The noise and tumult is indescribable. My heart aches for Texas," she
concluded.[38]

Many of those who descended upon the capitol and state treasury that
day resembled a ragtag lot of common thieves. Most of them had served in
units known variously as "Partisans" on the Texas home front. Some were
reported to be in the command of Captain Virgil S. Rabb, a notorious
leader and former member of George Flournoy's regiment who, alongside
Colonel James Duff, had overseen the hangings and shootings of many
German Unionists in the Texas Hill Country during the last three years.
At best, they were a desperate and undisciplined rabble.[39]

As darkness descended on June 14, a steady rain began to fall. But the thunderstorms failed to disperse the mob. What nature could not accomplish, however, an undermanned battalion of Confederate cavalry would. When General Jo Shelby and his Missourians approached Austin that night, they could see in the distance the lights of a dozen fires blazing around the capitol. As flames engulfed several buildings in the city's business district, members of a torch-bearing mob were battering down the doors of the state treasury. When Shelby's horsemen rode upon the scene of carnage their leader commanded them to scatter or even kill those who were plundering and looting. As Missourian John N. Edwards recalled the pandemonium in the treasury building, "Lights shone through all the windows; there were men inside gorging themselves with gold. No questions were asked." Gunfire erupted in the streets when some of the thieves attempted to escape with all the gold they could carry. According to Edwards, one of the looters who was shot dead near the capitol carried a "king's ransom" on him. Edwards saw others who were running away so hurriedly that coins literally spilled from their bulging pockets. Some locals would fittingly remember the shameful scene as the "night of shattered glass."[40]

Legend has it that the next morning Governor Murrah called on Shelby and pleaded with him to distribute what gold and silver remained in the treasury to his own brave men. But as Edwards recorded, although he and his fellow soldiers were ragged and hungry, with nothing to their name but their pride and dignity, Shelby declined the offer. The gallant general explained to both Murrah and his own officers that his boys had "entered the war with clean hands and they would go out the same way." He then purportedly lamented, "We are the last of the race, and let us be the best as well."[41]

By June 17 General Terrell and his party had arrived in Austin. Terrell called upon an ailing Governor Murrah, who insisted on accompanying his fellow Confederates to Mexico. In the last stages of consumption, the following morning the gaunt, ghostly figure of the last Confederate governor of Texas gathered a few belongings and, in the words of one observer, mounted his "tired old war horse and rode away dying to Mexico." The Rio Grande, and exile, would be his final wish.[42]

As for Shelby's column, they first headed southward toward San Antonio. Along their route, they observed many desperadoes lurking in the thickets. Bushwhackers, bandits, "brush men" brandishing weapons waited to ambush anyone with valuables—currency, horses, firearms and ammunition. It was as if marauding bands of robbers infested every stretch of wilderness, every turn in the trail as the stoic General Shelby led his column past the settlements of San Marcos and New Braunfels.

Once in San Antonio, Shelby's party rode through streets that were teeming with gangs of heavily armed hooligans. The column passed a dozen ransacked stores, several burned-out shops, and rows of boarded-up abandoned houses. It was a tragic sight awaiting Shelby and his men. They could not escape the haunting irony: lining the streets and alleys were thousands of bales of cotton stacked high and deep, the dirty white bundles serving as mute reminders of a once prosperous but now shattered Confederacy. At the request of the city's mayor, Shelby ordered his men to search several boarding houses, brothels, and barrooms known to be the dens of the worst bullies and cutthroats who terrorized the town. After sweeping the city for thieves and murderers, Shelby and his men joined other Confederate fugitives at the Menger Hotel on Alamo Plaza.[43]

There the evening turned into an emotional reunion and a memorable final farewell. The Menger brimmed with a throng of soldiers and civilians. The swelling crowd spilled into the lobby, courtyard, and nearby plaza, where a military band played popular Southern tunes of the day. Among the most recognizable officers in attendance was the tall, angular figure of General John Bankhead Magruder, former Confederate commander of the Department of Arkansas and later the Division of Texas, New Mexico, and Arizona. Magruder delivered an impromptu oration reminding the crowd that although they were leaving their homes and families behind for an uncertain future in Mexico, they should always remain proud of their Southern heritage and their service to the Confederacy. Also among them stood Missouri Governor Thomas Reynolds, likewise a defiant symbol of the Lost Cause.

General Shelby stood on a balcony overlooking the scene where a stooped white-haired old man moved anonymously through the lobby below, the brim of his hat turned down, partially covering his face. John Edwards recalled that the frail downcast figure had registered under the name "William Thompson." The "aged, bent" veteran appeared "spent with fatigue, and dusty as a foot soldier" as he quietly made his way upstairs, unnoticed by the crowd, and then retired into a guest room and closed his blinds. Moments later, however, General Shelby sent word to the conductor of the military band to play "Hail to the Chief," then "Dixie." At that point, the crowd erupted in cheers as the old man emerged from his room and acknowledged the outpouring of affection. Moved by the repeated chants of his name, a gaunt General E. Kirby Smith broke into tears. Even when the music and applause died down, Smith tried three times to speak, but each time his throat closed as he fought back his emotions. He could only wave and then salute the crowd before turning back into his room.[44]

For General Jo Shelby and his men, however, there was no turning back. More than 140 miles of mesquite-choked prairie lay between them and the border town of Eagle Pass. And like the trail behind them, the route ahead bristled with nests of brooding bad men, "war laggards" as Edwards labeled them, more menacing than the diamondback rattlesnakes that infested the region. One "motley band" of skulking renegades numbered as many as three hundred, Edwards estimated, their ranks composed of deserters, draft dodgers, Mexican vaqueros, Indian traders, and shiftless drifters from New Mexico and Arizona.[45]

As for General Kirby Smith, his recollection of the march to Mexico mirrored that of many of his fellows in arms. "You should have seen me in my traveling costume mounted on a mule, in shirt sleeves with a silk handkerchief around my neck *à la Texas*, with a revolver and a shotgun," he later wrote. "I carried all my worldly goods on my person. I actually possessed nothing but the clothes on my back. I had left everything behind except a clear conscience," he continued. "With a light purse, but a heavy heart, I trudged along over the desert plains and under the burning sun of the Rio Grande."[46]

Once Shelby and the remnants of his once-proud regiment camped within three days' ride of Eagle Pass and Piedras Negras, just across the river, General Smith, General Magruder, and General Hamilton P. Bee agreed to push ahead with a small escort. Perhaps a small advance party would prove less imposing to local Mexican officials; they could reassure them that their party of Confederates, while armed, was composed of soldiers and statesmen, not land pirates and filibusters. After all, only ten years had passed since a company of Texas Rangers under the command of James H. Callahan had burned Piedras Negras to the ground. Understandably, local residents would have good reason to fear the approach of what appeared to be another mob of mercenaries. On June 28 a haggard General Smith, who had discarded his faded gray uniform for a flannel shirt and denim trousers, led a small escort to the Rio Grande, which Edwards termed "high and rapid" owing to recent rains. After two of their party first swam the river to secure a ferry, Smith and his "staff" joined them.[47]

Early on the morning of July 1, General Shelby and his weary party rode upon the banks of the Rio Grande, below Eagle Pass and opposite the Mexican border town of Piedras Negras, which got its name from the black shale lining the riverbanks. After assembling several of his officers for a council, Shelby ordered Colonel Frank Gardere and twenty-one men to cross under a white flag of truce. For a short time they joined General Smith and parlayed with Governor José María Biesca of the state of Coahuila and the commander of local Juarista forces, reportedly numbering nearly two thousand.[48]

Meanwhile, General Shelby carried out one final act of defiance. John Edwards remembered that his commander ordered five of his officers to wade into the shallows of the Rio Grande with their tattered regimental flag, one of them holding aloft the battle standard that they had carried through the campaigns in southern Missouri and northern Arkansas. Before they drove the flagpole into the muddy bed of the river, Shelby dismounted, then pulled a trademark black ostrich feather from his slouch hat and carefully placed it through a brass hook holding the regimental colors. Several of the officers bowed their heads and observed a moment of silence. As the battle-worn banner unfurled in the wind, Shelby and his troops passed by their unit standard one last time, in tribute, as one remembered "before the swift waves of the Rio Grande closed over it forever." By noon the straggling Confederates had crossed into Mexico with their horses, mules, artillery, and wagons loaded with rifle carbines. They camped on the outskirts of Piedras Negras. But their journey was not over.[49]

Meanwhile, other Confederate fugitives, hundreds of them, made their way separately toward the border. Among them, General Alexander Terrell had taken a different route to the Rio Grande—but one equally as perilous. From Austin, his party, which included the pale figure of Governor Murrah, crossed the prairies west of Lockhart, keeping to the open plains while skirting east of the Balcones Escarpment near New Braunfels. From there they rode on to the San Antonio River and then the Nueces, which was swollen from recent rains. All the while, Terrell avoided settlements as well as thickets and timbers that hinted at danger. "Though anxious to avoid conflict, we agreed that we would not be arrested by Federal troops and forced to take an oath of allegiance." Still, as Terrell and his party scoured the countryside, they knew that they were constantly being watched by an unseen enemy, whether Union regulars, Mexican bandits, or Indian marauders.[50]

After ten more days on the trail, the tired horsemen, their threadbare gray tunics and frayed trousers covered with dust, came upon the Alamo Crossing of the Rio Grande, eight miles above the town of Roma. Terrell recalled that, on that morning in late June, no sooner had his party swam safely to the south bank than they were surrounded by a company of some thirty mounted Cortinistas. "They were a rough looking set of scoundrels," Terrell remembered. The Mexican troops detained them, interrogated their leaders, and even questioned their intentions. Then the *renegados* relieved them of their firearms, their ammunition and horses, and led them to an isolated camp. From there, Terrell and his men would be left to walk across the arid plains to Monterrey.[51]

Downriver, on the Mexican side, more marauding bands swarmed over the region. And most of these armed riders pledged loyalty not to Mexico, certainly not to the Emperor Maximilian, nor even to Benito Juárez, but to Juan Cortina. Missionary Melinda Rankin recalled the reception she received earlier that spring when she departed Bagdad for a bumpy six-day overland journey to Monterrey. All along the lower Rio Grande the Cortinistas, ostensibly fighting for the Juarista forces, had successfully bedeviled the French imperial army, for many months disrupting their supply lines, cutting off communications by intercepting cross-country mail, interdicting commerce bound for the border, or entering through coastal ports.

So when Cortina's *robadores* halted the stage carrying Ms. Rankin on the second day of her trip, the ensuing scene corroborated all the terrifying stories she had heard of the menacing border bandit. The horsemen swept down upon them and, at gunpoint, ordered them to a nearby camp. Before an hour had passed, Rankin remembered, a military band struck up a fanfare heralding the arrival of their commander. "Soon he with his bodyguard was before us. He was the complete personification of a guerrilla chief," she wrote of the legendary Cortina. "His Indian face and evil eye portrayed . . . [his] desperate character."[52]

Rankin's account of her encounter with Cortina suggested a racial and cultural prejudice common among Anglos on the border. Predictably, she failed to record an explanation as to why, if Cortina were indeed so "evil," he allowed the stagecoach—less its mail—to proceed on to Monterrey. And why its passengers were not harmed.[53]

Despite the ever-present threat of armed *robadores* ranging along the border, hundreds of Confederates congregated in Monterrey in late June and early July of 1865. They were a motley collection of soldiers of fortune, war criminals, politicians, planters and men of commerce. Among the most prominent of them were at least six former Southern governors, several members of the Confederate Congress, a handful of generals, and a number of other officers, including the infamous Colonel James

Duff, who had good reason to be on the run. Others, like Petra Kenedy, wife of South Texas rancher Mifflin Kenedy, and Isaac Surratt, son of accused Lincoln-assassination conspirator Mary Surratt, fled to Monterrey out of fear of reprisal for nothing more than their sympathy with the Southern cause, or their family connections. But their story must be told elsewhere.[54]

No one knows for sure how many Confederates escaped into Mexico during the final weeks of the war. Conservative estimates exceed one thousand. But one thing seems certain: only a few would find the treasures or the freedom they sought. Most, like Old Rip Ford, would cross back into Texas within a matter of months. Whether repentant or "unredeemed," they would go home and renew their lives as citizens of the country they had tried to leave behind. But no matter how far they traveled or what they did, for the rest of their days they would never be able to leave the war behind. For them, the fight would never be over. Their memories—and their prejudices—never left them. And their enemies would always be just over their shoulder.

4
Skinning Wars

As one bloody civil war ended north of the Rio Grande, another continued to rage south of the border. While Benito Juárez and his agents persisted in seeking U.S. aid in their war against the French-backed Emperor Maximilian, many Texans and other Southerners looked southward to a Mexico infinitely rich in resources. Still moved by the spirit of Manifest Destiny, these former Confederates gazed into Mexico and saw for themselves—and for their countrymen—an opportunity born of war and revolution. Their hope may have risen from the despair of their own defeat, yet they remained resolute in the conviction that their cause might not be lost if they could reestablish themselves in a Southern-style colony under Maximilian, or any Mexican authority willing to welcome them. For their generation, the allure of Mexico and the impulse of conquest remained just as strong as it had been for those who had crossed the Rio Grande with General Zachary Taylor and those who had occupied Mexico City with General Winfield Scott almost two decades earlier.

Following the American Civil War violence and disorder continued to grip the lower Rio Grande. The coastal plains of South Texas remained a breeding ground for some of the most lawless elements in both a discordant Lone Star State and a strife-ridden Republic of Mexico. If anything, four years of the Confederate experience had only served to reinforce the tragic traditions that had long ruled the border: the twin terrors of private violence and public vigilantism. To make matters worse, the lucrative commerce in contraband—most of it smuggled cotton, then later stolen cattle—had fostered widespread graft and corruption on both sides of the border. On the Mexican bank, the ongoing fight to oust the French-imposed imperial regime created a climate of fear and uncertainty, which in turn brought political instability. On the American side, brazen bandits and cattle rustlers remained elusive for Texas authorities and even more so for federal officials in Washington, D.C., who were now seeking to restore not just law and order but, in a larger sense, the Union.[1]

Compounding the problem, a six-mile-wide Zona Libre, or "Free Zone," existed along the lower Rio Grande. In 1858 the Mexican Congress had created, first for the state of Tamaulipas and later for the entire northern border with the United States, a free-trade zone where commerce was exempt from import duties. In theory, the measure would improve the fortunes of merchants on both sides of the border. The intent was to expand trade on the "northern frontier" by bringing relief from customs fees. As designed, the law established a commercial no-man's-land and a general climate where "imports" from the United States were exempted from trade restrictions, regulations and taxes. In practice, therefore, the Zona Libre translated into immunity for smugglers and cattle thieves who could raid across the river, then retreat to their sanctuaries on the south bank. There in isolated camps rustlers drove the animals into corrals, promptly slaughtered and skinned them, the hides, hooves, and horns then being transported to leather and tallow markets. Typically, butchers from the nearest Mexican border towns were on hand with cleavers and knives to do their bloody work in harvesting the meat. Los Matavacas, the Spanish-speaking people of the border called them—the "Cow Killers."[2]

After the close of the American Civil War the Rio Grande delta region remained a welter of conflict, much of it now centered on the competition for cattle hides. And the lowest common denominator of that competition was the crime of cattle theft. Even so, troubles along the border also resulted from long-running blood feuds that only amplified the cultural and racial struggle. Few were more candid in describing conditions on this unsettled river frontier than New Hampshire native Gilbert Kingsbury, a transplanted former teacher and farmer who had first arrived in South Texas in January, 1855. Living in Brownsville under the assumed name of "F. F. Fenn," Kingsbury had served the people of Cameron County first as county clerk, then as city secretary, and finally as postmaster. At the outset of the American Civil War, however, because of his Unionist sympathies, Kingsbury (or Fenn) had been removed from office, arrested, charged with sedition, and jailed by local Confederate authorities. On January 1, 1862, he had apparently escaped the city *juzgado* and fled across the river to Matamoros, where he lived in exile for nearly two years. During this time the banished civil servant had continued to aid the Union cause by spying on Confederate military activities in the Rio Grande district. Reporting all that he knew to Federal agents and civilian authorities on the south bank, then the Union command at Fort Brown beginning in November 1863, he had even corresponded on occasion with the *New York Herald*. His letters to the editor, which reported events along the border, consistently condemned the alleged villainies of Texans and crimes against Mexicans and Union loyalists alike.[3]

While awaiting expatriation, Kingsbury had remained an enemy of what he labeled the "Robber Army of Rebels," whom he variously described as "assassins," "thieves" and "stupid desperadoes" with "no morals or principles." In the process of revealing any rumors of Confederate military movements on the border, he had likewise remained an acrid critic of the Anglo power elite that had long dominated the economic and political landscape of the Rio Grande Valley. Although he had not dared to name these influential men for fear of retribution, he still excoriated the "ten millionaires" of the South Texas rangelands. He charged that these powerful barons had purportedly gained vast fortunes of wealth by exploiting wartime shortages and fears. Without question, he had in mind powerful and ambitious men like steamboat operators, landowners and livestock raisers Richard King and his partner Mifflin Kenedy, as well as Brownsville banker and merchant Charles Stillman, all of whom were ironically native to the North. But like "true Southern men" of Southern sympathies, Kingsbury claimed, they too had smuggled Confederate cotton into Mexico during the late war, and for their efforts they had reaped handsome profits. The allure of gold payments and powerful allies on both sides of the Rio Grande had simply proved too convenient and too lucrative for such opportunists to ignore. In his correspondence back east, Kingsbury had withheld some of his strongest invective for these "so called Union men" who were "more anxious to protect Rebels who came reeking with contraband trade which has visited us with robbery and blood" than to protect the citizens of the border.[4]

"No town on the continent has so large a proportion of millionaires, vastly wealthy men as Brownsville," Kingsbury estimated. "This monopoly of trade protects itself through corruption." Moreover, he alleged that following the war "a few capitalists remain in control of the financial and political and social interest of the community." After the Southern surrender Kingsbury lived in constant fear for his life—and for good reason. Hunting and harassing Unionists continued to be the favorite sport of many former Confederates, particularly those who continued to deny that their struggle for Southern independence was lost. Thus, as the momentous year of 1865 drew to a close, antipathy for former Union loyalists like Kingsbury remained strong, even deeply ingrained in the culture of South Texas, just as it was elsewhere across the Lone Star State and the American South.[5]

By the opening of 1866 the dynamic of the border conflict was changing dramatically. With the close of the war and the end of the Union

naval blockade, the highly profitable cotton trade was no longer funnel-
ing through the lower Rio Grande. Gone too were the personal fortunes
in contraband commerce that benefited many Confederate officials like
General Hamilton P. Bee. Now, in the months following the war, the
words "cattle" and "prosperity" were becoming synonymous. Whereas
the smuggling of cotton had represented great wealth during the war,
now the rustling of beeves and the profitable hide and tallow trade spelled
riches for anyone willing to risk his life stealing livestock and driving them
to the closest market. And that market was just across the river in the auction barns and slaughterhouses of Matamoros, Reynosa, Camargo, Guerrero, and Nuevo Laredo.[6]

Cattle for the Taking

The romance of the range cattle industry has always been central to the
Texan creation myth. As a popular adage put it, "Other states were made
or born. Texas grew from hide and horn." Alongside the fallen defender of
the Alamo and the intrepid Texas Ranger, the mythic cowboy has always
enjoyed a revered place in what might be aptly termed the Texan Holy
Trinity. Such mystique endures through the generations.[7]

The formula was a simple one. While several million head of longhorns
roamed freely over the rangelands of the Nueces Strip, a beef-hungry
American public awaited in the East. And anyone who could round up
a "fair share" of the drifting herds of bony longhorns and drive them to
market stood to figure up a fast fortune. All that separated Texans from
riches that would have seemed unimaginable just a few years earlier were
nine hundred miles of forbidding country, a harsh climate, a dozen Indian
nations—among them the fierce and far-ranging Comanche—and countless rivers and streams that in springtime swelled beyond their banks.

The rise of the great cattle kingdoms of South Texas offers a magnificent
though barbaric story, one that has been told and retold. That story does
not need to be repeated here. But the impact of the emerging range cattle
industry on the troubled border with Mexico, and on U.S.-Mexican relations, is another issue altogether, one worthy of reexamination. Fortunately,
contemporary participants and eyewitnesses left a trail of documentation,
although that trail is often difficult to trace owing to so many exaggerated
claims and impassioned counterclaims. But through the dense thicket of it
all, a story emerges, and that narrative often departs from the tracks left by

Walter Prescott Webb, folklorist J. Frank Dobie, and other iconic writers of previous generations.

Like the rest of Texas, after 1865 the Nueces Strip and the lower Texas-Mexico border still suffered from wartime shortages and postwar dislocations. "When the boys came back from the Civil War they found no United States currency, no gold, no silver," South Texas rancher John A. Loomis recalled. Of course, Confederate currency was now worth nothing more than a conversation and banks were nowhere to be found, at least nowhere south of San Antonio. Credit had dried up, much like the South Texas rangelands in summer. With it, the cotton trade had all but dried up as well. Even horses and mules were scarce. For the most part, the agricultural economy along the border had been reduced to a primitive system of barter. Most crops yielded by the land were harvested by field workers engaged in simple subsistence farming. As one traveler from England observed, "Times are awful. . . . Land is worth almost nothing, all private and public enterprise has been stopped and things generally are in a state of stagnation."[8]

Almost everything was in short supply—except firearms, livestock, and prejudice. Gunrunning aside, it was the drifting herds of cattle—an estimated six million, maybe eight million head or more—that presented the greatest opportunity and the greatest danger. Most beeves were longhorns that had been left, abandoned to range over the brush country of the Nueces Strip. Loomis called them "drift cattle." So much livestock—whether branded or unbranded—ran loose on the prairies, apparently unattended by any owner. This reality led rancher John McAllen to admit, "Every one became owners." The ability to round up the stock without drawing attention could quickly translate into legal title or, in the Anglo-Saxon tradition, simple possession, which was "nine-tenths of the law." All that was needed was a branding iron and enough shooting irons to protect the "investment." From San Antonio to Corpus Christi, downcoast to Brownsville and upriver to Laredo, the cattle wandered through the thickets in such numbers that a rider would almost never be out of sight of a small herd, or at least a few head. As for the animals, they did what they do best—they wandered, grazed, and multiplied. Since the ranges remained open and unfenced in those days, the lands were free for grazing. Of course, the cattle knew no boundaries, geographic, national, or otherwise. Neither did cattle rustlers—Mexican and Anglo alike—who recognized that the markets of Matamoros, Reynosa, Camargo, Guerrero, and other

Mexican border towns were much closer than the railhead towns of Kansas and Missouri. Better yet, they were on Mexican soil, safely across the river from Texan and American authorities.[9]

Over time, the vaqueros of the Rio Grande borderlands had become expert practitioners of their trade. From the Lipan, Mescalero, and other eastern Apache, they had learned to live off the land. From the Comanche they had learned their knowledge of horseflesh and their remarkable equestrian skills. From the Spaniard, they had learned the custom of the rodeo, particularly the practice of rounding up cattle, branding them and trailing them to distant markets. Now from the Anglo-Texan they learned the benefits of capitalism and the "free market."

Contrary to the Anglo-Texan Myth, not all cattle thieves of the post–Civil War era could be accurately described as "Mexican" in race or nationality, as previous generations of American writers have inferred. In fact, the ranks of rustlers included disgruntled Confederate veterans, some deserters from the Southern cause who were looking for a quick and easy way to "earn" a living. Traveler Thomas North offered a classic description of those he termed the "barbarian element" loose on the landscape of the Lone Star State, particularly those bad men who were the menacing refuse of the war. "In our five years' Texas experience we met this monster of the human heart in shapes . . . deeper, darker, and more vile than we had ever dreamed of before," he observed. Referring to the "renegade Americans" who were left after the war and who were now refugees from Reconstruction, he added that the most identifiable characteristic of these desperadoes was that they "value human life less than other people."[10]

John Linn recollected that in those days his fellow English-speaking Texans competed with Comanche raiders and rings of rustlers from Mexico in "appropriating the live stock left grazing on the prairies. Anything that belonged to a Mexican was legitimate game," whether north or south of the river, Linn confessed. "Immense numbers of cattle and horses were so seized and driven east for sale," many by those he identified as the "remorseless Gaels" of Texas.[11]

The breadth and extent of cattle rustling on the lower Rio Grande during the so-called Skinning Wars, and even the identity of many of the thieves, remains a matter of controversy. A century and a half later the debate continues as to the active role of fortune-seeking Anglo-Americans looking for a fast way to get rich. South of the Rio Grande people still insist that Texas ranchers stole their cattle and stocked their herds with longhorns from Mexico. North of the border, Anglo-Texans argue that cattle theft was long the chief enterprise of Mexican bandits who plundered the livestock of the Nueces Strip, and continued to do so with impunity until the Texas Rangers stopped them. To many Anglo-Texans, even today, just a hint or suggestion to the contrary amounts to nothing less than heresy. Not surprisingly, therefore, the answer as to who was to blame for rustling cattle and the attending violence still depends largely on which side of the river you are on.[12]

But little doubt remains that the worst criminals of both nations and of both races engaged in cattle rustling and assorted other crimes along the lower Rio Grande. Teamster August Santleben, who knew the cattle trails and trade routes of South Texas as well as anyone, recalled that the "thieves generally were organized to operate in gangs on both sides of the river and acted in collusion with each other by exchanging stolen property brought from Mexico for other property acquired in like manner in Texas." Smuggling weapons and ammunition was also as much a part of border culture as cattle and horse theft. Add to that the underlying racial tensions and nationalistic zeal of people on this unstable river frontier, and the situation remained highly combustible.[13]

Saving Frank Buckelew

To understand the border epidemic of cattle rustling in the mid-nineteenth century, a full account must first be made (if that is even possible) of the part played by those who were neither citizens of Mexico nor the United States. They were a people without a country, without land and livestock of their own, a destitute and desperate lot of refugees: American Indian tribesmen who had recently fled the punishing hand of the U.S. government and crossed into Mexico, taking up residence on the south banks of the Rio Grande. Scattered bands of half-starved Kickapoo and Lipan Apache, even stragglers of the Seminole, who like their new neighbors in Mexico now became dependent on a steady supply of beef from across the border. No doubt, in feeding their hungry families they believed that Texas cattle were their entitlement, and they agreed with the captain of the Mexican army who allegedly boasted when driving a herd of stolen Texas cattle back across the river, "the *gringos* are raising cows for me."[14]

Indian raids were nothing new on the borderlands of Texas. What was different about the Kickapoo villagers of Santa Rosa and their Lipan neighbors camped near the town of Zaragoza is that they enjoyed sanctuary and even support of officials, merchants, and rancheros south of the border.

As for the "Seminole Negroes," or "Seminole Maroons" as they were also termed, many Texans unfairly considered them a thieving bunch too, guilty by their racial association with and proximity to the Kickapoo and Lipan. Through the years both Texas and U.S. officials grew increasingly alarmed by the escalating reports of robbery, theft, and murder committed by Indian raiders crossing the Rio Grande. And they made no distinction among the native tribesmen, whether Lipan, Kickapoo, or Seminole. The record is filled with the testimony of scores of Texans who suffered ruinous losses at the hands of "Mexican Kickapoo." and Lipan raiding parties. What these depositions fail to disclose is just how destitute and hungry the Indian villagers were. Nor did the testimony acknowledge that, in the case of the Kickapoo, they were still stalked by memories of the Confederate Partisans who had tracked and attacked No-ko-aht's Coahuila-bound band near Dove Creek, a tributary of the southern branch of the Concho River, on January 8, 1865. The memory that the Kickapoo were carrying a white flag of truce that day when the soldiers shot some of them down like wild dogs only reinforced their argument that the Texans had first declared war on them.[15]

On December 6, 1866, Texas Governor James W. Throckmorton summarized his concern and frustration with the situation in a letter to U.S. commissioner of Indian affairs D. M. Cooley. Decrying the ongoing depredations along the border, particularly the theft of horses and cattle and the taking of captives, he complained that "it is needless to call upon Mexican authorities in their present anarchical condition." Then he warned that, if the Kickapoo were not removed to their former homes on the borders of Missouri, Kansas, and Indian Territory, the aggrieved citizens of South Texas would soon take matters into their own hands. If federal authorities failed to protect Texans along the lower Rio Grande from what he termed "this pest," these citizens would "not be restrained, but . . . [would] cross the Rio Grande and break up this camp of Indian robbers."[16]

In some cases, the evidence suggests that many marauders appeared to be disguised as Indians to conceal their identity. But there was no disguising the reality that the Kickapoo and Lipan living on the border not only poached cattle and drove them across the Rio Grande, they also engaged in another profitable trade—hostage taking and human trafficking. Records of the postwar years were replete with references to captives being taken from Texas border settlements, most of them children who were seized and either sold as slaves, swapped for goods, or held for ransom in Mexico. In such instances the exchange rate typically involved the currency of horses, cattle, and sometimes silver coins in return for the release of captives.[17]

The most celebrated of these cases in South Texas was that of thirteen-year-old Francis M. Buckelew, who was abducted by a Lipan raiding party in Bandera County on Sunday, March 11, 1866. "Frank" Buckelew and a black playmate named Morris were out looking for a lost oxen bell on the Ghoulson Place on the Rio Sabinal. The boys knew well the dangers of venturing into the wilds alone or in pairs. After all, only six weeks had passed since Frank's uncle, Barry Buckalew, had been murdered by Kickapoo marauders while hunting deer among the cedar breaks on the Little Seco in Medina County. Friends had later discovered Uncle Barry's body, stripped of boots and clothing, with two arrows buried in his back. In the case of little Morris, he had only recently escaped a similar fate when raiders had swept through the valley of the Sabinal and fallen upon a small party of cowhands caught in the open branding calves. That attack, which resulted in the killing of two young Texans and the capture of one child, had gone unavenged, though not forgotten.[18]

For the red-haired, freckle-faced Frank Buckelew and young Morris it all began like any other Sunday morning. But in the blur of a moment that changed. While walking across an open meadow, Buckelew thought he saw a movement in some distant redbud trees. "I kept watching the thicket. Looking around I thought I saw a hog, but a second glance convinced me that it was . . . an Indian, with war paint on his face, feathers in his hair, and a dirty greasy frocktail coat on his body." When the warrior rose up and released a chilling war whoop, Buckelew turned and ran as fast as his young legs could carry him. Looking back, however, the boy realized that the warrior was fast advancing, a bow and arrow aimed directly at him. "I stopped in my tracks and turned my face toward him."[19]

Being chased down had been harrowing enough, but what followed would be even more terrifying. The warrior marched Buckelew into a nearby tree line and then stripped him of his clothes and shoes. After that, the captor and three fellow raiders forced the boy to run barefoot alongside them, through the rocky wilderness, across a rugged terrain covered with briars and cactus. For more than a mile they trotted until coming upon an older warrior perched on a bluff. "It was evident from the action of the four savages," Buckelew remembered, "that he was more than an ordinary warrior."[20]

Buckelew soon learned that there was indeed nothing "ordinary" about the wizened old man with weathered skin. The aging chief spoke broken

English and had an "air of haughty dignity" about him. Commanding by his mere presence, he exuded an unmistakable majesty, though his sun-baked face and dingy deerskin leggings and tunic at first concealed that noble nature and "kindly manner." Only later did Buckelew learn the identity of the aging warrior who became his protector. Costelietos, his people called him; he was the principal chief of the Lipan Apache who had fled Texas more than a decade earlier and taken up residence on the Mexican side of the Rio Grande. It was the only place where they felt safe.[21]

Young Buckelew's journey to Mexico would be long and arduous. Along the route from the Sabinal to the upper tributaries of the Frio and beyond, across the hard lands of the Devil's River, then northward to the deserts of the Trans-Pecos they traveled. From one squalid camp to another his captors led him, sometimes treating him harshly, on occasions flogging him into submission with a rawhide quirt. As was the Lipan way, they dressed the boy like one of their own, in deerskin moccasins and frock, and offered him only enough water and rations to keep him on his feet and moving. At times, they forced him to gather firewood, prepare food, and make shelter—squaw's work.

For young Frank the weeks passed into months until he found himself living as a Lipan brave near the village of San Vicente, across the Rio Grande, a day's ride from Del Rio. By autumn he had been accepted fully into Lipan society. The adopted son of the warrior who had captured him, and by proxy the grandson of the venerable old Costelietos, Buckelew learned to hunt and handle horses the Lipan way. That included stealing ponies and breaking them.[22]

But Buckelew refused to let his captors break his spirit. He never stopped hoping to see his family again, and he never ceased planning an escape. That opportunity presented itself less than three weeks after his arrival at San Vicente in January 1867. During this trip, he somehow managed to tell his story to an old Mexican stranger, who in turn agreed to recruit a younger man who would be willing to rescue him and guide him across the river to safety.

For many weeks, reports of the "white boy captive" had already moved across the river into Texas and, unbeknownst to Buckelew, a benefactor stepped forward. Upon hearing of the fate of young Texan, Uvalde County judge Newman Patterson, himself a prominent stockman who had suffered losses at the hands of the Kickapoo and Lipan, persuaded frontiersman W. B. Hudson of neighboring Kinney County to secure the safe return of the boy. Based on his correspondence with Governor James W.

Throckmorton, Patterson had apparently promised Hudson that a bounty of $300 would be paid by the state of Texas for the return of Buckelew. For this purpose, Hudson recruited an unnamed Mexican vaquero to assist him in the dangerous mission.[23]

Buckelew later testified that one afternoon, while entering San Vicente with his captors, he was quietly approached by a Mexican acquaintance and a younger man who asked if he wanted to go home to Texas. Stunned but excited, he answered, "I sure do, if I can get there." A white woman living among the Lipan had already discouraged him from trying to escape, explaining that his home was "a way yonder," and that his folks were probably all dead anyway.[24]

But Buckelew did not waver. The older Mexican nodded his head when the boy reassured him again that he wanted to escape. "He told me that if I would get a good horse and come back to town that night, the young Mexican would take me to the home of Mr. Hudson, just fourteen miles down the river, and that he would take me home, and that we could ride to Bandera in five days. . . . About dark I caught the best horse in the herd and rode to town," Buckelew recalled. There, as promised, the younger man he had seen earlier in the day was to guide him across the Rio Grande. "I was riding bareback, but that made no difference to me, for I was going home," Buckelew remembered. Once on the Texas side of the river, he recollected, he could gaze back into Mexico and see that no Lipan were following him. Before the two horsemen rode on to Hudson's ranch, the Mexican also looked back across the river; until then, Buckelew remembered, the guide "had not ventured to utter a word . . . but turned to me and said, 'Indians, go hell—dam 'em!'" For the first time in nearly a year Frank Buckelew could laugh. He was a free man.[25]

A few hours later the two riders arrived safely at Hudson's homestead, and from there the boy was escorted on to Fort Duncan. Days later Buckelew returned safely to his family in Bandera County, where he lived in peace for the rest of his days. But that is another story.

Giving Diplomacy a Chance

The fall of 1870 turned out to be arguably the worst season for Kickapoo and Lipan raids that resulted in children being taken hostage. In September of that year during a week of the full moon a party of more than twenty Kickapoo raiders struck isolated cabins and homesteads as far north as the Nueces. On September 28 in McMullen County the marauders fell upon farmer Thomas Wesley Stringfield and his family, who were returning by wagon from Pleasanton to their homestead on the prairies near Loma Alta. Caught on the open plain by a party of armed horsemen, Tom Stringfield and his young wife, Sarah Jane, and three children tried to outrun the raiders. Finding themselves surrounded, the couple gathered eight-year-old Ida Alice, six-year-old Adolphus, and four-year-old Tommy and began running toward a nearby timberline. In an attempt to help his family escape, Tom Stringfield grabbed his rifle and tried to hold them off. But there were too many of them. Struck in the arm by a bullet, Stringfield stumbled and fell, then suffered a second gunshot wound, this one fatal.[26]

Several horsemen then chased down Sarah Jane, lancing and stabbing her repeatedly. "I saw them stab my mother in the heart," Ida Alice wrote years later. "I . . . screamed and started to my mother, but one of the men jumped between me and my mother. At that time another man picked me up before him on his horse and started to carry me away." As her abductor rode off, however, she bit him on the hand, causing him to toss her to the ground. Just then, another raider pulled her up onto his horse and attempted to gallop away. Again, she struggled and tried to pull herself from the horse by grabbing the limb of a small tree. At that point, the rider threatened her in broken Spanish, then threw her off his horse and began trampling her beneath his pony's hooves. Another raider then rode his horse over her repeatedly and finally thrust his war lance into her several times. Not satisfied that she was dead, a third horseman dismounted, grabbed her by the hair and pulled her head off the ground. She recalled that he spoke "not in English or Spanish" but in a tongue she had never heard and could not understand. Then he struck her over the head and left her for dead. "That was the last I knew for some time," she wrote.[27]

All the while, her brothers Adolphus ("Dolph") and little Tommy were carried off by the marauders toward Mexico. Only later did Ida learn that a Mexican family living nearby had found her alive but barely breathing. They took her in, tended to her wounds, and nursed her back to health until relatives came for her a few weeks later. It was then that she learned that the body of six-year-old Dolph had been discovered by a search party on the open range just days after the attack. The boy had been stabbed to death by his captors. As for Tommy, she never heard again of his whereabouts but was told that he had been taken across the Rio Grande and perhaps sold by the Lipan. But no one knew for sure.[28]

That same autumn, raiders stole away with other children and carried them off to Mexico, as evidenced by the abductions from the families of

Peter Schwandner and Henry Smith in Uvalde County. But in these cases the children were soon recovered after ransom payments were delivered by friends and agents of the families.[29]

Amid the growing depredations in South Texas federal officials determined to give diplomacy a chance. In the spring of 1871, U.S. Indian agent John D. Miles traveled from Indian Territory with instructions to negotiate the peaceful return of the Kickapoo to their reservation five hundred miles to the north, beyond the Red River. Arriving at Fort Duncan on April 11, Miles was accompanied by a fellow Quaker missionary and two self-styled "civilized" Kickapoo interpreters named John and Moses. Some sources contend that John was the respected chief known as No-ko-aht. After meeting with Major Zenas R. Bliss and the post chaplain, Edmund Butterick Tuttle, the peace party was joined by William Schuhardt, the U.S. consul at Piedras Negras, who briefed them on conditions along the border.[30]

Schuhardt must have offered Miles little hope for success. After all, he had already expressed his pessimism for the mission, referring to rumors that many Kickapoo were ready to return to their reservation as "utterly false." From all reports, he had insisted, "so long as the Kickapoo have the protection of the Mexican government and cross into Texas to loot, rob, and plunder, and as long as these acts are countenanced by citizens of Mexico, and as long as the Kickapoo can find a ready market for their booty they will never willingly quit."[31]

On a hot morning in May Major Bliss, Schuhardt, and a handful of Black Seminole scouts led by Sergeant John Kibbits escorted Miles's party across the Rio Grande and over the parched plains to Santa Rosa (now Múzquiz). The peace party could not have had a more reliable and resourceful guide than "Old Kibbits," as his fellow Black Seminole scouts called him. Sitetaastonachy, "Snake Warrior," his people had known him in the days of Osceola and the Florida Seminole Wars. He was more recently a protégé of the much revered—and feared—Chief Wild Cat as well as Chief John Horse, also known as Juan Caballo and "Gopher John" to people of the border. Kibbits could also boast of being a former civil chief of the Seminole "Maroons," or Mascogos, who had fled the United States following the war with Mexico, taking refuge at Nacimiento de los Negros, Coahuila. Stealthy, cunning, and resourceful, he knew the border country and the ways of the Kickapoo and Lipan. Just as important, his reputation as a tracker and a horseman was unequaled. The scouts who served under him obeyed his every order, without question. If he had a weakness, Bliss acknowledged, it was his fondness for the white man's whiskey. But when sober, there was no better or braver soldier than Old Kibbits.[32]

While the peace party was en route through the Mexican wilderness to Santa Rosa, a Kickapoo war chief rode out to meet them. Cheeno, the white men called him, and he turned out to be as colorful a character, every bit as impressive as Sergeant Kibbits. As Major Bliss drove his mule-drawn army ambulance beneath a rugged ridge, the old warrior literally rose from the rocks above them, unexpectedly, appearing suddenly like a lone apparition from the desert landscape. "He was a fine looking Indian, about five feet nine or ten inches and about fifty-five years old," Bliss recorded. "He had iron gray hair which was very curly and it was from this he got his name" from the Mexicans (*chino* meaning "curly" in Spanish). "He had a Roman nose and a very kind expression of countenance when in repose." As the old warrior approached the travelers, clutching a rifle in one hand and holding the other aloft in a gesture of friendship, Bliss and his Black Seminole troopers could see that he appeared to pose no threat. In fact, Cheeno shook hands with several members of the American delegation, though he "paid not the slightest attention" to the two "educated" Kickapoo.[33]

At first the meeting seemed awkward, but the tension soon eased. "I tried to talk a little," Bliss recalled, "but soon found I was not in accord with their custom, so I kept still. We sat there for several minutes with John and Moses looking dumb as two owls, and Cheeno the same." After a long silence Cheeno finally spoke in his native Algonquin; then Moses and John replied in kind. Major Bliss remembered that the three drew closer and enjoyed "a grand laugh and hand shaking and embracing. I think Moses was a relative of Cheeno. They had not seen each other for ten years and . . . at first they did not appear to know each other at all."[34]

It all seemed an auspicious beginning for the mission. Cheeno accompanied the peace party to Santa Rosa, where he had gathered a handful of Kickapoo braves. But these "spokesmen" did not actually speak for their band, which numbered no more than five hundred men, women, and children. Their principal elder chiefs, among them Macemanet, were nowhere to be seen. Before any talks could occur, Major Bliss and company were required to experience local hospitality and custom. "I went to the house of a Mexican agent," Bliss recollected. "It was nicely furnished and he asked the mother of the family to call the daughters. Three nice young girls came and greeted us cordially and after a while brought in their harp and guitars and played and sang for us very sweetly."

After a few minutes the father asked Bliss to accompany him to a nearby store and sample a glass of his native wine. Being gracious and polite, Bliss expressed delight at the wine, though it was too sweet for his taste. "He asked me to take some home. I accepted a bottle but he insisted on my taking a dozen, and after a good deal of persuasion I accepted. After a few minutes, we got up to depart and as I was going out he very politely told me I had forgotten to pay for the wine." Surprised, Bliss paid for the wine, which admittedly he liked even less now after he "had been inveigled into buying a dozen bottles I did not want."[35]

The wine proved even more unpalatable when Major Bliss and the others grew to realize that this guileful merchant was intent on hindering, not helping, them. Although "polite, friendly and diplomatic," Bliss later reflected, "this Mexican was doing all he could to prevent our succeeding in our mission." As for other local officials, the major remembered, in the coming days they too "did everything to assist me, but they were opposed to the Indians leaving the country, as they protected the ranches [below the Rio Grande] from incursions of hostile Indians," including Comanche crossing over from Texas.[36]

On their first afternoon in Mexico, Bliss and his companions also witnessed firsthand just how "business" was conducted between local magistrates and their Kickapoo neighbors. What the Americans saw in the picturesque and charming town of Santa Rosa should have come as no surprise. Through the shimmering heat and swirling dust of the surrounding desert the American delegation peered and watched in stunned silence as vaqueros drove a herd of Texas beeves, their brands clearly identifiable, through the streets of Santa Rosa to stock pens nearby, where the cattle were turned over to young Kickapoo braves who were brandishing weapons. With this delivery, the American agents later learned, came the promise of future rations of livestock.[37]

While awaiting a council with the Kickapoo, the American delegation called upon the alcalde of Santa Rosa, who received them "with a great deal of ceremony" as Bliss recalled. Treating them to a feast of food, wine, and an assortment of tequilas, town officials serenaded the Americans with mariachi music and invited them to dance with pretty señoritas. "The chaplain and Quakers stayed till the ball was over," Bliss recorded, "but of course did not dance, though I have no doubt they wanted to."[38]

The ensuing negotiations were less successful. "I had long talks with the Indians," Bliss recalled, "but could not get the promise to return to their reservation in the United States." When he inquired as to traveling to the main Kickapoo village to parley with their principal chiefs, Sergeant Kibbits took him aside and warned him "not to go to their camp . . . [because] they would kill me. He said he would not go for any [amount of] money, that it was certain death." Moses and John agreed that such a mission would be a fatal mistake, the colonel remembered, "so I finally gave it up." The council with Cheeno was one thing, they agreed, but walking into the den of disgruntled Kickapoo loyal to more militant chiefs was quite another matter.[39]

Within days of their arrival the peace party would cross back into Texas, returning to Fort Duncan empty-handed (or, in Bliss's case, with twelve bottles of unwanted wine). Tired and frustrated, though well fed and regaled, they could only acknowledge the failure of their mission. Miles later explained, "The people of Santa Rosa were so decidedly opposed to the removal of the Kickapoo, giving for their reason that the city and the whole community would be invaded at once by the Mescaleros and other marauding bands of Indians; that the Kickapoo were their only defense and . . . the Kickapoo trade was a matter of no mean importance to them." Miles could not have better summarized the whole matter.[40]

The Red Robber and the White Horseman

Understandably, South Texas stockmen and farmers—Texan and Tejano alike—grew increasingly weary of the unrelenting depredations. And they not only held Mexican officials responsible but also blamed the policies of their own distant U.S. government for driving the Indians across the Rio Grande and into border sanctuaries. Moreover, they bristled from the knowledge that so few troops—never more than 4,500 during the period—were stationed along the six hundred–mile lower Texas-Mexico border extending from Fort Duncan near Eagle Pass to Fort Brown. Seething beneath the surface of events as well was a deeply ingrained resentment resulting from racist attitudes that African American units were often assigned to garrison these posts. Texan anger also turned justifiably on officials in Austin who at best seemed slow to recognize the problem and at worst unable or unwilling to do anything about it. Specifically, the cash-strapped state legislature, embroiled in feuds over federal Reconstruction matters, balked at the very proposal to fund state troops, or mounted Rangers, to patrol the river frontier.[41]

To paraphrase historian Walter Prescott Webb, in the months that followed the American Civil War the frontier institution known as the Texas

Rangers again became little more than a memory, a mere historical expression. While the Reconstruction administrations of governors Andrew Jackson Hamilton (1865–66), James W. Throckmorton (1866–67), and Elisha M. Pease (1867–69) devoted little attention to frontier defense and border security, the Republican state legislatures of these years appropriated even less money for the protection of those living daily on the edge of danger.[42]

Therefore, in counties from the Red River bordering Indian Territory to the Rio Grande Valley, citizens organized committees of "public safety" to administer their own brand of frontier justice. Predictably, these vigilance committees seldom produced an impartial administration of the law. One northern visitor to South Texas noted of such a posse of regulators, "Each had his rifle, and as they sat on their horses, with long guns laid over their Mexican saddles, their broad sombreros, leather leggings, and tightly girdled blouses, they looked like they had come to have their portraits taken. After a steady stare, they rode away." The traveler observed that while there was a striking absence of skilled tradesmen and educated professionals among these vigilantes, there seemed to be no shortage of prejudice or firearms.[43]

Still, the traveler echoed the sentiments of citizens of the Lone Star State that "one regiment of Texans taken from the region near the Indians . . . is worth an army of regulars. They know the habits and haunts of the tribes, and they can strike them so fast and fatally." Sam Houston had never stated it more succinctly. In some respects, therefore, the frontier tradition of the "ranging service" remained alive and well in Texas, even if leaders in Austin failed to assist the border counties under siege. The people of Cameron as well as Hidalgo, Starr, Zapata, Webb, and other counties upriver were on the front lines of the violence, even if lawmakers and politicians tucked safely away in Austin were not. That disconnect only caused increasing discontent among the people of the border region, who viewed their state as at best feckless and at worst unconcerned if not openly hostile to their interests.[44]

By most accounts the largest ring of cattle thieves operating on the border was headed by the mythic "Red Robber," General Juan Cortina. A well-organized and extensive network of rustlers occupying a line of isolated cow camps strung along the south banks afforded bases of operation for armed rustlers who crossed into Texas with regularity and apparently with protection on the Mexican side. There, along the river most local officials—though not all—were loyal to Cortina and, by that association they were part of his system of patronage and favor. Regardless of who was in power in Mexico City, and who might control the state capitals in Tamaulipas, Coahuila, and Nuevo Leon, their allegiance was to Cortina, who gave them protection, status, influence, and a share of the profits from the cattle "trade" across the border.

Despite the perception that Cortina directed all cattle theft on the border, Texan August Santleben described the entire region as "infested with many outlaws," one of the "most notorious" being Alberto Garza. Known along the border as "Caballero Blanco," or the "White Horseman," because of his favorite mount, a white stallion, Garza had terrorized the river frontier since 1860. Santleben recalled that the ruthless, renegade vaquero had earned his "reputation of being a very brave man, but the cruelties he perpetrated on those who fell in his hands" provided ample evidence that he was not a bandit hero but rather a brutal highwayman. "He took special pleasure in humiliating the victims that were overpowered by his gang and robbed, by forcing them to dance at the muzzle of a six-shooter."[45]

More than a score of such thieves commanded armed gangs of bandits who were little more than soldiers of fortune. So feared was one "notorious" desperado, Manuel Telamantes, that officials in Eagle Pass were reluctant to order his arrest, especially since it was well known that he had put a price on the head of anyone who challenged his authority. Lawless elements infested every border town—on both banks of the Rio Grande—from Laredo to Brownsville. By all accounts they operated openly and with little regard to consequence or concern of arrest. Some lurked in the mesquite thickets, but many walked brazenly through the streets of border towns, unafraid of punishment by the laws of either the Lone Star State or Mexico. And they cared little whether Emperor Maximilian, his rival Benito Juárez, or anyone else claimed power in Mexico City. Like local warlords in a medieval feudal society, they were sovereigns over all they surveyed—or so they thought and acted at the time.[46]

Only three common threads connected men like Garza, Telamantes, and a dozen other thieves like them: they stole cattle from Mexicans and Texans alike; they typically sold them for their hides, horns, and hooves rather than for beef; and they apparently had no direct ties to General Juan Cortina and his ring of rustlers. If anything, they were Cortina's competition, not his confidants and compadres in the lucrative hide and tallow trade, then later the highly profitable commerce in beef cattle.

Another of the most popular myths of the era holds that the cattle thieves in South Texas were exclusively men of Mexican heritage. But the historical record indicates that nothing could have been further from the truth. In many cases, as documented by authorities in both the United States and Mexico, some border thieves were led and directed by an Anglo-American boss or his "ramrod," otherwise known as his *segundo* (or second in charge). Like their counterparts from south of the border, these men sought nothing more and accepted nothing less than the chance to profit from the illegal trade in hides and beeves. If that meant plunder and killing along the way, then that was simply accepted as part of the "business." In sum, all criminal elements along the lower Rio Grande—Mexican and Anglo alike—saw fortunes to be made in stealing cattle.

Just as there was no shortage of "drift cattle" on the grasslands of the Trans-Nueces, there seemed to be no end to the supply of mercenaries, thieves, and cutthroats who would kill for any cause—especially money. And in those days, that translated into livestock. On February 6, 1869, Cameron County judge Jeremiah Galvan offered the adjutant general of the state of Texas a grim assessment of the prospects for peace and order on the border. Reporting that "the unfortunate condition to which our exposure as a frontier [and border] county has reduced us . . . to lawlessness and violence at the hands of strangers," he blamed corrupt Mexican officials for both negligence and complicity. He even alleged that authorities on the south banks of the Rio Bravo provided protection for cattle rustlers and gangs of bandits that ranged freely north of the river.[47]

"Our jail is constantly full of criminals," an exasperated Judge Galvan complained. "No sooner has the District Court . . . sent a score of them, strangers to our habits, languages, and laws, to the penitentiary," he warned, "a new batch takes their place." To state it in terms that authorities might understand, Galvan pleaded that his constituents' isolation on the border placed them in the position of being "sentinels to the tier of counties . . . [north] of the Nueces."[48]

Other local officials could provide even more personal testimony to support such claims. In September 1869, former Cameron County judge Stephen Powers and Sheriff James G. Browne both filed complaints that their own mounts were stolen and carried into Matamoros. In the case of Judge Powers, his horse was later "found in the possession of the son of the second alcalde" as Rip Ford recalled, and "could not be recovered." Not long thereafter, a posse headed by Eugenio Benavides, special inspector of hides and animals in neighboring Hidalgo County, clashed with a party of cattle thieves, reportedly led by notorious rustler Desiderio Villareal, near Salt Lake. During the gunfight Villareal was wounded and a butcher from

Matamoros named Casario Salinas was captured, while several of their fellow raiders escaped across the river. After the fight, Benavides reported that 129 beeves bearing Texas brands were recovered and returned to their rightful owners.[49]

So grave were the mounting problems of cattle theft and horse stealing that Judge Galvan led Cameron County residents in forming a stock raisers' association for the purpose of documenting losses and recovering livestock. Galvan even served as chairman of the Cameron County Stockman's Association, and while in office he formed a company of ranchers, commanded by Louis Renand, to patrol the river and recapture stolen stock. Neither Galvan nor anyone else on the Texas side ever documented whether these armed "regulators" actually crossed the Rio Grande to "reclaim" their cattle. What Galvan did document, however, was a detailed record of the number and estimated value of the animals recovered and sold at auction, the proceeds being divided equally among the ranchers and the vaqueros who recaptured their stock. Beginning in August 1869 and continuing until June 1871, Galvan listed the recovered stock, the brands on the animals retaken, the names of the "captors," and sales receipts. No record surfaced suggesting that some of the vaqueros who received bounties for returning stolen stock might have been the same men who took the animals to begin with, or if they were at least in league with those who did.[50]

A Reign of Terror

In many instances during Reconstruction, acts of violence erupted not from range wars between cattle ranchers and common rustlers but instead from unresolved disputes and even hatred between former Confederates and "Union men," including many who had recently arrived on the border. One such feud involved Cameron County sheriff Rudolph Krause, a German immigrant who owed his appointment to the Republican Governor E. J. Davis, and the editor of the anti-Republican *Brownsville Sentinel*, who happened to be the most famous man on the South Texas border— John S. Ford, Old Rip himself. Ford had not minced words in his editorials when directing vitriolic criticism of the Reconstruction policies of the Congress, President Grant, and now Governor Davis.[51]

On the evening of February 16, 1870, the bad blood between Krause and Ford led to a confrontation that turned violent and near deadly. The Miller Hotel on Elizabeth Street, only a block from the Matamoros ferry, was the most respectable gathering place in Brownsville. A two-story structure owned by proprietor Henry Miller, the popular hotel offered the closest thing to elegance and comfort on the river frontier; its downstairs dining hall and fashionable barroom were said to be the finest south of San Antonio. Old Colonel Ford liked to frequent the establishment, where he could engage in social conversation and talk about any subject from contemporary politics to his memories of past military campaigns, from Mexico to the Rio Grande to Comanche country in West Texas and Indian Territory. A raconteur of renown, he always drew a crowd of the curious, most of them admirers. Everyone on the border knew his name, and most knew of his fame. And all who knew him understood that while he might have grown gray, stooped, and tired after years of service to Texas, neither his charisma nor his fiery temper had dimmed. He could still regale audiences with accounts of his fighting days. Some said most of Ford's favorite stories were about himself and particularly his own exploits as a Ranger. Or possibly, Ford just told his listeners what they wanted and expected to hear.[52]

Regardless, on this Wednesday night, while playing billiards with friends, Ford was not the one doing the talking. He was approached by two men who saw only a faded hero, a fallen leader of failed causes and past wars. No one later clarified whether Ford had been drinking that evening. If he had, no one, not even Ford, could have predicted how he might react to the insults of lesser men. According to newspaper accounts, Sheriff Krause and Deputy Cruise Carson—both armed—walked into the Miller Hotel. Witnesses claimed that, without provocation, Krause began to insult Colonel Ford. Repeating the language, described as a personal affront to the old Ranger, Krause walked closer to Siebert's Cigar Stand near the pool tables where Ford stood holding only a cue. Witnesses agreed that Krause was the aggressor.[53]

The *Brownsville Daily Ranchero* reported what happened next. "The Sheriff renewed his insults. . . . Colonel Ford caught him by the throat" and shoved him against the wall. Krause then drew his pistol and fired at point-blank range, striking Ford in the hand. Before Krause could discharge a second shot an unnamed bystander pushed the revolver aside and witnesses separated the two combatants and wrestled them apart. Splattered with his own blood, Rip Ford knew it had been a close call. But it was not the first time he had faced down death.[54]

The matter did not end there. Editor Henry Maltby of the *Daily Ranchero* publicly shamed Sheriff Krause and called for his arrest and prosecution. Brownsville Mayor Jeremiah Galvan tried unsuccessfully to persuade U.S. military officials, from Fort Brown to San Antonio, to intervene. Galvan even issued an arrest warrant, but Sheriff Krause had apparently already fled to avoid prosecution for attempted murder. Within days, however, Krause turned himself in to the Republican state district court judge Henry Haupt, who then released the lawman after he posted bail. Apparently, no formal indictment was ever issued in the case, and the legal matter was closed.[55]

For Ford and other "unredeemed" Confederates it was far from over. The incident only served to breed more local resentment toward the "Radical Reconstruction" administration of Governor Davis. Perhaps Maltby best summarized the sentiments of many of the citizens of South Texas when he editorialized, "When the time has come that the sheriff of Cameron County can enter a hotel and insult an honorable citizen and attempt to take his life with impunity, we are solemnly reminded of the propriety of keeping one's thoughts to himself, lest he himself may be the subject for the licensed blade of the assassin."[56]

During this same time, Ford ended up in the middle of the growing turmoil swirling around cattle theft and associated border violence. As editor of the *Sentinal*, he reported on the spreading contagion of cattle rustling. In one article during the summer of 1870 he alleged that more than seven thousand head of Texas beeves had been driven into Mexico in just one week, though he failed to offer evidence for the number claimed. Even federal military authorities were reportedly seeking his advice and assistance with their patrols "against cow thieves and other disturbances of peace and quietude."[57]

During the next year, little changed to "quiet" the border troubles. Early in 1872 federal authorities impaneled a U.S. grand jury in Brownsville to investigate the epidemic of plunder and violence that had long plagued the lower Rio Grande. No one was surprised when jurors chose John S. Ford to serve as foreman and spokesman for the panel. It took the federal grand jurors only nine days to issue subpoenas, consider testimony and collect evidence of what they termed the "reign of terror" that existed in the Rio Grande Valley. Before the end of March, they had handed down fifty-seven bills of indictment, in the process charging that an average of five thousand Texas cattle were rustled across the river each month and sold in the hide and tallow markets at Matamoros, Reynosa, Mier, Camargo, Guerrero, Nuevo Laredo, Piedras Negras, and other Mexican border towns. They documented multiple cases of horse theft and the murder of livestock inspectors and other local magistrates. Moreover, the jurors alleged that one bandit chief, who had "written the history . . . of this side of the Rio Grande in letters of fire and blood," was responsible for most of these outrages. That man was the governor and military commander of the Mexican state of Tamaulipas, General Juan N. Cortina.[58]

The federal grand jurors concluded that lawlessness along the lower Rio Grande had reached such a level that they had no choice but to implore U.S. government officials to act immediately and decisively in response to the "armed invaders" who continued to pillage the settlements and rangelands of South Texas.[59]

If anything, during the coming weeks the grim situation grew even worse. On February 10, 1872, the *Daily Ranchero* carried a report that no doubt reflected the attitudes of many Texans in the Rio Grande Valley. "There are many persons on this side [of the border] who maintain themselves by cattle stealing. The peculiar character of our Mexican population, combined with the advantages of a very scattered [Anglo] population and dense thickets, makes . . . cattle stealing a very profitable business." Those who perpetrated and carried out such crimes, the article continued, "cannot be reached by our tribunals" because they have "many able friends" in positions of power south of the border. Then the report announced that two accused rustlers, identified as Pancho Blanco and Cipriano Guerrero, "were caught and hanged from a mesquite tree by rancheros" only the previous week. The newspaper further claimed that the two dead vaqueros were "thieves known by the rancheros for a long time as robbers of great notoriety." Last, the editorial offered a shocking remedy for the growing epidemic of violence and lawlessness. Referring to the lynching of Blanco and Guerrero, the publisher grimly proposed, "We approve of . . . [this] way of disposing of all suspicious characters the whole length of the frontier." Hang suspected rustlers first—lynch them in the name of the law—the writer urged the citizens of South Texas. Then let authorities investigate later.[60]

Some citizens of South Texas may have hoped that such news would have a chilling effect on border bandits and rustlers. But if they believed that vigilantism might bring an end to the lawlessness, they were wrong. The cattle thieves and cutthroats of the river frontier were confident, even brazen, in their belief that they could steal and murder with impunity. And they would remain so until they knew that they were being hunted, tracked by men who were determined to kill them.

5
Robb's Commission

N o story of conquest can ever be told only in terms of wars, treaties, and territorial gains. The calculus of history demands more complex metrics, vectors, and common denominators. But history is not scientific. There are no formulas, no equations that explain the ascendance of one nation over another. In sum, history cannot be calculated or weighed with any more precision than the future can be predicted.

Following the American Civil War, however, one thing should have been predictable, if not inevitable: the appearance of the railroad on the lower Rio Grande frontier. The locomotive of American progress, its smokestack and cowcatcher symbols of greater days to come, had already begun to churn its way westward across the landscape of the Lone Star State. By 1872 ribbons of steel rails stretched through the Piney Woods of East Texas, and in the coming months, construction of lines to Dallas, Austin, and San Antonio were inching toward completion.

But across the state progress was slow, even slower on the lower Rio Grande. At the close of the war, U.S. Army crews had constructed a railway from Brazos Santiago to Boca Chica Bay and from there twenty-three miles across the shallows and salt flats to White's Ranch. The boggy terrain made building the railroad a most difficult task. So did the sweltering humidity and outbreaks of malaria. Even when completed, the line later proved unprofitable in private hands. Then the narrow-gauge railroad was washed away, destroyed by a hurricane that slammed into the South Texas coast in October 1867.[1]

Not until 1870 was the Rio Grande Railroad Company chartered to reopen the spur and finish linking the Gulf of Mexico to Brownsville and thus the Mexican border. It was only a matter of time now before the Rio Grande Valley would become truly connected by rail to the outside world. But investors remained cautious. The unremitting violence and lawlessness along the river frontier were discouraging enough. So was the continuing political instability in Mexico, even after the capture and execution of Emperor Maximilian in June 1867 and the restoration of President Benito Juárez and his Liberal nationalist government.[2]

Not unlike refugees from the fallen Confederacy, romantic and opportunistic investors from the North looked to Mexico for the wealth the country promised. As one railroad builder and entrepreneur from Philadelphia declared in 1872, "God, in his generosity, seems to have given a share of all his best gifts to Texas." But the Lone Star State, he added, was but "the vestibule of rich Mexico. . . . All that is needed now is a firm, bold American hand to open the door to countless treasures so long kept from the world at large, and as yet scarcely touched by civilization." Indeed, the sixteenth-century conquistador Hernán Cortés never stated it more bluntly or candidly.[3]

Perhaps the New York–born and Harvard-educated banker John Austin Stevens best expressed American ambitions south of the border following the Civil War:

> A railroad from Point Isabel to Brownsville, and from Matamoros, on the opposite bank, to Monterey, would turn the whole of the supply of this rich and fertile country into American hands. . . .
>
> The northeastern states of Mexico, encouraged by our sympathy, would put forth new efforts, and inspired by the noble example of the patriots of the Rio Grande districts, would throw off the yoke of the invaders and reassert their ancient liberties.
>
> With the rebellion vanquished, the Union re-established, never again to be assailed, and Mexico once more a free and vigorous Republic, what power or combination of powers would dare stop the western course of Empire?

So in the aftermath of the American Civil War, despite their seething resentment and antipathy for the Yankee nation of the North, most Texans—like their predecessors a generation earlier—agreed that the road to Mexico lay open, and the gateway to this road to riches was South Texas.[4]

McNelly Arrives

Five months after a U.S. grand jury impaneled in Brownsville issued fifty-seven bills of criminal indictment against border outlaws and rustlers and petitioned state and federal authorities to dispatch more troops to the border to suppress the lawlessness, they at last received an answer. On July 9, 1872, Governor Edmund J. Davis ordered state police captain Leander H. McNelly to lead a company of some thirty mounted men across the Nueces "for the purpose of arresting criminals and breaking up the cattle and horse stealing prevalent in that locality." Perhaps in anticipation of trouble with armed "citizens' committees" in the counties of South Texas, and knowing the reputation of his state police for inciting former Confederates and Democratic partisans, Davis instructed Captain McNelly to ensure that his company was "kept under control, orderly and active, and that persons engaged in legitimate business . . . [were] not molested." Moreover, the governor directed McNelly to offer aid and assistance to local civil officials in their efforts to apprehend "murderers and other criminals evading arrest."[5]

McNelly had handpicked his recruits, many young men he had known from the farming communities of Brenham, Burton, and the Brazos River bottomlands of Washington County, Texas. Some he had even served with in the Louisiana and Gulf campaigns of the late war. In Davis's words, McNelly selected them because they were men "upon whom he could rely in all respects." Described as "thoroughly equipped and armed," the recruits assembled in Austin on the grounds of the state capitol on the afternoon of July 10 to hear Governor Davis issue his charge and offer words of caution. A correspondent for the *Austin State Journal* recorded Davis's address, "Boys, I authorized Captain McNally [*sic*] to select thirty good, honorable, brave men as policemen for the purpose of sending them out upon the Rio Grande frontier to chastise and bring to justice the numerous horse thieves and outlaws that are depredating upon the good citizens of that portion of our State." Then the governor offered praise to them and their captain for their willingness to serve Texas.[6]

But most of the governor's address may not have been received as warmly by the audience. Davis announced to the police recruits that during their expedition to the Rio Grande they would no doubt encounter people who were of a different culture, race, and nationality, people who did not speak "our language." He cautioned that all Texans of Mexican heritage were not enemies but rather "fellow citizens and as such must be treated by you as friends." Then he issued clear and unmistakable words of warning: "I do not send you out to make war upon Mexico, but to preserve citizens in their rights and to bring to justice . . . the scoundrels of whatever nationality . . . who are now infesting that section." As for American Indians on the border, however, he offered little mercy. "Should you come across or encounter any of the Indians, you need not stop to ask whether they will surrender," he concluded, "but bring them down by the shortest means." Davis thus avoided the complexity that many of the border raiding parties included both Mexicans and Indians. Some even counted among their ranks men as white as Davis himself.

Finally, knowing the Texans' hatred for their Yankee and Mexican counterparts, Davis reminded McNelly and his enlistees that they should set aside any remaining grievances toward Union men, no matter their color. Acknowledging that many of them had fought on the Confederate side against him, Davis urged them now to leave behind any lingering bitterness. The War between the States was behind them, he counseled. Whatever loyalty they had held during that conflict made no difference now, he reminded them. That matter was closed.[7]

Texas adjutant general James Davidson, a temperamental and ambitious Scotsman, did not issue the formal order for McNelly's march to the Rio Grande until July 13, the directive commanding the unit to proceed to the border "for the purpose of arresting criminals, breaking up horse & cattle stealing & restoring & enforcing the laws in that section of the state." Davidson further ordered "all sheriffs & other civil officers, police-men & other persons . . . to assist Capt. McNelly & his detachment in the discharge of . . . [their] duties." On July 16 McNelly's force arrived in San Antonio. According to newspaper reports, they were "well armed and mounted," but they may not have been well behaved during their short stopover in the Alamo City. The *San Antonio Herald* announced that the morning after their first night's stay in town, the men of McNelly's police were still "sloshing around" the streets of San Antonio. Moreover, the edi-tor of the *Herald* wrote that one member of the detachment, John Beck, "didn't get enough soldiering in the war," so he had joined McNelly's company for the apparent sport and amusement of tracking down and killing suspected bad men. Before the expedition to the border would be completed, McNelly would dismiss one other member of the command, John Dorman, for "drunkenness and absence without leave."[8]

All things considered, despite such references to unruly recruits, Lean-der Harvey McNelly turned out to be an excellent choice to command this expedition. Born on March 12, 1844, in Brook County, Virginia, the son of Peter J. and Mary Downey McNelly, young Leander had moved to Texas with his family in the autumn of 1860. Some said that he had aspired to become not a farmer or a soldier but a Methodist minister. Or at least his mother had hoped he would become a preacher of the gospel. Then the war came.

Like so many farm boys of his generation, young McNelly had enlisted in military service. He joined the Fifth Texas Mounted Volunteers com-manded by Colonel Thomas Jefferson Green. For the next three years, he experienced the hardships of war, all the while learning the art of unconventional tactics, the value of deception, the importance of surprise, and the necessity of good mounts. Following the Battle of Valverde in New Mexico near the upper Rio Grande in February 1862, Private McNelly served as Green's personal aide. He had seen action at the Battle of Galveston on July 1, 1863, and was reported to be among the first—if not the first—of the Confederate raiders who had stormed aboard and captured the Union gunboat USS *Harriet Lane.*[9]

But it was during the Red River campaign in Louisiana the following year that McNelly truly distinguished himself as a guileful and bold commander of Confederate guerrillas. Commissioned a captain on December 19, 1863—at the age of twenty—he had returned to Texas only long enough to raise a company of mounted rifles, most of his young recruits coming from the fertile bottomlands of the lower Brazos. By all accounts he had played a significant role in Confederate efforts to turn back the advance of General Nathaniel Banks's twenty-five thousand Union troops in their march up the Red River. Although seriously wounded at the Battle of Mansfield on April 8, 1864, Captain McNelly had recovered to the point that he was able to rejoin his command. After General Green's death at Blair's Landing on April 12, McNelly had been reassigned to General John A. Wharton's regiment. Only weeks later, he had crossed the Atchafalaya and led his raiders through the marshes and cane breaks of the Lafourche country to spy on Union movements. Near Brashear City his mounted irregulars, numbering fewer than one hundred, had effectively interdicted enemy supply lines, disrupted communications by cutting telegraph lines, harassed and even captured Yankee pickets, and created diversions by baffling Union commanders with a series of bold attacks, flanking movements, and rapid retreats. On one occasion, while operating behind enemy lines that June, a few dozens of these "McNellys," as this unit of Confederate scouts came to be known, had even created confusion among Federal commanders by riding back and forth across a bridge to simulate the sounds of a larger force. All the while, their captain and other officers shouted commands to imaginary rebel units, creating the illusion of an entire regiment that appeared to be surrounding a Union camp. Remarkably, this simple feint resulted in the surrender of as many as eight hundred Union troops. So many of the bluecoats had been captured that young McNelly and his band of marauders could hardly provide for them, or even guard them, until reinforcements arrived on the scene.[10]

The *Galveston Weekly News* carried a report on July 5 that, in view of later events, struck a tone of irony. During one encounter in the woodlands southwest of Baton Rouge, the newspaper announced, the intrepid McNelly and his raiders had bedeviled the Second Texas Union Cavalry, commanded by none other than Colonel Edmund J. Davis of South Texas. According to Confederate chronicler Theophilus Noel, McNelly's guerrilla operations had brought him in direct contact with the so-called Texas traitors, Unionists from the southern borders of the Lone Star State. It was the same E. J. Davis who as "Radical" Republican governor of Texas seven years later enlisted the services of McNelly in his much-hated state police, formed to carry out the laws of the Reconstruction government of Texas. Oddly enough, Noel notes another development that, if true, likewise proved ironic. Hinting that the brave captain was soon reassigned because he was allegedly "not working to suit someone," Noel recalls that McNelly and his raiders were "ordered out to hunt Jayhawkers [i.e., suspected Union sympathizers] on the Calcasieu."[11]

No official record exists explaining the reason for McNelly's transfer to East Texas during the final months of the war. But one fact seems clear. Early in 1865 McNelly gained his first experience in law enforcement work. Among his duties, while headquartered in the town of Hempstead, he tracked down Confederate deserters and disgruntled Unionists who threatened to collaborate with Federal officials at the war's end.[12]

Through it all, McNelly had proved that he was the kind of commander who would not order men into a fight but would lead them into battle. This his commanding officers had recognized during the war. As one serving with him had observed, "He won the highest confidence of soldier and officer." Confederate Major General James Major had commended McNelly for "gallant and meritorious conduct," extolling his "daring courage and consummate skill" in the face of the enemy. The late General Thomas Green had referred to him as "one of the best soldiers and the most daring scout in the cavalry service." Brigadier General C. S. Andum had called him "sagacious and dashing," a remarkable young man of "superior qualifications," adding that "there is not an officer in my division who is his equal as a scout, and *not one* who does not ardently desire his promotion." No less than General E. Kirby Smith had acknowledged McNelly's "gallantry and good conduct in the field" while authorizing the nineteen-year-old private to receive a field commission as captain.[13]

In Virginia people may have spoken reverently of John Singleton Mosby, the celebrated "gray ghost" of the Confederacy. In Missouri the stories of William Quantrill and his much-feared raiders may have already gained iconic status. In Tennessee even the mention of Nathan Bedford

Forrest might have caused proud Southern men to swell with pride. But in the Lone Star State, especially in the valleys of the lower Brazos River, the legendary Louisiana swamp fox, Leander McNelly, was the name on the lips of so many Texans.

Now, in 1872, a frail but handsome, clean-cut man of twenty-eight, sporting a neatly trimmed mustache and goatee, McNelly looked and sounded like anything but a soldier. He was a man of few words, and his voice was thin and piping. But he let his actions speak for him. Little wonder, therefore, that during his five weeks in South Texas in the summer of 1872, he apparently issued to state adjutant general Davidson only two terse reports of his activities. Even then, he had to be repeatedly pressed by Davidson to file a final, formal report detailing his actions and providing a firsthand assessment of the situation on the border. If he did so—and no evidence suggests that he did—that report did not survive.[14]

One fragment of evidence does survive, however. According to prominent cattleman Levi English of Dimmit County, McNelly's detachment of police accompanied him in trailing a herd of his own cattle—allegedly numbering some one thousand head—to the Rio Grande, only to discover that they had already been driven by thieves into Mexico. Other than the fact that McNelly first traveled to Laredo and then patrolled upriver in search of rustlers, little is known about what has been termed McNelly's "Rio Grande expedition" of 1872. Only one fact seems clear: before leading his force safely back to Austin in mid-August, McNelly had tracked rustlers to the Rio Grande and, in compliance with his orders, he had stopped at the water's edge on the Texas side. Three years later, however, when McNelly would return to the lower Rio Grande at the head of a special force of Texas Rangers to suppress cattle rustling and lawlessness on the border, it would be a different story.[15]

Robb Tours the River Frontier

By the time Captain McNelly rode off to the Rio Grande on the orders of Governor Davis, President Ulysses S. Grant had also weighed in on the growing crisis in the Nueces Strip. On May 7, 1872, President Grant appointed a three-member commission to investigate conditions in South Texas and to recommend appropriate responses to the growing disorder. Headed by Colonel Thomas P. Robb of Savannah, Georgia, the commission also included Republican partisans Richard H. Savage of California and Fabius I. Mead of Mississippi.[16]

Grant's choice of Colonel Robb to lead the commission seemed, at best, politically motivated, at worst an example of the president's poor judgment of character. By most accounts a product of the Republican Party patronage system, seemingly distinguished by his lack of qualifications, Robb had earned his reputation for controversy and corruption while serving as collector of customs for the port of Savannah. The fifty-two-year-old native of Bath, Maine, spoke no Spanish, and he knew little if anything about Mexico or the lower Rio Grande country. His experiences were varied, including the operation of a wholesale grocery warehouse in Chicago, a stint as a merchant in Sacramento following the gold rush of 1849, and a term as mayor of Sacramento. Following his service in the Union army during the American Civil War, Robb had established the first Republican newspaper in Savannah, the *New Era*, which championed the so-called Radical Republican agenda. Like so many other "Radicals" he formally endorsed Ulysses S. Grant for president and even attended the 1868 Republican convention in Chicago pledged as a Grant delegate. For his support, spoilsmen of the Republican Party had awarded him with an appointment as federal postmaster for the city of Savannah before his promotion to the even more lucrative position of head of the port authority there. Apparently, in considering Robb, President Grant ignored the fact that his well-traveled supporter and partisan operative had recently faced a federal indictment on charges of embezzlement and conspiracy to defraud. Though a Chatham County jury never convicted him of the charges, Robb still shared the disgrace that one of his deputies had been found guilty of having been "short in his cash in the amount of $2,000." As for Robb himself, he was deemed negligent and responsible for presiding over "loose, disreputable, and demoralizing" practices that characterized the collection of customs duties. Despised by Southerners as a "carpetbagger," the spoilsman was described by one contemporary as a "two-faced political hypocrite" with vaulting ambitions.[17]

None of that dissuaded Grant, who on the recommendation of such party bosses as Wall Street banker Levi P. Morton and Senator John A. Logan of Illinois, named Robb to lead the presidential commission to the border. Robb first convened the commission in New Orleans on July 5, 1872, and several days later proceeded by steamer down the Gulf Coast to Point Isabel, across the inner coastal channel from South Padre Island. Not until July 30 did the Robb Commission commence public hearings in Brownsville. During the next two months, the commissioners traveled up the Rio Grande on the tug steamer *San Juan*, stopping at Texas border villages and outposts to accept testimony, interview officials, and gather evidence of the increased incidence of cattle rustling along the river. Their inquiry soon revealed a shocking picture of banditry and bloodshed on the border. Dozens of witnesses, including many Spanish speakers, told the commissioners of the heavily armed bands of cattle thieves who were raiding South Texas ranchos and settlements with greater frequency and "astonishing boldness." All too often, and too easily, they explained that rustlers crossed the river and evaded U.S. Army infantrymen stationed at outposts from Fort Brown to Fort Clark near Brackettville. At times the thieves even penetrated more than one hundred miles to the Nueces River before retiring with entire herds of cattle to their rendezvous points south of the Rio Grande.[18]

While touring the border, Robb, his fellow commissioners, and their interpreter soon discovered that Mexican bandits, often joined by Texas outlaws and former Confederates, intimidated law-abiding citizens on both sides of the Rio Grande. All too often the thieves threatened border residents to remain silent, to flee their homesteads or face certain death. Members of the commission also confirmed what Texans already knew: marauding bands of renegade Kickapoo and Lipan Apache had laid waste to the frontier above Rio Grande City, leaving the region scorched and denuded. During their forays, they not only rounded up livestock but also torched the South Texas prairies before retiring back across the border to their villages in the foothills of the Santa Rosa Mountains.[19]

The commissioners likewise learned of the frustrations of both U.S. military and civilian officials. Remote army outposts situated along the border were located too far apart and were undermanned, garrisoned with small detachments of infantry units, which were no match for the swift and elusive marauders. Moreover, even when military patrols, federal customs officers, or local livestock inspectors trailed rustlers to the Rio Grande, they could only watch in frustration from the Texas side as the thieves mocked them from the other bank. Even more irritating, according to the testimony received, apathetic and sometimes corrupt officials in Tamaulipas and Coahuila offered more contempt than cooperation or, worse yet, protected the raiders and allegedly even shared in their profits.[20]

To complicate matters further, witnesses complained to the commissioners that Mexican trade policies had only encouraged the depredations along the U.S.-Mexico border. Since 1858, the government in Mexico City had formally recognized a six-mile wide Zona Libre, or "Free Zone," a narrow strip of land paralleling the south bank of the Rio Grande where all commerce and trade remained exempt from Mexican federal import duties. Such a policy, the commissioners were reminded, had only promoted smuggling into Mexico, and in so doing had ensured the profitability of cattle theft and the protection of cattle rustlers and horse thieves along a three hundred–mile frontier from Matamoros to Piedras Negras.[21]

As Robb and his colleagues soon learned, the summer of 1872 proved to be a season of simmering anger and seemingly random violence on the lower Rio Grande. The testimony of one prominent stockman bore witness to that. Among the Texans who offered a deposition for President Grant's commission stood the short club-footed figure of Richard King, owner of the Santa Gertrudis ranch near the waters of the lower Nueces. On August 26, the flinty, rough-hewn Captain King testified that less than a month earlier, on the evening of July 31, while traveling across the Wild Horse Desert on the old Corpus Christi road "for the purpose of appearing before the commission" in Brownsville, wagon driver George Evans, fellow traveler Franz Specht, and he were approaching San Fernando Creek. Suddenly, with no warning, they were ambushed by a party of gun-wielding Mexican bandits, "eight or ten in number." Before King could pull a rifle from beneath his seat, the raiders fired several rounds, one mortally wounding the hapless Mr. Specht, who was merely traveling with the party to the border to conduct personal business. King all but admitted to the commissioners that he had been a target of assassination before, and that he typically traveled across the ranges of the Nueces Strip with a larger escort of mounted bodyguards. Not this time, however. King acknowledged that he had been shot at before, and admitted that he would always suspect that the bullet that killed Specht was meant for him. Not even a $600 reward posted by Governor Davis would ever produce information leading to the arrest of the killers responsible for Specht's death.[22]

Considering the nature of the continuing blood feud between King and the rancheros south of the Rio Grande, such a scenario seemed plausible. After all, with the fall of the Confederacy, Captain King, like hundreds of other prominent Texans, had fled into Mexico. For a few months, while living in exile in Monterrey, he had become familiar with his Mexican counterparts south of the border. He had observed their creative methods of growing their herds by rounding up "lost" livestock. So it was not surprising that Mexican authorities had long accused Ricardo King, as Mexican stockmen called him, of hiring thieves to round up cattle—whether unclaimed or branded—and drive them across the river into Texas. Some even charged that one of the largest hubs of horse and cattle theft on the border was King's own Santa Gertrudis, and that the old hacendado had hired a notorious renegade, Atilano Alvarado, to manage his rustling operation near Guerrero, south of the border. Allegedly, the chief purpose of this ring of rustlers was to mark calves not only with Captain King's widely recognized "Running W" but also with other brands that the captain had registered in Brownsville with the Cameron County hide and brand inspector (a perusal of these records in the Cameron County courthouse revealed that King had more than two dozen brands registered—far more than any other stockman running cattle in Cameron County).[23]

That General Juan Cortina, commander of the line of the Bravo in the state of Tamaulipas, held nothing but enmity for gringos like Captain King was well chronicled. It was even widely known, or at least rumored, that Cortina had publicly sworn to capture and hang the owner of the Santa Gertrudis, though such boasts were typical of the Red Robber. The much-feared "bandit chieftain" had always made it clear that he considered Captain King and other Texan cattlemen as well as Anglo merchants and bankers in Brownsville to be bigger thieves than even the most brazen of rustlers who regularly crossed entire herds of Texas cattle into Mexico.[24]

Cortina's determination to defend and even encourage Mexican cattle thieves seemed less personal than financial, more motivated by profit than patriotism. Robb and his colleagues gathered more than sufficient evidence to support the charge that Cortina was behind much of the mischief and mayhem on the border. Following the death of President Benito Juárez in July 1872, Cortina fell from the favor of the new president, Sebastián Lerdo de Tejada, who ordered his removal from military power and even his arrest. But the aging jefe still wielded enormous influence on the border, especially among those who stood to gain from stealing Texas cattle.[25]

Among the mountain of depositions received by the Robb Commission, one of the most intriguing testimonies was offered by a former Cortina "soldier," Apolinario Hernandez, who corroborated other testimony implicating the Red Robber as the principle chieftain of a vast and well-organized cattle-rustling operation. While Hernandez admitted that he never actually saw Cortina attending regular "bull-slinging feasts" at Rancho Canelo, upriver from Matamoros, he knew that the vaqueros in charge—namely Sabos Garcia and Segundo Garza—stood "high in Cortina's confidence." At one recent "rodeo" south of the river, where steers were butchered and heifers and calves were rebranded, he observed as many as two thousand head of Texas cattle carrying the marks of more than a hundred different ranchers, including ones he recognized as those of Captain King and Mifflin Kenedy. While Hernandez could only mark his signature with an *X* on the deposition, his account attested to the breadth and extent of cattle rustling along the border.[26]

Until September 6, 1872, Robb and his fellow commissioners had only heard allegations and reports of cattle rustling along the border. That morning, however, they learned firsthand of the location of one purported nest of thieves. While steaming up the river aboard the tug steamer *San Juan*, they slowly rounded a sweeping bend some fifteen miles below Rio Grande City. They then observed the theft of a herd of Texas cattle in progress. In stunned silence, they watched as a few naked vaqueros swam more than fifty head across the river to the slippery south bank where armed and mounted men drove the animals into the thick underbrush and corrals nearby. Also standing on board the river tug that morning was cattleman Mifflin Kenedy, longtime partner of rancher and steamboat operator Richard King. Kenedy informed Robb and the others that half a mile below the crossing was the Rancho Las Cuevas, operated by Juan Flores Salinas, who reportedly boasted of his own private army of mounted riflemen as well as the support of Cortina's *rurales*.[27]

After inspecting the Rio Grande border as far north as Ringgold Barracks near Rio Grande City, the Robb Commission returned to New Orleans, then to Washington, D.C., by train. On October 11 Robb and Savage met privately with President Grant in the White House for what the *New York Times* reported to be a "long interview." No doubt they briefed the president on the gravity of the situation and offered a summary of their preliminary findings and recommendations. In short, they concluded, nothing short of an increased American military presence would deter cattle rustling on the border.[28]

Robb's Inquest Continues

Meanwhile, reports of disorder and violence on the lower Rio Grande continued to stream in. On October 5, 1872, just one week before Robb and Savage's meeting with President Grant, the *New York Times* published an account from San Antonio of a company of Texans, heavily armed vigilantes numbering about twenty, who followed a band of Mexican cattle thieves into Mexico, a few miles upriver from Eagle Pass. According to an unnamed source, Lieutenant John Davidson and soldiers from Fort Clark near the town of Brackettville were ordered to do nothing more than patrol the border and observe the movements of Texan regulators as they crossed the Rio Grande and attacked an enclave of suspected rustlers near the village of La Resurreccion, sometimes called Villa Nueva. The article reported further that the Texans had killed several Mexican marauders while losing two of their own during the clash. More shocking, the newspaper alleged that the Texan militia had burned the home of a local alcalde "with him in it."[29]

What this newspaper account failed to mention was an even more disturbing allegation. The Texan raiders, purportedly led by a man labeled by one Mexican source as a "notorious assassin" named McWeber, disguised themselves by painting their faces black to appear to be "Seminole Negroes" and their Kickapoo neighbors living south of the Rio Grande. Worse yet, the Texans—rumored to include several prominent stockmen from Uvalde County—crossed the border on the night of September 27 for the sole purpose of murdering the alcalde of La Resurreccion, identified only as a Señor Aguilera. Still more unsettling was the news that a woman and child were among the victims of this raid.[30]

Newspapers across the Lone Star State swiftly condemned such wanton violence perpetrated against innocents, but nevertheless strongly urged the citizens of South Texas to continue organizing their own local posse to patrol the border from Brownsville to Eagle Pass. On October 27, the *Galveston News* joined in the growing chorus of righteous indignation. Urging ranchers of the lower Rio Grande to band together and form vigilance committees for mounting expeditions against suspected thieves and rustlers, the editorial announced: "If our stockmen catch . . . [Juan Cortina] or any of his sort on this side of the Rio Grande, they should swing them from the nearest tree."[31]

Such reports of Texans threatening to take the law into their own hands must have been fresh in the minds of Robb and the other commissioners when, on December 10, 1872, they submitted a formal preliminary report to the Congress. The document could only be described as a catalog of crimes and cruelty. The commissioners included more than 350 depositions that had been accepted as evidence of the violence and depredations that had plagued the Rio Grande frontier since 1848. Each of the pages dripped with bloody accounts detailing murder, theft, bribery, corruption, and the destruction of private property. Always, the report concluded, these crimes were committed by raiders from northern Mexico against residents of Texas. Among the impressive parade of witnesses who corroborated this record of barbarism stood law enforcement officers of the South Texas border counties, hide and brand inspectors, stock raisers, diplomatic representatives, such as U.S. consul Thomas Wilson at Matamoros, and military officials, including Colonel Ranald Slidell Mackenzie of the Fourth U.S. Cavalry, recently assigned to Fort Clark, and Colonel A. M. McCook of the Tenth U.S. Infantry, commanding at Fort Brown. Of course, cattlemen the likes of Captain Richard King and John McAllen appeared before the panel. Robb even solicited testimony from arguably one of the most respected Texans of them all, Old Rip Ford.[32]

By all indications, the work of the Robb Commission was cut short after the $6,000 appropriated by Congress the previous spring had been expended. After their discussions with President Grant, therefore, Robb and Savage waited in Washington, D.C., for additional funds, while Mead resigned his post and returned to Mississippi. Before the end of the year Congress passed a supplemental appropriations bill. Then on January 11, 1873, Robb received orders from the president to return to Texas. The work of the commission was not yet finished.[33]

Accompanied by new commission appointee Thomas O. Osborn of Illinois, Robb and Savage returned to New Orleans, where in late January they were joined by federal judge John H. Howe, selected to serve as secretary to the commission. Delays, frustrations, and even tragedy stalked them in the weeks ahead. For several days, severe winter storms prevented them from departing for the Rio Grande. What Robb termed "irregular communications" also hampered their efforts to notify Texas and U.S. officials of scheduled public sessions in Brownsville, Corpus Christi, and Laredo. Worse still, once they arrived in Texas heavy rains turned their overland route into a quagmire, at times slowing travel to less than ten miles a day. Then on April 3, 1873, Judge Howe, whom Robb called an "efficient and worthy secretary," died of consumption in Laredo before the commissioners left for San Antonio.[34]

Rip Ford, who accompanied Robb's party on their second tour across South Texas, recollected one odd incident on the trail. After the commissioners departed the Rio Grande, reports of rattlesnakes and stinging reptiles in the weeds prompted a nervous Mr. Osborne to carry a Spencer carbine each day. On at least one occasion, Osborn—who Ford recalled even feared being bitten by "noxious insects"—jumped from the wagon and, while walking ahead of his escort, began swatting at horseflies and bull gnats. Then, without warning, he opened fire, waiving his rifle wildly and aiming into the tall grass, moments later explaining that he thought he had seen a snake slithering away into the brush.[35]

When the commissioners stopped in several hamlets along the route to San Antonio, eyewitnesses to depredations too often failed to come forward, for whatever reason. Further complicating their efforts, conflicting accounts offered by the witnesses who did testify often confused rather than clarified issues. Still more frustrating, the commissioners were not even authorized to subpoena or cross-examine witnesses, and much of the testimony received was simply submitted in written depositions instead of firsthand testimony under cross-examination. Ford later admitted that most of these accounts became convoluted when the claims of cattlemen were founded largely on the projection that their livestock lost—presumably to rustlers—would have increased their herds in numbers by at least one-third per year. In other words, as even Ford later confessed, the estimates of losses by South Texas stockmen might have been greatly inflated. If true, then at least some of the evidence presented by ranchers claimed the loss of more cattle than the cowmen had ever even owned to begin with.[36]

Despite such obstacles, setbacks, and controversy, the Robb Commission completed public hearings in San Antonio by mid-May, one year and one thousand depositions after its appointment by President Grant. In a voluminous report issued the following year, the commission described conditions on the Rio Grande border as growing increasingly more desperate and chaotic. Robb and his fellow commissioners cataloged a staggering $48 million in claims by those who allegedly suffered at the hands of Mexican bandits and marauding Indians who enjoyed refuge south of the Rio Grande. They stopped short of recommending punitive and preemptive military strikes across the border into Mexico, but did urge the U.S. Department of War to fortify further and patrol more closely the Rio Grande below Eagle Pass. They even proposed that the state of Texas assume more responsibility by raising an entire regiment of Rangers, provided that these volunteers were commanded by officers of the U.S. Army. Apparently, they hoped that such professional leadership and military discipline would restrain angry and vengeful Texans from committing atrocities against Mexicans living on both sides of the river.[37]

In the end, commission members agreed that, alone, the U.S. government remained powerless to suppress lawlessness on the border. Only with the increased cooperation of leaders in Mexico City could that be accomplished, they maintained. But as long as the Zona Libre existed south of the river, particularly along the stretch bordering the states of Tamaulipas and Coahuila, they predicted that peace would remain as elusive as the scattered bands of rustlers who ranged freely over the land. Almost as significant, they insisted, not until Mexican officials removed the much-vilified General Cortina from the Rio Grande frontier would order be restored to the entire region.[38]

In summary, Robb and his colleagues reported that "it is for the government of the United States to . . . [offer] those who live under the shadow of its flag on the distant Rio Grande that protection which they deserve." For too many years, the commissioners concluded, the South Texas border country had been "depleted by the arrow of the Indian and the knife and pistol of the Mexican assassin." At last, they strongly recommended, the time had come for action, not words.[39]

Controversy unsurprisingly followed Robb's commission to San Antonio that spring. Gauging by the reaction of citizens of the Alamo City, journalist and freelance writer Edward King, on assignment from *Scribner's Monthly* to write a series of articles on post-Reconstruction Texas, observed that "opinion seems somewhat divided as to the extent and nature of the damage done the cattle-raising interest by the Mexicans, some Texans even asserting that Texan claims are grossly exaggerated." After visiting with San Antonio residents during the Robb Commission's brief stay there, Mr. King even reported that most believed that there was "much stealing on both sides of the Rio Grande." While he concluded, based on interviews with stock raisers and others, that the herds of cattle grazing in South Texas had been depleted by two-thirds or even three-fourths since 1866, he insisted that Mexican bandits may not have been the principal cause. Marauding Comanche from the High Plains of Texas as well as Lipan Apache and Kickapoo living south of the border were responsible for carrying off "immense herds," he claimed, and they did so with the approval and even encouragement of corrupt Mexican authorities in the border states of Tamaulipas, Coahuila, and Nuevo León."[40]

Then King turned his pen on the U.S. Department of War and the Grant administration. After interviewing local officials in San Antonio, he echoed their belief that the U.S. military presence on the border was woefully inadequate. To begin with, Federal posts along the lower Rio Grande were too few and positioned too far apart. The horse troopers and their grain-fed mounts were "but poor matches" for the Indian raiders and their war ponies that were raised to graze off the land. Moreover, without telegraphic communications between forts, and with headquarters in San Antonio and Washington, D.C., commanders on the Rio Grande were usually completely unaware of the movements and depredations of Indian raiders, Mexican bandits, and Texan regulators bent upon taking matters into their own hands. In other words, there seemed greater coordination and cooperation between the marauding bands than the troopers of the U.S. cavalry and infantry.[41]

As some Texans liked to muse, the swift and elusive Indian raiders were more likely to laugh themselves to death than to be killed or captured by the mule-mounted infantry stationed at federal posts along the line of the Bravo. A more mobile cavalry force, and more of them, were desperately needed, Texans demanded.

The Mexican Response

As the Robb Commission worked to complete its inquest, what might be aptly termed a propaganda war erupted between the United States and Mexico. In anticipation of the Robb Commission's findings, officials in Mexico City had already acted to preempt the argument that only Mexicans were responsible for the widespread lawlessness and plunder that had long plagued the border. Knowing that the commissioners appointed by President Grant would surely blame Mexican federal officials as well as local authorities in Tamaulipas, Coahuila, and Nuevo León for allowing marauding bands of cattle rustlers and horse thieves to operate north of the border, President Lerdo de Tejada had appointed his own investigative commission on September 30, 1872. Headed by Ignacio Galindo, the commission had also included Antonio Garcia Carrillo and Augustin Siliceo. The three had first gathered in Monterrey, where they adjourned on November 14, before traveling to Matamoros to begin a formal inquiry into the nature and causes of border violence and lawlessness.[42]

Known officially as La Comision Pesquisadora de la Frontera del Norte, or the Commission of Investigation of the Northern Frontier, Galindo and his fellow commissioners traveled more than 450 miles along the south banks of the Rio Bravo, visiting towns and ranchos from Matamoros and Mier to Reynosa and La Resurreccion. In the process of interviewing more than three hundred witnesses and compiling evidence of countless crimes committed by Anglo and Mexican alike, the commissioners produced copious documentation that the quagmire of Texan claims against citizens of Mexico was greatly exaggerated and, in some instances, the accusations were false and without merit. While traveling upriver, the Mexican commissioners, who had also invited American citizens to testify before their tribunal, only heard about their counterpart, the Robb Commission. They had no opportunity, therefore, to read the Robb report before issuing their own findings, though they doubtless heard rumors of the American claims. The conclusions of Galindo and his commission were thus not a response to the charges from the American side of the border but an independent assessment of the perils plaguing a five-hundred-mile-long frontier for nearly two decades. Still, the final report of La Comision Pesquisadora, which included more than 17,600 pages in manuscript form, documented—from the Mexican view—a litany of criminal acts and atrocities along both sides of the border dating back to 1848. Literally hundreds of instances of theft, robbery, murder, and plunder filled the volume with countless claims, most of them implicating Anglo-Americans, and particularly Texans, in creating instability and lawlessness along the lower Rio Grande.

One year after undertaking their investigation, on May 15, 1873, members of La Comision Pesquisadora submitted their findings to President Tejada. Most of the report dealt with Indian depredations along the border, which had commanded so much of the commissioners' attention. Predictably, Galindo and his colleagues offered a stinging indictment of U.S. Indian policies. For decades, they argued, policymakers in Washington had waged a campaign to drive American Indians westward. This ongoing racial war had forced American Indians to flee into Mexico to escape the sword of the U.S. Army, they reasoned. Any depredations into Texas, therefore, resulted from the misguided efforts of officials in Washington to solve the "Indian problem." In the end, although American policymakers in Washington had failed the Indians on moral grounds, they had succeeded in one respect—creating a border problem for both Mexico and the United States.[43]

In general terms, the Mexican commissioners blamed U.S. officials for negligence and for malevolent policies, specifically the forced removal, subjugation, and concentration of Indians onto reservations. As for the spread of cattle rustling and the wave of banditry on the border, La Comision Pesquisadora reached conclusions strikingly different from those offered by Robb and his companions. In focusing not upon thieves operating from bases south of the border but upon Texans who had allegedly carried out acts of aggression against the nation and the people of Mexico for the past two decades, they turned their criticism toward the Lone Star

State. "The old and modern history of Texas, filled with calumnies, out-rages, invasions and ambition against Mexico, is a lesson which should . . . [require] all the energy of the Mexican government, in order to afford its long-suffering inhabitants a respite from their continual struggle against open and secret enemies [no doubt a reference to filibustering and diplo-matic intrigues]." Blaming a "restless spirit of the floating population of Texas which is ever dreaming of revolution [and] enterprises inconsistent with the maintenance of peace and harmony between the two nations," the Mexican commissioners charged that a "spirit of invasion" had been fostered north of the Rio Grande, and that an impulse toward aggression still prevailed on the "gringo's" side of the border. They concluded, too, that the "society in Texas" was "utterly demoralized and corrupt" and that its worst elements had "spread its pernicious influence to the regions of the Bravo and the Nueces." They also stressed that Texan "cow hunters" had long honored the established practice of claiming unbranded calves as soon as they were weaned, no matter that the calves followed cows carry-ing clear markings and brands. In so doing, the Mexican commissioners argued, Texan cattlemen stole from their neighbors, and they did not let any border or boundary stop them.[44]

The members of La Comision Pesquisadora insisted that, as long as South Texas remained a breeding ground for armed criminals and ambi-tious adventurers, the northern frontier of Mexico would be left exposed to predations and violence. While agreeing that the border counties of Texas along the north banks of the Rio Grande were prey to excessive vio-lence, they provided evidence that they were no more so than the remain-der of the Lone Star State, where few people of Mexican heritage resided. In other words, the tribunal emphasized the lawless nature of Texas, and it dismissed the allegations that Mexican citizens were primarily responsible for acts of robbery and plunder near the north banks of the Rio Bravo. They even offered published statistical evidence to support their argument. And they did not stop with numerical tables. They identified—sometimes by name—hide and brand inspectors, lawmen, and judges in Texas border counties, charging them with graft and corruption. As for Texans accused of alleged acts of theft and plunder, the list read like a who's who of the Nueces Strip. And at the top of that list was a familiar name—Captain Richard "Ricardo" King. The report claimed that the New York–born ranchero, who had grown up the son of poor Irish immigrants, now laid claim to being the king of the cattle trade in more than name only. But they also alleged that he had built his vast ranching empire in Texas with *ñañinta*'s ("grandmother's") cattle. No matter the property laws of the Lone Star State, the people of Mexico refused to look upon him or his sort as legitimate. And they never would.[45]

So Mexican rancheros, and even Texas stockmen of Mexican heritage, believed that they were well within their rights to retrieve King's cattle and return them to their native land, or to the highest bidder for beef and hides. They insisted that it was only justice, and it was good business. After all, little stood in their way but a crooked river, and its waters were not much of an obstacle.

As for Anglo-Texans—whether cattlemen, farmers, politicians, or soldiers—they saw the matter much differently. Convinced of their own cultural superiority, and their Manifest Destiny to spread American institutions and ideals across the continent, they held the land by right of conquest and, they dared to suggest, by providence. Even so, an increasing number of them agreed with their Mexican counterparts on at least one thing: they looked upon the Rio Grande not as an international border but as just one more river to cross.

Colonel Edmund J. Davis.
Courtesy of Texas State Library
and Archives Commission.

Colonel John S. "Rip" Ford.
Courtesy of Lawrence T.
Jones III Collection, DeGolyer
Library, Southern Methodist
University.

General Lew Wallace.
Courtesy of Prints and
Photographs Division,
Library of Congress,
Washington, D.C.

"Cattle Raid on the Texas Border." Courtesy of Prints and Photographs Division, Library of Congress, Washington, D.C.

143

General Juan N. Cortina.
Courtesy of Texas State
Library and Archives
Commission.

Captain Richard
King. Courtesy of
Texas State Library
and Archives
Commission.

Colonel Ranald S. Mackenzie. Courtesy of Western History Collections, University of Oklahoma Libraries.

The Return March, by Frederic Remington. Author's collection.

General Edward O. C. Ord.
Courtesy of Prints and Photographs Division, Library of Congress, Washington, D.C.

Captain Leander McNelly.
Courtesy of Western History Collections, University of Oklahoma Libraries.

John S. "Old Rip" Ford.
Courtesy of Texan Institute
of Cultures, University of
Texas at San Antonio Libraries
Special Collections.

George Durham. Courtesy of
Western History Collections,
University of Oklahoma
Libraries.

Leander H. McNelly.
Courtesy of Albert and
Ethel Herzstein Library,
San Jacinto Museum of
History, La Porte, Texas.

McNelly's Rangers in camp. Courtesy of Walter Prescott Webb Papers, The
Dolph Briscoe Center of American History, University of Texas at Austin.

John B. Armstrong.
Courtesy of Western
History Collections,
University of Oklahoma
Libraries

John King Fisher. Cour-
tesy of Western History
Collections, University of
Oklahoma Libraries.

6
Mackenzie's Raiders

Even before the Robb Commission had completed its investigations
in the spring of 1873, U.S. War Department officials had reached
their own conclusions about conditions on the border. Early that year
President Grant had announced redeployment of the Fourth U.S. Cavalry from the upper Brazos to Fort Clark, stationed near the lower Rio
Grande. Their mission was to suppress Indian marauders and border bandits who continued to stage attacks from the Mexican side of the river. On
February 5, 1873, General William Tecumseh Sherman had written to
General Christopher C. Auger, commander of the Department of Texas,
headquartered in San Antonio, affirming that the president "wished to
give great attention to affairs on the Rio Grande frontier, especially to prevent the raids of Indians and Mexicans upon the people and property of
Southern and Western Texas." Sherman had further informed Auger that
President Grant insisted that the daring cavalry commander he had once
anointed the "most promising young officer" in the entire U.S. Army be
chosen for the task. That officer was Colonel Ranald Slidell Mackenzie.
"In naming the 4th for the Rio Grande," Sherman had explained, "the
President is doubtless influenced by the fact that Col. Mackenzie is young
and enterprising, and that he will impart to his Regiment his own active
character." In other words, Mackenzie would be bold, even aggressive, in
carrying out the mission. And that is precisely what both President Grant
and General Sherman intended.[1]

To that end, from his headquarters at Fort Concho, near the muddy
waters of the Rio Concho, a quiet, though confident, Colonel Ranald
Mackenzie issued marching orders to five companies of his regiment, three
under his immediate command at Fort Concho, two others still posted
at Fort Richardson near the Northwest Texas town of Jacksboro. On the
morning of March 4 a column of more than three hundred army bluecoats
thus mounted up and rode southward toward Mexico, their handsome,
dignified thirty-two-year-old commander in the lead. Four long weeks
on the trail led Mackenzie's expedition across more than three hundred
miles of Comanche country, through some of the most unforgiving and
inhospitable land in all the Lone Star State. From Fort Concho to Fort

McKavett on the upper San Saba, then through the rugged wilds of the Edwards Plateau to the Nueces they rode. Weary, dust-covered and saddle sore, Mackenzie's troopers at last arrived at the border post of Fort Clark near the town of Brackettville on April 1. All Mackenzie knew at the time was that he was to relieve the post commander, Lieutenant Colonel Wesley Merritt of the Ninth U.S. Cavalry, an all-black unit of "buffalo soldiers," as the horse Indians of the Southern Great Plains termed African American troopers.[2]

Already word had preceded Mackenzie that he would soon be assigned a dangerous mission of the greatest importance, and that he would have the backing of none other than the highest authority of the U.S. government. General Sherman had recently confirmed that the Grant administration held Mexico strictly accountable for Indian raids into Texas, depredations conducted by marauders enjoying safe harbor on the south bank of the Rio Bravo. If the government in Mexico City would not act swiftly to halt these raids, Sherman had vowed, the U.S. Army would. President Grant had tired of the insolence of border bandits and Indian renegades, and so had Sherman. Now both men fully expected U.S. regulars to punish the marauders who had been raiding across the border with impunity.[3]

Meanwhile, in the solitude of his quarters at Fort Clark, a brooding Colonel Mackenzie had anguished over reports that the border raids were not only continuing but increasing in intensity. Throughout early April army patrols scouting along the Texas side of the river had revealed an escalation in banditry, he had learned. And the source of many raids, as reported by spies operating south of the river, was not Cortina's bandits but renegade Kickapoos and aligned Lipan Apaches holed up in villages as deep as sixty miles across the border, in the foothills of the Santa Rosa Mountains.[4]

Indeed, just six weeks earlier, while Thomas Robb and his commissioners were wrapping up business, discussing only their pending recommendations to President Grant and the U.S. Congress, officials of the Department of War and the U.S. Army had ceased talking about continuing border depredations. They were preparing to act. Just days after his arrival at Fort Clark Colonel Mackenzie rode northward to San Antonio to meet with U.S. secretary of war William Belknap and General Philip Sheridan, famed commander of the far-reaching Department of the Missouri. On the afternoon of April 11, 1873, Secretary Belknap and General Sheridan, accompanied by Colonel Mackenzie and a small cavalry escort, arrived at

Fort Clark. Still exhausted from their overland trip from St. Louis, then from their bumpy wagon ride from San Antonio, Belknap and Sheridan had been dispatched to the Rio Grande by no less than President Grant.[5]

Both Secretary Belknap and General Sheridan enjoyed little time to rest. On the evening of their arrival Colonel Mackenzie and Lieutenant Colonel Merritt hosted a formal military ball in honor of the dignitaries. The clapboard post headquarters was festooned with decorations, the regimental band provided patriotic music, and ladies dressed in all their finery joined their husbands in greeting their distinguished guests. Afterward, Sheridan and Belknap retired for the night into the wooden structures that served as officers' quarters. If not for the presence of two visitors of such celebrity, and the fact that Colonel Mackenzie had arrived with five companies of the Fourth Cavalry only ten days earlier, all might have seemed routine. But the quiet of that balmy spring night belied the fact that something truly big, something out of the ordinary appeared to be imminent.[6]

Events the following day only confirmed that fact. Understandably, rumors quickly spread throughout the post that the unannounced appearance of Secretary of War Belknap and General Sheridan meant that a major military operation was most likely in the planning. All signs pointed to a campaign against the marauding Kickapoo and Lipan, who for years had conducted their raids as far as 150 miles and more into the interior of Texas. Despite such speculation, no one except Secretary Belknap and General Sheridan knew for sure. And they were not talking, at least not yet.

Mackenzie must have been somewhat uneasy about meeting with Sheridan, a man known widely for his unpredictable nature and his legendary temper. Sheridan's dislike for the Texas frontier had already preceded him to the Rio Grande border. One report persisted that, while in Galveston several years earlier, Sheridan was told by an eastern gentleman, "If only there was plenty of water and good society" in Texas, it would be "equal to any part of the Union." A surly Sheridan reportedly growled in response, "Those are the only two things they lack in hell, water and good society."[7]

Accordingly, upon his arrival at the dusty outpost of Fort Clark and the neighboring town of Brackettville, the general found little water and even less evidence of good society. Early on the morning of April 12 an impatient General Sheridan, with the secretary of war at his side, held a formal review of the troops of both the Fourth and the Ninth. Little else happened that day, certainly nothing to indicate that preparations would soon be made for arguably the most daring military operation along the border since the war with Mexico a quarter century earlier. On the night of April 12 both Secretary Belknap and General Sheridan held another private meeting with Colonel Mackenzie, a war counsel that turned out to be as mysterious as it was stunning in its implications. As Mackenzie later related the substance of the discussion, Sheridan began by instructing him, "I want you to control and hold down the situation [on the border], and to do it in your own way." Sheridan explained that he wanted Mackenzie to "be bold" in pursuing and punishing Indian raiders, and he made it clear that the president, the secretary of war, and he all agreed that the Rio Grande should not be considered a political obstacle or geographic barrier in chasing and chastising the marauders. Mackenzie needed to attack them in their lairs south of the Rio Grande. Sheridan further ordered that only an aggressive "campaign of annihilation, obliteration, and complete destruction" would eliminate the Indian threat along the border, and thus bring some relief to the South Texas rangelands. Then the irascible general concluded bluntly, "I think you know what I want done."[8]

Although not present at the meeting, Lieutenant Robert G. Carter, temporary quartermaster of the command, learned of the conversations later that night when Mackenzie summoned him to his quarters. Pacing back and forth as he explained Sheridan's instructions, the normally calm Mackenzie appeared nervous and even agitated, and rightfully so. He told Carter that when he had asked under whose authority he was to cross the border to attack Indian "hostiles," a visibly angry General Sheridan had bristled. "Damn the authority," the general exclaimed, slamming his fist on a table. "You are to go ahead on your own plan of action and your authority and your backing will be . . . [President] Grant and myself." Then when a startled Mackenzie had raised the question of when he should expect official orders, Sheridan had brusquely refused to promise such instructions in writing. If Mackenzie moved quickly to "clean up the situation," Sheridan had promised, he could "rest assured of the fullest support." He need not wait for orders in writing.[9]

Carter remembered that the typically stoic Mackenzie seemed "intense in speech and action" as their conversation continued until dawn. During their talk—with the red-eyed Mackenzie doing most of the talking—the colonel spoke in anger of the massacre at Howard's Well the previous year, of the slaughter of men, women, and children there along the San Antonio–El Paso Road, and of the death of Lieutenant Frederick Vincent. He also talked of the report that Colonel Merritt had received only two nights earlier that a raiding party, made up of Kickapoo and their Lipan Apache allies, had struck the Dolores Ranch only eight miles downstream from Fort Clark. The marauders had purportedly made off with thirty-six stolen horses, and they were believed to be heading northward across the Devil's River and then into Mexico.[10]

A grim-faced Mackenzie admitted that a punitive expedition across the Rio Grande, though necessary, would carry great risks. Then he wondered aloud whether he and his subordinates might be court-martialed if they failed, especially since no written orders would be issued. Mackenzie explained that he would appear to be acting on his own. He was prepared to accept the responsibility, he continued. That is what leaders are supposed to do. But he obviously was agonizing about his men being exposed to grave danger. Granted, troopers were trained to accept that death in battle was always a possibility. Many if not most of the men of the Fourth Cavalry had seen their share of it on the killing fields of the American Civil War. But if any of them were captured during an action across the river, torture at the hands of the "savages," or a final moment of terror in front of a Mexican firing squad could await them. Such a daring raid into Mexico would require much preparation and coordination. And the staging would take time, more time than might be allowed.

At that point, Carter interrupted his commander and reassured him that their men were well trained for such a mission, and he acknowledged that they would need only a few weeks to ensure that their mounts, some of the best animals in the army, were rested and well fed. He also concurred that the colonel would need reliable information on the location of Indian villages across the river, specific intelligence regarding the relative strength of the enemy and their numbers in arms. Trusted guides who knew the country on both sides of the river and a scouting party of able "Seminole Negroes" would be essential to ensure a successful raid into Mexico. Mackenzie agreed.[11]

That Mackenzie paced nervously until sunrise surprised Carter, who greatly admired his intrepid commander. After all, during the American Civil War and the Indian campaigns that followed Mackenzie had earned his reputation as a fearless warrior. A natural leader who carried what one enlisted man described as a "dignified presence," Mackenzie was all soldier. "Gallant and distinguished," one trooper remembered his handsome, dark-haired commander. A proper gentleman who lacked neither confidence nor courage, Mackenzie had every reason to exude pride in his accomplishments as an officer of the U.S. Army. A West Point graduate in the class of 1862, he had always demanded much of his men, and even more from himself.

He carried the wounds of the late war as proof of his bravery. At the Battle of Second Manassas in 1862 he had suffered from a gunshot to the torso. Two years later, during the bloody siege of Petersburg, he sustained another wound, this one blowing away most of the index and middle fingers of his right hand, leaving only stubs in their place. Owing to the latter injury, the Comanche and Kiowa of the Southern Plains later named him "Bad Hand."[12]

Now on that April night at Fort Clark a troubled Colonel Mackenzie provided his subordinate only a vague outline of his mission to cross into Mexico. No doubt, years later Captain Carter remembered only some of the context and details of their conversation. What seems certain, however, is Mackenzie's determination to keep his plans secret. Before the sun rose over the desolate plains of South Texas, Mackenzie insisted that Carter not tell anyone of their discussion. No one, neither Colonel Merritt nor Mackenzie's own staff—not even Carter's wife—was to be informed. Not a word was to be said. Carter acknowledged the order. Still, he later remembered, "I left his quarters at daybreak, a very much burdened soldier."[13]

Carter could not help but notice that on a stained and brittle map unfolded on the table between them, the deserts south of the Rio Grande and east of the Santa Rosa Mountains were identified only as *terreno desconocido*, or "unknown territory."

Little wonder that Colonel Mackenzie seemed more nervous than usual.

Mackenzie Crosses the Border

Upon his arrival at Fort Clark two weeks earlier, Mackenzie had found the post to be primitive, almost inadequate, even by army standards. Lieutenant Carter described the fort as "dilapidated," barely fit for the troops assigned there. Situated on a windswept forty-foot bluff overlooking Las Moras Creek (named for the nearby grove of mulberry trees), the rustic post commanded an undulating plain that lay stark and denuded for much of the year. "There is scarcely any top soil, but feeble patches of grass rest the eye, and a few stunted trees bear testimony to the utter barrenness of the plateau," wrote Lieutenant Eugene B. Beaumont of the Fourth Cavalry. The cantonment, which was dignified by the name of a fort, consisted of a scattering of log barracks and adobe structures built twenty-one years earlier to accommodate only a small contingent of the First U.S. Infantry. The dingy outpost had been abandoned by Federal troops at the outset of the Civil War, and the general condition of neglect was apparent everywhere on the grounds. Below the heavily eroded limestone ridge and beneath the weathered clapboard buildings, more than a hundred faded and tattered campaign tents stretched toward the creek. In most cases the incessant winds had ripped the canvas covers from their poles, tearing the fabric to ribbons. Still, the tents provided the only temporary quarters some of Mackenzie's pony soldiers would have. Just beyond the stream, the bustling town of Brackettville sprawled out, its barrooms and brothels inviting the young troopers to seek any form of entertainment known to "civilization." Such woeful conditions and open temptations seemed to belie the importance of their mission, Mackenzie must have feared.[14]

Mackenzie had earned his reputation as a stern disciplinarian, a man hardened by battle and tempered by command experience. He cared little if his men saw him as overbearing, harsh, and even callous. He would demand much of them, but even more of himself. For five weeks, the colonel pressed on with preparations for the dangerous task that lay ahead. Scattering the companies of his command into four separate camps, both to provide adequate forage for the horses and to avoid the appearance of a large force staging for an offensive, Mackenzie ordered that his mounted soldiers perform wheeling movements and rehearse skirmish tactics each day. He insisted that his troops hold carbine practice regularly and that frequent inspections be conducted to ensure that shoulder weapons and side arms were cleaned regularly and kept in good working order. Every morning farriers shod horses and repaired saddles and tack. Troopers ground their swords and sharpened their knives. All the while, no officer spoke of an expedition across the border, and Mackenzie said nothing about their mission to anyone except Adjutant Carter, not even to the other officers of his own staff. But rumors and speculation circulated in the camps that an attack upon an enclave of Indian raiders was imminent, and that those marauders enjoyed the sanctuary of Mexican soil. Some troopers even whispered the word "invasion," while others spoke in hushed tones about the possibility of another war with Mexico.[15]

Soon at least some of the rumors would be dispelled while others would be confirmed. New to the border and lacking familiarity with both the Spanish language and the geography of the region, Mackenzie, a New York native, fully understood the importance of gathering reliable intelligence. Before he could launch an assault against the Kickapoo and Lipan renegades responsible for recent raids into Texas, he must first have information—accurate information—about the exact location and strength of the enemy. He must know of the best river fords and what trails offered the best route to the Indian villages beyond and the safest return to the Rio Grande. Just as important, he must know how many Indian warriors to expect, and what resistance he might encounter. The success of the operation would depend on the element of surprise. For that purpose, he turned to the grizzled post guide, Isaac "Ike" Cox, a forty-year-old frontiersman who had ridden dispatch for the army for seven years before becoming a scout. Cox claimed to know more about the Mexican side of the river than any man on the lower Rio Grande. To accompany him, he recommended Green Van and Art McLain, both local "half-breed" rancheros who—like Cox—had recently lost hundreds of livestock to the Indian marauders. "Both [were] first class men," Carter noted, "who knew the country even better than Cox." Both were "part Indian" by admission. In a sense, so was Cox, who even claimed that he could "smell an Indian a mile away." Described by one contemporary as a "peculiar character," Cox spoke a strange hybrid language of English, Spanish, and Comanche (Shoshone). He had been captured by Indians as a boy, and he grew to understand their ways. Anglos of the border considered him more Indian than "white," while the Indians saw only his white skin. Like Van and McLain, Cox loathed the Lipan and Kickapoo raiders, not for their race but because of the cattle and horses they had stolen. Understandably, he welcomed the opportunity to recover his livestock—and bring back Indian scalps, trophies in compensation for his losses. More than restitution, what he sought was revenge.[16]

In late April, as soon as the prairie grasses turned green, providing ample forage for the horses, Mackenzie dispatched his three "reliable and trustworthy" scouts to scour the south bank of the Rio Grande, both upstream and downriver. Within two days of crossing into Mexico, Cox and his two companions rode into the Seminole village of Nacimiento. Cox knew of the Seminole's intense hatred for the Kickapoo, with whom they had long been at war, and their dislike for the Lipan. He guessed correctly that these descendants of runaway slaves and renegade warriors exiled from the Florida swamplands would gladly reveal all they knew about their enemies. What the Seminoles apparently disclosed led Cox and his fellow scouts more than seventy miles upriver, where four days later they observed Indian villages scattered out beyond the town of Remolino (meaning "whirlwind"). Situated on the parched plains near the headwaters of the San Rodrigo

River, more than thirty-five miles northwest of Piedras Negras, the villages had provided the beleaguered Kickapoo with much-needed sanctuary, a haven where they could live under the protection of the Mexican state of Coahuila. Alongside them, their former enemies, now allies, a scattering of Lipan and Mescalero Apache, also enjoyed the refuge afforded by the waters of the Rio Grande.[17]

After more than two weeks of tracking their enemy, Cox and his party returned to Fort Clark and met with Colonel Mackenzie on the evening of May 16. They reported that they had located the Indian villages. Hearing this, Mackenzie issued marching orders. Riders from Fort Clark galloped into the night with the urgent message that the troopers must be ready by sunrise to saddle up and move out with full packs. In the predawn darkness the four camps that were scattered for several miles along the waters of Las Moras Creek awakened to the news that final preparations for a march must be completed in the glow of campfires and under the faint light of a half moon. The six company commanders only then learned from Mackenzie's courier where they would rendezvous with their commander—and that they were heading across the Rio Grande into Mexico.[18]

Shortly after 8:00 A.M. on May 17, along the Las Moras some three miles downstream from Fort Clark, Mackenzie gathered his company commanders for a briefing. He then addressed the troops for the first time about their mission and how it carried great danger. Some of them might not return, he explained. Death and scalping at the hands of Apache or Kickapoo braves, or possibly capture and torture, might be their fate. Maybe an equally violent end while being "stood with back against a wall riddled with bullets" would await some if they surrendered to Mexican *federales.* Mackenzie's normally halting speech and slight stammer seemed to disappear as he spoke confidently of the secretive and controversial nature of their raid across the Rio Grande. Into Mexico he would lead them, the colonel promised. And back to Fort Clark, God willing, they would return.[19]

Mackenzie failed to tell his men the full truth: he had no direct, official written orders to cross into Mexico. As the sun rose at their backs, the troopers rested their horses and made final preparations for the march. After a breakfast of hard biscuits and dried beef, the much-anticipated order came. "Stand to horse!" an officer shouted the first command. "Lead out!" the second order followed. "Count by fours! Mount!" Slowly and deliberately, without fanfare the column moved toward the border. Later in the day, by the time the sun fell before them on the western horizon,

Mackenzie's raiders had covered twenty miles of rugged terrain in eight hours. Through the chaparral and mesquite thickets they wound their way beside Las Moras Creek, following Mackenzie's detachment of eighteen Black Seminole scouts all the way to the cane breaks running along the Rio Grande. Within thirty minutes of the column's arrival at the river-banks, night had fallen. "It was now too dark to distinguish anything but the dim forms of moving horses and men," Carter recalled.[20]

Soon after 10:00 P.M. the troopers began to cross by twos. Leaving some of their mules and pack trains safely on the Texas side, the column filed into the river. "The double line of horses made a living dam across the stream," Lieutenant Beaumont remembered. Although the ford cho-sen was shallow, in the riverbed lurked the danger of quicksand. So each pair of riders remained immediately behind the pair just ahead of them. By midnight all had crossed safely. Quietly, the officers then directed their men to draw rations from their saddlebags and eat while they could. There would be no time for food the next day, they were forewarned.[21]

The night march turned out to be serene, though somewhat eerie. Beau-mont described the ominous sight of a "blood red" moon that rose in the sky, its glow being filtered through the prism of dust stirred by winds blow-ing in from the Gulf of Mexico. Otherwise, the canopy of stars shone clearly in the heavens as Mackenzie's column rode, in silence, past isolated jacales and dark farmhouses, only a few of which were illumined by crackling fires. Little more than the creaking of leather saddles, the jingle of equipment, and the muffled timber of horse hooves broke the quiet monotony of the march. Only the occasional barking of dogs in the distance interrupted an otherwise-uneventful advance toward the objective.[22]

It was an almost soothing calm. But no one expected that to continue once the sun rose over the Mexican plain.

Day of Screams

"Daybreak disclosed a creek in the valley," Beaumont remembered. But Lieutenant John Bullis's Seminole scouts had apparently miscalculated the distance, and the dust-covered troopers remained far short of their desti-nation. Six more miles along a dry streambed and an estimated four more miles through the thickets and underbrush finally brought the regiment to four Indian villages that spread out before them.[23]

Despite the delay, Mackenzie and his pony soldiers had apparently arrived undetected. The sun stood low in the eastern sky when Mackenzie ordered three companies to encircle the villages and cut off any chance of escape to the west. Led by Lieutenant Bullis and his Black Seminole scouts, the remaining two companies advanced at a lope, then a full gallop.[24]

Mackenzie could not have asked for a more fearless warrior to lead the charge than Lieutenant John Lapham Bullis. Like his commander, a native of New York and a veteran of the War of the Rebellion, Bullis was the consummate professional soldier. Despite having been raised a pacifist of Quaker faith, he had never backed down from a fight. Short, muscular, with a drooping handlebar mustache and receding hairline, the thirty-two-year-old Bullis commanded the respect of enlisted men and commissioned officers alike. More important, his Black Seminole scouts adored him. And they would have followed him through the gates of hell. For his ferocity in battle and for his bulldog-like tenacity, Bullis had earned the moniker the "Fighting Quaker." The Apache people's name for him has been variously translated as "Thunderbolt" or "Whirlwind," likewise a tribute to his lightning-like quickness in the attack and the suddenness of his strike against an unsuspecting enemy.[25]

During his distinguished military career, Lieutenant Bullis had proved himself in battle many times. Simply put, he was a leader, a motivator, and a good judge of character. And he had every reason to trust the courage and skill of his Seminole scouts. After all, Bullis had trained them, or some might argue they had trained him.

The Black Seminoles rode as if they had been born in the saddle, and they could read horse tracks like handwriting. No one could question their bravery, or their cunning. Their ranks would include Sergeant John Kibbits (also spelled Kibbets in some sources) and three future Congressional Medal of Honor recipients: John Ward—listed on the rolls as twenty-six years old—and two younger members, Pompey Factor and Isaac Payne, who both had yet to reach their twentieth birthdays. All three, like the rest of their column, were of the Moscogos—the name for those Seminole who were of mixed race, both Indian and African. As some observed, they may have been African in appearance, but Indian in their dress, customs, and ways. If, as some in the army liked to claim, "it takes an Indian to catch an Indian," then the Seminole scouts seemed well suited for their task.[26]

On that fateful spring morning near Remolino, Bullis and his Black Seminole scouts struck swiftly and without warning. In a matter of minutes, Mackenzie's troopers swept in and captured stores of supplies and munitions and rounded up the pony herd, most of the more than two hundred animals bearing Texas brands. As the gunfire subsided the bluecoats had captured more than forty men, women, and children, rounding them up and herding them together like livestock. Among the captives stood the frail figure of the principal Lipan chief, old Costelietos. Seminole scout Renty Grayson had tossed a lariat over the old man as he attempted to escape. Stooped and wizened, the elder chief's wrinkled face had been baked by the sun and dried hard by the wind. But that appearance belied the fact that, only the previous year, he had led the raid on Howard's Well.[27]

Descendants of the Lipan Apache would remember Mackenzie's attack as the Día de los Gritos, or "Day of Screams." While the Indian dead by Colonel Mackenzie's count officially numbered nineteen, Captain Carter remembered the actual number to be much greater. He even later admitted that, owing to confusion during the attack, women and children as young as two lay among the dead. In his words, they were "badly shot through their bodies." Some of the wounded were literally dragged from their tepees by the pony soldiers. In the swirl of confusion no one had time to count the corpses that were strewn across the field, seemingly everywhere in sight. As the gunfire subsided Mackenzie was told that most of the young Lipan and Kickapoo men—the warriors—were away, maybe on a spring hunt, or perhaps a raid. He also learned from the scouts that as many as a hundred others, mostly women, children, and old men, were fleeing to the west toward the Sierra Madre Mountains.[28]

Disappointed and perhaps even angry at the news, Mackenzie yelled, "Fire the villages!" The shrill, terrified cries of women and children continued as troopers dismounted and gathered bundles of long grass Lighting them, the soldiers moved from one lodge to another, torching each of them. Carter recalled vividly the chaotic scene as the Indian hovels, their thatched roofs "as dry as tinder, flashed up and roared and burned like powder. The fierce crackling of the flames mingled strangely with loud reports of carbines, sharp cracks of rifles, cheers and yells." Clouds of smoke rose over the sandy plain as the fire consumed everything in its path.[29]

Meanwhile, amid the choking dust and smoke, two of Lieutenant Bullis's Seminole scouts rode up with a young brave they had captured. What happened next turned out to be the most bizarre and surreal moment of all. The mounted Indian warrior appeared agitated, even defiant. But not until he found himself among women and children under guard did he realize that he was a captive of his enemies. More remarkably, the scouts had failed to disarm their young prisoner, who brandished a rifle in his hand. Carter remembered the moment: "I was facing the Lipan Indian whom the Seminole had just brought in, and watching his face and every movement. The moment I saw the look of rage at what he had witnessed come over his face, I feared trouble."[30]

Then it happened. Realizing that armed troopers now surrounded him, the young warrior leveled his rifle at Captain Clarence Mauck, "who had just ridden up," according to Beaumont. At that point Mauck slid from his saddle and shielded himself behind his horse, frantically wheeling the animal around to avoid getting shot. Just then, Carter cocked his carbine and, without time to aim, fired. "He gave a loud, piercing yell," Carter recalled of the young brave, "threw up his gun, which went off in the air . . . [as he] toppled off his pony, dead before he touched the ground."[31]

During the attack, Captain Napoleon B. McLaughlin, a "sturdy and intrepid old soldier," as Carter remembered him, also tempted death. His company had led the advance of regulars that morning, and it was McLaughlin who had ridden to the front as his pony soldiers roared into the Indian camps. Firing his service revolver, McLaughlin taunted the enemy at point-blank range. At one point, as the fight moved through the village, McLaughlin—whom Carter called the "best pistol and carbine shot in the Army"—rode up, with revolver drawn, and approached a young Kickapoo brave sprawled on the ground. Just as McLaughlin came to within a few feet of the apparently lifeless body, the warrior rolled over, raised his rifle and fired. Fortunately for McLaughlin, the shot missed its mark. As his terrified horse twisted and spun away from the rifle blast, Captain McLaughlin still managed to reach around and squeeze off a round from his service revolver, killing the young man instantly.[32]

As plumes of gray smoke drifted over the Mexican plain, the specter of carnage was everywhere. The gunfire had stopped, but the wailing of women and the cries of children had not. "Ruin and desolation" lay all around, as Carter recollected. "A cyclone could not have made a cleaner sweep." Realizing that his soldiers had destroyed the principal Kickapoo village and one Lipan village but that another two stood almost a quarter of a mile away still unharmed, Mackenzie considered his options. Informed that hundreds of "hostiles" were fleeing westward toward the Santa Rosa range, Mackenzie refused to divide his command to pursue them. Instead, he ordered a retreat. No doubt as the horse soldiers fell back toward the border an alarm would be spread quickly that the hated gringos had violated sovereign Mexican territory. Word of the attack would surely move rapidly up and down the river frontier. Armed *rurales*, perhaps even Mexican federal forces and Lipan and Kickapoo raiders would soon assemble to cut off their path to the Rio Grande. From Remolino and past a dozen other, smaller hamlets, toward the border they would ride. There was no time to waste. Mackenzie understood that.[33]

The colonel also knew that the rugged terrain would make their retreat to the border difficult enough. As it turned out, he was right. Retracing their route to the Rio Grande in daylight—and with dozens of prisoners—proved to be even more challenging and dangerous than advancing by night. While the column began a slow withdrawal, the glare of the sun now revealed what Carter called a "dreary, almost waterless waste of mountains and trackless deserts." As they pulled back toward the Rio Grande, with their captives under heavy armed guard in the rear, they traversed the parched and featureless plains of eastern Coahuila. Past isolated adobe towns and farms, they pushed on. Carter recorded that "everywhere we met the black, malignant scowls" of leering Mexicans who gazed upon the troopers with obvious disdain. To compound matters, a stifling heat hung in the air.[34]

Fearful of ambush at any time, Mackenzie sent Lieutenant Bullis and his Seminole scouts ahead at his flanks and front. A few of the Seminoles remained behind the column to protect the rear. Still, nightfall on May 18 found them a full day's ride from Texas soil. "As darkness settled about us our anxiety increased," Carter recalled. "We did not feel safe and we fully realized the worst was before us." Uncertainty stalked them through the night. If not for a glowing moon that illumined the landscape, their path would have been completely obscured by the darkness. "We wearily rode on," Carter recollected. "The heavy, overpowering clutch of sleep was upon every officer and man." No wonder, as this marked the third night that most had no sleep, no opportunity even to rest for more than a few minutes. "It was a long, long night," Carter remembered. Ever so slowly the hours passed, but no ambush came.[35]

Some troopers slumped over, fast asleep in the saddle. Heads bobbed with each bounce of the horses' steps. A few men, exhausted and spent, even tumbled from their horses. Others found by their officers to be nodding and swaying had to be shaken to keep them alert. As for the captives, some women and children riding two or three to a pony, they had to be lashed to their horses, not to prevent their escape but to keep them from sliding from their mounts and toppling onto the trail.[36]

Sunrise on May 19 brought the welcome sight of the Rio Grande. Never had the muddy waters of the great river looked so good to the soldiers of the Fourth. Men and horses alike plunged into the cool, refreshing relief provided by the stream. Once safely on the Texan side, they ascended a bluff some distance back from the riverbanks, where Captain Henry Lawton and a supply train filled with rations from Fort Clark awaited to greet them. For the first time in two days, the troopers were ordered to strip the saddles from their mounts, fill their canteens, and pitch camp. The heavily lathered horses, every bit as fatigued as their riders, were at last allowed to drink their fill and forage on the fresh carpet of luxuriant grasses. Then for the first time since leaving Texas, Mackenzie allowed his men to bed down for a well-earned rest while sentries took turns standing guard. The river was at their back now, between them and their enemy.[37]

Still sensing the threat of snipers and *guerrilleros* stalking them, Colonel Mackenzie ordered his best sharpshooters to establish a picket line above the cane brakes and among the dense chaparral that ran along the riverbanks. For the remainder of the day the thickets on the Texas side bristled with .50 Spencer carbines and .45 Smith and Wesson service revolvers. But that show of force failed to stop a scattering of angry Mexican gunmen and armed Indian warriors from sporadically firing across the river, without effect. For more than an hour Mackenzie's men listened to threats, taunts and epithets being hurled from the Mexican side. Finally, one of Mackenzie's troopers shouted back across the waters, in Spanish, inviting the enemy to "come on over." But their pursuers never crossed the narrow ford to the Texas bank. "We heard no more of this boastful, gasconading rabble," Carter recollected.[38]

Later that morning cattleman and guide Green Van appeared at Mackenzie's campsite with several containers of newly made mescal, a product of the agave plant that was, in Carter's words, a "very potent Mexican drink." The friendly ranchero suggested that he could bring more for the enlisted men, even all they could drink. But Mackenzie refused to allow the mescal to be passed around to any of his men. In their exhausted and hungry condition, they might become wild and unruly, maybe even sick and further dehydrated by the alcohol.[39]

That evening after sundown Mackenzie called together his company commanders and other officers of his staff. Captain John Wilcox and Lieutenant Leopold Parker joined Mauck, McLaughlin, Beaumont, and Carter. At first, their casual conversation covered mundane logistical matters regarding the return trip to Fort Clark, including the disposition of the captives. But then the talk turned to an even more serious topic that generated more heat than the campfire that flared up between them. Beaumont began by asking Mackenzie if he had ever received written orders to lead the command across the border into Mexico. Without hesitation, Mackenzie answered that he had been issued no such orders. Stunned and angered, Beaumont confronted his commander, calling their operation "illegal," even going so far as to demand what would have happened if Mackenzie's withdrawal back to the Rio Grande had failed. Would he have simply left the wounded and captured behind "to be hung or shot by a merciless horde"? Mackenzie bristled, admitting that he had, in fact, considered that possibility. At that point, an outraged Beaumont interjected, "Your officers and men would have been justified in refusing to obey your orders." Then Beaumont defiantly confessed, "Had I known that you had no orders to take us over the river, I would not have gone!" Carter, who witnessed the entire exchange, recalled that a stoic Mackenzie then rose to his feet and snapped, "Any officer or man who had refused to follow me across the river I would have shot!" To that, McLaughlin interjected, "That would depend, Sir, on who shot first!" Mackenzie glared back at his speechless subordinates.[40]

"There was absolute silence for some minutes," Carter clearly remembered. "The silence soon became painful, and great was the relief when first one and then another withdrew from the flickering light of the mesquite bivouac fire and, rolling himself in his blanket, sought relief from such a terrible condition." Beaumont never mentioned his quarrel and near confrontation with Mackenzie in his memoir of the raid on Remolino. Apparently, McLaughlin likewise left no written record of the angry words he traded with his commander. Perhaps in the coming years neither man continued to harbor any ill will. Maybe both came to understand that the issue of written orders proved academic in the end. After all, only one fellow trooper—Private Peter Carrigan—had died in the assault on the Indian villages, while two others were seriously wounded and carried back on litters. But the rest, almost four hundred men, had returned safely to Texan soil. And they probably had their commander to thank for that.[41]

Early the next morning, while the troopers prepared to move out to Fort Clark, the Seminole scouts gathered the Lipan and Kickapoo captives. What a sad and pitiful sight the prisoners were. Huddled together, their faces drawn with fear, they suffered from hunger and exposure to the elements. Some looked sick. Others shivered in the morning chill, their half-naked bodies covered with dirt, their hair mostly matted with grime and infested with lice. They were no threat to anyone.

One Lipan boy caught the attention of Lieutenant Carter: "Here was a child of but five or six years. By custom, his head had been shaved smooth,

except a tuft or stiff scalp-lock, a crest running from his forehead over back
to his neck." Like other boys his age, his face was painted for war, Carter
observed—but with one striking difference. "His infantile warrior spirit
had given away. Young though he was, he fully realized that he was a captured prisoner of war, in the hands of a hated white man, and separated,
as he believed, forever from his Indian home. The tears had coursed down
his face, over the paint and sweat," Carter continued. "His rigid form,
bolt upright, but added to this strange, impressive spectacle. All faces wore
that dull-gray, ashy, deathlike appearance, indicative of overworked nature
and the approach of exhaustion and physical collapse." Carter admitted to
being forever haunted by the picture of terrified children clinging to their
mothers. The images of the captives forever seared into his memory. The
scene remained vivid, even decades later, "one never to be forgotten in a
lifetime."[42]

Covered in dust, sunburned, and saddle scalded, Mackenzie's raiders
rode back into Fort Clark around noon on May 21. They returned to what
Carter termed an "anxious garrison" churning with false rumors that the
entire command had been wiped out, "cut to pieces." The sheer terror
caused by such rumors of disaster showed on the faces of every army wife
at Fort Clark. But as these women dashed toward Mackenzie's long column of bedraggled troopers approaching the post, their fears soon turned
to great joy upon seeing their loved ones back from the field. But there
was no joy in the faces of the captives who now found themselves dis-
placed, separated from their loved ones. The legends of the Lipan would
long remember the youngest of them, the children, as the "Lost Ones."
Within days, they along with the others would be driven like livestock to
San Antonio and there temporarily held under armed guard until their
forced removal north of the Red River to Fort Gibson and then westward
to Fort Sill, Indian Territory.[43]

By almost every white man's measure, Mackenzie's daring raid across
the border could be judged a military success. That is, by almost everyone
except Colonel Mackenzie himself, who had a different standard of success. A quiet and serious man, not given to celebration, he seethed over
the fact that most of the Lipan and Kickapoo men—the true marauders
and warriors—had been away on a hunt or a raid when he struck their
villages near Remolino. The last thing he wanted was to be known as a
woman killer, a slayer of boys and old men, a captor of children. There
was no honor in that. Mackenzie's "victory," as military officials would
describe it, had been pathetic, not a source of pride. There was nothing

noble about capturing the hungry and helpless. A troubled Colonel Mackenzie knew that, though he remained publicly silent on the matter.

Perhaps that is why Mackenzie desperately hoped for another chance to deal the Indian raiders a lethal blow. For the three days after the return from Remolino reports persisted that a large force of Mexican soldiers and Indian renegades was gathering on the south bank of the Rio Grande and staging somewhere near the town of Villa Nuevo for a possible counterattack on Texan soil. On the morning of May 24 Mackenzie personally led a small reconnaissance party from Fort Clark to the Rio Grande, and for two days and two nights he scoured up and down the river for any signs of such a threat. Finding none, Mackenzie returned to Fort Clark on the afternoon of the 26th, only to find his soldiers still nervous and uneasy about the prospect of an attack launched from Mexico.[44]

The anxiety that gripped Fort Clark only escalated that evening as a squall line blew in, bringing fierce winds and brilliant streaks of lightning. As the thunderstorms rumbled across the plateau overlooking Las Moras Creek, the skies flashed, went completely black, and lit up again with bright flashes that caused soldiers and civilians alike to scurry for cover. A howling gale whipped across the plain and brought sheets of rain that quickly transformed the post into a quagmire. Throughout the worst of it, Mackenzie's sentries, clad in slickers and floppy-brimmed hats, hunkered down at their stations, as if accepting a beating from a stern parent. Their commander had ordered them to maintain their watch and to be on the alert for an enemy no doubt bent on revenge. Surely no Mexican or Indian would conduct a raid in such fearsome weather, the young men of the Fourth Cavalry must have reassured themselves as the rains pummeled down.[45]

As it turned out, the only retaliation that Mackenzie and his regiment suffered was from nature's fury. Dawn on May 27 brought clear skies and the soothing symphony of songbirds that were rejoicing. Like their human counterparts, they were relieved that the storm had passed, even if the danger of a worthy adversary intent on revenge had not.[46]

Hanging by a Thread

Despite Department of War claims to the contrary, Mackenzie's expedition across the Rio Grande only complicated the long hemorrhaging diplomatic relationship between Mexico and the United States. As expected, Mexican officials soon expressed outrage over the violation of their territorial sovereignty. However, U.S. officials, now armed with the conclusions of the Robb Commission, expressed pleasure and even support for Mackenzie's action. General Sheridan voiced his approval in no uncertain terms when he reaffirmed to Mackenzie on May 28 that "there is in my opinion only one way left to settle the Mexican Frontier difficulty, that is, to cross the Rio Grande and recover our property, and punish the thieves." Several days later, in a letter to Secretary of War Belknap, the irascible Sheridan repeated that sentiment in still stronger language: "For twenty years there has been no safety for life or property on the Rio Grande, and at last we are driven by a necessity . . . [namely] the protection of our lives and our property, to cross a very crooked river to exterminate the murderers and robbers." Sheridan continued that defiant tone in a dispatch to the U.S. adjutant general on June 5: "There should be no boundary line when we are driven to the necessity of defending our lives and property."[47]

The flinty General William Tecumseh Sherman agreed, responding to Secretary Belknap several days later: "The invasion of the territory of a Friendly [*sic*] power in *hot pursuit* of an aggressive or robber force would be warranted by the Laws of Nations." Unless the government of Mexico protested more vehemently, Sherman urged, "there is no need of our making further enquiries." As for Mackenzie, who was quickly commended by the Texas state legislature, he defended his own actions and even vowed to strike again across the border "if my friends on the other side of the river . . . will not act promptly to prevent depredations."[48]

In the weeks and months that followed, no one stood more unwavering in support of Mackenzie than General Sheridan. "Send word to Mackenzie that he is all right and will be sustained, that he has done a good thing," Sheridan reassured General Christopher C. Auger on May 27. General Sheridan even prophesied, "I consider the Mexican border troubles as drawing to a close." But he could not have been more wrong. Over the next two years the cycle of violence continued uninterrupted. Heavily armed bandits ransacked settlements in the lower Rio Grande Valley with even greater frequency, often leaving their victims facedown in the dirt, their bodies riddled with bullet holes. In each instance the assailants galloped back into the brush and toward the protective waters of the Rio Grande, leaving behind a trail of blood—and a menacing fear.[49]

As for Colonel Mackenzie, while the scorching summer of 1873 droned on, he waited impatiently at his post in Fort Clark. Convinced that renegade bands of Kickapoo and Lipan Apache were preparing to launch more raids across the border, he remained ever vigilant, eager for another opportunity to attack them in their sanctuary, even if that meant war with Mexico. On May 29 Mackenzie wrote General Auger that Governor Victoriano Cepeda Camacho of the state of Coahuila held the "greater share of the blame" for continuing depredations in South Texas. On June 2, he again expressed his eagerness for another opportunity to strike the enemy in their lairs. "If there is a good chance, please let me attack the Apaches . . . or if the Kickapoos won't now come in, let me hit them if a first rate opportunity offers." That same day, Mackenzie penned a letter to "His Excellency," Governor Cepeda, charging him with negligence and even complicity with the Indian marauders, and he went so far as to suggest that Cepeda was personally responsible for "causing innumerable outrages on this side" of the Rio Grande.[50]

On June 30 Mackenzie revealed his innermost feelings about the border problems, expressing his sentiments about the neighboring nation to the south and its people. Again, he reported to General Auger that marauders were staging near the towns of Santa Rosa and San Fernando. Then he admitted, "So far as the Mexicans are concerned, I have for their individual character not the slightest respect, and for that very reason I regard a war with them if it cannot be honorably avoided . . . as a very great calamity. We don't want their miserable population [or] any of their territory. They are not fit for any government but an absolute one, and we could not govern them in that way." In the end, however, Mackenzie confessed, "If there is war with Mexico . . . whether in my opinion it is right or wrong, when it comes I wish to have my share in it."[51]

Only later did Colonel Mackenzie learn that General Sheridan had ordered him into Mexico at the same time that the Bureau of Indian Affairs had dispatched a "peace commission" across the Rio Grande into Coahuila to negotiate the removal and safe return of the Kickapoo to Indian Territory. Led by commissioners Henry M. Atkinson of Nebraska and F. G. Williams of San Antonio, the mission, which included a small military escort, was left stranded in Múzquiz, where in late May and early June, they claimed, their lives were left "hanging by a thread." Despite the tension, however, the talks continued. And so did the raids and recriminations on both sides of the border.[52]

But Mackenzie had little interest in diplomacy or politics. A war of words did not suit his restless nature or his penchant for action. Soldiers were trained to fight, not to debate or argue or question orders from their superiors. Still, as the situation on the border continued to deteriorate, and U.S.-Mexico relations devolved into an even more caustic exchange of insults, accusations, and threats, Mackenzie could not keep his opinions to himself. His only duty was to keep his superiors informed of the imminent threat of marauders lurking just beyond the border. All that was left to do now was to wait for another opportunity to deal the Kickapoo and Apache renegades a more lethal blow—while U.S. and Mexican officials talked and negotiated and postured.

But swarms of border bandits, Indian marauders, and gangs of rustlers waited for no one. Throughout the next eighteen months the cycle of violence and bloodshed continued unabated along the river frontier. If anything, raiding parties and bands of rustlers crossed the Rio Grande into Texas with greater frequency than before. This reign of lawlessness along the lower Rio Grande took its toll.

No wonder that a young cavalry officer stationed at Ringgold Barracks wrote the U.S. adjutant general early in 1875 that the entire Rio Grande frontier was "panic stricken" and that it would "take the whole army of the United States to effectively stop it." Later that year another army officer stationed in South Texas confirmed that the region was in the "wildest state of excitement." Texas Governor Richard Coke echoed that assessment when he warned General Edward O. C. Ord, newly appointed commander of the Department of Texas headquartered in San Antonio, that the "imminence of a sanguinary border war" had caused the depopulation of several South Texas counties. Ranchers and farmers alike were fleeing northward alongside Mexican peones to some place, any place, of safety. In the process, they had little choice but to abandon their herds on the range and their crops in the field. As Coke explained the urgent situation in a message to the Texas state legislature, "The energies of that country are paralyzed, its commerce destroyed, its wealth reduced."[53]

Like most fellow Texans, especially the citizens of South Texas, an impatient Governor Coke feared that the surge of violence along the border would dissuade immigration into the state and would thus inhibit trade, prevent capital investment, and, most important, prohibit railroad construction through such an immense and promising country. Coke remained determined to prove wrong those skeptics who claimed that the borderlands of Mexico were godforsaken.

Whether the Almighty had given up on the lower Rio Grande and abandoned it to the devil's designs, as some suggested, Coke refused to consider. With the support of the legislature in Austin, he determined that a "special force" of state troops—Mounted Rangers—could be raised to rid the region of marauding bandits and their violent ways. Coke needed the right man to accomplish such a daunting task: A man willing and able to lead young troops south of the Nueces, to the banks of the Rio Grande and beyond if necessary. A leader able to track down and capture—or kill—the worst of the border bad men. One who could match the bandits in their bravado and brutality. One who would meet violence with violence, cruelty with cruelty, and terror with terror. One who would not be stopped by threats or by force of arms, and certainly not by a crooked river.

7
McNelly's Rangers

Throughout 1874 swarms of border bandits struck farther into Texas, and with greater boldness and frequency. Everywhere they rode, they left a trail of blood and destruction. The month of May proved the most terrifying and deadly yet. On May 5 some twenty-five miles west of Corpus Christi, highwaymen held up a young man named Watson and two fellow travelers. After tying them up, the bandits robbed all their belongings and left them barefoot on the prairie with nothing more than their underclothing. That same day between the Olmito and Lampasito ranches, about seventy miles southwest of Corpus Christi, bandits ambushed a French traveler named Martinet, making off with his boots, baggage, and a reported $4,800 in cash. Before riding away, the *bandidos* stole his horse, lashed him to a tree, and left him alone to face the elements.[1]

But these men were fortunate compared to other victims of the spreading violence. On May 9, at the Rancho Penescal near the Nueces County and Cameron County line, not far from the Martinet robbery, a band of some thirty armed outlaws fell upon a country store owned by John F. Morton and Michael Morton. At gunpoint they robbed the store's firearms, ammunition, and other valuables. Then they brutally murdered both proprietors as well as three others, identified as P. F. Coakley, John M. Fletcher, and Herman Tilgner, before stealing their horses and escaping into the brush. Later, a federal inquest reported that, when captured, one of the raiders, Armando Lerma, confessed to being a party to this crime and admitted that he and his fellow bandits had crossed into Texas from Mexico. As an accomplice to the killings, Lerma was swiftly tried and convicted of murder. But because he agreed to "turn evidence" against his fellow bandits, he was sentenced to life in prison. One report insisted, however, that he was soon hanged in Corpus Christi by vigilantes before he could be imprisoned. The circumstances of his execution were not documented and remained "unexplained."[2]

The rest of that year along the border brought only more cattle rustling, robbery, and murder. The following year predictably brought still more terror. Early in 1875 border violence quickly escalated to a new level. On January 18 Albert Dean and Joseph Dunn, both Starr County customs inspectors stationed in Rio Grande City, came under attack while investigating a herd of cattle being driven toward the Rio Grande. Five Mexican vaqueros armed with Winchesters opened fire on the two officers as they approached the scene. Although the five presumed thieves escaped across the Rio Grande, Dunn and Dean reported that the caballeros possessed all the rawhide ropes, brands, and other paraphernalia considered "useful" in their craft and trade.[3]

Just over a week later, on January 26 bandits attacked a patrol of the Ninth U.S. Cavalry near the Solis Ranch in Starr County, killing two black troopers and one Mexican scout, stripping them of their boots, service revolvers, and carbines. Then on February 27 marauders fell upon a general store seven miles downriver from Edinburg (present-day Hidalgo) in Hidalgo County. The mounted gunmen confronted Mauricio Villanueva and shot the young clerk through the head and then turned their guns on the popular proprietor of the post, J. L. Fulton, who also served as the local brand inspector and justice of the peace. Fulton, a former officer of the Thirty-Sixth Infantry and veteran of the Union army, apparently had wrested a pistol from one of his assailants during a scuffle and seriously wounded him. But Fulton's defiance was greeted with several blasts from the robbers' revolvers. Fulton was later found facedown, the back of his head blown off, his body shot through with several other bullet holes.[4]

Then, on March 23 Alexander Morel of Hidalgo County was gunned down and killed when he rode upon a party of rustlers who were in the process of practicing the art of rounding up "lost cattle." As Brownsville resident William Neale recalled, "Many a good man was sent to the silent land by these ruffians." All along the river frontier, cattle thieves and land pirates seemed to be as ever present as the mesquite thickets. But such events as these would be but a prelude to the infamous Nuecestown raid.[5]

The Raid on Nuecestown

For the people of the lower Nueces, March 26, 1875—Good Friday— was a day to remember. It all started that morning when several bandits rode up to the Campbell Place near Tule Lake and stole several horses at gunpoint. A few miles away, the raiders "made a clean sweep of everything valuable" at the Page Ranch, even carrying off Mr. Page as a hostage. Not long thereafter, at Rancho Juan Sais, some nine miles upriver from Corpus Christi, an even larger party of *robadores* sacked and looted George Franks's store, taking the proprietor captive in the process. As it was later reported, "They took everything they wanted, exchanged their old clothes

for new and even stripped Franks to his underclothing." Even more terrifying, while plundering the store of everything from saddle and tack to
weapons and ammunition, the bandits seized more than a dozen prisoners, including several women and children. The marauders even executed
one captive, hanging an elderly Tejano who worked for Franks, when he
refused to join the raiders. For his efforts in trying to save his hired hand,
Franks was brutally beaten. After completing their bloody work there,
the heavily armed bandits continued to Nuecestown, twelve miles inland
from Corpus Christi, by one account herding their hostages before them
"like sheep."[6]

Arriving at Nuecestown later that afternoon, the mounted gunmen surrounded the general store and post office, then confronted merchant and
postmaster Thomas J. Noakes and his wife, Martha (born Maria Lud-
wig, the daughter of German immigrants). Tom Noakes later recounted
their harrowing experience in chilling detail. "I was kept busy all day," he
began. "After finishing [sorting] my letters I made up the mail in readiness for the carrier who was about due." Just then, a local tradesman
named John Smith entered the store to pick up a parcel. At that point,
Noakes remembered, "I noticed three Mexicans ride up and fasten their
horses to the rack in front of the store." Noakes saw that the riders were
"heavily armed" as they approached the door. "I said nothing to Smith
of the circumstance, but walked hastily to the sitting room at the back
of the store to get my Winchester." No sooner had Noakes grabbed his
rifle than Smith ran into the room, pursued by "a savage looking" bandit
brandishing a six-shooter. Turning the pistol on Noakes, the intruder took
aim. "But before he could shoot, my bullet had penetrated his chest and
knocked all the fight out of him." While Smith escaped out the back door
of the building, Martha Noakes rushed to her husband standing over the
wounded bandit. Terrified, she explained that she had handed their infant
daughter to her older brother and sister and told them to run out back
toward the riverbed, where their two older brothers were playing. "Seeing
the wounded Mexican could shoot no more," Noakes continued, "I made
ready for the next to follow him."[7]

But what followed was more than Tom Noakes bargained for. "Having
seen but three Mexicans, I felt . . . able to cope with that number. . . . I
stepped to the door leading into the store to see where they were, and was
taking aim at the fellow nearest me when my attention was attracted by the
number outside the store, which appeared to me to amount to a hundred
Mexicans." Realizing the hopelessness of the situation, Noakes looked for

his wife, but "she was nowhere to be found." Panicked, he dashed into his office and escaped through a hidden trapdoor, one of three that he had built into the floor, then he crawled into a trench beneath the house, where he encountered Smith, who was understandably "very excited." Noakes motioned for Smith to remain quiet while he scrambled to the front of the store, where he could get a better view of the bandits. From his concealed position, he noticed that the outlaws had already seized several prisoners, among them town residents Mike Dunn and Tom Nelson. Then when the unsuspecting mail rider approached on the Corpus Christi road, the bandits captured him and his two horses loaded with mail bags. "I determined at once not to be taken alive, so I passed back to a place where I could command the store with my rifle." Certain that neither he nor his family would see another sunrise, Noakes would never forget the expectation that he was about to witness a massacre.[8]

What he saw next struck him with an unimaginable fear. Several bandits had surrounded Martha Noakes, two of them taunting her with pistols aimed at her face. To raise his Winchester and fire now would only ensure her death. So he slowly trained his rifle on the gunmen and waited for what seemed like an eternity. He could only watch as a defiant Martha pleaded with her tormentors, begging them not to burn down her home or kill her husband. "Several times when they had lighted a fire in the store my wife put it out, and the first time by throwing a pitcher of water on it," Tom recollected. Eventually, the bandits succeeded in setting the store ablaze. The flames spread quickly.[9]

As this horrifying drama played out, Noakes heard several rifle reports from behind the store. Peering out from beneath the building, he saw a fleeing John Smith stagger and collapse to the ground. As the flames roared above his head, Noakes finally escaped and dashed through the wall of smoke that billowed from the store. "I passed by Smith soon after leaving the house," Noakes remembered. "Being on his face and covered with blood, and as I thought, dead," Smith was shot to pieces. Known to locals as "lying Smith" for his aversion to the truth, he could not talk himself out of this hopeless situation.

Only when Noakes squeezed through an opening in his fence and scurried into a clearing could he see Martha motioning to him. She had made her way to safety as their home was consumed in the flames. "When she left the house, as she ran down the hill towards the river, the two Mexicans who had killed Smith rode after her." As they reined in alongside her and leveled their pistols, however, "she begged them to spare her life for the sake of her baby, and they let her go." Several minutes passed before Tom and Martha were reunited with their five children on the opposite bank of the Nueces. Miraculously, all were safe.[10]

Perhaps even more remarkable, during the confusion, Martha had managed to save a light wagon by pulling it away from the burning house. Despite being lashed with a quirt by a particularly sadistic bandit who sported a large scar on his cheek, she had also dragged a mattress and blanket from the home before the roof collapsed. She had even gone back into the blaze to retrieve her sewing machine. But despite her heroism, Martha—described by one contemporary as "the spunkiest woman I ever saw"—was unable to save her home.[11]

"While the house was burning I had to stand and watch from my retreat . . . the huge tongues of flame shoot heavenward, knowing that they were licking up the fruits of ten years' toil, and everything except ourselves that I valued in this world," Tom Noakes lamented. The heat from the blaze was so intense that several calves penned up near the building were burned alive. All things considered, the experience for the Noakes family could hardly have been more traumatic.[12]

By now dusk was settling over the Gulf coastal plains. Other than the roaring fires that engulfed the Noakeses' store and home, burning the clapboard building to the ground, no other sound could be heard as nightfall approached. An eerie quiet returned to the scene of the carnage. In the meantime, the bandits had ridden away, headed southward toward the Rio Grande, but not before they had made off with several more captives and helped themselves to at least three horses, eighteen new Dick Heye saddles (studded and inlaid with distinctive silver conchos), scores of rifles and revolvers, and some two thousand cartridges. It had been a productive day for the *robadores*.[13]

Noakes waited until the last light of day to walk back up the hill to sift through the smoldering ruins of his home and store. To his astonishment, a severely wounded John Smith was lying about one hundred yards from the site of the store, still alive. He must have crawled some distance from where he first fell. As Noakes knelt over him, Smith was barely breathing but able to ask for water. He had lost so much blood. All that was left to do was to comfort the dying man.[14]

The violent fury continued well into the night and even through the next two days of Easter weekend. As word of the terror spread, two companies of volunteers had formed in Corpus Christi to track down the bandits. One posse was led by Nueces County sheriff John McClane, the other by a local merchant named John Swanks. "A brave man," according to Noakes, Swanks raced ahead of his party of ten volunteers as they caught up with the thieves near a timberline known as "the Motts," not far from Nuecestown. While leading a charge against the bandits, Swanks was gunned down. His friends, who turned their horses and retreated, later returned to the scene, only to find Swanks lying dead in a pool of blood.[15]

As a postscript to the Nuecestown raid, that evening back at Noakes's store, while volunteers were preparing John Smith's body for burial, they heard a faint voice in the distance. Beneath a tree along the roadside, they found a "half dead Mexican" wrapped in a sheet. Still clutching a knife, the blood-soaked bandit, the same man who had been wounded earlier by Tom Noakes, remained defiant to the end. Like a cornered bobcat, he fought for his life, cursing his enemies in Spanish as he was captured alive. The wounded man who had been left behind by his fellow thieves, abandoned to face the certain wrath of the Texans, was carried off to the Nuecestown jail that night. As was the custom in the Nueces Strip in those days, several nights later the prisoner was turned over to a mob and hanged from the nearest tree.[16]

Not long after riding away from Noakes's store, the bandits also held up two other stations that Friday evening. Once the raiders decided to ride back into the brush and head toward the protective waters of the Rio Grande, they realized that their captives—more than a dozen in number—were of little value. In fact, the hungry prisoners were now a burden. Looking to flee with only enough loot to allow them to travel light and fast, and to reach the border undetected, the outlaws finally released all their hostages unharmed.[17]

But the citizens of Corpus Christi and nearby Nuecestown were still not satisfied. All things considered, it had been a horrific weekend, an Easter never to forget—the kind that filled "good Christian people" from the Nueces to the Rio Grande with a terrible resolve. In a tradition as old as the ancient Roman *posse comitatus* ("power of the community" or "force of the county" in Anglo-Saxon common law) local officials in South Texas resorted to forming volunteer militia to curtail banditry and protect their homes and families. Such "citizen's safety committees," typically raised or appointed by county sheriffs, resembled the recent gangs of regulators or vigilantes of the Civil War years when "Judge Lynch" reigned along the border with Mexico. Rather than any legitimate, regulated militia mustered into service for law enforcement, these mounted volunteers rode into the rangelands of the Nueces Strip bent on settling scores and avenging recent atrocities, as well as "adjudicating" long-standing rivalries and unresolved hatreds.[18]

A Complicated Man

Still the raids continued. Less than a month after the attack on Nuecestown, another large party of bandits swam their horses across the Rio Bravo below Rio Grande City and rode more than fifty miles to the village of Carrizo, or Redmond's Ranch, where they surrounded the adobe house of Dr. David D. Lovell, the town postmaster. Robbing his station of a reported $7,000 in goods and cash, they left Lovell in the doorway of the depot lying dead with multiple gunshot wounds. During this time the enterprising *bandido* Alberto Garza, the White Horseman, resumed and even expanded his depredations in Duval County, where for the past year he had robbed and ransacked trading posts from Concepcion to Los Olmos.[19]

As one young army officer summarized the situation, the whole country south of the Nueces was "panic stricken" and another confirmed that the region was in the "wildest state of excitement." Texas adjutant general William Steele went so far as to describe it as a "state of war" being waged upon the people of Texas. Reflecting the racial prejudices of many Anglo citizens in South Texas, Steele even bristled that the federal "Negro Cavalry" and black infantry units stationed along the border line of defense were "worthless for that service." Governor Richard Coke shared that assessment when he warned General E. O. C. Ord, commander of the Department of Texas, that a "sanguinary border war" had caused a rapid depopulation of several South Texas counties. Ranchers, herdsmen, and farmers alike were fleeing northward, abandoning their stock and crops in the fields, he cautioned. As Coke explained further in his annual message to the Texas state legislature, "The energies of that country are paralyzed, its commerce destroyed, its wealth reduced." The situation along the border had reached a state of crisis.[20]

Fearing that the border violence was fast spiraling out of control, Governor Coke dispatched Texas adjutant general William Steele and state senator Joseph E. Dwyer into the Nueces Strip and the Rio Grande Valley to gather evidence of the ongoing crimes and atrocities. Their report the following summer not only corroborated the Robb Commission's conclusions but also blamed much of the recent lawlessness on local volunteer militia and "citizens' safety committees" that were engaged in "private killing." In their frustrations and fierce determination to punish those who plundered, these vigilantes administered swift frontier justice at the end of a rope, lynching any suspected rustler from the nearest tree, burning a homestead because cattle, presumed to be stolen, were grazing on the unfenced ranges nearby, or shooting a man dead who might have had the misfortune of unwittingly buying a stolen horse. Moreover, these "regulators" committed these deeds in the name of the law. Dwyer summarized the tragic acts of such self-appointed avengers, pointing out that "instead of exterminating the banditti who invaded Texas, the vengeance fell upon the poor and unfortunate" living in the border counties north of the river. Almost inevitably, he concluded, these victims of vigilante violence were Tejanos, or Mexican Texans farming and ranching on the Texas side of the border.[21]

Dwyer's conclusion was chilling, and his candor was admirable. While charging that many of the border bandits considered "the killing of a Texan something to be proud of," he also admitted that "there is a disposition on the part of some Americans not to respect the property of Mexicans," and a "considerable element in the country . . . that think the killing of a Mexican no crime."[22]

Only the previous year, Coke and the Texas legislature had reconstituted state Ranger forces—termed a "mobile constabulary"—to protect the frontier from Comanche raiders and thieving bandits. The Frontier Battalion, consisting of six "permanent companies" of seventy-five men each under the command of Major John B. Jones, had been scouring the borderlands of northwest Texas in search of Indian raiders and desperados. Only Captain Neal Coldwell's Company F had been assigned to the borderlands of South Texas. A separate organization, a single company of Washington County volunteers led by Captain Leander H. McNelly, had been ordered into DeWitt County to suppress a local orgy of gunpowder and lead known as the Sutton-Taylor feud. McNelly's "special force" of state troops had—by their mere presence—restored order and quiet to the rangelands surrounding the town of Cuero and the farming country along the lower Guadalupe River. There more than three hundred hired killers, among them a young gunslinger named John Wesley Hardin, had been waging one of the longest and costliest blood feuds in Texas history. But that story must be told elsewhere.[23]

Even before receiving a final report from Dwyer and Steele, Governor Coke instructed his adjutant general to order Captain McNelly to ride southward into the storm of violence along the lower Rio Grande. Coke could not have made a better choice. Already McNelly had earned the reputation as one of the most feared lawmen in all Texas. Known to the members of his company simply as "the Captain," he was a leader in every sense of the word. A man who inspired respect, confidence, and most of all loyalty, he was justly recognized as a formidable foe by even the worst of bad men. As Ranger Napoleon Augustus Jennings later recollected, "I never saw him lose his temper or heard him raise his voice in anger. Although the life of the Rangers was exciting enough for the rest of us, it seemed tame to our Captain after his war experiences." Jennings further observed that "a more cool and collected individual under fire it would be impossible to imagine." Another member of the company, William Callicott, likewise remembered his captain as "a man that seldom got mad and never did get excited. He always handled his men like a father would his children. . . . Whenever he gave a command, it certainly had to be obeyed." But perhaps Ranger George Durham put it best: "I never have yet figured out what there was about the Captain that worked such a spell over his hands. . . . When he spoke, we hardly breathed. Leastwise, I didn't. Even the horses seemed to quit swishing and stomping."[24]

Since the war years, the legend of Leander McNelly had only continued to grow. Both enemies and admirers viewed him as something of a devil figure, an apparition on horseback, a fearless man who would stare death in the face without flinching. As one contemporary put it, he never "blinked at the sight of danger."[25]

But McNelly was a most unlikely hero. Handsome, clean cut, barely thirty years old, he was the son of a sheepherder. Some who knew him said killing was against his gentle nature. They observed that there appeared to be a kindness and softness to him, though he seldom allowed himself to reveal that side to his men. After the Civil War, the quiet and unassuming McNelly married a pretty farm girl named Carrie Cheek, and together they settled down on a place west of Brenham, near the hamlet of Burton. There McNelly and his young wife took up the plow, raising one hundred acres of cotton and a son named Leander, or "Rebel" to his father. Ranger George Durham described his captain as a "little runt of a feller" who spoke in a thin, piping voice that at times sounded like a "coughing whisper." At first glance, he seemed frail, timid, humble, "preacherish" in Durham's words. His dark gray-streaked mustache and goatee made him look older than he really was, and his neatly trimmed facial hair only partially concealed a boyish face and kind blue eyes.[26]

Most would have taken him for a circuit-riding minister. After all, along with a Colt revolver and a Sharps carbine, he carried a Bible in his saddlebags and read it almost every evening. But his voice and appearance were deceiving. Simply put, he lived by the Old Testament injunction "an eye for an eye." And if necessary, he was prepared to die by it. Like his Old Testament God, he was quick to judge and slow to forgive.

Many perpetuated the story that McNelly had looked death in the face so many times that he was not afraid of dying. It was said that he simply wanted to die well in a worthy cause someday. What few people knew about the storied Confederate guerrilla fighter was that he was already dying—of consumption. Ever since his boyhood in Virginia, he had suffered from tuberculosis. Now his lungs were completely wracked with the dreaded disease. He knew it was a death sentence. But he concealed it well, just like he hid, beneath the harsh exterior and brusque manner of a lawman, his love for his family and his stout Christian faith.[27]

McNelly was a hard man to know, even harder to understand—especially if you were a bandit or a rustler. The way he moved, the way he spoke, his quiet strength: unlike so many leaders who simply exuded confidence, there was something else about him, something about his manner that distinguished him from others, something intuitive and difficult to define. Those who rode alongside him in the ranging service swore that he seemed to know, almost instinctively, things that no one else knew. They claimed that it was uncanny how he could sense danger before anyone else. Even before he led his company of Washington County volunteers southward to the lower Rio Grande, some were already saying that he was the last of his kind, and that they would not see his like again.

A man to be respected, no one doubted. Even more, he was a man to be feared. After all, when McNelly accepted the governor's commission to raise a company of state troops and ride into the range wars of South Texas, he had nothing to lose. Nothing but his life, and that issue had already been settled. All this and more the *robadores* and rustlers of the Nueces Strip would soon learn. They might as well have been stalked by *el diablo*, the devil himself. At least Lucifer would have offered mercy for those who surrendered to his will and followed him into darkness, or so some said. But not Captain McNelly.

Men Who Would Take Orders and Fight

In the spring of 1875 McNelly's Rangers appeared to be anything but battle ready. Resembling a mob of rowdy renegades more than a company of law enforcement officers, they wore no uniforms, no insignia or badges, no evidence of rank. "Most of them gave you the idea they had fought in the war," Durham recalled, "On which side was their business." "They looked like men who would take orders and fight," and showed every evidence of the "wear and tear of a hard life," he added. "Somehow you wouldn't pick a one of them to push around." Unshaved and unwashed, with weather-beaten faces, soiled clothes, scuffed boots, and sweat-stained hats, they were a surly-looking lot. In fact, their horses were the most well-groomed members of the company. Jennings remembered them as "beardless boys, full of deviltry and high spirits, and ready at a moment's notice to rush into any adventure." A few, no doubt, were "on the dodge," running from the law. But each was armed to the teeth, a veritable arsenal on horseback in possession of every conceivable instrument of death, from bowie knives to repeating rifles, to six-shooters and shotguns. And to a man, they reflected their Captain's grim determination to rid the region of rustlers and thieves—by any means.[28]

McNelly handpicked his recruits for their willingness to unquestioningly follow his orders. They looked like an odd collection of cowboys and plow-boys. Only a handful were seasoned fighters, mostly former Confederates like their captain. A few were even city "dandies" dressed (or overdressed) as frontiersmen. Few were native Texans, as the captain preferred to enlist men who claimed no "kinfolk" nearby, no one they might have been more loyal to than to him. As was the custom and tradition in those days, all furnished their own firearms, mounts, saddle and tack. They seemed a fair representation, an appropriate cross-section of the youth and pride of the Lone Star State, though most had been born elsewhere.

Astride his favorite horse, a roan he had named Old Ball, twenty-two-year-old Private William Crump Callicott had grown up in the cotton country of the lower Brazos River bottoms. Like most, he had little formal education. As he liked to say, he had not been "vaccinated" with much book learning. Most of his knowledge had been acquired in the saddle or by walking behind his father's plow horse. A farm boy as well, eighteen-year-old Private George Durham had only recently left his native Georgia for the wilds of Texas. As with Bill Callicott, picking cotton was not his career choice. Tall, stocky, a strapping kid still inexperienced in the ways of the Texas frontier, he aspired to a greater adventure in life. Hunting outlaws and cattle thieves appealed to his youthful sense of the romantic. Like many his age, he welcomed danger, and Captain McNelly liked that about him.[29]

The only member of the company younger than Durham was Private L. B. "Berry" Smith of Lee County, known affectionately to his fellow Rangers as "Sonny." Only seventeen by most accounts, he too dreamed of riding in pursuit of border bandits, the more and worse the better. He held little fear of bad men—too little fear. In his short time on this earth he had had no reason to be afraid. After all, his father, D. R. "Dad" Smith, had also joined up with McNelly that spring. The oldest member of the company, he served as camp cook and "wagon boss." Then there was young Tom Sullivan, McNelly's interpreter. Other than the captain's favorite scout, Jesús "Old Casuse" Sandoval, Sullivan was about the only one among them who could "speak Mexican." Other men in Company A, Washington County Volunteer Militia, appear as mere names on incomplete muster rolls or in the faded memories of the participants who recorded their accounts decades later. Corporal William L. Rudd, Corporal Roe P. Orrell, privates M. J. "Polly" Williams, Spencer J. Adams, Matt Fleming, Thomas McGovern, Horace Maben, H. G. "Deaf" Rector, Shadrach Nichols, J. R. Wofford, and the captain's nephew, John McNelly, were but a few.[30]

More is known of Captain McNelly's officers. Lieutenant T. C. Robinson, a newspaper correspondent and aspiring poet from Virginia, had signed on with Captain McNelly the previous year in DeWitt County. His name on McNelly's muster roll read "T. Chanders." Curiously, the amiable Robinson penned dispatches from the field for the *Austin Daily Democratic Statesman* under the pseudonym "Pidge." He was not the only member of the company who preferred to hide his identity behind an alias or a pen name. At least he was candid about his own limitations. At twenty-eight, he was older than most men in the company, but judging by his letters, "Chanders" or "Pidge" admitted to no previous experience in either law enforcement or the military, and he even joked about being uncomfortable with firearms and afraid of wild horses. In some respects, the self-effacing and enigmatic Robinson seemed to be hunting down more stories for the newspaper than outlaws and cattle thieves for the state of Texas. In sum, he was anything but the Hollywood image of a Texas Ranger.[31]

Not so of brothers Lawrence Baker Wright, age twenty-five, and Linton Lafayette Wright, twenty-three, who both served in the rank of sergeant. Like Durham, they were transplants from rural Georgia. And like Durham, they had traded in the mule and plow for a horse and a Colt revolver. They were both brave men, maybe too brave, especially since they were about to head into a country far more dangerous and unforgiving than any they could imagine.[32]

Sergeant John Barclay Armstrong might have been the most able among them. Tall, well proportioned, with dark hair and a bushy mustache and goatee that accentuated his handsome features, the twenty-five-year-old Tennessean certainly looked the part of a lawman. He even carried an air of confidence and a swagger that set him apart from the others. Armstrong was a big man, broad-shouldered, with a chiseled physique. Napoleon Jennings described him as "a dashing fellow, always ready to lead a squad of the Rangers on any scout that promised to end in a fight." McNelly saw much promise in Armstrong, who possessed the two most important qualifications that the captain admired in a man: an unwavering loyalty and an unflinching nerve.[33]

On April 18, 1875, Adjutant General Steele received a telegram from Sheriff John McClane of Nueces County: "Is McNelly coming? We are in trouble. Five ranches burned by disguised men near La Parra last week. Answer." Four days later, McClane got his answer. In the early gray of the morning on April 22, McNelly and his men crossed the Nueces, the captain and his young Rangers ready to a man to administer gunpowder justice.[34]

Already, even before McNelly's company crossed the brackish Nueces en route to the border, word had preceded them of the captain's method of bringing back bodies, not prisoners. As Ranger Bill Callicott wrote to historian Walter Prescott Webb years later, "[McNelly] had orders to deal with . . . [the bandits] the same way that Major [John] Jones dealt with the Indians; if caught on this side of the river with stolen cattle, kill them." Durham likewise recalled the Rangers' brutal method of shooting first and investigating later. Other Ranger captains before McNelly had "tried to fight according to the books as written in Austin. The military had to fight by the books as written in Washington. But those Nueces outlaws didn't fight by any books," Durham charged. "Neither did Captain McNelly. They made their own rules, and the Captain made his. They didn't mind killing. Neither did Captain McNelly. They didn't take prisoners. Neither did Captain McNelly."[35]

As a haunting reminder of the task before them, McNelly and his Rangers passed the body of a Mexican vaquero hanging high in a pecan tree as they rode quietly into Corpus Christi. The captain's first order of business was to disband the gangs of armed vigilantes roaming the rangelands of South Texas. Everywhere he rode, McNelly's word traveled ahead: regulators who took the law into their own hands and committed crimes would be considered no better than bandits. In short, they would be hunted down and shot on sight.

McNelly said as much in a written order that he issued publicly on April 27 from his headquarters at the Gorillas Ranch in Nueces County. What the *Corpus Christi Daily Express* critically termed a *"pronuncia-miento"* was vintage McNelly, short and to the point. "In consequence of the most recent outrages committed in this portion of the country by armed bands of men acting without authority of law, I find it necessary to notify all such organizations that after the publication of this order I will arrest all such bands." Then the order announced, "Nothing but the actual presence of some duly accredited officer of the county or state will protect them." No one could have mistaken the meaning of the message.[36]

Not all Anglo-Texans reacted favorably to McNelly's published order decreeing that all local militia companies stand down. The *San Antonio Daily Express* denounced the open letter as imperial and aimed at the wrong parties. "This is an extraordinary proclamation emanating from a Captain of a Corporal's guard sent by the so-called Governor of the State to the Rio Grande to extinguish the Mexican raiders," the editorial read. The stinging public indictment charged further that "it seems to be directed not against the Mexicans, but against the Americans." Calling the action "high handed," and referring to McNelly as "Captain of state police," the newspaper recalled the much-hated Radical Reconstruction administration of E. J. Davis: "Martial law had some semblance of author-ity then; but McNelly issues orders like an Emperor."[37]

Despite such criticism, McNelly stuck to his plan. He quickly recog-nized that companies of mounted vigilantes who prowled the brush coun-try south of the Nueces were not providing protection but were, in fact, part of the problem. "The acts committed by Americans are horrible to relate," he admitted to Adjutant General Steele. "Many ranches have been plundered and burned, and people murdered or driven away; one of these parties confessed to me as having killed eleven on their last raid." McNelly knew about the conclusions of Adjutant General Steele, who had observed the previous summer that "there is a disposition on the part of some Amer-icans . . . not to respect the property of Mexicans" and "a considerable ele-ment in the country . . . that think the killing of a Mexican no crime."[38]

At Sol Lichtenstein's dry-goods store on Chaparral Street in Corpus Christi, Captain McNelly met with Tom Noakes and Mike Dunn. Care-fully, the captain listened to them recount the recent raid. "He wanted all details," Durham recalled. "Captain seemed mighty concerned about those eighteen Dick Heye saddles," the young Ranger remembered. "He also asked Mike to describe the man who quirted Martha Noakes. Mike told him he was a two-pistoled American dressed in all the mail-order finery. 'Some taller than usual,' Mike added." Dunn explained that the fair-skinned, brown-haired bandit "had a heavy, deep scar, reaching from his hairline to the point of his chin, on the right side."[39]

Standing alongside McNelly, "Old Sol" (merchant Moritz Lichtenstein) interrupted the questioning and pointed out that he had some of those same saddles on order, but they had not come in yet. Young Durham remembered that the captain thought for a moment, then rasped, "When they come, don't sell a one until I tell you." Then he turned to Sergeant John Armstrong and instructed in a soft but commanding voice, "Describe those saddles to the Rangers. Make sure they understand exactly. Then order them to empty those saddles on sight. . . . Empty them. Leave the men where you drop them, and bring the saddles to camp." No other words were spoken, or needed. They understood the order.[40]

A quiet fell over the room as McNelly chewed on an unlit cigar. After several minutes, he turned to Old Sol and said apologetically, "The Legislature didn't give me a dime, but I've got to have some supplies." Before McNelly could say anything more, Lichtenstein explained that he had the biggest stock of firearms, ammunition, and field equipment between San Antonio and Brownsville. "Pick out . . . all you want," the storekeeper insisted. McNelly countered that Sol might have to wait for his money, and considering the fickle politicians in Austin he might not even get paid. "Let me worry about that," Sol reassured him.[41]

Then turning the conversation specifically to his supply of rifles, Sol encouraged McNelly to consider Henry or Winchester repeaters, or even Spencer carbines, the same type the U.S. Army contracted for its troopers. "How about Sharps?" McNelly inquired. Puzzled, Old Sol admitted that he had more than thirty in stock, but those were only of use to buffalo hunters. They were big game weapons, .50 caliber no less. "I want them," the captain answered. Sol responded that the heavy single-shot breech loaders might be perfect for hunting bison that would "not shoot back," but less than ideal in a fight with heavily armed bandits on horseback. A man would have to reload after every shot, Sol offered. McNelly interrupted, "I don't want men who miss."[42]

Upon first handling one of the Sharps, Durham remembered his first impression of the cumbersome but lethal rifle—McNelly's weapon of choice. "They were boogers. . . . That fifty-caliber bore looked big enough for a gopher to crawl through." As for the flat-nosed bullet, it was "as big as your thumb. It was plenty wicked. But no second chance." It was a sobering thought for a farm boy from Georgia who had never felt the sting of battle, or even thought much about killing or dying. If anything, Durham understated the case. The Sharps was a powerful weapon with an effective range of eight hundred meters. The border outlaws had nothing to match that, and Captain McNelly knew it.[43]

After procuring the Sharps rifles and enough cartridges for the campaign ahead, McNelly directed Lichtenstein to load his wagon with staples and cooking supplies: dried beef, beans, corn meal, flour, coffee, and various other victuals and incidentals. Then the captain issued a cryptic verbal warning to anyone who presumed the right to take the law into his own hands. Any posse or civilian militia in the field must be disbanded, by sundown. After that, any armed bands that his Rangers encountered would be considered outlaws. There would be no effort to discriminate between bandits and vigilantes, "deputized or not." All who were armed would be shot on sight, the captain announced in his wheezing voice. No exceptions.[44]

Delaying less than a day in Corpus Christi, McNelly and his men moved out, heading west. The captain ordered riders to the front and flanks of the column. For two days and nights squalls of heavy rains rolled into the region, bringing torrents that turned the ground into what Durham described as a "sticky gumbo." Along the trail, D. R. "Dad" Smith's wagon sank so deep into the thick bogs that the team of mules had to struggle to free the mud-caked wheels. Men and their mounts became rain soaked, but still they slogged on. As the flat coastal plain sprawled out ahead of them, there was nowhere for the waters to drain. Even when the horsemen rode upon high ground they were forced to compete with cattle, deer, and rattlesnakes that sought refuge there. At times the water on the ground was ankle high, which forced the Rangers to dismount and lead their mounts on foot. With the prairies almost impassable, McNelly and company could cover no more than five or six miles a day.[45]

Early on their third morning in the saddle they came upon the Little Oso, twelve miles south of Corpus Christi. What they found there, where a railroad trestle crossed the stream, was as disturbing as anything McNelly's young recruits could have imagined. Two Mexican vaqueros were hanging from the wooden trestle. Their necks were stretched, their heads bent to the side, their bodies left dangling and swinging in the ocean breeze.

As the Rangers rode slowly over the bridge, not a word was spoken. Not until the captain pulled up and announced that this was not the work of bandits or outlaws. A posse of vigilantes had strung up these two young men, no doubt. That is what self-appointed enforcers did when they were determined to "work off an old grudge," the captain explained without any emotion.[46]

Later that day, the company rode into the country crossroads of Banquete, an abandoned outpost with a population of one: William "Old W6" Wright, he was called, because his livestock bore the brand "W6" on their hips. Some said that the old man had just appeared one day with a branding iron and a .30 Winchester—and he knew how to use them. "Nobody knew where . . . [he] came from," Durham mused, "because nobody asked. You didn't ask such questions. It wasn't polite, and it was sort of risky. Where a man came from and what his maiden name was before coming to Texas was reckoned as his own affair."[47]

Wright approached Captain McNelly and explained that a stage driver from Austin had dropped off a package for him the day before. The box contained a stack of books, the curious Wright explained, as the captain reached in and withdrew one tome as thick as a mail-order catalog. The cowman chuckled that he was not in the book. He had looked to make sure. "The Book," as the Rangers came to call the heavy volume, was not the Bible, but you would not have known that by the way McNelly handled it, first thumbing it, then reading and studying it. He would carry it with him in the weeks and months ahead, right alongside his Holy Bible. He even shared copies with his lieutenants and sergeants, expecting it to be *their bible*, too. It was a directory of sorts, a catalog of criminals and fugitives from justice, page after page of wanted men from throughout the Lone Star State, bad men who had outstanding warrants for their arrest. The worst of the worst and all the rest—all were there—and the adjutant general of the state of Texas had compiled the book for his Ranger captains as well as local law enforcement officials.[48]

McNelly's company continued some twenty-five miles to Captain Richard King's Rancho Santa Gertrudis. There Captain McNelly and his men were greeted by the old hacendado himself. No more than five feet, six inches in height, maybe 130 pounds after a good meal, the clubfooted, gruff-looking Captain King limped up and introduced himself. "He wasn't too much to look at the first time," Durham recalled of the brown-haired, bearded cattleman. He did not appear to be the captain of anything, certainly not the king of any far-flung empire, not even one of short grass and beef cattle. But appearances were deceiving. The legendary rancher standing before them was the very same remarkable man who had acquired his well-deserved reputation as a resourceful though sometimes ruthless *empresario*, a man fearlessly determined to leave his "Running W" brand not only on his cattle, but also on the rangelands and the history of South Texas. There was a certain reserved dignity about him, a manner of propriety, yet a rough-hewn earthiness that made him more human than mythic. In sum, Richard King was not the kind of man to be underestimated.[49]

Neither was McNelly. As the Ranger captain and his men dismounted and pulled their saddles from their weary mounts, King commented on how poor the animals looked. "How in the world did you get this far on these nags?" he chuckled. "You must have had to walk some." McNelly sheepishly joked that the horses were all they had, and all that the state legislature would provide. He had a hunch that King would remedy that.[50]

Before dusk Captain King first made sure that McNelly's "boys" had the grand tour of the ranch house, which towered more than sixty feet above the plain, its steeple commanding a view of the rangelands for miles around. King showed them his personal arsenal—racks of repeating rifles, shotguns, and revolvers, any weapon even a Texan could imagine. Stacked boxes of cartridges also filled the room, giving the place the appearance of a fortress. Then Captain King ordered his kitchen workers to feed McNelly and his troops the only square meal they had eaten in two weeks. Afterward, he directed them from the "grub house" to a long bunkhouse, where rows of mattresses complete with bed linens and pillows lined the walls. The night must have been welcome to young men who had been sleeping on the ground, with nothing more than a blanket for a bedroll, a saddle for a headrest, and a canvas tent for a roof.[51]

The sun rose too quickly. At the first light of morning, McNelly and his Rangers awakened to the sounds of Captain King's cowhands rounding up horses in a nearby corral. Los Kineños, the vaqueros proudly called themselves, and they were exceptional horsemen. With King shouting orders in Spanish, the ranch hands were cutting out the best of the lot. Tossing a lasso over each animal and leading them into an adjacent barn, the vaqueros were preparing the horses for the long ride ahead. Fresh mounts, and new or repaired saddle and tack, would be provided any man who needed them, King bellowed. As for Captain McNelly, King personally selected a large, magnificent bay. Segal, they had named him, and he stood out among the bunch. Tall and well formed, like the rest of the horses, he could take a rider as far as he needed to go—to Mexico, or even hell and back if necessary.[52]

As was the case with Old Sol's Sharps carbines and cartridges in Corpus Christi, McNelly had no authorization to promise King that the state of Texas would ever reimburse him. But that mattered little to King, who explained that he would rather McNelly and his Rangers than the border bandits ride off on his best horses. But the big bay that King had saddled for him must cost $500, McNelly interrupted. Shaking his head, King bitterly complained that the thieves had stolen enough of his stock. Even if he never saw a dime of payment, he would be no worse off. The soft-spoken Captain McNelly thanked him.[53]

Perhaps George Durham put it best. As the Rangers rode out of Santa Gertrudis early in the morning, they appeared "a lot different outfit from the motley crew that Captain had flung together" more than two weeks earlier in Burton. "We were forted and ready for anything." On a more personal level, Durham remembered, "I felt mighty chesty. For the first time in my life I had a prime bit of horse flesh between my knees, and that always does something to a man."[54]

The Paint Horse Gallows

Captain McNelly led his company of young Rangers southward toward the border. Over the next several days they skirted the "Big Sands" of the Wild Horse Desert, which sprawls along the Gulf Coastal Plain for more than seventy-five miles. Along their route, they observed much evidence of the recent range war: an occasional burned out and abandoned cabin, cattle roaming unclaimed, Tejanos with all their worldly belongings piled into mule-drawn carts and wagons heading to some place of safety. Most disturbing, however, was the grisly sight of another Mexican vaquero dangling from a mesquite tree, a noose around his neck. No doubt, McNelly knew, the young man had been the victim of vigilante vengeance, just like the other two left hanging from the railroad trestle near Banquete.[55]

Heavy spring rains continued to turn the coastal plain into a quagmire, slowing McNelly's advance. Not until May 14 did Company A, Washington County Volunteers, McNelly's Special Force of Rangers, ride into the village of Edinburg (then located on the river). Tired, drenched, his boots covered with mud, McNelly dashed off a letter to Adjutant General Steele that afternoon, informing him that the company was now camped within ten miles of the Rio Grande. "I met [Ranger] Captain [Neal] Coldwell yesterday," McNelly began, "but think he is disinclined to take chances in crossing the river (which is not a ten foot rise). [General Juan] Cortina was on the opposite side yesterday and hung an alcalde and another Mexican for killing one of his cattle thieves. Can't say anything yet about the conditions of affairs here," he continued. "Everyone says that stealing is going on constantly, but Captain Coldwell thinks most of the reports are false."[56]

As it turned out, Coldwell, commander of Company F of the Frontier Battalion, was the one who was wrong. Perhaps at first only McNelly sensed that. But soon, every one of his Rangers would as well. Each day McNelly's scouting parties returned to camp with more reports of rustlers crossing the river into Mexico, trailing huge dust clouds of cattle bearing Texas brands. Allegedly, these cattle thieves were in the employ of General Juan Cortina, the same "Red Robber of the Rio Grande" who had long been the chief nemesis of Anglo-Texans on the border. By mid-May, McNelly had bivouacked at Rancho Las Rucias in Cameron County, a few miles upriver from Brownsville. For the next two weeks, he worked to establish a spy network, one that would bring him all the reliable information he needed. During the first week in June, acting on information gathered by his spies operating above and below the river, the captain ordered seventeen of his Rangers to ride off to La Parra, north of Brownsville. The next day McNelly's scouts picked up the tracks of a small party of raiders herding cattle southward to the banks of the Rio Grande. Within forty-eight hours the Rangers had trailed and then captured two of the suspected bandits.[57]

Both prisoners suffered the misfortune of being turned over to Jesús Sandoval, one of McNelly's spies recruited for his prowess as a tracker, his knowledge of the river and his resolve to kill bandits. It soon became apparent that Sandoval's skills also included torturing captives into confessions—and he enjoyed his work. The cattle thieves could not have had a more terrifying enemy. "Old Casuse" (pronounced "Casoose"), as the Rangers butchered his name, was a rangy, brooding figure, with shoulder-length auburn hair and a beard speckled with gray. Durham recollected that Casuse was "what you would call spooky" in appearance. "He looked like a crazy man," Durham remembered—a man who lived only to kill and to have his revenge against Cortina's rustlers, who had reportedly raided his Rancho Estero Grande, some fifteen miles upriver from Brownsville the previous year. By some accounts, during Sandoval's absence from the ranch, raiders had raped his wife and fifteen-year-old daughter, burned his barn and ranch house to the ground, and stolen his livestock, all the time threatening that they would soon return to kill him and his family if they continued to cooperate with "gringo" officials. His "fierce, glittering eyes," as Ranger Napoleon Jennings recalled, revealed the hate that he harbored and the terrible vengeance he sought. It was rumored that, just days before joining up with McNelly, Sandoval had hanged four alleged thieves from the same tree near the river, leaving their corpses dangling as a reminder to other bandits who crossed the border.[58]

Now Old Casuse used the same gruesome method to extract information from the two captives taken near La Parra. Sandoval took each to an isolated tree, tied a rope around the prisoner's neck, tossed it over a limb, then hoisted the man two to three feet into the air, strangling him for several moments before lowering him back to ground. Casuse repeated the grisly ritual several times until the suspected spy had apparently told all that he knew. "As far as we knew," Callicott speculated, "this treatment always brought out the truth."[59]

After McNelly was satisfied with the confessions, he left the captives with Casuse, who tied a hangman's noose, looped it over each prisoner's head, and one at a time forced them to stand in the saddle of his tall paint horse. Then Sandoval walked behind the animal and slapped him on the backside, causing him to dash away, thus strangling the life from the victim. "Captain McNelly didn't like this kind of killing," Callicott insisted, "but Casuse did." As Callicott remembered further, "We caught several spies on that scout . . . and Casuse dealt with all of them alike, showing no partiality—he always made them a present of six feet of rope."[60]

Years later Ranger S. N. Hardy, who served under Captain McNelly, confirmed stories of the "paint horse gallows" to famed folklorist J. Frank Dobie. "One night while we were camped on the Rio Grande, I was in charge of the guard," Hardy recalled. "Sandoval was keeping watch, and along about midnight I heard him cursing a blue streak in both Mexican and English. I went down to see what the trouble was." What Hardy described next was a ghastly scene. "When I got near the river," he recollected, "I saw an empty skiff, which had come over from the Mexican side. Also I saw Sandoval on a horse riding against a taut rope that was hitched to his saddle horn. The other end of the rope was tied to the neck of a Mexican . . . [whose] feet were tied to a mesquite bush. After he got through pulling, he dismounted and showed me another Mexican whose throat had been cut to the bone." Before young Hardy could inquire about their crimes, Old Casuse "explained that these two victims were the last of the gang who had burned his home and ruined his wife and daughter. I did not say anything to Captain McNelly until months later. Lots of things happened on the Rio Grande that never got into the ranger reports," Hardy admitted.[61]

The well-dressed and fair-complexioned Sandoval spoke with a kind voice, in a tone befitting a priest. But what little English he knew revealed the truth behind his mild manner. Bill Callicott insisted that, other than a few choice phrases like "God damn them" and "kill them all," Sandoval stuck to his native Spanish. Jokingly, some of the boys insisted that Casuse could speak two languages—Spanish and profanity.[62]

No wonder. What English he attempted was so badly mangled that few could even barely understand him. The ranchero would come to call his fellow Rangers, most of whom he only knew by name, simply "*muy bravos hombres*"; by that, he meant *valientes*, or "fearless." Of the scraggly-looking Sandoval, Durham wrote, "His skin was dry and parched, and his light blue eyes seem to throw off sparks." Napoleon Jennings later described Casuse as a thin, angular figure in a panther-skin vest, as "sinewy and strong and as active as any man I ever saw." An "extremely graceful rider and a daring one," according to Jennings, Sandoval "did not differ from hundreds of Mexicans on that border, except he was rather taller." He carried a "haughty bearing," as if he somehow believed himself to be better than others of his nationality.[63]

Lieutenant T. C. Robinson recorded that Sandoval appeared to be the "perfect Chesterfield in politeness; he puts us to shame by the elegance of his manners." Robinson further observed that, even on the occasions when Old Casuse "officiated" at a "tucking up," or hanging, he insisted on proper decorum. "He is so kind and considerate that it . . . [would] almost be a pleasure to be hanged by such a nice gentleman."[64]

The reality, however, was no joking matter. It was well known that the seemingly meek Old Casuse had a score to settle with the border bandits. Despite being named for the Prince of Peace, he earned his reputation as McNelly's "hangman." One Mexican newspaper from the border state of Tamaulipas carried a chilling account of Sandoval's method of executing prisoners. *Voz del pueblo* (voice of the people) of Matamoros published a report accusing McNelly's Rangers of summarily lynching captives "with impunity." The article even singled out Jesús Sandoval by name as McNelly's chief executioner. Based on accounts from purported eyewitnesses, the newspaper offered in graphic detail how Sandoval "enjoyed his work." The article described how he would tie the hands and feet of a captive, then placing a noose around the vaquero's neck, he would remove his hat, drop to his knees, and make the sign of the cross. Offering a few words from the scriptures and a short prayer, he would call the victim by name, pronounce him guilty, and "grasp his hand, telling him, *adios* my good friend, goodbye." With that short ritual, the newspaper claimed, Sandoval conducted his executions with the knowledge and approval of his captain, also identified by name—McNelly.[65]

Perhaps General Edward O. C. Ord, commander of the Department of Texas headquartered in San Antonio, stated it most succinctly. Obviously with some knowledge of lynching conducted by Texas state troops, he confessed that McNelly "had a big advantage" over the U.S. Army "mainly because he employed means of getting information from prisoners that was denied the military. His prisoners would talk. Ours wouldn't."[66]

In the border city of Matamoros, local legend has it that an enigmatic blind woman walked the dusty streets and crowded markets in those days. Some said that, despite the cataracts that clouded her eyes, the wizened old lady could see things that others could not. They claimed that she possessed a gift of prophecy. Whether she could see and predict the future, many believed that she possessed some unexplained mystical power. Some feared her, and a few even heeded her message of impending doom. Like a modern-day Jeremiah, the aged woman with gnarled fingers and white hair stringing to her shoulders presented a striking, even strange figure on street corners and in the public squares. No matter if bystanders stopped to listen to her admonition of the coming of the end days, the self-proclaimed seer still spoke of an impending apocalypse—the final judgment that was at hand. All must repent of their sins and prepare now, she warned her listeners, for the time foretold in St. John's Revelations was upon them. The Almighty had allowed her a glimpse of hell's fury. She had seen the dreaded reaper of Satan, or so she claimed. Death was coming, and coming soon, she cried, and he was riding alongside the devil on a pale horse. And as the scripture proclaimed, "Hell followed with him."[67]

Of course, the soothsayer's lamentations that the horsemen of the apocalypse would soon descend and bring wrath and judgment upon the land never materialized, at least not in a literal sense. But in the spring of 1875 some of the more superstitious people on both sides of the border must have wondered. For when McNelly and his Rangers arrived on the Rio Grande word quickly spread of the presence of Los Rinches. Within days of reaching the border McNelly left camp at Las Rucias with a small escort of Rangers by his side and traveled to Brownsville to interview local authorities about the ongoing contagion of cattle theft and violence along the river. No doubt, late in May when he rode through the streets of Brownsville astride a tall spirited bay steed named Segal, with the ghostly looking figure of Jesús Sandoval and his paint horse alongside, the news had already preceded them: "Los Diablos Tejanos," the Texas Devils, had returned to the border, and hell would follow with them.[68]

8
Texas Devils

In springtime the prairies of South Texas unfold before the traveler like a colorful quilt of wildflowers and other native blooms. By April the land awakens as the huisache trees with their yellow blossoms come alive and giant yuccas with their white spires reach upward toward the heavens. The red-blossomed Indian paintbrush and beautiful bluebonnets blanket the landscape, as do patches of white and yellow daffodils, daisies, and a dozen other colorful plants that grow in the wild. The green palmetto comes alive, too, its leaves fanning out like the feathers of a wild turkey. Even the thickets of mesquite begin to bear fruit, or more accurately beans, which sustain wildlife and livestock alike. The prickly pear cactus, the withered creosote, and the stunted chaparral survive the mild winter and promise the traveler difficult passage through this dreary landscape of rolling dunes and scrub brush. Despite its scars and its imperfections, each April and May the Wild Horse Desert, an apt name for this desolate swath of coastal plain, retains a certain charm and appeal. Everywhere there is proof that even in this forsaken land there is beauty.

No wonder that Anglos and Tejanos alike who live there take such pride in their home. The country holds a grandeur and mystique all its own. This semiarid Big Sands country, which crawls southward from present-day Falfurrias to Raymondville, could also be called foreboding and unforgiving. During summer the sunbaked dunes radiate enough heat to blister both men and animals. In those long afternoons, when the sun arcs high, even rattlesnakes avoid the sprawling sands. But the diamondbacks are somewhere out there. Huddling in the sparse shade, the white-tailed deer avoid the heat of day. The short-legged javelina—the wild hog native to this country—also roots and takes cover from the searing heat. So do the elusive coyotes that dart about the thickets, then disappear from sight. Equally shy cougars and bobcats prowl, usually at night. But they too are there.[1]

Swooping overhead, the red-tailed hawk and its cousin the Cooper's hawk command the skies. Majestic predators, they keep watch from above, forever searching for field mice, lizards, snakes, and any living creatures that might be unaware of their presence. An occasional turkey vulture hangs in the air, gliding, swinging, and sometimes descending to the earth, reminding pilgrims that the harsh land has claimed another victim.

Danger is always lurking somewhere south of the Nueces. For many miles, there are few waterholes along the way, and they are far between. What pools that exist are often brackish owing to briny sediment and the salt-laden ocean air. Some of the adventurous who have traveled across this inhospitable landscape have likened it to a purgatory, a place of punishment, suffering, and remorse that precedes the entrance to hell. The summer heat is oppressive and impartial, and the soaring temperatures are only made worse by the stifling humidity that sticks in the air. Something about this land defies description in anything other than the most common of terms: open, spacious, strange, and remote.

But perhaps only one word best captures the distinct character of the country: emptiness. There is an inexplicable void there, a sense that a traveler is nowhere and yet, somehow, between somewhere and somewhere else. It is no ordinary land.

During the rainy season the downpours never seem to stop. Then during the dry season the drought never seems to end. As some cowboys liked to muse about the Big Sands, whatever grows from the ground will stick you, and whatever crawls and slithers across the parched earth will either sting you or bite you. To be sure, this desolate country is no place for the meek and mild mannered. It is not a country for the timid. Understandably, in the spring of 1875 when Captain McNelly and his men rode through the Wild Horse Desert, headed for the "Lower Country," as some Texans termed the Rio Grande Valley, they must have sensed that danger.

As it turned out, an inferno of violence and lawlessness awaited the Rangers, and their captain knew that, even if the boys in his company did not. Some of his young recruits may have sensed it. But they had not been where McNelly had been. Most had never seen death firsthand. Still, they must have wondered, at least to themselves: how could the captain be so reserved, so calm, so detached, so certain of himself and yet so uncertain and seemingly unconcerned about what lay ahead? Perhaps they thought, or even whispered to one another, that the captain had seen so much death while fighting Yankees during the Louisiana campaigns a decade earlier, that he had stared down the barrel so often while in the service of Governor Davis's state police, that he had been immunized from fear. After all, some of the Rangers had been with him in DeWitt County when he had faced down the hired gunslingers of Creed Taylor and William Sutton the previous year. It was almost as if the captain had stood in the crosshairs of danger his entire adult life. And now, they realized, he was slowly dying of the "lung fever," or "consumption." To such a man as Leander McNelly, who had experienced so much more than his thirty-one years, death was not a stranger but a constant companion.[2]

McNelly was not afraid to meet his Maker. But he was not cut out just to sit and wait for him. He would rather ride out, unafraid, and meet him on his own terms.

McNelly's Spies

To his credit, Captain McNelly understood well that courage alone would not defeat the border bandits. They were brave men, too. He needed information, reliable information about their movements, their methods, their habits, their hideouts. He wanted to know the locations of their favorite river crossings, the fords where they swam cattle across the river into Mexico. He wanted to know who hired them, who paid them, and how much. He wanted to know who bought their stolen livestock, and where the herds were being driven to market. He wanted to know where the bandits slept, what they ate, and what they feared most. He wanted to know everything about them.

To that end, he developed a network of spies—men he could trust—to infiltrate Juan Cortina's cattle rustling operations south of the river. He needed agents who would bring him all the information they could gather, and he did not care how they obtained it. George Durham remembered that not long after McNelly established camp near the Laguna Larga at Rancho Las Rucias, about midway between the towns of Edinburg and Brownsville, several men appeared that he had never seen before. One of the mysterious figures politely introduced himself in his native Spanish as Jesús Sandoval.[3]

Another unfamiliar rider who showed up one day at the captain's tent was the large sandy-haired figure of Herman S. Rock. The Rangers had no idea yet that "Old Rock" was a mounted inspector of hides and brands for Cameron County. All they knew at first was that he appeared to be working for or with the captain and against the cattle thieves. The muscular, chiseled Herman Rock was aptly named. Physically imposing but quiet, even distant, he seemed to suit his name. The young men of McNelly's company no doubt noted that he was the type who ruled this country, the kind who showed others that the land belonged to those who were determined enough to take it.[4]

As much as anyone, Herman Rock became the foundation of McNelly's network of spies. Unlike the captain, he cursed like a mule skinner, even to the point that his profanity almost became an art form. Like Jesús Sandoval, "Old Rock" knew every cattle trail and backcountry trace in the county. He also knew every foot of the river and every turn in its channel. Rock brought with him another able scout, just as familiar with the terrain and landmarks along the river. His name was Lino Saldana, and he also served as Cameron County deputy sheriff. Being of Mexican heritage, speaking his native Spanish and English, he held an advantage in this country. Other locals who were enlisted by McNelly included Macedonio Longoria, Timoteo Solis, and Matias Serata, all Tejanos who volunteered to help the captain track down Cortina's rustlers.[5]

But the most successful of McNelly's spies may well have been one of his own recruits, Sergeant George A. Hall, who had served with McNelly in the state police. The fact that Hall successfully embedded himself in Cortina's inner circle of cattle thieves that summer lends credence to Mexican claims that so many of the cow thieves were citizens not of Mexico but of the United States, and specifically Texas. Remarkably, the amiable young Hall managed to blend in with the bandits, gaining their trust and even helping them supervise the shipment of cattle to markets as far away as Cuba, the greater Caribbean, and Central America.[6]

McNelly also relied on daily scouting parties. His experience during the late war had taught him that a good commander needed riders in the advance to be his eyes and ears—daring horsemen always willing to venture out on a reconnaissance, sometimes in pairs, or even alone if necessary, regardless of the peril. The captain wanted men who could be relied on, men who possessed cunning and daring that equaled or even exceeded that of their foes.

Meanwhile, on May 19 Captain McNelly rode into Brownsville, and for three days he met with local officials and interviewed victims of the border violence. While no record exists of any conversations with the legendary sage of Brownsville, John S. Ford, Old Rip must have been consulted for advice. As thorough an investigator as McNelly would not have missed the opportunity to gain insight from the graying former Ranger captain who knew more about the border troubles than any man alive. After all, as a young volunteer in the war with Mexico, Rip Ford had been schooled in the unconventional military arts by none other than the most famous Ranger of them all, Colonel John Coffee "Jack" Hays, *el diablo* himself. Beginning in 1868, for a few years Ford had served as hide and brand inspector for Cameron County. In 1872, he had been elected foreman of a federal grand jury for the Eastern District of Texas and in that capacity

guided his fellow jurors to demand more U.S. cavalry forces to patrol and
protect the lower Rio Grande from predators who crept up from Mexico.
In 1874 he had even been elected to the post of mayor of Brownsville for
one term, surprising his family and friends alike that he had the stomach
for politics, even at the local level. Anyone who read the *Brownsville Sentinel* in recent years could not have escaped the message of its editor, John
S. Ford, that the border bandits must be hunted and confronted. Nothing
less than force would restore law and order to the north banks of the Rio
Grande and the Nueces Strip beyond.[7]

During his stay at the Miller Hotel on Elizabeth Street, McNelly also
spoke with Cameron County sheriff James G. Browne, city marshal
Joseph P. O'Shaughnessy, and Major Henry C. Merriam of the Thirty-
Eighth Infantry stationed at Fort Brown. Then he interviewed other
prominent citizens of Brownsville about the border crisis. McNelly was
a good listener, and what he learned during his first days on the border
only convinced him that the situation was, if possible, even worse than he
had been led to believe. Not surprisingly, most town leaders, among them
Cameron County justice of the peace Cornelius Stillman, encouraged
Captain McNelly to strike the bandits whenever and wherever they could
be found. No doubt some local citizens suggested that the Rangers might
have to carry the fight across the Rio Grande, into Mexico. Maybe longtime Brownsville merchant William Neale best summarized the frustrations and determination of many of the town's people when he described
the "years of terror" on the lower Rio Grande, noting that "a man's life
was only worth his backbone . . . [since] his life depended on how quick he
was on the trigger." Always reminding others that Cortinistas had brutally
gunned down his own son, William Peter Neale, during the Brownsville
disturbances of 1859, the elder Neale admitted that he still slept with
loaded firearms beside his bed. "There was no telling when one of these
cold-hearted murderers would kill you for fifty cents," he later recalled.
Neale's conversations with McNelly, like those the captain likely had with
Rip Ford, must have been a clear call for action.[8]

Local leaders provided McNelly with the same perspective that would
be reflected several months later in the report of a so-called Permanent
Committee of Safety appointed at a town meeting of Brownsville residents
one month before McNelly's arrival. In sum, as reflected by the committee's composition, their interest in "public safety" was closely entangled
with their determination to protect the commercial interests of local merchants, stockmen, and steamship owners. Other than Old Rip Ford and

Sheriff James Browne, the body included district customs collector John L. Haynes, county hide and brand inspector Herman S. Rock, banker Francisco Yturria, former postmaster Robert B. Kingsbury, and storekeepers and landowners like Jeremiah Galvan, William Neale, Adolphus Glavecke, and Treveno Garza.[9]

For their first three weeks patrolling the border, McNelly's spies returned almost daily with only general information about the activities of cattle thieves staging south of the river. That changed on Saturday, June 5. After receiving word that a raiding party of sixteen rustlers had crossed the Rio Grande some eight miles below Brownsville, McNelly ordered eighteen of his Rangers under the command of Lieutenant T. C. "Pidge" Robinson to scour the river in hopes of intercepting them. On June 8, near a ford upriver from Rancho Palmito, Robinson's scouts rode upon and captured a suspicious vaquero, Rafael Salinas, who admitted that he and his fellow rustlers had crossed the river near La Parra with the intention of stealing a drove of cattle. Three days later a second raider fell into the hands of Robinson's scouts. Identified as Encarnacion Garcia, another known Cortina associate, the prisoner was also persuaded to talk, and he corroborated the story that Salinas had told. No doubt, after their "interview," both captives soon confessed to their interrogators. Fortunately for the prisoners, Old Casuse was not among this scouting party, or else they might not have lived to be turned over later to the custody of Sheriff Browne. Few captive rustlers that summer escaped the infamous paint-horse gallows. Apparently, Salinas and Garcia did.[10]

In the meantime, Captain McNelly returned to Brownsville, in part to talk to more witnesses, in part to rest and recuperate with his wife, Carrie, and son, Rebel. William Neale of Brownsville remembered the pleasant June evening when he was sitting with McNelly and others on the porch of the Miller Hotel, long the finest establishment in all Brownsville. In the presence of several local leaders who were relaxing with the captain, one of McNelly's spies, Matias Serata, galloped up with word that a band of rustlers was driving a large drove of cattle near the Reparo Ranch north of town. The thieves were herding the beeves toward the river, he reported. Neale recalled that McNelly said little, then rose from his chair, walked down the street to the telegraph office located in the Yturria building, and sent a message to his command encamped at the Hacienda Santa Maria, near Las Rucias. The Rangers were to assemble, saddle up, "put spurs" to their horses, and meet him before sunrise at the Reparo Ranch on the Palo Alto Prairie. The men should come prepared for action. While no record of the telegram has survived, the captain no doubt inferred that men were going to die the next day, and that he planned on the cow thieves doing all the dying.[11]

The Palo Alto Fight

For Captain McNelly there could have been no better place for bloodletting than the Palo Alto Prairie. After all, the plain was the sight of the inaugural battle of the war with Mexico in 1846. Maybe it was fitting, therefore, that what happened early on that Saturday morning, June 12, 1875, was a running gun battle smaller in scale but equal in ferocity to that earlier campaign. After trailing the bandits through the predawn darkness, McNelly moved in and located them at a salt marsh soon after sunrise. By then, an early morning fog had lifted, and McNelly could look out through his field glasses upon the waters of a sprawling *laguna* and the surrounding wetlands. "On arriving I found . . . [the raiders] drawn up in a line on the south side of a marsh about six hundred yards wide, filled with mud and water, eighteen to twenty inches deep," McNelly later recorded. The rustlers had driven their herd onto a small island surrounded by the boggy plain. The captain surveyed the scene through his telescope; then he ordered his men to form a skirmish line, but did not yet allow them to unsling their Sharps carbines or draw their pistols. McNelly commanded the column to advance slowly, at a deliberate pace, toward the cattle thieves. As soon as the Rangers closed to within four hundred meters, the bandits dismounted and opened fire with repeating rifles, but their rounds fell harmlessly in front of their pursuers who continued forward at a slow gait to within one hundred meters. As Durham recalled, the thieves were "well forted for a standoff," as if they were expecting help. Then, just as McNelly's men moved to within pistol range, perhaps fifty meters at most, the thieves leaped upon their horses, wheeled around, and galloped away. Attempting to escape, they even abandoned their cattle as they raced toward the Rio Grande. In anticipation of such a retreat, however, the captain had already ordered three of his best riders and sharpshooters into a timberline to flank them and "force a stand."[12]

What followed was a series of skirmishes extending over five or six miles. When the bandits broke out in groups of two or three and scattered over the prairie, the Rangers spurred their mounts in pursuit, Captain McNelly leading the way, urging his men to move in and "powder burn" the enemy at close range. Durham remembered that the captain's big bay, Segal, "took off like a turpentined cat," mud flying up from his hooves as the chase began. At a full gallop, McNelly's men raced after the rustlers. One by one the Rangers gunned them down, several of the raiders first having their horses shot from under them. "I have never seen men fight with such desperation," McNelly later reported. "Many of them, after being shot from their horses and severely wounded three or four times, would rise on their elbows [in the mud] and fire at my men as they passed."[13]

McNelly overhauled one of the fleeing raiders, shooting his fleet mount several times, sending the horse tumbling into the mud. The injured rider staggered to his feet and scrambled through the ankle-deep water toward the tall marsh grass known as Spanish dagger. As the captain dismounted and approached the vaquero, the man suddenly emerged from the brush wielding a knife. Apparently, the bandit had emptied his pistol and thought McNelly had done the same. He was mistaken. Calmly, while the rustler raced toward him brandishing a large blade McNelly aimed his revolver and, in Callicott's words, "placed the last shot he had between the bandit's teeth as if he had put it there with his fingers."[14]

The boyish "Sonny" Smith was neither as experienced nor as lucky as his captain. After one bandit fell from his horse and lay motionless for a few moments, apparently dead, young Smith slid from his saddle, holstered his pistol, and approached the lifeless body. But when Smith came near, the wounded man suddenly turned over and shot him dead, then crawled into a pond a few feet away and disappeared into the thick marsh reeds.[15]

Meantime, Captain McNelly had shot and mortally wounded another rustler, who had been thrown from his horse. The captain disarmed the wounded man, later identified as Guadalupe Espinosa. Removing his black beaver hat and placing a hand on the dying man, McNelly paused to recite scriptures to the injured vaquero as he drew his last breaths. Moments later, however, when McNelly arrived at the lagoon several hundred yards away, he saw Sonny Smith's body and learned that the boy's killer was hiding somewhere in the marsh. Visibly upset, the captain paced back and forth. He calmly asked where Smith's killer was hiding. One young recruit pointed to the nearby pond that was filled with tall reeds. McNelly scanned the lagoon, then seeing a slight movement in the murky water, he ordered every Ranger present to surround the area and open fire on a suspicious looking clump of rush grass. When the shooting finally stopped, the bandit's thrashing body floated to the surface, bloodied and riddled with bullets. William Neale of Brownsville remembered that the man's carcass was so full of holes that "you could almost use him as a sieve to sift flour."[16]

By the time the shooting had stopped, Old Casuse had ridden up in hopes of catching the rustler alive. But he was too late. That, however, did not stop him from tossing a lariat over the dead man's head, tying the rope to his pommel horn and dragging the body from the water, then across the muddy plain.[17]

By late morning the Palo Alto fight was finished. Carefully, the Rangers tied young Smith's body across his horse and led him back to Brownsville, where they prepared to bury him with full military honors. Dad Smith was inconsolable. Later in the day his son's remains were laid out in the camp chapel at Fort Brown, and an undertaker was called in to prepare the corpse to be placed in a handcrafted pine coffin.[18]

As for the dead raiders, they were treated with less respect. The Rangers roped their bodies, dragged them through the mud for more than a mile, then with the help of Brownsville city marshal Joseph P. O'Shaughnessy piled them into a wagon. Later that afternoon McNelly and his men rode into the Brownsville town plaza, unloaded the corpses, and in the words of George Durham, "stacked them like cordwood" for all to see. This act was Captain McNelly's unmistakable message to other cattle rustlers: steal livestock and be prepared to suffer the consequence.[19]

As word spread of the ghoulish display, so did anger and sorrow. Most, if not all, of the dead had family on both sides of the river. McNelly's sentries guarded the bodies through the night, not allowing grieving relatives and friends to claim them and carry them away. It was a *noche triste*, or "night of sorrows," that the people of Brownsville would not soon forget. Threats of reprisal were quick in coming from Matamoros, and wild rumors circulated even in Brownsville that the deceased—several of whom resided in town—were all respectable citizens of the border. So incensed was General Cortina that he reportedly threatened to lead his private army of as many as five hundred armed men across the river to avenge the deaths of his brave vaqueros. Jennings recounted that McNelly sent word to Matamoros that "he would be waiting for" Cortina. But that showdown never happened.[20]

The physical evidence gathered by Captain McNelly and local authorities told a different story from that of Cortina and his loyalists. The cattle rounded up at the Palo Alto Prairie all bore Texas brands, notable among them the famed "Running W" of Captain King's Santa Gertrudis Ranch, and all the animals were later confirmed to be stolen. The Rangers also retrieved eight unique Dick Heye saddles, unmistakably among those taken from Tom Noakes's store during the recent raid on Nuecestown.

One of the corpses, an Anglo marked by a distinctive crescent-shaped scar on the right cheek, was later identified as an outlaw known as Jack Ellis, the same man who had flogged Martha Noakes when she had resisted the raiders while they looted and burned her home. Still another dead outlaw was even wearing the same new suit of clothes that had been stripped off the body of a murdered stockman, schoolteacher and former county sheriff's deputy William McMahan, north of Brownsville only days earlier. The bandits had tortured the helpless McMahan, reportedly cutting off his hands and feet and putting out his eyes before they shot him in the head. The horribly mutilated body was later discovered by justice of the peace Cornelius Stillman, who reported that he gathered up and buried the scattered remains where he found them.[21]

One of the vaqueros shot down at the Palo Alto was reportedly found alive, although barely. Jennings recorded that José María Olguin, known to locals as El Aguja, "the Needle," was transported to the Brownsville jail where, according to some accounts, he later died of his wounds. But other evidence suggests that Olguin escaped jail (if he was ever there at all) and later returned to his thieving ways before finally being arrested, convicted of cattle rustling and sentenced to prison in Huntsville, where he died in 1880. William Neale remembered, however, that a bandit named Librado Mendez later testified that Olguin had brutally murdered poor McMahan, and that the Needle had escaped the battle at the Palo Alto Prairie, only to be captured months later and shot by a Ranger while "trying to make his escape." Like so many others, he was a victim of *la ley de fuga*, or "the law of flight." But historian Jerry Thompson insists that a badly injured "Holguin" crawled away from the Palo Alto fight and crossed the river to Matamoros, where he recovered from his wounds. How did the Needle meet his end? As people say along the border, "*Quién sabe?*" But it seems certain that the hapless cattle thief did not long continue weaving and threading his way through danger. One way or the other, he found an early grave.[22]

There is little controversy, however, that the dead rustlers included Camalo Lerma, the apparent leader of the outfit (later identified as Smith's killer) and, like Espinosa and Olguin, a known associate of Juan Cortina. If anyone expected Captain McNelly to express any regrets or offer any apologies to Cortina or anyone else, they simply did not know him. Late that morning following the fight, the gun smoke had hardly cleared the air when Cameron County sheriff James G. Browne rode upon the scene. Still stinging from the fact that two of Captain McNelly's men had mistakenly arrested and detained one of his deputy sheriffs, Lino Saldana, the previous day, Browne unloaded his complaints, exchanged words with McNelly, and then insisted that the captain provide him with a full account of the gunfight at the Palo Alto. But McNelly had no intention of doing that. He knew that he had the backing of Governor Coke, and more important he had forty well-armed and mounted Rangers behind him. He simply did not need to worry himself with such demands. Besides, diplomacy was not his strength, nor his concern.[23]

On the night of June 12 one that was in Durham's words "heavy with fight," at the Brownsville town plaza a squad of McNelly's Rangers stood guard over the corpses. A quiet tension gripped the town. Still, as Durham recalled, "Nobody came to try and get one [of the bodies], and none of the dead bandits tried to leave." The rustlers' decomposing remains were left on display until the sun was high the next day.[24]

The smell of death still hung in the air the following night. Confident that he had brought in bandits, not honest businessmen, on June 14 McNelly telegraphed Adjutant General Steele in Austin: "Had a fight with raiders, killed twelve and captured two hundred and sixty-five beeves. Wish you were here." Characteristically, the captain was a man of few words. He preferred to intimidate the border rustlers with actions. That, McNelly insisted, was the only language the bandits truly understood.[25]

McNelly's next opportunity for a show of force came several days later. Sonny Smith's funeral turned out to be a scene befitting a fallen hero. After a public viewing of the body at city hall, the Rangers placed the flag-draped casket on a flat wagon. Smith's horse, empty saddle and all, was tied to the rear of the wagon. An honor guard that included Major Merriam and the legendary Ranger Captain John S. Ford headed the solemn procession, with McNelly's entire command following the cortege. The captain and his young Rangers walked two abreast, their revolvers strapped to their hips in plain view. A military band played a dirge and a few stirring refrains in tribute to the deceased, but few other fanfares and flourishes marked the event, only quiet, gawking crowds lining the streets. No sounds to interrupt the silence could be heard other than the muffled clomping of horse hooves. Through the town to the market square they marched, and back to the Fort Brown cemetery for internment. All along the way, some in the crowd, mostly those of Mexican heritage, glared at Los Rinches as they passed. Still, all things considered, it was a sad but impressive spectacle, in Bill Callicott's words the "finest funeral that had ever taken place in the little town of Brownsville."[26]

In contrast, the dead bandits were buried together in a shallow grave outside town. They received no ceremonies, memorials, or headstones. McNelly made sure of that. In the hot summer weeks that followed, McNelly's spies continued to slip across the river to learn more about the movements and activities of Cortina's vaqueros. In the meantime, however, the captain made no effort to hide his intentions. His Rangers made themselves plainly visible patrolling the river both above and below Brownsville. On at least one Saturday night, a group of rowdy Rangers crossed the river to Matamoros. Apparently, several of them imbibed more than their share of tequila and went looking for a few señoritas, and for trouble. Predictably, the Texans ended up turning a festive fandango into a wild fistfight. The pistol-wielding Rangers were even accused of using decorative luminaries and coal oil lamps for target practice. As Jennings later summarized their summer of "fun," McNelly's men were purposefully carrying out "a set policy of terrorizing the Mexicans at every opportunity." Jennings even admitted, "McNelly assumed that the more we were feared, the easier would be our work of subduing the Mexican raiders; so it was tacitly understood that we were to gain a reputation as fire-eating, quarrelsome dare-devils." He concluded, therefore, "We accomplished our purpose. In a few weeks we were feared as men were never before feared on that border." In other words, McNelly wanted the people along the lower Rio Grande to know that the Texas Devils were patrolling the river, and that their judgment was swift and final.[27]

In the aftermath of the Palo Alto fight the border remained quiet for many weeks. So quiet, in fact, that McNelly's dispatches to Austin usually mentioned little more than the monotony of daily patrols to reconnoiter the region for rustlers who apparently were no longer there. The Palo Alto fight was over, but it was far from forgotten. [28]

Not until July 9 did Governor Coke write McNelly a congratulatory note. The text of the letter should put to rest any doubts about the governor's unequivocal approval of the captain's recent actions. "The conduct of yourself and the officers and men under your command in discharge of the arduous duty of defending the Rio Grande border . . . merit the highest praise," Coke reassured McNelly. "The pride of true Texans in the historic fame of the Texas ranger is fully gratified in the record your command is making." Then he concluded, "You have done well. Continue the good work."[29]

McNelly had every intention of doing just that—at least as long as his weakened body and his support from the politicians in Austin held out. As for his health, he placed his soul in God's hands. His fundamentalist faith and belief in predestination would not allow him to do otherwise. The appointed day and hour of a man's death was already decided, he believed. The scriptures said so, at least as he interpreted them. He trusted the Almighty's final judgment. As for the politicians in Austin and Washington, he did not trust a one of them. He knew from past experiences, both in war and in peace, that he could not turn his back on anyone, especially politicians who no longer had any use for him and his troops.

Other than his Maker, McNelly trusted only his scouts. They brought him reliable intelligence about the rustlers' operations. For that reason, he kept patrols in the field for most of that summer. For McNelly, the operation against the bandits amounted to war, nothing less. Not surprisingly, he insisted on the strictest discipline. As Jennings recalled, it was as if every man in the company was a "shadow" of the captain. No alcohol was allowed in camp, no card playing, no gambling, and no complaining. Only on occasion were the raucous young Rangers allowed to leave camp on patrol or to go into Brownsville and Matamoros. Even then, they all knew that they should not dare disappoint Captain McNelly, and that if they did, they should not bother returning to camp.

On occasion, the daily monotony and boredom of camp life was interrupted when scouts brought in suspected spies who were turned over to Jesús Sandoval for interrogation. Durham recounted one particularly horrible incident that summer, which ended with the barbaric decapitation of two captives. "By the time we got there each bandit had been pulled loose from his head," Durham vividly recalled the grisly scene. "Bound tight, each had been lashed to a tree by the neck; then Casoose had looped the feet with his rawhide lariat and slapped his horse. That was it." Afterward, Old Casuse "put his hat on the ground and was looking up, crossing himself. White foam was drooping from his chin, and his eyes were blazing fire."[30]

Such savagery was not consistent with Sandoval's reputation as a mild-mannered gentleman. But the record remains clear on one point: Sandoval was a man-hunter, unforgiving in his judgment and malevolent in his methods. George Durham remembered Sandoval not as a gentleman but as the "most vicious, merciless killer" that he had ever met. Little wonder that Sandoval was a marked man on the Mexican side of the river, and that Juan Cortina had reportedly placed a price on his head, something that Old Casuse had admitted in sworn testimony before a U.S. circuit court earlier that spring. "I have been a peaceable citizen of the United States since 1853. . . . I have many enemies in Mexico," Sandoval explained as a translator recorded his statement. "They say I am Americanized and consequently a criminal—a traitor to Mexico. They have persecuted me, threatened my life and attempted to assassinate me," he claimed. "For seven months I have not slept in my house. I have slept in the chaparral and have been a solitary sentinel over my own person." Well dressed, at times even elegant and well spoken, Sandoval hardly sounded like a cold-blooded killer as he testified before a federal judge. But appearances were deceiving.[31]

During the sweltering days of July, McNelly moved his camp back to Rancho Las Rucias. As the summer days droned on, the South Texas prairie shimmered like a hot anvil's edge. Each day the grasses burned up beneath the Texas sun, and a searing, furnace-like heat rose from the sands and chaparral. For days on end, no rain was in sight, not a drop. Eventually, the unforgiving heat took its toll on the ailing captain. Confined to his tent for days at a time, he lay coughing, wheezing, occasionally even spitting up blood. His face appeared ashen, and his strength and his life seemed to be slipping away.

In September, with autumn approaching, the captain's lungs still labored. His cough became more spasmodic. He remained in his tent most of the time. None of his men should have been surprised when in early October the pale and frail figure of Captain McNelly returned to his farm in Washington County. Some of the young Rangers wondered if they would ever see him again.[32]

Still, while McNelly had already made peace with his God, he was not yet ready to make peace with the border bandits or to surrender to the disease that was sapping his strength, though not his will. He still had fight left in him, and he had at least one more river to cross.

After convalescing at home for more than three weeks, the captain returned to the border during the second week in November, by all appearances renewed and revived in spirit, if not in health. Soon after rejoining his company near Brownsville, he learned from his scouts that General Cortina had recently contracted to ship at least eighteen thousand head of beeves to the Cuban hide and meat markets by the beginning of the year. McNelly knew that surely meant that the bandits would be busy. So on November 12, 1875, in Brownsville he penned a note to Adjutant General Steele, clearly revealing his intentions: "I will move up the river tomorrow and think that I may be able to do something. Major [A. J.] Alexander [commanding cavalry officer at Fort Brown] says that he will instruct his men to follow raiders anywhere I will go. I hope to be able to put them to the test in a few days," he vowed, concluding that "I should think myself in bad luck if I don't find some . . . [bandits] on this side or the other side of the river." The phrase "or the other side of the river" drew attention to what some have speculated were McNelly's actual designs and ulterior motives.[33]

The *Rio Bravo* Affair

During McNelly's monthlong absence from the border one intriguing development provides an important clue about the captain's actions that autumn. McNelly aside, the enigmatic episode also sheds more light on the intentions and ambitions of the Grant administration and, more specifically, some officials in the Department of War, including commanders on the scene. To be sure, the border intrigue known as the "*Rio Bravo* Affair" adds to the mystery of the extraordinary events that would soon unfold that autumn and bring the United States and Mexico perilously close to war.[34]

In the aftermath of the infamous Nuecestown raid the previous March, Governor Coke and the citizens of South Texas had increased their demands for federal military action to suppress border banditry. Coke had gone so far as to warn President Grant of the "depopulation of the lower Rio Grande country" unless the administration stepped up its efforts to protect and pacify the border. Later in May the governor amplified his concern and his sense of urgency in another admonition: "Citizens are being murdered, thousands of cattle being driven across the Rio Grande, the roads are infested with bands of robbers." In almost threatening language, he even predicted the "imminence of a sanguinary border war." In other words, he implied that, if Washington failed to address the problem with greater military force, Texans would defend themselves by whatever means available to them.[35]

The citizens of Beeville directed their frustrations and anger not merely at the recent failures of the Republican Reconstruction government but to the cigar smoking president himself. "Thanks be to God, Grant can no longer blind the people with smoke from Havana. . . . [The people of South Texas] are oppressed on the one hand by a band of carpetbaggers that would divest us of every vestige of liberty, while on the other hand by a nation of brutes, who pride themselves in robbing the citizen of his labors." On April 24, 1875, the *Corpus Christi Gazette* had threatened that a "war of retaliation will be prosecuted until the Government of Mexico and the United States again clash arms to settle the difficulties." Moreover, such a war should end in nothing less than a "cession or purchase of [Mexican] territory." On June 5, the *Gazette* echoed the growing sense of outrage and impatience with the apparent ineptitude of the federal military: "The American people of Texas will not much longer allow themselves to be trampled upon and their earnings indiscriminately appropriated. Redress will be sought and the Rio Grande will be no barrier."[36]

Against the backdrop of such growing war fever, General E. O. C. Ord, commanding the Department of Texas, made his case to General Sheridan, requesting more support for his troops on the border—not in the form of additional cavalry regiments but a "light draught Iron Clad . . . with sufficient number of steam launches to patrol the river Rio Grande." To that end, General Ord traveled to Washington in early June and met with President Grant, apparently convincing him of the need for some gunboat diplomacy on the lower Rio Grande.[37]

Four months later, on October 12 Lieutenant Commander Dewitt Clinton Kells of the U.S. Navy moved up the mouth of the Rio Grande aboard the steam-powered USS *Rio Bravo*, recently outfitted with four small howitzers and one thirty-pound rifle cannon. By sundown, Commander Kells and his crew of more than fifty officers, seamen, and marines had puffed into Brownsville, dropping anchor in the shallows below the Fort Brown earthworks. A somewhat antiquated side-wheel steamer, the twenty-year-old former Alabama commercial vessel *Planter*, now reconditioned, repaired, and renamed, had been purchased during the past year by the Department of the Navy and converted for use in river patrol.[38]

Meantime, president of Mexico Sebastián Lerdo de Tejada had attempted to diffuse the tensions on the border and offer hope that the crisis had passed. Fearing the outbreak of a general war with the United States, President Lerdo had ordered the arrest of General Juan Cortina, and on July 1, less than three weeks after the Palo Alto fight, Lieutenant Colonel Parrat of the federal army of Mexico captured Cortina and jailed him in the artillery barracks in Matamoros. Four days later, under armed guard, Cortina was transported to the port of Bagdad, then aboard a steamship down the coast to Vera Cruz. From there President Lerdo's *federales* escorted the legendary caudillo more than 350 miles by train across rugged mountainous terrain to the Prisión Militar de Santiago Tlatelolco on the outskirts of Mexico City. Charged with smuggling, horse theft, cattle stealing, murder, and most important, with being an enemy of the Lerdist "revolution," the

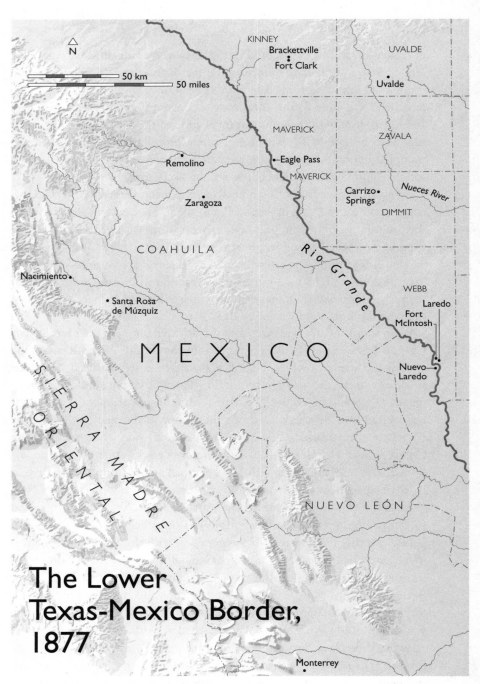

The Lower
Texas-Mexico Border,
1877

Cartography by Carol Zuber-Mallison

mythic "Red Robber of the Rio Grande" could only sit alone in a dark prison cell and ponder that his long reign on the border was over.[39]

But, even with Cortina removed from the lower Rio Grande, events still hastened toward a possible armed conflict between the United States and Mexico. The arrival of the impetuous Commander Kells at Brownsville all but ensured that. From the moment he set foot on Texas soil, Kells seemed to exhibit an eagerness to provoke the Mexican federal government into open hostilities. According to at least one source, the daring and adventuresome career naval officer from New York solicited citizens in Brownsville to expedite the imminent conflict by arranging "to have this vessel fired upon by a party of Texans from the Mexican bank" during the *Rio Bravo*'s first trip up the river. In such a case, Kells allegedly reasoned that he would then "have an excuse to return the fire, destroy adjacent Mexican ranches and land and occupy Mexican soil, ostensibly to avenge the insult to the U.S. flag, and thus precipitate an armed conflict with Mexico." John L. Haynes, one-time Unionist, now U.S. customs collector in Brownsville, confirmed Kells's scheme, adding that the impulsive naval commander even suggested that Captain McNelly's Rangers might be enlisted in the ruse.[40]

Across the river in Matamoros, on October 14 U.S. consul Thomas Wilson expressed his fears in a confidential dispatch to Secretary of State Hamilton Fish. He charged that Commander Kells had the audacity to recruit Texans on the border for his enterprise. Moreover, Wilson described Kells's potential compatriots as "men of means, who expect to reap large profits in case a war with Mexico takes place." Believing that the impulse for war on the Texas side of the river was reaching a crescendo, Wilson advised Fish that the reckless Commander Kells should be monitored closely, restrained, and if necessary removed from command. As a result, on November 5 Kells received a telegram from the Department of the Navy ordering him to remain in Brownsville until further notice.[41]

Still, two days later Wilson became even more anxious about Kells's rumored plot to ignite a war with Mexico. That afternoon Wilson and John L. Haynes observed Commander Kells and Captain McNelly together, conferring aboard the *Rio Bravo*. When Wilson boarded the steamer and approached the two men about their plans and intentions, reminding Kells of his standing orders not to continue patrols upriver, the commander informed him that he was preparing to launch a patrol *downriver*. The following morning a near-frantic Wilson telegraphed Secretary of State Fish that Kells was embarking on a river patrol, in direct violations of his orders, and that "Captain McNally [*sic*] was going with him, and . . . they were to cooperate with a force of cavalry which had been sent out from Fort Brown by Col. Potter during the night." Their presumed objective, Wilson speculated, was a large party of rustlers reportedly preparing to cross a herd of Texas cattle into Mexico. Or at least that rumor was being broadcast by Kells, perhaps as a pretext for his actions.[42]

Adding to the drama, an increasingly paranoid Wilson expressed the belief that his own life was in danger. Fearing for his personal safety, he emphasized in his communications that his warnings to Secretary Fish must remain confidential. "There are so many lawless and desperate persons on the Texas frontier who are ready to engage in any enterprise, especially one likely to provoke war with Mexico," he warned. Such soldiers of fortune "would be equally ready to resort to any violence to prevent any interference" with their plans. In other words, Wilson seemed convinced that Commander Kells and his collaborators were so zealous in their cause that they might even order his assassination to silence him and thus protect their plot.[43]

By all indications, Wilson's worst fears were somewhat irrational and probably unjustified. But if his suspicions were true, that Kells and McNelly had in fact conspired with local army commanders to cross into Mexico and create a provocation for war, events in the coming days thwarted their plans. The departure of the *Rio Bravo* from Brownsville was delayed by one day as the steamship's experienced pilot failed to show. Then on the morning of November 8, no sooner had Commander Kells launched the side-wheel steamer than the vessel ran aground in the shallows, even before clearing the first bend in the river within sight of Fort Brown. Another day passed before Kells and crew freed the *Rio Bravo* from the muddy bed and snarls of tree limbs. By then, Kells had received yet another telegram from the Department of the Navy—this one ordering him to stand down and remain at Fort Brown. Finally, on November 15 Commander George Remey of the U.S. Navy reported to Fort Brown and assumed command of the *Rio Bravo*. In the end, owing to diplomatic pressures, Kells had been replaced by a naval officer more to the liking of the U.S. Department of State.[44]

As to whether the private collaboration between Captain McNelly and Commander Kells amounted to a plot to goad Mexican officials into attacking American forces on the north banks of the Rio Grande, the issue remains open to conjecture. The evidence seems intriguing yet less than conclusive. On November 9 McNelly had cabled Adjutant General Steele a cryptic note that read simply, "The Affair has proved a failure." But the captain had failed to explain the reference to "the Affair"—or maybe he never intended to explain in a public record owing to the secretive nature of the matter.[45]

Perhaps Commander Remey provided the best perspective about the rumored intrigue. In the end Remey concluded that Consul Wilson's allegations seemed "a little strong" and even fraught with exaggeration. "I think the consul was justified in forwarding his statement," Remey admitted. "Yet I am induced to think that Kells is or was disposed to talk more than to act in such matters." To be sure, the ruggedly handsome Kells not only looked like he belonged on the Shakespearean stage rather than in the navy, but his theatrics were enough to convince anyone of his sincerity about almost anything, even a plot to start a war with Mexico. In sum, the garrulous Commander Kells was a great actor who could entertain listeners with tales of adventure and heroism, most especially his own. In the end, while the loquacious naval officer cut a swath across the Brownsville social scene, he seemed much less likely to cut a path across northern Mexico or border history.[46]

Still, no less than historian Walter Prescott Webb concluded, "There can be little doubt that McNelly had some deep scheme in mind, and it seems his purpose was to bring on a war with Mexico." Historian Michael G. Webster agreed that the plot to incite war would have played out had Thomas Wilson, Secretary of State Hamilton Fish, and others in Washington not intervened and "frustrated the scheme of a few strong-willed men bent on forcing a confrontation between Mexico and the United States." Webster even went so far as to argue persuasively that prominent Texans on the border were intent upon war and that many of them "still harbored ambitions to extend the Lone Star domain to the Sierra Madre."[47]

But as far as Captain McNelly was concerned, the truth may be far less romantic, the reality not so grandiose in design. As cattle theft and violence during the summer and fall of 1875 showed few signs of abating, McNelly maintained his resolve to track down and kill rustlers and recover stolen cattle, nothing more. If he had to lead his men across the Rio Grande to do that, he would do so. But by all indications no impulse of territorial conquest motivated him. And neither diplomatic interference nor political intervention would stop him. Perhaps, in the end, that is why diplomats and politicians in Washington should have been more concerned about McNelly than the bombastic, boastful Commander Kells.

By mid-November a bitter chill gripped the lower Rio Grande. The sun-splashed days and blue skies of summer seemed to fade to gray as autumn promised cooler days and colder nights. Again, the featureless landscape surrendered its beauty and charm as the afternoon shadows grew longer and the siege of winter awaited. McNelly and his men waited meanwhile for the opportunity to follow yet another band of cattle rustlers—wherever the trail might lead. They would not have a long wait.

9
Crossing the Jordan

Captain Leander H. McNelly was a Bible-toting man who not only read and recited the scriptures but tried his best to live by them. He was thus no doubt familiar with the gospel hymns of his day, particularly one that had become a popular spiritual ballad in the early 1870s. "Wayfaring Stranger" tells the story of a young man "traveling through this world of woe." The lyrics speak of the promise of God's kingdom of heaven, where "there's no sadness, toil or danger in that bright land to which I go." The verse also holds the hope that the pilgrim will soon pass over one last river to see his beloved mother and father who have gone before him. "I'm going there no more to roam," the words conclude. "I'm just crossing over Jordan. I'm just going over home." Lieutenant Robinson recalled that his fellow Rangers liked to sing around the campfire at night, and sometimes even joined in song to entertain their captain and bring some comfort and peace of mind to all. Robinson also remembered that one of the Rangers' favorite hymns told the story of crossing the Jordan. "One Wide River" was one song that "Pidge" recalled. Whether another might have been the lament of the wayfaring stranger is not known. But on November 18, 1875, as McNelly's Rangers gathered along the north banks of the Rio Grande, some fifteen miles downriver from Rio Grande City, the lyrics could not have been more appropriate for the occasion.[1]

Captain McNelly was also familiar with the Old Testament story in the book of Joshua about the young warrior who led the ancient Israelites in their conquest of Canaan. The scripture also could not have been more fitting for the captain and his troops as they pondered the imminent danger that awaited them on the other side of the Rio Grande. The passage reads:

> Then Joshua rose early in the morning; and he and all the sons of Israel set out . . . and came to the Jordan, and they lodged there before they crossed.
> And it came about at the end of three days that the officers went through the midst of the camp;
> and they commanded the people saying, "When you see the ark of the covenant of the LORD your God . . . then you shall set out from your place and follow it."[2]

No doubt, McNelly knew the scripture well. Soon after returning from his convalescence at his farm in Burton, he also knew that his days on this earth were numbered—that his appointed day with the Almighty was drawing nearer. Maybe that is why he seemed even more determined to go after the cattle thieves without further delay. There had been enough scouts north of the Rio Grande, enough reports, enough talk about rustlers and robbers holed up in their havens south of the river. Now, he determined, the time had come to trail them across the Rio Grande. He did not need the encouragement—or approval—of any U.S. naval officer or anyone else. Whether he had received tacit consent from U.S. military officials for his "invasion" of Mexico remains unclear.

But one thing seems certain. Neither Colonel Joseph H. Potter, commanding a detachment of the all-black Ninth U.S. Cavalry ("buffalo soldiers") stationed at Fort Brown, nor General Edward Ord, nor Texas adjutant general William Steele tried to stop him. They may have even privately approved of McNelly's legendary attack upon the Rancho Las Cuevas on the morning of November 19, 1875. Unfortunately, historical documents do not always provide the final answers to such questions.[3]

On November 15, four days before McNelly's crossing into Mexico, his scouts had reported that more than a hundred head of cattle had been driven across the river, no more than a mile below Ringgold Barracks near Rio Grande City. Within the next three days they also informed McNelly that two additional droves of stolen cattle, numbering as many as five hundred head, were rustled across the river a few miles below Brownsville. In each case the bandits had eluded U.S. Army regulars, seemingly with little difficulty. According to George Hall, Jesús Sandoval, and other "spies," the herds were being driven to the Rancho Las Cuevas, where the livestock was cut out and sold to buyers for shipment to Bagdad, and from there on to Cuba and other distant markets. Moreover, Hall informed McNelly that the proprietor of the rancho, as well as *comandante* of local *rurales* and the apparent jefe of the rustling operation headquartered there was Juan Flores Salinas, a longtime associate of General Cortina.[4]

Now having this information, Captain McNelly decided to cross after the thieves, said to number in the hundreds. Motivated neither by political ambition nor by a sense of history, nor by a desire to incite a war or to conquer territory, McNelly simply set out that evening to punish a small army of bandits and to recover a few hundred head of Texas cattle. That was what Governor Coke had sent him to the border to do. So when he positioned some thirty of his Rangers on the north bank of the river opposite the Rancho Las Cuevas on November 18, 1875, he sought nothing more than to strike a blow at the bandits who had been preying on the people of South Texas. And he would settle for nothing less than the opportunity to finish the job Governor Richard Coke had assigned him.[5]

Regulars and Rangers in Pursuit

While McNelly was preparing his Rangers to strike, troopers of the Eighth U.S. Cavalry were also on the trail of the Las Cuevas cattle thieves. More than one week before the storied river crossing by McNelly's Rangers, Colonel Robert H. Potter had ordered forty-three-year-old Captain James Franklin Randlett to scour the river between Rio Grande City and Edinburg. As directed, on November 9 Captain Randlett commanded Company H under First Lieutenant Henry J. Farnsworth and Company D under Second Lieutenant J. W. Williams to pursue and punish any rustlers found in possession of stolen cattle. While Farnsworth led his command upriver to Ringgold Barracks, Captain Randlett and Lieutenant Williams camped just outside Edinburg on the night of the November 11. Only three days later an unnamed ranchero from the Texas side rode into camp and alerted Randlett that a band of rustlers from south of the river had passed his rancho several days earlier, heading eastward. Randlett agreed that the thieves likely intended to cross back into Mexico with a drove of stolen cattle.[6]

On the afternoon of November 15, Captain Randlett telegraphed Fort Brown and communicated to Colonel Potter that he would break camp the next morning and head toward the Rio Grande in hopes of intercepting the raiders. Colonel Potter's response probably gratified the captain and may have even surprised him. Potter had dispatched thirty men of Company M under Lieutenant O'Connor to scout and trail the raiders. Their orders were to get between the rustlers and the river. Potter instructed Randlett to rendezvous with Lieutenant O'Connor and "if you catch the thieves, hit them hard. If you come up with them while they cross the river, follow them into Mexico." The commander of Fort Brown likewise informed Randlett that Captain McNelly's state troops were also camped near Edinburg. "Try to connect with him and take a Sheriff or deputy with you. . . . Keep me advised of result," Colonel Potter instructed.[7]

Captain Randlett left camp that evening with a troop escort and rode some sixteen miles upriver where he searched out John Thompson, the mounted customs inspector for Edinburg and Hidalgo County. Randlett, a native of

New Hampshire, could not have found a better source of information. Few men had earned the reputation of being more knowledgeable about the people of the border, their customs, their habits, their concerns and fears than the earthy Thompson. And fewer still knew more about that stretch of the Rio Grande, its channels and currents, the best fords for crossing, indeed every bend in the river. From Thompson, Captain Randlett learned that the thieves recently spotted by scouts appeared to be headed for the Las Cuevas crossing located near Camargo, and about midway between Ringgold Barracks and Reynosa, downriver on the south bank.[8]

By midafternoon on November 16 Captain Randlett ordered his men to mount up and move out toward the river ford across from Rancho Las Cuevas. Shortly after 4:00 P.M. the troopers arrived at the river's edge in time to see at least thirty vaqueros on the opposite bank roping and pulling the last of a longhorn herd out of the mud. From the Texas side Captain Randlett commanded his men to open fire on the thieves as they scattered and disappeared into the brush, leaving two of their dead companions behind. Not willing to ford the river in daylight, and unable to locate a safe crossing before nightfall, Captain Randlett waited until the next morning.[9]

But Randlett wasted little time in dashing off a terse communication to the alcalde of Camargo, Diego Garcia. He later reported his demands that Mexican authorities return the stolen cattle "at once," and he insisted that the rustlers be turned over as well, even identifying ten of the raiders by name. He later admitted that his letter was written hastily and "without regard to form of law or military etiquette." Not expecting the bandits' leaders and patrons to comply, however, he remained convinced that proper etiquette and good social graces would accomplish nothing. Only a coordinated attack upon the rustlers *on their side of the river* would "finish up the job." In that regard, Randlett would soon find a natural ally in McNelly.[10]

Apparently, Captain Randlett's immediate commander on the scene, Major David R. Clendenin, would view matters differently. After arriving at camp on November 17, he cautioned Randlett that crossing into Mexico would constitute a "warlike invasion of a country with which our own was at peace," and that Randlett's orders "would not justify . . . recovering the cattle." To Randlett, such instructions seemed to contradict Colonel Potter's orders issued the previous week.[11]

On the morning of November 18 Captain Randlett received a response from the alcalde, Diego Garcia, that the police of Camargo had recovered some of the cattle, but only after a shoot-out with several of the rustlers. Still skeptical, he proceeded with plans to attack the cattle thieves, even if he and his men had to swim the river to get to them. Then John Thompson's Tejano scouts brought Randlett word that still another band of rustlers was headed for a different river crossing several miles upriver with a herd of several hundred beeves. Apparently, Thompson's posse had been unable to intercept them.[12]

In the meantime, early that afternoon McNelly and his own scouts rode into Randlett's camp and the Ranger captain "at once declared his determination to cross the river and called upon . . . [the army] to give him assistance when he called for it." For McNelly, the opportunity had at last arrived. No more waiting, no more discussions, no more reports or delays. Now the time was right to hit the raiders on their own ground.[13]

Ranger Lieutenant T. C. Robinson recorded that shortly after 1:00 P.M. a courier galloped into the Ranger camp near Rancho Los Burros in southern Hidalgo County. The rider carried orders from Captain McNelly instructing Robinson's command to "ride rapidly" to Las Cuevas, or "Robber's Roost." "We obeyed them to the letter," Robinson claimed, "We rode fifty-five miles in six hours, each man carrying one hundred rounds of ammunition." Along the route, at more than a dozen ranchos, vaqueros glared at them and watched in silence as the Rangers rode past, the observers seemingly realizing as Robinson noted that the "jig was up." The Rangers assumed from their appearance that "most of them . . . [were] in sympathy with the raiders from the other side," as Robinson recalled. "As we came to the main telegraph route, we could see where the detachment from the gallant Eighth [cavalry] had passed, and heard from the frightened rancheros that the fight was progressing." Shortly after dusk, the Rangers looked ahead and saw a "hideous object waving in the night breeze, fearful to look upon." A dead caballero "swung . . . [from] the tree in full view of the road." But Robinson recalled that the young Rangers "did not seem to mind it much" as such grisly sights had become all too familiar.[14]

Another two miles in the darkness brought Robinson's column to an encampment of the Eighth U.S. Cavalry at Rancho Loma Alta, or "High Hill." Nearby an impatient Captain McNelly waited with two dozen Rangers, including Old Casuse, several scouts and interpreter Tom Sullivan. McNelly explained that he and his mounted troops had arrived from Reynosa at 2:00 and that they had ridden hard for more than forty miles, trailing after a band of rustlers with a large drove of cattle. But after chasing them all the way to the banks of the Rio Grande, they had arrived at the water's edge too late to prevent the thieves from crossing into Mexico with the entire herd.[15]

After the briefing McNelly questioned Robinson about the company's readiness to cross the Rio Grande and embark on their most dangerous mission yet. He demanded to know if Robinson had brought enough provisions and supplies for a campaign across the river. Robinson explained that his men were carrying enough cartridges to fight their way to Mexico City. McNelly bristled. "I suppose you have rations with you." Robinson answered, "No sir." What about salt or coffee, McNelly pressed? Surely Robinson and his troops had not come all that way with nothing in their haversacks but sand. How did Robinson expect his men to survive on the other side of the Rio Grande? Robinson claimed that he joked that he did not expect to live long enough to worry about food. Then he apologized to his commander and explained that he had followed orders by hastening to rendezvous with the rest of the company. Then McNelly asked about the condition of their horses? The mounts were heavily lathered and exhausted, Robinson reported, in need of water, forage, and rest. McNelly nodded in agreement. When Robinson again offered to account for how many cartridges that his men carried, his captain abruptly stopped him. Robinson remembered that McNelly growled and threatened that, if he mentioned cartridges one more time, he would have him arrested and tied up on "this side of the river." Robinson said no more. "I thought it would look too bad to *say anything,*" he recollected.[16]

After the Rangers unsaddled their horses Captain McNelly called them all together. Silent for a moment, he began to speak: he would not *send* them into Mexico; he would *lead* them. The brief speech sounded more like a sermon than a war council. Durham recalled that the captain "was starched up as neat as any military officer. His britches were fresh ironed and washed, and so was his jacket. . . . He even had on a little black necktie." As Durham remembered the moment, McNelly appeared to be heading to church rather than into battle.[17]

The captain reassured his men that, if any among them wished to resign and ride away from certain danger and possible death, it would not be held against him. McNelly told them in a calm voice that theirs would likely be a "fight to the death." No quarter would be given to the bandits, he stressed, and none would be expected from them. A company of cavalrymen from Ringgold Barracks was camped nearby, he reminded his men. Although armed with two Gatling guns trained on the south bank, the U.S. troops were under strict orders from Colonel Potter not to cross the border. Anyone unwilling to follow him into Mexico and assume the real risk that they might not return alive should therefore step aside, he repeated. The frail, consumptive captain chewed on the end of a cigar and promised that he would pray for them. When he finished, to a man the young Rangers expressed their enthusiasm for a fight—and they reiterated their confidence in McNelly. As a testament to the captain's charisma and ability to inspire others, not one Ranger asked to be dismissed.[18]

Shortly before 1:00 A.M. on November 19 McNelly led what would be the first border crossing of Texas Rangers in fifteen years. McNelly first ordered five of his Rangers under Sergeant John B. Armstrong to swim their horses over to the Mexican side. Minutes later Armstrong sent back word that the currents and the quicksand along the south bank made a crossing on horseback too risky for both the men and their mounts. Heeding that warning, McNelly ordered the remainder of the party to leave their horses behind; they would paddle across in a small commandeered rowboat, he explained. And he would be among the first to cross.[19]

With an old Mexican boatman steering them, three and four at a time, the Rangers rowed in silence. Lieutenant Robinson remembered the long wait at the river ford with his typical sense of the morbid. Recalling his fear and his belief that he would not live to see another sunset, he claimed that a calm Captain McNelly sensed his anxiety and ordered him to wait on the Texas side until the other Rangers had crossed. "He advised me to come over in the last boat," Robinson recollected; then the captain added that the wait would afford his second in command enough time to write his last will and testament. "He seemed to take a malicious delight in making me feel as bad as possible," Robinson wrote of his commander. "I was not very long in writing my will—simply directing that my effects should be packed in a cartridge box and sent to the Second Sergeant . . . to be distributed among the poor." No doubt, in view of their conversation earlier that day, McNelly appreciated Robinson's grim reference to a cartridge box.[20]

McNelly, Old Casuse, and Tom Sullivan were the first three to climb into the leaky rowboat and paddle across the river. "What a tub to cross the Jordan in!" Robinson wrote in jest. "One could punch a hole through it anywhere with a finger." But it was no joking matter at the time as the Rangers were forced to bale water constantly to keep the little boat afloat. Only by pulling the launch upon the riverbank and turning it bottom side up every few minutes could they prevent the boat from filling too fast. The Rangers appropriately called the craft their "sinking fund."[21]

The soft moonlight reflected dimly off the river as the Texans crossed. By 3:00 A.M. on November 19, all had made it safely to the south bank. Once on the Mexican side, they huddled in silence. At first, the darkness seemed eerie, but as the night wore on it grew more menacing. The thickets along the river prevented the young Rangers from seeing anything beyond their own hands in front of them. A chill settled into the night air, and a heavy dew blanketed the ground, covering the men and making the minutes and hours pass ever so slowly. Death would have to wait until morning.[22]

The Attack on Las Cuevas

At the first gray light of dawn a young Mexican guide led McNelly and his men through a fine mist and into a bank of heavy fog, then down a narrow cattle trail, through tall grass and thick brush. Only the creak of leather could be heard as the Rangers followed their captain's hand signals. When the Rangers came to a split rail fence no more than half a mile from the river, McNelly motioned for the tall figure of Sergeant Armstrong to ride ahead. Not long thereafter, Armstrong returned and signaled to McNelly that the slumbering cow camp appeared just beyond a timberline.[23]

The much-anticipated attack commenced. Out of the morning mist McNelly's Rangers charged, shouting like demons as they roared through the camp, spraying gunfire in every direction. Strangely enough, Robinson remembered, several workers at the compound casually continued to smoke cigarettes and perform their chores as the shooting erupted all around them. It was over so quickly that an old woman cooking breakfast in one jacale never even stopped pulling tortillas from her cooktop. In less than a minute, five Mexican vaqueros lay dead around a woodpile. While the smell of gunpowder still hung in the morning air, the Rangers' young Mexican guide admitted his mistake to McNelly. This was not the infamous Rancho Las Cuevas but a small line camp called Rancho de Cucharas. The Rangers had attacked and shot up the wrong camp.[24]

The advantage of surprise now gone, McNelly and his men then advanced more than half a mile across a sprawling plain to the cluster of huts and corrals known as Las Cuevas, where an estimated three hundred armed riders had been alerted and were assembling for a counterattack.

Bill Callicott remembered, "It was all open ground between us and the ranch. . . . We were lined up in the edge of the woods in plain view of the Mexicans." Luckily for McNelly's men, who were almost all on foot, the first enemy volley sailed harmlessly over their heads. "Such fiendish yells I never heard," Lieutenant Robinson remembered. "I could see very little; where the smoke came from the guns it hung like a pall." Quickly assessing the hopelessness of his situation, the captain commanded his Rangers to fall back in an orderly retreat, the fog covering them as they dashed back through the thickets toward the river.[25]

At the water's edge Captain McNelly ordered his company to make a stand behind the river's natural earthworks of mud and brush. He figured correctly that the leader of the rustlers, Juan Flores Salinas, would assume that the fleeing Rangers might attempt to swim the river back to Texas and, while in the water, would thus be exposed as easy targets for his rifle-wielding *rurales*. But as Flores led a charge toward the Rangers he was greeted by a thundering volley from the thickets along the riverbank. On the opposite bank, Captain Randlett's Gatling battery opened fire, providing cover for McNelly's troops. Among those who fell dead in the initial assault was Flores himself, who was shot at least twice. He was said to have fallen with a silver-plated Smith & Wesson pistol still in his hand. Ranger Callicott remembered that through the roar of gunfire he could hear the distinct voice of Old Casuse Sandoval shouting, "Son a bitch, keel 'em."[26]

By McNelly's count as many as two hundred horsemen were repulsed by the murderous fire from the Rangers' Sharps rifles and Randlett's rattling repeating guns. Even with Flores dead on the field, twice again the vaqueros charged the Rangers' makeshift fortification. Both times the Mexican home guard retreated, leaving more than two dozen dead and dying scattered over the field. Remarkably, the Rangers did not suffer a single casualty. Neither did Captain Randlett's regulars on the Texas side of the river.[27]

Within an hour of the initial exchange of gunfire, in defiance of his direct orders, Captain Randlett ordered a platoon of his regulars to cross the river in support of the besieged Rangers. Fearful that McNelly and his men might be overrun and that the Texans were "in danger of annihilation," he led about forty troopers of Company H of the Eighth U.S. Cavalry to take up positions alongside the Texans. Leaving their mounts behind, Randlett's regulars crossed in a skiff and dug in beside McNelly's troops. The scene now seemed reminiscent of military operations during the so-called Cortina War of 1859–60, when Rip Ford's Rangers fought alongside U.S. regulars on Mexican soil.[28]

Late that morning a strange quiet fell over the river. But no one expected it to last. The standoff continued through the afternoon. Pinned down by the continual crack of gunfire, with their backs to the river, the Rangers peered over the natural breastworks as Mexican *rurales* lined the timbers beyond an open plain. A far as the captain and his men could see, the brush seemed to bristle with rifle barrels, the muzzles flashing and puffs of smoke rising from the tree line. "I am in temporary earth and have refused to leave until the cattle are returned," the captain scribbled in a telegraph to Adjutant General Steele. "The Mexicans in my front . . . [number] about four hundred. What should I do?"[29]

News streaked by telegraph to Brownsville, to Austin, and even to the nation's capital that the company of thirty Rangers had been cut off and reportedly surrounded. Within hours McNelly received his answer: couriers delivered cables from the U.S. consul Thomas Wilson at Matamoros, Colonel Potter, and even Secretary of War William Belknap, who had also been informed of the situation. The messages urged McNelly to turn himself over to the Mexican authorities. But the word "surrender" was not in the captain's vocabulary.[30]

George Durham remembered having read the message from Colonel Potter to Captain McNelly, and he recorded his commander's defiant response and refusal to comply. In his account, Napoleon Jennings later cited Potter's actual orders, which stated, "Advise Capt. McNelly to return at once to this side of the river. Inform him that you are directed not to support him in any way while he remains on Mexican territory. If McNelly is attacked by Mexican forces on Mexican ground, do not render him any assistance," the note admonished. "Keep your forces in the position you hold now and await further orders. Let me know whether McNelly acts upon your advice and returns."[31]

But the captain had no intention of complying. Simply put, his boss was Texas adjutant general Steele, who answered directly to Governor Coke and to no one else. The defiant reply to Potter and the others was vintage McNelly: "I shall remain in Mexico with my Rangers until tomorrow morning—perhaps longer, and shall recross the Rio Grande at my own discretion. Give my compliments to the Secretary of War and tell him and his United States soldiers to go to hell."[32]

Still dug in along the riverbank, McNelly's Rangers could only watch and wait for a counterattack. Hours passed, with no further exchange of gunfire. Then late in the afternoon, Ranger Callicott alerted the captain that three riders had appeared from the tree line carrying a white flag of truce. McNelly, Lieutenant Robinson, and Sergeant Armstrong, pistols strapped to their hips, rode out to meet them. Leading the party to parley with the Texans were three distinguished-looking, well-dressed gentlemen who appeared to be anything but common bandits. One was an unnamed civil official, identified by one source as the "governor," the second was dressed in military uniform, the third—the spokesman for the group— an amiable gray-bearded physician, Dr. Alexander Manford Headley. An English adventurer who had immigrated to Arkansas during his youth, some said in quest of diamonds, Headley had taken up residence in Camargo and was now practicing more than medicine. Some said that he had held retainer as an employee of Cortina himself, and that he was even in partnership with the cattle thieves.[33]

Jennings described Dr. Headley as a "tall, handsome man, about forty years old, but his hair and long beard were as white as snow, giving him a most patriarchal appearance at a little distance." But a "closer view showed he had a youthful, ruddy complexion and deep, soft blue eyes. He wore a fine, white linen suit and a broad white *sombrero*." Hardly the image of a common criminal, Dr. Headley exuded the presence of a refined gentleman and a respectable citizen of the border.[34]

Several versions of Headley's parleys with McNelly and his Rangers have been passed down. These accounts sharply differ as to details. But as to the outcome, there is little disagreement. Whether Dr. Headley and his entourage first rode out and met under a flag of truce with a small escort that included Lieutenant Robinson and Sergeant Armstrong but not McNelly matters little. Whether the meeting or meetings occurred on the first afternoon of the siege along the river also remains unclear and just as unimportant. The issue of whether the old English physician and soldier of fortune held talks with the Rangers' leaders only once, or twice, or even three times as Callicott recalled, also remains open to debate. Captain Randlett reported to both Major Alexander and Colonel Potter that he too met with the negotiators from Camargo on the first day of the standoff, and that he also issued written demands for the return of the cattle as well as the surrender of the band of rustlers responsible for stealing the beeves. What no one questions, however, is that McNelly met personally at least once with Dr. Headley and the Mexican delegation, and that he stood his ground and never retreated from his demands.[35]

Another night passed without further event—and without a resolution to the stalemate. During this time McNelly apparently crossed back to the Texas side of the river and telegraphed both Austin and Washington, updating officials about his standoff with Mexican forces. The following day, Saturday, November 20, during the continuing negotiations a curiously jovial Dr. Headley politely restated his request that he be given the privilege of recovering Juan Flores's body and other remains from the field. But before he could finish asking permission, a resolute McNelly interrupted him, again demanding that the Mexican party surrender all stolen cattle in their possession as well every rustler responsible for their theft. Stunned, one of the negotiators asked how many men McNelly had with him. "Enough," Lieutenant Robinson snapped. After Headley offered to share a bottle of mescal with the Texans, McNelly brusquely declined. Headley then unfolded a message and politely handed it over to the captain. Addressed to "the commander of the invading party from Texas," the communication from the alcalde of Camargo, Diego Garcia, again demanded the surrender or withdrawal of the Texan force. Otherwise, they would be shown no mercy or immunity.[36]

After talking for a few minutes while passing the bottle of tequila, Headley and the "peace party" appeared to be stalling for time. When Lieutenant Robinson alerted McNelly that he saw Mexican snipers slipping toward them through the brush on their right, the captain instructed his men that, if anyone fired on them, their counterparts under the white flag of truce were to be killed. By one account, Dr. Headley reportedly laughed at the command and jokingly asked whether McNelly intended "to have us all murdered." Then when he asked McNelly if he knew how many citizens of Mexico his Rangers had already killed, the captain snapped, "No." Headley informed him that twenty-seven *rurales* and state police, including Flores, lay dead. McNelly showed no emotion. Apparently, he communicated in a few words that if Headley and his compadres believed that there had been enough killing, they should turn over the stolen cattle and the rustlers who had taken them. No more needed to die, McNelly insisted, but there would be more killing if necessary. Eventually, Headley and his fellow negotiators agreed to turn over the herd of cattle at 10:00 the following morning at the ferry crossing some fifteen miles upstream, opposite Rio Grande City. But they equivocated about any thieves that might be in their custody or jurisdiction. Then Headley's party turned their horses around and rode back into the tree line.[37]

Satisfied that his terms had been met, McNelly returned to the river-bank. Only after sunset did he finally order his troops back to the Texas side. Among the controversies surrounding the Las Cuevas affair few remain more puzzling than Captain Randlett's defiance of Colonel Potter's standing orders by crossing the Rio Grande to aid the Texas state troops. Amid the trail of military correspondence about these events on the Rio Grande, a report from Major Andrew J. Alexander penned ten days after the events sheds some light on the chronology of the border standoff. Alexander reported that by the time he and two companies of the Eighth Cavalry had arrived on the scene at 4:30 P.M. on November 19, Captain Randlett and forty troopers had already joined McNelly's Rangers on the Mexican side of the river. Soon thereafter, Alexander received a dispatch from Randlett, explaining that a truce had been negotiated for the "suspension of hostilities" until 9:00 A.M. the following morning. "The United States forces were at once withdrawn to this bank," Randlett scribbled, "but Capt. McNelly who was not under my orders declined to withdraw until the Mexican authorities delivered up the stolen cattle and thieves." According to Alexander, after receiving the dispatch from Colonel Potter on November 20 "advising Capt. McNelly to withdraw to this side, which he did," the crisis appeared to have passed.

But the matter was far from finished—and the danger far from over. After midnight on November 20 McNelly and a handpicked escort of ten men saddled up for the ride to Ringgold Barracks, some fifteen miles upstream. The following morning, Sunday, November 21, Captain McNelly and several of his men boarded a flatboat and crossed the Rio Grande to receive the stolen cattle, as had been arranged and promised. Dubbed McNelly's "Death Squad," they included Lieutenant Robinson, sergeants Armstrong and Hall, Corporal Rudd, and privates Callicott, McGovern, Maben, Pitts, and Durham. No one was on the other side to meet them.[38]

Visibly angry, but with the tone of a proper Southern gentleman, McNelly dashed off a formal yet sternly worded note to Diego Garcia, the reigning magistrate of Camargo. "The agreement of yesterday with your representatives . . . was that as many of the stolen cattle in your possession should be delivered to me at 10 ock [*sic*] today. Upon this understanding all troops were withdrawn to the right bank of the river. This agreement has not been complied with." Then McNelly reminded Garcia that U.S. regulars also awaited his response. "I would be glad if you would inform me of the earliest hour at which you can deliver the cattle and any of the thieves you may have apprehended." Then he closed, "I have the honor to be Your Obedient Servant. Very respectfully, L. H. McNelly, Capt. Comg. [*sic*] Texas Rangers."[39]

Clearly, the only obedience McNelly respectfully observed was to the state of Texas. Before noon several local Mexican customs officials at last appeared and explained through an interpreter that the Rangers must wait another day, because such business as the transfer of a herd of cattle was not normally conducted on the Sabbath. An angry exchange ensued. Robinson remembered that a customs collector from Camargo even demanded to know if the Texans had a permit to transport the cattle into Texas. McNelly fired back that the rustlers needed no permit to drive the animals across the river into Mexico. Durham recalled that, at that moment, more than one of the Mexican officials reached for their revolvers, but before any of their pistols cleared leather Ranger Bob Pitts shot the first one to draw, dropping him dead in his tracks. At the same moment, McNelly was on the customs official "like a cat," according to Durham. The captain kneed the man in the stomach and pistol-whipped him to the ground as the squad of Rangers kept their guns trained on the others. Grabbing the agent by the collar and pulling him to his feet, the captain explained through an interpreter, "Tell this man to order his hands to deliver his cattle over [the river] in an hour or he dies. Tell him also if any rescue is tried, he dies. Tell him." As Robinson recalled, "The ominous 'kerchack' of the carbine levers as the long, murderous looking cartridges were chambered home, satisfied them as to the permit and the cattle were allowed to cross over." "Such is the power of a fifty caliber argument, such the authority of Sharps on international law," Robinson concluded. Durham agreed that the customs official from Camargo, a mere bureaucrat with no stomach for bloodshed, was a "plumb scared hombre. . . . He savvied, and he sure believed [McNelly's threat]." The heightened tension of the moment left every man shaking, everyone except McNelly.[40]

Pale and trembling after stumbling over the body of his dead comrade, the customs official from Camargo ordered his men to deliver the cattle. Bill Callicott remembered what happened next: "If ever you saw cattle put across the river [in a hurry] they did it in less than five minutes." Durham remembered the scene the same way. "It wasn't long till the cattle were started down to the river. Nobody was trying any monkey business." The standoff ended with no further event.[41]

While the legendary "Las Cuevas War" was over, the border problems that brought on the incident were not. In the coming months cattle rustling continued along the river frontier, though not as frequently as before, according to some. In the aftermath of McNelly's bold attack, even with Cortina now far removed from the border, other bandit chieftains were "still at their old business," in the words of General Ord. On the diplomatic front the reaction from Mexico City to McNelly's incursion seemed mild in comparison to similar border incidents of the past. No doubt, a single company of Texas Rangers—with the help of Randlett's bluecoats—had struck a hard blow against one nest of cattle thieves. Still, other bases remained at the border town of Guerrero and farther into the interior of Mexico. Certainly, the river crossing had secured Leander McNelly's place in the pantheon of Texas Ranger lore—for Anglos and people of Mexican heritage alike. But the affair only caused more apprehensions and confirmed the tensions and deep divisions between people on both sides of the border.[42]

If anything, the Las Cuevas affair amplified the ill will, resentment and mistrust between Los Norte Americanos, or gringos from the north banks, and the Spanish- speaking people some Anglo-Texans labeled "greasers" from the Mexican side of the Rio Grande. The currents of antipathy between them ran even deeper and stronger than the meandering river that had long separated them. In sum, McNelly had not altered the course of cattle rustling and crime along the border any more than he had altered the crooked course of the Rio Grande.

No Sign of Relief

Ironically enough, some of the most stinging criticism for both McNelly and Randlett came not from Mexican authorities but from the U.S. consul in Matamoros. When informed of the Rangers' crossing at Las Cuevas, Consul Thomas Wilson referred to the state troops as "menacing" Las Cuevas. Moreover, he predicted that the motive for the assault was to "precipitate a conflict" with Mexico. At the same time, he advised Secretary of State Hamilton Fish that U.S. regular forces should only cross the Rio Grande in what diplomats and military officials termed "hot pursuit" of raiders, literally meaning in cases where the army chased them into Mexico. In other words, border incursions after the fact, or preemptive attacks across the river constituted egregious violations of Mexican national sovereignty and territorial integrity. Running fights that carried across the river were a different matter. Then, and only then, when the army captured criminals on Mexican soil should they turn them over to Texas authorities so that they might be brought to justice.[43]

Still, Wilson concluded his letter to Fish with one stunning admission. "The moment it is thoroughly demonstrated that the Rio Grande no longer forms a line within which cattle thieves can find . . . shelter and protection, that moment cattle stealing as a profitable and comparatively safe avocation will cease." On at least that point Wilson could agree with both Captain Randlett and Captain McNelly.[44]

Not surprisingly, the *Heraldo del Bravo* in Matamoros condemned McNelly's raid, referring to the attack as a "filibuster invasion" carried out by "miserable pirates" from Texas. Reinforcing the claim that before McNelly's "invasion" Mexican rural police had already defeated the thieves of Las Cuevas and had recovered seventy-five stolen beeves, the newspaper further asserted that the police from Camargo were still in the process of investigating the matter and that more arrests were forthcoming. Of course, hardly anyone on the Texas side of the river believed that.[45]

McNelly's decision to lead his troops across the border may have been questioned and even criticized by some on both sides of the border, but his exploits were generally hailed by others, both in Texas and back in the East. On December 1, 1875, the *San Antonio Daily Express* went so far as to call for an entire regiment of "fearless rangers" to be raised and deployed on the border to deal effectively with the raiders, described as "a disaffected class throughout the northern part of Mexico." The article called the bordering nation to the south "that God-forsaken and unhappy country," which was incapable—or unwilling—to control its "thieving population" along the border. The time had come, therefore, for leaders in Washington to renew the call for negotiations to acquire the Mexican borderlands of Tamaulipas, Nuevo León, Coahuila, and Chihuahua, the proposed boundary running along the crests of the Sierra Madre range. In conclusion, the newspaper pronounced, "We do not consider the border thieves as the Mexican Republic. Against these marauders we entertain a most inveterate hatred." The time had thus arrived "for every man of them to have met the ends of justice."[46]

In a separate column the following day, the publisher of the *Daily Express* reprinted a recent report from Horace Greeley's *New York Herald* that implied that, should diplomacy fail, Captain Leander McNelly might be just the right man who could accomplish the task by force of arms. "What Texas intends to do for her own protection may be gathered from the recent actions of Captain McNally [*sic*]. She proposes to protect herself if the United States government will not protect her," the newspaper editorialized. Describing McNelly as "energetic, cool, brave and possessed of wonderful physical endurance," the article declared, "He has already pursued into Mexico bands of thieves, recovering the stolen property and showing no mercy to the robbers. His last exploit proves of what stuff he is made, and shows that he will not hesitate to 'carry the war into Mexico.'"[47]

The public campaign of the *Daily Express* did not end there. On December 2 the publisher followed with a sarcastic rebuttal to the recent claims of the *Heraldo del Bravo*. The editorial simply referred to the "mean pride and insolence" of their counterpart south of the border. That same day in Brownsville McNelly dictated a report to Adjutant General Steele expressing his grave concern about the state of affairs on the border. "The condition of this frontier is pitiable in the extreme," he began. "The lives and property of our citizens are entirely at the mercy of the Mexican hordes of robbers that infest the banks of the Rio Grande." Claiming that three-fourths of the Mexican population between Piedras Negras and Matamoros benefited from the illegal "cattle trade," he reported that the thieves were "getting bolder than ever." The raids were sure to continue, he warned, until the thieves understood that there would be no refuge, and that American forces would follow them into Mexico to punish them for their outrages. "The policy pursued so long by our government, of policing our border so ineffectually that the raiders may cross cattle as they please, must now be admitted by the most obtuse of its stupid originators to be a miserable failure. Criminal, I call it, for it has permitted our people to be robbed and impoverished, our men to be murdered and our women outraged."[48]

For the normally unemotional McNelly, the report was unusually impassioned in its appeal. The words were those of a lawman whose frustrations were reaching a breaking point. "Although our state is poor—not yet recovered from the effects of the war—I will warrant that enough men and money can be raised to put a stop to these diabolical outrages." Vowing to do just that, McNelly declared, "These are American citizens, Texans. They are being murdered, robbed, driven from their homes. . . . Shall we wait for the political clock to strike the hour for putting a stop to it? When will the hour come? When?" he demanded. "We have waited ten years, and ten long years they have been to the people of this desolated border; and still no . . . sign of relief. God help the frontiersmen if they have to wait ten years more!"[49]

McNelly saved his most ominous words for last: "With my present force, I can do but little." Pointing to the fact that many of the thieves often struck seventy-five to a hundred miles from his camp, he informed Steele, "By the time I receive the information and get to the crossing, the raiders are over the Rio Grande and safe." Now, after his attack upon Rancho Las Cuevas, he predicted, "They are anxious to have revenge." With two hundred more Rangers, he insisted, he could locate and intercept the rustlers more effectively. "Unless this can be done," he warned, "I would respectfully recommend that this troop be ordered elsewhere, or disbanded. It is too humiliating to follow the thieves to the bank of the river and see our stock on the opposite bank, and have the raiders defy us to cross." Crossing again with his present force, he admitted, would only lead to "destruction."[50]

On December 10, 1875, the *Daily Express* reported that Captain McNelly had arrived in Brownsville aboard the steamer *I. G. Harris* the previous day, presumably to continue his fight against the border bandits. Only a passing reference was made to the fact that he was "slightly unwell."[51]

The report understated the truth about the captain's deteriorating health. His crackling lungs were beginning to fail. He now appeared even more pale and sickly than the last time he had visited town a few weeks earlier. He was losing weight and his strength was fast waning. It seemed like only a matter of time before the wretched disease of tuberculosis would claim him as it had so many others.

On December 20 McNelly was still well enough to attend a town meeting in Brownsville where the ongoing problem of cattle rustling was the central topic of discussion. Major Tom Parker had called the gathering and gaveled it to order. Promptly, those in attendance elected the graying figure of John S. Ford to preside. With McNelly an observer and Old Rip directing the meeting, the citizens of Brownsville selected a committee of eleven citizens to petition Governor Coke to maintain state troops on the border and even to increase the Ranger presence on the lower Rio Grande to two hundred men. The assemblage also chose Colonel John L. Haynes to chair that committee and, along with McNelly and Ford, to carry their collective concerns to Washington, D.C. Near the end of the meeting McNelly was called upon to speak. According to one observer, he made "a few terse remarks" promising that he would do his best to continue to serve the people of Texas and take the fight to the cattle thieves. After McNelly concluded, the entire audience erupted in thunderous applause. The ailing Ranger captain could not have asked for a warmer reception, or for more reassurance and public support.[52]

Whether he had sought such acclamation, McNelly had now gained it. He had simultaneously become an almost mythic hero to many in South Texas—and a villain to others. Regardless of what the politicians might say now, he had earned the admiration and respect of those Texans who had found themselves on the front lines of the border wars for the past quarter of a century. To them, the thin figure of Captain McNelly stood even taller than his growing legend.

McNelly Goes to Washington

Even before the events at Las Cuevas, McNelly had already commanded the affection and loyalty of his young Rangers. Now his name and reputation quickly reached beyond the borderlands of South Texas and the farming country of the lower Brazos, though, as biographers Chuck Parsons and Marianne Hall Little acknowledged, "little had been achieved" by the recent campaign. Even so, George Durham remembered that many people in the Rio Grande Valley and across Texas "thought Captain McNelly was magic. They'd heard about him crossing over and fetching back a herd of cattle. Those folks thought he was bigger than the President of the United States. Some of them even believed that he'd won the Battle of San Jacinto."[53]

On December 23, 1875, McNelly departed the lower Rio Grande for Washington, D.C., to answer the questions about the border troubles and, specifically, his decision to cross into Mexico. Whether Carrie, little Rebel, and baby Irene traveled with him remains unclear. But it was clear that he was a sick man. Durham remembered how shocked he was at the sad sight of the "pint sized" Captain McNelly on the eve of his trip to the nation's capital. The captain was already "leaving the outfit to the other officers. He didn't give his wife as much trouble as he used to in keeping him out of the weather and eating the good food she cooked for him." Even in camp a weakened McNelly now required the comfort of a feather mattress in the back of his own wagon, and his final days in Brownsville were spent mostly in the Miller Hotel, near an apothecary and a doctor. "You didn't have to get too close to see the sprinkling of gray in his beard," Durham recalled. "There wasn't as much spring and bounce in his walk. He was sort of hunkered over and walked slow. He wasn't dead by a long sight, but . . . he was taking it easy." Like others serving under McNelly, the young farm boy from Georgia could not help but notice that the captain's lungs rattled more and his chest at times seemed to heave with every breath. As Durham summarized his commander's condition, the "lung fever" had left the captain "puny" and "wilted."[54]

Rumors circulated through the Ranger ranks that Captain McNelly might not return to duty, that his body could no longer hold up to the demands of service in the field. Some even quietly speculated that Governor Coke was under increasing political pressure to remove the captain from command. They whispered that officials in Austin were growing impatient with McNelly, who failed to file enough reports—and file them often enough—to suit Adjutant General Steele. George Durham remembered, "The fact is that captain didn't like to write. . . . He'd said in so many words that all he wanted was dead bandits. He didn't want prisoners. He didn't want reports." Durham also recalled McNelly saying that "other Texas Ranger outfits had failed to halt banditry. They all made lots of reports, but Captain said reports weren't what bandits needed. He held that a well-placed bullet from a Sharps did more for law enforcement than a hundred reports."[55]

But if anyone thought that McNelly was done, they simply failed to take stock of his extraordinary will to finish the job that he had started. After all, he had not come to South Texas to practice politics. He had not come to recover his health. He had come to hunt down and kill bandits and rustlers.

By the time McNelly departed South Texas, no one had to explain to him that the consumption was a death sentence. He understood that when he boarded a steamship bound for the nation's capital.

10
Catching Hell

For Captain McNelly and his Rangers it promised to be a dreary winter, cold and wet. For the cattle thieves, it would be no different. The business of stealing livestock typically tapered off during December and January as many of the rustlers simply went into hibernation and waited for the first signs of warmer weather and green grasses to provide forage for their horses. In Napoleon Jennings's words, "The raids practically ceased," and the bandits seemed "completely cowed." Even so, the New Year of 1876 promised to bring with it the reality that Texas state troops—Rangers—were no longer just patrolling the river. McNelly's men, even just forty of them, were still poised to cross the border to punish the most brazen bandits. Some thieves were continuing to splash across the Rio Grande into Texas, reports confirmed, but in fewer numbers than the previous year. Unlike then, now the raiders seemed to be looking for an occasional small remuda of horses or a few cows rather than entire herds of cattle. Little wonder some residents of South Texas openly discussed whether McNelly's services were still needed.[1]

As for McNelly, he paid little attention to such talk. When he departed for Washington, D.C., two days before Christmas he had only one thing in mind—his testimony before Congress. In McNelly's absence Lieutenant Robinson assumed temporary command of the company, just as he had when the captain had left camp and returned home earlier in the fall. Still, Company A, Washington County Volunteers, remained McNelly's Rangers, even in the captain's absence. After all, he had recruited them. He had signed them up and trained them. He had taught them to follow their best instincts to avoid danger, to keep their eyes open and ears trained at all times, and to trust the Ranger next to them. He had taught them the importance of a good mount, of caring first for their horses because their own lives might depend on it. He had also taught them to make the first shot count because they might not get a second. But mostly, he had taught them the absolute necessity of obeying orders if they were to stay alive in bandit country.

It was as if the captain had put his own brand on each of them. As Durham put it, the "boys" were still forty of "McNelly's little shadows," and they always would be. As December turned to January, the patrols along the river seemed to be less productive, and less necessary. After the job of returning stolen cattle to their "rightful" owners was finished, not much else occupied the Rangers except morning, noon, and night. "There just wasn't any more Ranger business," Durham remembered. "We rode patrols far and wide without once taking our carbines out of the scabbard." For days at a time the weather dictated that the Rangers remained huddled near the warmth of their fires at Camp Retama in western Cameron County. The tall spreading Spanish oaks provided some shelter from the north winds and from the showers that frequently moved in from the Gulf or from the mountains of Old Mexico. Just as comforting, from nearby ranches and farms law-abiding Anglo and Mexican families brought the Rangers fresh bread, milk, and eggs. "We soon settled into an easy camp life and were living high on the hog," Durham recollected.[2]

Sometime after the first of the year, for whatever reason, Lieutenant Robinson apparently moved the company to a site called Laguna de las Calabazas. From there, on January 15 "Pidge" filed his next dispatch with the *Daily State Gazette* in Austin. The letter published four days later was a long, rambling narrative describing the events surrounding the Las Cuevas incident. Oddly enough, Robinson provided far more details about the raid to the newspaper publisher than McNelly had to Adjutant General Steele. But the lieutenant wrote nothing in the article of the Rangers' movements and activities since November 21 of the previous year. Not one word. It was as if he too believed that the lull in the border violence would continue, perhaps indefinitely.[3]

While Robinson remained a writer of considerable flair, he was apparently no better at filing official reports than his captain. Perhaps Robinson, like the others, actually believed that their mission had been accomplished and that the time had come to pull back and even let down their guard. Maybe no more reports were in order now because the job was all but finished, or so it seemed.

It would soon become apparent that Captain McNelly was perhaps alone among his men in believing that the border troubles were far from over. He understood the bandits better than anyone. He knew that they would return seeking vengeance, and that when they did state mounted troops—Texas Rangers—must be there to meet them.

Congressman Schleicher's Inquest

Few people outside South Central Texas had ever heard of Gustav Schleicher before his election to the U.S. Congress in 1874. A native of Darmstadt, Germany, he had studied civil engineering at the University of Giessen. Like so many German Lutherans who had immigrated to the Lone Star State in 1847, and no different from emigrants from many nations, the twenty-four-year-old romantic and intellectual viewed Texas as a boundless new land of new beginnings. Texas was an almost mythic place of limitless opportunity, he had heard, an untamed country where anyone could find a chance to start over again and make a better life and future for one's family. A surveyor and entrepreneur who had first settled in Indianola, he had helped to lay out the route for the first railroad from Port Lavaca to San Antonio. For a brief time, he had operated a shingle mill on the waters of the Guadalupe near Huaco Springs, west of New Braunfels. By 1850 he had moved to San Antonio, where he had helped to found the Guadalupe Bridge Company and the San Antonio and Mexican Gulf Railway. While in Alamo City the young German visionary had also tried his hand at the restaurant and tavern business, though without much success.[4]

In 1853 fellow citizens and neighbors had elected him to the Texas State Legislature, one admirer labeling him a "firm and consistent Democrat." For much of the next decade he had also served as surveyor of the Bexar Land District, which stretched more than four hundred miles from San Antonio to El Paso. In 1859, a year after he had served as cofounder of the San Antonio Water Company, Schleicher won a seat in the Texas state senate representing the sprawling county of Bexar and surrounding districts. During the troubles of 1860–61, Schleicher—a large, amiable man of considerable girth—had risen in stature as a leading supporter of Governor Sam Houston and a voice for Unionists throughout the state. But when the Civil War came he had shifted his allegiance to the Confederates. During the conflict, he had even served the Confederacy as a captain of engineers in General John B. Magruder's brigade. Following 1865 he had surveyed lands for the construction of a rail line from the port near Indianola to a site in DeWitt County where Sandies Creek empties into the Guadalupe River. It was there at the confluence of these streams that he had founded the town of Cuero in 1872. During this turbulent time, he had maintained a law practice in San Antonio, and his network of contacts grew with the city.[5]

When he arrived in Washington in March 1875, fifty-one-year-old Representative Schleicher was no stranger to responsibility. No sooner did the ambitious Schleicher take his seat in the House than he began to position himself to wield considerable influence on behalf of the people of his South Texas district. Remarkably, he requested and received appointments to three powerful House committees, all relevant to the concerns of his constituents—Foreign Affairs, Indian Affairs, and Railroads and Canals.[6]

What soon became clear was that behind the rhetoric of border defense was his true passion and political priority: railway construction and capital investment to spur the growth and expansion of the South Texas economy. But before that could be realized the border troubles with Mexico had to be resolved and the river frontier made safe for further settlement. To that end, he had lobbied the House leadership and colleagues on both sides of the isle, even pleading with the newly elected Speaker of the House Michael Kerr (D) of Indiana to appoint a special committee to investigate depredations and violence on the lower Rio Grande. Only if that country could be made safe would investors have confidence, Schleicher insisted. Without that, there would be no more railways to the border, no economic security for the river frontier.[7]

On January 6, 1876, the House of Representatives passed a resolution calling for formation of such a select committee. Within days Kerr appointed the Special Committee on the Mexican Border Troubles, with Gustav Schleicher (D) as chair. Aside from the ambitious Texan, the committee also comprised Stephen A. Hurlbut (R) from Indiana, Lucius Q. C. Lamar (D) of Mississippi, former Union general Nathaniel P. Banks (I) of Massachusetts, and Alpheus S. Williams (R) of Michigan.[8]

The weather was especially bitter on January 24 when Captain McNelly arrived at Capitol Hill to testify before the committee. An arctic blast had plunged temperatures to below 20 degrees as gusts of north winds exceeded thirty miles per hour, and the gray skies threatened more snow. But the weather was of less concern to McNelly than the bitter political climate in the halls of Congress. McNelly had traveled to Washington in the hope of meeting with President Grant, but apparently that never happened. The captain only learned of the appointment of Schleicher's special committee after he had arrived in town. Nevertheless, he had come well prepared to make the case on behalf of the people of the lower Rio Grande for a stronger border defense. Even though he preferred a private audience with President Grant, this would be his opportunity, and he knew that he had to make the most of it.[9]

Dressed in his best beaver hat, finest dark suit, a starched white shirt, black string tie, and polished Sunday boots, McNelly raised his right hand and took an oath to tell the whole truth, and nothing but the truth. For the next two and a half hours he did just that. Chairman Schleicher began, "Have you just come from the Rio Grande?" McNelly answered yes. When asked how long he had been there and to explain his occupation, the captain informed the committee that he had been dispatched by order of the governor of Texas to command a company of "state militia" for the purpose of "breaking up" the roving bands of cattle thieves that had been preying upon ranches and settlements on the north side of the Rio Grande. A man of few words, not known for his patience with legal or legislative proceedings, McNelly must have considered his time on the witness stand to be one of the longest and least gratifying days of his life. But members of Congress and the administration must know the situation, he may have reminded himself. The citizens of Cameron County would not have sent him all the way to Washington just for appearance's sake.[10]

Schleicher asked how McNelly had gained firsthand knowledge of these ongoing raids and his "means" of obtaining reliable information about the rustlers. For several minutes, the ailing Ranger captain unloaded on the committee members. He testified that, "after being on the river for some weeks, I found that I could employ, for money, Mexican cattle thieves as spies." In this way, he explained, he could "sell them to their companions, tendering them handsome rewards." McNelly added that he "promised to pay more than they could make by raiding." In effect, he admitted that he paid the spies bounties for each thief that the Rangers killed or captured, with ten dollars a head being the standard rate and fifteen dollars for the most notorious thieves. Besides, the captain added, he vowed to place the spies on the state payroll for sixty dollars a month once they proved themselves to be reliable and trustworthy (that was more than the thirty-dollar salaries of his own troops, or forty dollars for officers). Of course, McNelly made no mention of Old Casuse's paint-horse gallows. That was one truth, he decided, that best remained undisclosed.[11]

With such a network of well-paid informants, McNelly reported, his Rangers had been able to track down and "turn loose" three to four herds of cattle each month. Typically, he continued, when small bands of thieves realized that the Rangers were closing in on them, they simply abandoned the livestock and rode casually toward the river. "When we would come up we would find the cattle in the bush," he testified, "we could not find the men who had been driving them. The country is filled with numbers of armed Mexicans; and it is a most common sight to see four or five or six men, well-armed and mounted, whose business no one knows." When asked their business, McNelly informed the committee members, these vaqueros would answer that they were "trading stock" or that they worked at a nearby ranch or one twenty miles into the interior. "We know nothing of them," the captain continued, "and if we take them to the ranch to which they say they belong, the servants . . . generally, without hesitation, verify their statement; in many instances from friendship, most frequently from fear."[12]

So many of those who worked cattle on the Texas side were friends or relatives of the rustlers, McNelly explained. "They are their kinfolk, their cousins, uncles, and brothers—for it seems to me as if all the Mexicans on both sides of the river are related." Congressman Hurlbut interjected, "That or *compadres?*" McNelly responded, "Yes, relatives or *compadres,* which is a little nearer with the Mexicans." Then he added, "I find that I can trust none but the Mexican owners of the ranches. . . . I do not know of any Mexican who owns a ranch on this side of the river and who lives in Texas whom I do not consider to be a good citizen. . . . They all want to see the laws enforced, and they all want to see this raiding broken up."[13]

McNelly next turned his attention to the daily dangers of life on the lower Rio Grande. "I am willing to take a good many chances," he continued, "but I would certainly not live on a stock ranch west of the Nueces River, at any point from the mouth of the Devil's River to the mouth of the Rio Grande. I think the risk is too great—so great that scarcely any compensation would pay for it." Then he admitted, "My position in command of a company of [state] troops I do not consider half as hazardous as that of those . . . living on ranches." Most of those on the front lines of the danger, he informed the committee, were "excellent Mexican citizens" of Texas, many of whom were third-generation rancheros and proud of their heritage, their land, and their citizenship of the United States. The fact that almost all had families on both sides of the border did not diminish their loyalty to their adopted country north of the river.[14]

When Congressman Schleicher asked McNelly if he was aware of any raiders from the Texas side who had crossed the border into Mexico, the captain answered that he had "not heard of a single charge" to that effect. Why? Too dangerous, the Texan explained, even for the most daring of desperadoes.[15]

Congressman L. Q. C. Lamar followed the chairman by asking if McNelly meant to imply earlier that an armed force of five hundred Americans could not remain on Mexican soil for more than two or three days without being overpowered and outgunned? "I speak as a soldier," McNelly responded, speculating that such a military force of "our best troops" could not cross more than four miles into Mexico and remain there for even twenty-four hours without being annihilated by the "rural police" of Mexico. By that, he meant the *rurales* who were local forces typically commanded by the owner of a large ranch, or his "superintendent" as McNelly described the foreman. When pressed to elaborate, the captain informed the committee members that "these frontiersmen are armed with Winchester rifles and carbines, and quite a number of them with Spencer rifles," apparently purchased from the Texas side of the river.[16]

When questioned as to the number of Mexican federal troops stationed along the line of the lower Rio Bravo, McNelly testified that, to the best of his knowledge, detachments from three regiments of Mexican cavalry and a full-strength regiment of infantry were stationed in Matamoros. But he could not estimate the numbers of troops. As to their readiness, however, he described the cavalry forces as "indifferently armed and mounted." Aside from their uniform military cap, these Mexican troops typically wore a wide assortment of attire ranging from tattered and dingy dungarees to mismatched woolen tunics and outdated military blouses. Some even appeared to the "shamefully naked," as McNelly described, without field boots or even winter coats. In appearance, and in fact, they did not seem to pose the same threat as the border *rurales*, or irregulars, who were commanded and paid by the rancheros of the river frontier and who could doubtless "whip" the federal troops "three to one," in McNelly's words.[17]

When Mr. Hurlbut questioned whether these *rurales* ever apprehended cattle thieves and turned them over to Texas authorities, McNelly responded, "No sir; on the contrary, we have applied to the authorities on the other side again and again. . . . The Mexican authorities promise to capture them and turn them over; but they have never done so." Then McNelly revealed that his sources had provided ample evidence that the rustlers were "almost exclusively" from the very same rural police, or *rurales*, that he had been discussing moments earlier. For the most part, he had learned, they were not deserters from the local guard but well-paid mercenaries working for wealthy rancheros south of the border. In other words, they performed double duty as police and cattle rustlers.[18]

McNelly apologized that he had not come prepared to offer the committee statistical information supporting the estimated number of Texas cattle that were being driven across the border into Mexico each month. He noted that he had kept a log back in Texas with such information and that he recalled reporting to Colonel Potter that thieves had driven some two thousand head across the Rio Grande during the past November. With that, the committee adjourned for the day.[19]

Schleicher again recalled McNelly to the stand on Saturday, January 29. When the chairman resumed the questioning about the "character of the population" on the Texas side of the Rio Grande, McNelly answered: "Probably nine tenths of the people living . . . [outside] the towns are of Mexican origin." Owners of the land and the cattle, they were good citizens of Texas and the United States. But many of the workers on these ranches were part of a "floating population," he continued. They hired on as cowhands for temporary or seasonal employment, rounding up the cattle, branding them, building and repairing fences, wrangling horses, and performing other chores. Of these vaqueros and their known loyalties and allegiances, the captain stated, "They are Mexicans, decidedly, for all their habits and feelings," and they held what he termed a "violent antipathy for the *gringos*, or Americans."[20]

Most of McNelly's testimony that day focused on the disingenuous nature of local Mexican officials, who continued to pledge cooperation but repeatedly failed to live up to their word. Among the most egregious offenders, he alleged, was the duplicitous Colonel Cristo, *comandante* of the *federales* garrisoned in Matamoros. "Have you ever known of any instance in which Mexican authorities on the other side, either civil or military, have endeavored to restore stolen property?" asked Mr. Hurlbut. "No sir; not one," McNelly responded. After discussing the wide-ranging network and influence that General Cortina had wielded for more than fifteen years, McNelly recounted his recent experiences with rustlers who were remnants of his cattle-thieving operation.[21]

When questioned by Schleicher about the difficulty in determining the personal identity of the raiders, McNelly responded, "All of these men are known by public reputation; we know all of them, or nearly all of them. . . . They are identified on this side by the citizens of Texas, and they are known on the other side. They live there publicly and do not conceal their business." Brazen and confident, the thieves did not "attempt any concealment" of their crimes, he reported. Like the farmworkers of the border, they had families on both sides of the river, which made their apprehension more difficult.[22]

Mr. Hurlbut then turned to the question of authority. He asked if "sufficient power" existed under Texas law to allow state troops to detain and investigate criminals on mere suspicion of the theft of livestock? McNelly answered, "No sir; there is not." But he added that martial law was not the answer, either. Without specifically mentioning Reconstruction, he claimed that such extraordinary measures placed a greater burden on law-abiding citizens than on the lawless criminal element.[23]

McNelly made it clear that there were no easy answers—and perhaps no answers at all. The central government of Lerdo de Tejada seemed too preoccupied with putting down revolts in the interior of Mexico to patrol and police the border effectively, he agreed. Only with political and economic stability in Mexico, and only with cooperation from Mexico City and the state capitals, could that be done. Admittedly, a force of four hundred to five hundred highly mobile troops would be required to recapture most stolen livestock driven across the lower Rio Grande, and that assumed swift raids across the border, with the consent and assistance of the Mexican government, McNelly stated. Then Congressman Hurlbut inquired, "I suppose that you are aware that sending a body of troops under the flag of the United States, into a country with which we are at peace is a declaration of war."[24]

A defiant Captain McNelly finally bristled, and the exchange turned more contentious. "I do not know of any writer on international law who does not agree . . . [with] the principle that where a nation is unable or unwilling to restrain its turbulent population from depredating on a neighboring . . . [nation] that the . . . [offended country] has the right to pursue these robbers across the line, and there to punish them for their offenses." When congressman Hurlbut tried to lecture the Texan on the causes of the war with Mexico and the consequences of American troops crossing the Nueces in 1846, McNelly quickly replied that Mexican officers had been leading troops across the Rio Grande for years, advancing into Texas and committing outrages against the people of the Lone Star State. When Hurlbut pressed him to produce evidence to that effect, McNelly clarified that by "Mexican troops" he was referring again to rural police, who had continually violated sovereign U.S. and Texas soil since 1848, in violation of the peace of Guadalupe Hidalgo. He even alleged that there had been "instances" when Mexican federal troops had crossed into Texas as well. Hurlbut asked whether they were under orders from Mexico City. "I do not know anything about their orders; but they have certainly crossed, and that fact is proved by the Congressional committee [the Robb Commission] that was down there."[25]

Captain McNelly took aim one last time. "The people of the frontier do not want war; they want peace. I have followed fifty herds of cattle to the bank of the Rio Grande, and I would see the stock on the opposite bank. The Mexicans would dare me to cross the river and take them. They would say: 'Here are the cattle. Come across if . . . you dare.'" At that point Congressman Hurlbut's tone changed, and he wanted to know if McNelly believed that commanders on the scene should be given more "extraordinary powers" to deal with the cattle thieves. "Who can give that authority?" McNelly asked rhetorically. "The President can," Hurlbut answered. With that, McNelly concluded by acknowledging that he and his family resided in Washington County on the lower Brazos, more than three hundred miles from the Rio Grande. As for his primary occupation and his financial interests, he stated simply, "I am a planter; I own no property on that frontier." The official record of the Texan's testimony ends there.[26]

McNelly had never retreated from a fight in his life, and he did not withdraw that day from some tough questioning. As he had done so many times before with border bandits and outlaws of the worst type, he stood his ground.

Two weeks later, after McNelly picked up his beaver hat, walked out of the Capitol, and departed Washington, General Edward O. C. Ord appeared before the House select committee. From his perspective as commander of the U.S. Military Department of Texas he offered a sober assessment of the border troubles. But his testimony seemed dispassionate, even detached in comparison to McNelly's appraisal. In a formal narrative befitting a military report, General Ord surveyed the recent raids into Texas and countermeasures by both Texas mounted troops and U.S. regulars, focusing specifically on the controversial Las Cuevas affair. He spoke of troop strength and the distribution of forces on the river frontier. He also meandered through a myriad of issues, ranging from the terrain, climate, and culture on the lower Rio Grande, and to the need for a stronger extradition treaty with Mexico. He talked about the political instability in Mexico City and how that contributed to blurred lines of jurisdictions and fragmented authority on the local levels of government. Only briefly did he raise the issue of racial divides along the border when he mentioned replacing "colored troops" of the Thirty-Eighth Infantry at Fort Brown with all-white units that would be looked upon more favorably by the "Mexican population" on the Texas side of the river. But he seemed to have nothing in the way of recommendations.[27]

Surprisingly, the one issue General Ord skirted—and the one that committee members failed to pursue during his testimony—was the source and extent of cattle rustling. But in keeping with military protocol in such hearings, General Ord instead submitted several reports and copies of communications intended to shed light on the problem. Such was not the case when longtime Cameron County resident John L. Haynes took the stand on February 14. Collector of customs for the District of Brazos de Santiago, which included the counties of Cameron, Hidalgo, and Starr, "Colonel" Haynes enjoyed an uncommon vantage point. After being sworn in, he spoke briefly about his thirty-years of living in the Rio Grande Valley. Even with former general and congressman Nathaniel P. Banks present with the committee members that day, Haynes made no mention of his Unionist activities during the late war, or his longtime association with former Governor E. J. Davis. Being the chief federal customs official for the ports of Brownsville, Point Isabel, and Brazos Santiago, he spoke with authority about the problem of smuggling along the entire line of the lower Rio Grande. When asked if the Zona Libre, the free zone along the south banks of the river, contributed to the growing industry of cattle theft, he answered, "I think it has. The establishment of the free zone has always been regarded by the people of the frontier as a hostile measure on the part of Mexico." He confirmed that the policy had created a tinderbox of troubles for the Texans and the U.S. troops as well as residents of the lower Rio Grande. With safety and a duty-free zone awaiting them south of the border, the rustlers and their patrons had been operating without constraint.[28]

Haynes also discredited allegations leveled by the Mexican commission appointed by President Lerdo de Tejada three years earlier. "I have read the report," Haynes testified, "both in Spanish and English. The report is very ingenuous and plausible," he admitted, "but it is full of fallacies and misrepresentations." That Anglos coveted the lands of South Texas following the Treaty of Guadalupe Hidalgo did not necessarily mean that the gringos and their courts swindled Mexicans out of their claims. Such allegations were "absolutely false," he insisted. The justice system (and Miller commission of 1853) had in fact confirmed the land grants of scores of South Texas rancheros of Mexican descent. Resentful of the charges that every Anglo-Texan was a filibuster or a moral degenerate, he declared that cattle rustling had long been a contagion on the border and that corrupt Mexican officials had been complicit and even in league with the thieves for more than two decades.[29]

As the committee members listened intently Haynes submitted the final report of the "Permanent Committee" that had been appointed by the citizens of Brownsville on April 17, 1875. The report chronicled recent outrages committed against citizens of South Texas by bandits crossing the border. Hardly any of this information was new, however, most of it being contained in previous congressional testimony and reports. What made the Brownsville committee's remonstrance remarkable was the acknowledgment that Anglo-Texans had committed wrongdoing against the persons and property of Texans of Mexican descent through the years. But these misdeeds and outrages were the result of individual criminal acts, the report stated, not the organized actions of groups designed to subjugate and oppress Tejanos. The committee report then pointed to the fact that Anglos were in the minority in the South Texas counties according to the 1870 U.S. census, no more than one in nine residents between the Nueces and the Rio Grande being "American."[30]

Of the committee members who had signed the Brownsville report, thirteen of the sixteen were Anglo citizens of South Texas, and only three were of Mexican heritage. Still, in the end their conclusions offered no hint of racial strife on the border or the cultural divide that separated both peoples, only the importance of the need for cooperation in creating a peaceful country where people might no longer live in the shadows of terror. "It is to the interest of our government and people, especially of the people of this frontier, to preserve amicable relations with the government and people of the neighboring Republic of Mexico." The report then referred to the "large trade passing through this frontier" and to the painful reality that "our commerce as well as our local industry in stock-raising has been seriously injured by the disorders." Whether merchants, herdsmen, workers, landowners, or steamship operators, Texan and Tejano alike, all shared the same interest—a safe and secure border where all people could live and work together, free from fear, and to share the same water and the same land, in peace.[31]

Captain McNelly could not have agreed more, except for one thing. When he returned to Cameron County, Texas, that April to resume command of Company A, he wanted the rustlers and bandits to live in fear. And the only way to ensure that was to let the word travel ahead that he was back to track them and hunt them down—the worst of them, and the rest of them. With that in mind, on May 17, 1876, McNelly again saddled up Segal and led his company back into the field.

The Captain Returns

On May 25, 1876, McNelly and his men rode into the border town of Laredo. Napoleon Augustus Jennings, a nineteen-year-old "greenhorn" from Philadelphia, never forgot the moment when he first set eyes on the legendary captain and his Texas Rangers. Standing on a street corner that morning, Jennings was contemplating the fact he was a long way from home and down on his luck. "Looking up the street, I saw a troop of horsemen coming toward me. As they approached I saw that they were Americans, and for a moment I thought they were cowboys. But what, I asked myself, were so many cowboys doing together? I counted them as they rode by. There were forty-two of them."[32]

As the riders drew closer, Jennings could not help but notice that one of the men stood out. "At the head rode a man who was surely not a cowboy, whatever the others might be. The leader was rather under the average height and slimly built, but he sat so erect in the saddle and had such an air of command he seemed like a cavalry officer at the head of a company of soldiers." But as young Jennings looked past the first rider and surveyed the rest of the horsemen it became apparent that these were not U.S. regular troops. "It was easy to see these men were not soldiers. They were heavily armed, to be sure, but they wore no uniforms, and were nearly all beardless youths. The leader himself seemed not more than thirty years of age, although he wore a heavy dark brown mustache and 'goatee,' which, at first glance, made him look slightly older."[33]

Still wondering who these men were, other than so many strangers in a strange land, Jennings observed the lead rider hold his right hand above his head. Without a word, the entire column halted. Even the horses seemed to stand motionless as the commander turned to the man behind him and spoke so softly that Jennings could not hear him. Then the leader wheeled his horse down a side street, leaving the officer behind him to shout the command "Forward march!" For Jennings, the entire scene only raised his curiosity. He could not help but ask a Hispanic gentleman standing nearby if he knew the identity of this armed company of mounted men. "Why, those are McNelly's Rangers," the man responded in English. "They are heading down the river."[34]

Young Jennings had heard of the storied Texas Rangers and of their fearless Captain McNelly. But he had assumed that they would look larger than life, just like they were pictured in the press back east—surly-looking, bearded hellions who were armed to the teeth with everything from Bowie knives to Colt revolvers. The dime novelists and journalists had depicted them as the devil's horsemen who were the scourge of bad men, border-land bandits, and marauding Indians. And yet here were the real Rangers, for the most part looking hardly more than schoolboys on a Sunday morning ride.

Little wonder that Jennings thought to himself, "Why shouldn't I join the Rangers?" Down on his luck, having bounced from one job to another, young Jennings was dressed in dirty faded clothes, scuffed boots, and an old sombrero that was "somewhat the worse for hard usage." But he had nothing to lose, so he worked up enough courage to seek out McNelly and offer his services.[35]

His encounter with McNelly would be brief and to the point. Entering the little hotel where the captain and his family were staying, Jennings asked to speak with the commanding officer. Soon he received word that McNelly would meet him upstairs in his room. "I found him sitting by the window, talking to his sweet-faced wife," Jennings remembered. McNelly looked him over, sizing him up, perhaps thinking that the young man looked more like a half-starved ragamuffin than a Texas Ranger. "I have come, sir, to ask you to take me into your Rangers," he began. "I should very much like to join . . . if you'll take me." The captain asked his name and then inquired, "You from the North?" First hesitating, Jennings confessed, "I am a Philadelphian." McNelly asked, "What brought you into this country?" Jennings replied, explaining that he had come to Texas to make money and to lead a life of adventure. "If you join my troop you'll see all the adventure you want," McNelly answered. "Can you ride?" When Jennings assured the captain that he could, he was told to come back at 3:00 in the afternoon. With that, his interview was abruptly over.[36]

What Jennings learned later that day left him at first eager, then anxious. The captain had decided to take him on, he heard from one local resident who knew McNelly. Jennings recalled, "As it was near the appointed hour, I went to the little hotel. The Captain was standing in the doorway." McNelly told him that he had decided to let him sign up, but he added, "You'll have to get a horse, saddle and bridle, a couple of blankets and a six-shooter. The state furnishes your carbine." Before turning and walking back into the hotel, the captain informed him that the company would strike camp early the next morning and move downriver. "If he had told me the entrance fee to his troop was ten thousand dollars in gold, it would not have staggered me more. . . . The money would have been as easy to obtain," Jennings remembered his desperation. "I was completely disheartened."[37]

As it turned out, a short walk up the street and a chance encounter with Mounted Customs Inspector H. A. Burbank changed the course of Jennings's life. Burbank, who had befriended the adventuresome young romantic recently arrived from the East, recognized the young man's predicament and offered to help. He would procure the horse and gear for the youth in exchange for a written agreement to have Captain McNelly send ten dollars a month from the Ranger's pay (a private's salary was a generous thirty dollars per month). In just a few minutes, therefore, Jennings mounted up and rode off to muster into Company A, Washington County Volunteers. He was now a Texas Ranger, in name if not yet in deed and experience.[38]

But like the rest, while Napoleon Augustus Jennings would find the adventure of a lifetime, it would not be as romantic or as rewarding as he had envisioned. Meanwhile, on May 31, while resting in his hotel room Captain McNelly wasted little time in informing Adjutant General Steele that he planned on going after arguably the most notorious nest of bandits bedeviling the Rio Grande border. Without revealing too many specifics to his troops, and without much fanfare, he sent word to prepare to saddle up for a difficult march the following morning. This time the company would be heading back north toward the hard lands of the upper Nueces.[39]

Not until McNelly and company arrived in the Dimmit County settlement of Carrizo Springs a couple of days later did it become apparent that Company A, Washington County Volunteers, had left the "Lower Country" behind. Now their services were needed on another front line, one every bit as dangerous and violent as the rangelands of Cameron and Hidalgo Counties.

This reality McNelly explained to Adjutant General Steele in a communication that depicted the situation on the border as nothing less than grave: "You can scarcely realize the true condition of this section, from Oakville to this point. The country is under a perfect reign of terror from the number and desperate character of the thieves who infest this region." Describing the river frontier as still being "rich in stock, but very sparsely settled," the captain concluded that the "opportunities and inducements to steal are very great." He then confided to his boss that "some of the oldest and best citizens told me that, in all their frontier experience, they had never suffered so much as from these white robbers. For weeks past they have not dared to leave their homes for fear of being waylaid and murdered."[40]

McNelly continued, "Every house in this part of the country has been repeatedly fired into by armed men, from fifteen to twenty in number at a time." Their horses and cattle driven from the fields, their cowhands and wranglers gunned down on the range, the ranchers along the border were understandably left fearful and "destitute of means." For those who had enough courage to protest or complain to authorities, they received death notices if they failed to abandon their ranches and leave the country. As for those who did not heed these warnings, McNelly reported, they were brutally murdered by the worst outlaws the Nueces Strip had ever seen. Gangs of the bullies—the refuse of Reconstruction and revolutionary Mexico—swarmed throughout the Nueces Strip, threatening and intimidating law-abiding citizens at gunpoint. "No witnesses can be found who will dare to testify against the desperadoes," McNelly wrote. "I am told by the Circuit Judge that he is convinced no jury in three counties—Dimmit, Maverick, and Live Oak—can be found to convict them."[41]

The largest and perhaps most vicious band of cutthroats and assassins, reportedly numbering in the hundreds, preyed openly upon law-abiding citizens from Goliad on the San Antonio to the headwaters of the Nueces River. Let there be no mistake, McNelly implored the adjutant general, these outlaws held no allegiance but to crime and they respected no authority, not even that of the Almighty. And they understood only one thing, McNelly implied—the business end of a .45 Colt or a Sharps rifle.[42]

Just four days after Napoleon Augustus Jennings joined McNelly's command, the word spread through camp that the company was heading to an outlaw hideout on Pendencia Creek, some ten miles northwest of the town of Carrizo Springs. The young Rangers learned from their officers that there, near Lake Espantosa, the most notorious horse thief and cattle rustler in all the borderlands was holed up. John King Fisher—the very name struck terror into every decent man and woman in seven counties: the Rangers had all heard the name. Everyone agreed that King Fisher was one dangerous man. But the boys reassured young Jennings—Captain McNelly was equal to the task.

Catching King Fisher

To settlers and stockmen in the region, Lake Espantosa—meaning "haunted" or "fearful" in Spanish—is a place to be avoided. In the words of historian Charles Robinson, it is "a sort of ghost lake" formed from old channels of the upper Nueces. Local lore has it that strange spirits lurk there, sometimes appearing through the fog of night or rising in the morning mist that clings like a dark cloak to the shallow marshes. Some say that lost souls wander there, and that the murky waters are guarded by the apparitions of the dead; some say that the lost souls are those who disappeared there without any trace, presumably murdered by bandits from both sides of the Rio Grande. Alligators have been known to swim and splash along the water's edge. Mysterious voices and unidentified noises are said to fill the darkness, alongside the mournful howls of coyotes and the lonely wailing of wolves. No wonder that outlaws would find such haunts to be a perfect place to hide from the law—and an ideal ground for burying the bodies of their victims. No witnesses lived there; only the dead stayed behind—and they could not testify in a court of law.[43]

Whether McNelly had heard the legends of this "haunted" lake is not known. But even if he had, it would have made no difference. Death and stories of ghoulish spirits scared him no more than the crude sign that stood at a fork in the trail crossing the prairies west of the lake. "This is King Fisher's Road," the placard read. "Take the other one."[44]

During the first week in June, McNelly had no time for ghost stories. He spent his days and evenings interviewing locals, gathering more information about Fisher's sprawling empire built on stolen horses and cattle from Mexico. Already, through the efforts of A. L. Parrot, one of his spies, McNelly had learned much. Parrott, who had posed as a photographer and portrait artist that spring to gain the thieves' confidence, rode into the Rangers camp one day and dumped an entire saddlebag filled with pictures into McNelly's lap. The captain wasted no time in moving against Fisher and his gang. Now, he even knew what they looked like. Locals who had been victimized by Fisher and those not loyal to him or his operation also supplied more details, enough, in McNelly's view, to merit arrest warrants. To McNelly, the evidence he had was enough to apprehend and bring to justice the young outlaw chieftain and his "hired hands."[45]

George Durham thus remembered how surprised he and his fellow Rangers were when they heard their captain explain to them that, on this raid, they were not to fire their weapons unless they were first fired upon. It smacked of interference from the politicians and bureaucrats in Austin and Washington, he thought. After all, before Las Cuevas the captain had "said in so many words that all he wanted was dead bandits. He didn't want prisoners. He didn't want reports. Captain said he was sent in by the governor not to write reports." Durham also recalled that McNelly made his feelings clear that "other Texas Ranger outfits had failed to halt banditry. So had the military. They all made lots of reports, but captain said reports weren't what bandits needed. He held that a well-placed bullet from a Sharps did more for law enforcement than a hundred reports."[46]

But the days of "shooting first and asking questions later" were over— or at least were supposed to be over. Times were changing. Even so, as Jennings acknowledged, McNelly's Rangers could not have been more confident in themselves and in their captain, and for good reason. "Our success on the lower Rio Grande gave us the feeling that we were invincible," he remembered. Armed now with new .44 Winchester repeating rifles (the now-famed 1873 model) shipped to them weeks earlier by Captain Richard King, they were convinced that twenty-five Rangers could hold off an entire army of bandits. The lever-action rifles were lighter and easier to wield than the cumbersome Sharps. Best of all, like their Colt six-shooters, the Winchesters could fire rapidly and accurately, even from horseback, and up to ten rounds without reloading if necessary.[47]

Riding out of their camp near Carrizo Springs on the morning of June 6, the column followed Pendencia Creek through the open ranges west of town. McNelly first divided his patrol into two squads and advanced slowly through the dense chaparral and tall Spanish grass. Not until they approached to within a quarter mile of Fisher's hideout did the columns converge. Realizing that the outlaws had not yet detected their presence, McNelly commanded his men to form one long battle line. Durham recalled the scene: "He opened us up into a skirmish formation and moved us slow till he sighted the main house, nested under a cottonwood grove surrounded by thick brush." From there, McNelly and his troops could see several men playing cards, apparently still unaware of the Rangers' approach.[48]

At that point, McNelly raised his hand, and on his prearranged signal the Rangers rode full speed toward the ranch compound. The dirt and dust flew as McNelly spurred Segal into a dead run, with his troops following in line. The Rangers maintained their intervals between riders, just as their captain had taught them, as they fanned out across the plain. Then, unexpectedly, a rock-and-rail fence rose ahead. But in Jennings's words, "The horses went over it like so many hunters after the hounds."[49]

By the time McNelly and his mounted troops galloped up to the cluster of clapboard buildings the poker-playing outlaws had scattered. As the Rangers flew from their saddles with Winchesters and revolvers drawn, King and his men scrambled into the cabin and nearby outbuildings. Since McNelly had ordered his troops not to shoot unless they were fired upon (perhaps a result of the perceived criticism they had received from Austin for their attack upon Las Cuevas the previous November), no gunfire punctuated an otherwise chaotic scene.[50]

Then a tense moment threatened to break the morning quiet. "Darting around the house," Durham recollected, "Parrot came flush up with Frank Porter." Recognizing young Parrot, Porter raised his rifle and yelled, "You're that damned picture man." But after a moment the outlaw realized that the Ranger "had the drop on him." After a brief standoff, Porter lost his nerve, dropped his rifle to the ground, and raised his hands.[51]

Moments later at the doorway of the main house a dapper-looking King Fisher found himself face to face with Captain McNelly, who as usual was dressed in his starched Sunday finest. What followed would have disappointed anyone expecting a showdown between two of the most lethal gunmen in all Texas. First identifying himself by name, rank, and affiliation with the state Rangers, McNelly ordered Fisher to lock his hands behind his head and turn around. Fisher complied and stood motionless as McNelly carefully slid two pistols from his holsters. The captain handed the ivory-handled silver-plated revolvers to one of his Rangers and instructed Fisher to turn around.

Although King Fisher was smirking and his lips curled into a smile, McNelly found no humor in the moment. Before the captain could question his prisoner, he found himself cornered not by an outlaw but, even worse, by an angry woman. Fisher's bride, Sarah, "a pretty girl, with wonderfully fine, bold black eyes," as Jennings remembered, moved between her husband and McNelly. Insisting on an explanation, she demanded to know why Texas Rangers had come to her home with guns drawn. McNelly calmly drawled, "He's under arrest." When she pressed to know why, insisting that "he's done nothing," King Fisher interrupted and politely motioned for her to step aside. Then, as Durham recalled, just as Fisher had begun to challenge McNelly to explain the charges against him, the captain snapped, "You're going to jail."[52]

While McNelly's men were rounding up and disarming seven more prisoners, who all surrendered without a fight or even a whimper, the captain could not help but take stock of his overdressed prisoner. A Hollywood scriptwriter could not have created a more colorful character than John King Fisher. Dressed more like a circus performer than an outlaw, the young gunslinger was in Jennings's words "the most perfect specimen of a frontier dandy . . . I ever saw. He was tall, beautifully proportioned, and exceedingly handsome. He wore the finest clothing procurable, but all of it was the picturesque, border, dime novel kind." Atop his head rested a broad-brimmed sombrero festooned with gold and silver lace and a band made of rattlesnake skin encircling the crown. His black-and-gold embroidered Mexican vest, white silk shirt, and crimson sash around his waist must have brought to mind a successful pirate, which is exactly what Fisher was. His unique striped chaps made from the skin of a Bengal tiger were sewn down the seams with fringed buckskin. His distinct boots, of the "finest high heeled variety," accentuated his wardrobe, as did the stylish spurs decorated with silver bells that jingled when he walked.[53]

The dapper Fisher and all the others "gave up without a struggle," Jennings recalled. In all, McNelly and his Rangers had caught nine prisoners that morning without firing a shot. It was a remarkable feat, especially considering the desperate character and dreaded reputation of the outlaws. Burd Obenchain, alias Frank Porter, may have been the worst of the lot; a vicious killer who reportedly specialized in murdering Mexican vaqueros, he claimed to have ridden with Quantrill's Raiders during the war. The whole posse were listed in "the Book" for a varied assortment of crimes: Bill Templeton, a notorious horse thief with outstanding warrants in both Texas and Mexico; Warren Allen, wanted for the brutal murder of a black trooper at Fort Clark; and Will Wainwright, Jim Honeycutt, Al Roberts, and Wes Bruton and his son, Bill.[54]

Though the nine outlaws had surrendered meekly, McNelly understood that they were anything but harmless. This was especially true of Fisher and "Porter." Reportedly, only several weeks before their capture, the two thieves had stolen a herd of cattle from six vaqueros east of Eagle Pass. According to McNelly's sources, they disarmed the herdsmen and marched them to the prairies near Lake Espantosa, where they shot them execution-style. Rolling the bodies into a narrow shallow grave together, they left the corpses for the carrion-eating birds and animals. Locals came to call the field—appropriately located near the infamous "haunted" lake—"Frank Porter's Graveyard." As for Fisher, the twenty-six-year-old outlaw claimed persuasively that he had killed a man for every year of his life, "not including Mexicans," he boasted. An exceptional horseman who bragged that he could ride any of a thousand mounts he had stolen in Mexico, Fisher sported the skills to back up the claim.[55]

No one needed to convince Captain McNelly that these were bad men, probably beyond "reform." But McNelly also had a dilemma on his hands. He had not had any experience holding prisoners since the war in Louisiana. So he decided to fall back on the old Spanish tradition, *la ley de fuga*. He called out for Sarah Fisher and offered her a terse warning. As Durham recalled the moment, the captain calmly told her, "I'm taking these men to Eagle Pass. They're under arrest." Then he asked her to pass along the word to others, "If any rescue is tried they all die." In anger and disbelief, she replied, "That's your law. . . . We've heard you make your own law, but let me tell you—" she threatened, "if you kill my husband . . ."[56]

Having enough of her insolence, McNelly walked away, without another word. He turned to Lieutenant Lawrence Wright and instructed him to select a squad of Rangers and escort the prisoners to Eagle Pass. He would follow the next day and meet them at the office of the Maverick County sheriff. Everyone could see that he was too sick to saddle up, and they knew that he would be riding a few hours behind them in a wagon. Besides, none of them ever questioned the captain's orders.

Around noon the next day Lieutenant Wright and six Rangers, including young George Durham, rode into Eagle Pass with their prisoners. Captain McNelly's wagon, driven by Ranger Jim Wofford, arrived no more than an hour later. If McNelly or any of his men expected a welcome from local law enforcement, they would be mistaken. Durham remembered that when the captain entered the office and presented his prisoners to Deputy Sheriff Vale he found himself on the wrong end of the interrogation. Fisher's lawyer and Vale were more interested in questioning him than in incarcerating the prisoners—all of whom they knew personally. On whose authority did he make the arrests? Did he have warrants? Court papers? Did he come to present witnesses against these men? "No," the captain conceded. What specific evidence could he produce against these men? He had nothing more than their names listed in the adjutant general's list of known fugitives, the thick volume known as "the Book." Could he guarantee that Maverick County would be reimbursed for jailing and caring for those men until they were claimed by authorities of Texas or other states?

Again, McNelly answered simply, "No." Deputy Vale informed McNelly that, without proper court orders, he would have to set the prisoners free. By now exasperated, the captain turned, pointed to his prisoners and ordered Lieutenant Wright to give them back their guns and release them. It was a stunning defeat for McNelly.[57]

But he was not prepared to walk away quietly. As a grinning King Fisher began to strap on his pistols McNelly stepped out the door and waited for him. Durham witnessed what happened next. Confronting the cocky gunslinger and horse thief, McNelly proceeded to deliver a stern lecture and warning. Fisher may have dodged the law until now, but the day was coming when his luck would run out. He should go home to his pretty young wife and give up his crooked ways. When Fisher boasted that he already was a "law-abiding man," McNelly fired back, "Make damn sure you stay law-abiding."[58]

Finally, as Durham witnessed, the captain left Fisher with some chilling words of advice: "You could make a good citizen," McNelly encouraged him. "You'd also make a good corpse. All outlaws look good dead. . . . But it's up to you."[59]

Fisher chuckled and, with that, he rode away a free man, at least for now. McNelly told Lieutenant Wright to order his men to return to camp on the Carrizo. He would be along in a day or two. He had to attend to some matters, he said. But Wright and his fellow Rangers knew the truth. Their captain's health was quickly deteriorating. He had been coughing up more blood lately and needed to see a doctor. Besides, Carrie insisted that her husband seek treatment.[60]

Even when the ailing captain returned to camp, looking more rested and comfortable, he still appeared listless. "He never pranced or fidgeted any more, or rolled that soggy cigar butt," Durham recalled. "We hands saw little of him, as he rode in the big wagon."[61]

Dress and Act like Gentlemen

Catching King Fisher had been one thing. Bringing him to justice was quite another. Realizing that authorities in Maverick County were as corrupted by cattle and horse thieving as any officials on the Mexican side of the river, McNelly's young Rangers must have wondered if their captain would figure out how to take care of these outlaws in his own way. Then word spread through camp that the company would be packing up and

260 A Crooked River

heading to San Antonio. Rumor had it that the captain was under scrutiny from Austin, and that is why he insisted that his men be on their best behavior in Alamo City. Their reputation, the Rangers' reputation, and that of their captain would be on the line. It was an election year, and officials in Austin seemed sensitive about the stinging criticisms leveled at McNelly and his methods. More specifically, the Rangers' recent raid into Mexico had met with a storm of controversy. From Matamoros, Monterrey, and Mexico City to Austin and Washington, D.C., the boys had heard, McNelly had been "catching hell" for his actions.[62]

No one knew for sure why they were going to San Antonio, and no one asked. But most in the company agreed that the time there would be a welcome break from life in the field, a chance to dress and act like gentlemen. Most of all they understood that they could not let their captain down now.

On June 15, 1876, Captain McNelly and Carrie arrived in San Antonio and checked into the Menger Hotel. Carrie had heard that a physician in town, Dr. George Cupples, might offer some new hope in treating consumption. Her husband was only thirty-two years old—too young to die, even in such a harsh country as this.[63]

McNelly left word with his sergeants that during their stay in San Antonio his Rangers must report to him at the Menger Hotel twice a day. Obviously, despite his confidence in the officers, he still wanted to keep track of his troops. He understood that they were under no small measure of public scrutiny, so he agreed to an interview with a reporter from the *San Antonio Daily Express*, who apparently seemed more interested in asking about reports of misdeeds by the Rangers than outrages and crimes committed by the bandits. Insisting that his recruits could "ride longer, stand more hardships, eat less" than any regulars or partisans in the field, he emphasized that they were "most obedient" to his commands. Like any good leader, he accepted responsibility for his troops, and he reassured the reporter and his readers that the Rangers were not a bunch of young ruffians but men of character and integrity. "I allow no whiskey in camp. . . . I allow no obscene language. . . . When any of them violate these rules they are dismissed. I can bring my men to your city," he continued, "and they would be so quiet you would never know they were about. They know better than to get drunk, shout, [and] ride their horses through town."[64]

Even that short interview must have been exhausting for McNelly. The already-legendary Ranger captain remained in his hotel room, out of the public eye. Only a physician and his trusted officers had access to him. That is why Private George Durham's opportunity to visit proved an exceptional honor. After finally recognizing a well-dressed, groomed, and shaven Durham wandering through the hotel lobby, Corporal Rudd asked the lanky kid from Georgia if he would like to look in on the captain. Assuring Durham that McNelly would be happy to see him, Rudd led him upstairs and to the end of a long hallway. Durham remembered that Carrie opened the door and whispered that the captain was in bed sleeping. Just then, McNelly rose and rasped, "Who is it?" When he realized that it was young Durham, a smile broke over his face. "He was the same color as the sheets," Durham recalled. Breathing in "short gasps," McNelly joked that Durham should save some of his paycheck. Governor Coke would probably be "thrown out" in the November election, the captain predicted, and the special force of Rangers most likely would be tossed out with him. He even urged Durham to look for other work, not because he had done anything wrong but because he had faithfully followed his commander's orders, just like the captain had followed those of Governor Coke.[65]

While McNelly labored to talk, the brief conversation proved even more difficult for Durham. Looking at McNelly, who was a mere ghost of his former self, Durham could not help but think back to the gallant image of the captain a year earlier, mounted on old Segal, leading his Rangers into battle at the Palo Alto Prairie. He pictured him reading scriptures to that dying cattle rustler. That is how he wanted to remember him. Not like this.

Durham admitted that when he walked out of the Menger Hotel that day, he "sort of puddled up." He understood that his captain was dying and that he had probably seen him for the last time.[66]

Epilogue
Postscripts from Purgatory

J esse Leigh Hall would have stood out in any crowd. He was head and
shoulders taller than most men, and his auburn hair curled over his
collar, accentuating his angular face and lithe frame. His waxed handlebar
mustache, turned up on the ends, and his neatly trimmed goatee gave
him something of a chivalrous appearance. His soft Carolina accent, gen-
teel manner, and fashionable wardrobe contributed to an almost elegant
presence, at least by Texas standards. Little wonder that famed western
artist Frederic Remington would later describe him as "a gentleman of the
romantic Southern soldier type."[1]

A native of North Carolina, Hall had changed the legal spelling of his
middle name when he immigrated to North Texas in 1869. "Lee" Hall,
as he was known to the folks of Grayson County, taught school for a time.
Then he found his life's calling in law enforcement, serving first as deputy
sheriff in Denison on the Red River, then as the city marshal of nearby
Sherman. Later, as sergeant of arms for the Texas state senate, he cultivated
political alliances with lawmakers and other government officials who were
as ambitious as he. No one should have been surprised, therefore, when
the well-connected "Red" Hall received the favor of Governor Coke and
Adjutant General Steele, both equally determined to address the unrelenting border banditry and livestock theft along the lower Rio Grande.[2]

Holding a commission from the adjutant general, Lieutenant Hall
joined Company A, Texas State Troops, McNelly's Rangers, at their camp
in Oakville on August 10, 1876. While his rank placed him as second in
command, the reality could not have escaped the young Rangers, some of
whom privately resented Hall from the day of his arrival, even though they
joked with him and complimented him on his choice of horseflesh. Captain McNelly might be laid up in San Antonio, the troops understood. But
Sergeant John B. Armstrong should have been placed in charge, or maybe
Lieutenant T. C. Robinson, most of them believed. No doubt, many of
the company saw Hall's appointment as strictly political. As Durham later
confessed, "We didn't fall over ourselves welcoming Lieutenant Hall."
"He was a good man," Durham admitted grudgingly, "but he wasn't
Captain McNelly."[3]

Just days after Hall's arrival in camp, a convalescent McNelly sent a dispatch from San Antonio, ordering him to Goliad to aid the Dewitt County sheriff in investigating a recent bank robbery. To the men of Company A, that mattered little. As far as they were concerned, no one could replace their captain, not "Red" Hall or anyone else. Lieutenant Hall would have to earn their respect and trust, and that would take time. He would need to prove himself. But Governor Coke and Adjutant General Steele had given him and the Rangers little time to conduct a "big round up" of bandits across the brush country of South Texas.[4]

Despite the sense of urgency, time passed slowly at the Rangers' camp near the settlement of Oakville in Live Oak County. Throughout September life was dull, even monotonous compared to the past two years. Sleeping, cleaning their firearms, getting fat on pork loins, lamb stew, and lots of beans, cornbread, and dried beef, the men had it easy. Then one afternoon in late September all that changed. Sergeant Armstrong called them together and passed the word: the troops had ten minutes to saddle up and get ready to ride. It would be a long and difficult march, Armstrong explained. For days, his scouts had returned with reports that rustlers were trailing droves of cattle and captured horses up from Northern Mexico to the Nueces River country. There was no time now to pack provisions, Armstrong hurriedly told them, only plenty of ammunition.[5]

Following a backcountry trail up the Nueces River, Armstrong led two dozen Rangers through thunderstorms that rumbled overhead. "All day long the rain poured down in torrents," Jennings remembered, "wetting us to the skin." Their progress was slow as their horses slogged across the muddy prairies, with water rising all around them.[6]

To prevent the bandits from learning of their approach Armstrong ordered that every man they met on the trail be taken prisoner. By sunrise on September 30, Armstrong and his troops had captured five suspected thieves, all presumed to be King Fisher's associates. Durham wrote bluntly, "We persuaded them to talk." One of the captives, a young horse thief named Noley Key, agreed to do just that, and even to lead his captors to the rustlers' stronghold, although he insisted that Fisher and his gang were no longer there. Determined to check it out for himself, Armstrong demanded that Key guide him there anyway. When the Rangers closed in on Fisher's home that morning, they expected a shoot-out. But they were disappointed, as only women and children were present, just as Key had said.[7]

Armstrong pulled Key aside again and asked him to take a walk. Jennings recollected that his sergeant "took Key aside and drew from him the information that a band of horse thieves were in camp on the [west] banks of Lake Espintosa [*sic*], six or seven miles distant." Durham provided more detail on just how Armstrong "persuaded" Key to tell him what he wanted to know. The prisoner "saw things our way when we heisted [*sic*] him a couple of feet off the ground" with a rope around his neck. Interrogated and under duress, Key disclosed the location of the camp where seven men waited with as many as fifty horses recently stolen in Mexico. A terrified Key further disclosed that his partners in crime were preparing to head north where they could sell the stock.[8]

Knowing more now, Sergeant Armstrong divided his company. He ordered eighteen of his men to a second "desperado settlement," as Jennings termed it. The remaining six, including Rangers Jennings and Durham as well as Thomas J. Evans, Thomas N. Devine, A. L. Parrot, and George Boyd, headed out with Armstrong and Key for the thieves' camp at Lake Espantosa. By now the rains had passed over and a full moon illumined the landscape. After riding for an hour, a roaring campfire came into view, and Key pointed to the location of his colleagues in crime. Armstrong signaled for his men to dismount.[9]

Quietly, the sergeant instructed Evans and Devine to remain behind to guard Key and the horses. Then Armstrong and the other four Rangers slipped through the tall brush, closing in on the bandits with rifles in hand. They could hear voices and see the silhouetted figures darting about in the night, their images reflecting off the lake waters nearby. Only when Armstrong moved to within twenty-five yards did the horse thieves discover them.

Armstrong first thought that he had caught them off guard, but he was wrong. Before he and his men closed in, all hell broke loose. One of the bandits yelled a warning to the others then a single shot pierced the night air, followed by a roar of gunfire. By Jennings's estimate, two hundred rounds were fired in the next four or five minutes. A hailstorm of lead engulfed the camp. Durham remembered, "We sprayed the camp good." As the fight broke out, Armstrong shot one bandit dead in his tracks. Bullets flew in every direction, creating a terrifying whirring sound like the hum of swarming hornets. Their backs to the lake, several of the outlaws had little choice but to jump into the waters in a frantic attempt to escape. It was a chaotic scene, one that the humble Sergeant Armstrong later described as "a lively little fight."[10]

Both Napoleon Jennings and George Durham offered eyewitness accounts of the shoot-out, and for once they agreed on one thing: the most memorable moment during the gun battle was a knife fight. One of the outlaws, a massive figure named John Martin, had spent all his cartridges and was backing up toward the water's edge, brandishing a large knife. Facing off with Martin (known by the alias "One-Eyed John"), Ranger George Boyd raised his Winchester and squeezed the trigger, but the rifle jammed. Just then, Martin charged him, and the two became locked in a death struggle. Boyd, a man of average height and build, managed to pull his own knife as the two tumbled to the ground. Back on their feet, both combatants slashed and flailed at each other, each drawing blood. Since Martin's left eye had been gouged out years earlier, Private Boyd slouched and kept circling on his opponent's blind side. Then suddenly Boyd leaped on Martin's back and the two fell to the ground again, this time rolling and thrashing into the lake. Durham remembered that when Boyd thrust his blade into Martin's ribs he could "hear the bones crunch." When it was all over, the wiry young Boyd staggered to his feet, covered in blood. As for One-Eyed John, he lay dying at the lake's edge.[11]

Armstrong later reported that, in addition to Martin, Jim Roberts and George Mullen were among the dead bandits. Armstrong recorded that they and the others were "undressed and in their blankets" at the outset of the attack, although they still managed to open fire with six-shooters before being killed. During the shoot-out, Private Jennings dropped another known desperado, identified as Jim McAlister, shooting him through the mouth and blowing away part of his jaw. Jennings claimed that the severely wounded McAlister later recovered in jail, albeit with part of his jaw missing. Purported to be "reformed," the one-time horse thief and gunslinger with the deformed face was easily recognized while stalking the streets of San Antonio in future years.[12]

When the smoke and smell of gunpowder drifted away, it became apparent that Armstrong's raid had been only a partial success. During the confusion three of the bandits had apparently escaped into the night while the entire herd of stolen horses had broken free and gotten away, although fifty of the ponies would later be rounded up.

Then Sergeant Armstrong learned that he had lost his prisoner and informant. Returning to where he had left Evans and Devine with the Rangers' horses, Armstrong asked, "Where's Noley Key?" "Dead," Devine responded. When pressed by Armstrong, Devine explained that as soon as the shooting started, Key had jumped up and tried to run away. Both

Evans and he had fired at the fleeing prisoner, and one bullet had struck the boy in the back, killing him. Armstrong looked over and saw Key's body sprawled facedown in the grass.[13]

Perhaps most disappointing of all, Armstrong would have to report that King Fisher and the worst of his gang were nowhere to be found. Sources later told the sergeant that the outlaw leader was delivering a large herd of stolen horses for sale somewhere in the wilds of the Devil's River country. Once again, the self-styled king of the South Texas outlaws had escaped the long arm of Texas law. But his reckoning would come another day.

As Captain McNelly's reputation and that of his Rangers grew to Texas-sized proportions, so did the criticism. Not all of it came from Austin or Washington. Noley Key's grieving mother, Angelina B. Key, demanded that the state of Texas account for the Rangers' use of deadly force at Lake Espantosa. Writing Adjutant General Steele, apparently more than once, she accused: "McNally's [*sic*] men murdered my Son. And Armstrong's only justification at the inquest held was that his Instructions [to Devine and Evans] covered the case." By that, she charged that the men left to guard their prisoner were under orders to shoot to kill if Key tried to flee. "The only excuse rendered at the Inquest was that He attempted to escape—and who was there but his two murderers to see that?" Then she insisted that Armstrong and his men never had the authority to arrest her son in the first place, much less disarm and detain him without a warrant, and finally kill him with no pretext other than the allegation that he was attempting to run from the scene of a gunfight.[14]

"McNally [*sic*] and his troop have been lauded & praised by the Authorities of the State, for What?" Ms. Key asked. "For taking one deaf Boy seven or eight miles unarmed—in the dark hours of the night, shooting him all alone, . . . then killing three other Boys sleeping quietly in their Camp." Perhaps her reference to the "deaf Boy" suggests that she not only believed that her Noley, only sixteen years of age, was incapable of wrongdoing but that he was also unable to hear the Rangers commanding him to stop running. That question remains unanswered since the trail of official correspondence and the inquiry into the matter of Noley Key's death ends there.[15]

But the ongoing political controversy about McNelly's Rangers did not. Specifically, Adjutant General Steele seemed to face a dilemma. Medical expenses for the ailing captain mounted faster than the arrests of outlaws. In sum, McNelly's declining health made it unlikely that he could ever return to the field. His medical bills had amounted to half the funds expended to keep the entire company in service. Besides, by November, Lieutenant Lee

Hall was already serving as acting commander of Company A. No doubt letters of complaint from a grieving mother and family may have made the decision easier for Steele.[16]

To members of the company, however, especially those who had been with Captain McNelly through the violent border campaigns of the past two years, there was more to the decision than simply medical expenses and letters from a few angry citizens. George Durham weighed in on the matter, "All of us, including Captain himself, knew he was down to be fired. His kind of law enforcing wasn't good politics."[17]

Few were surprised, therefore, when the word came down on January 31, 1877. Leander H. McNelly received his letter of discharge from the ranging service. At least Carrie would have "Lee" to herself now. And ten-year-old Leander, or Rebel, and eight-year-old Irene could at last spend more time with their father, even if that time was fast fleeting.

The Crooked River Rolls On

Any river knows its source, and the Rio Grande is no different. Just as the great river owes its origins to the melting of a thousand snows streaming down from the San Juan Mountains of Colorado and the Sangre de Cristo Range of northern New Mexico, so the ongoing border conflict owes its source to generations of mutual mistrust and underlying racial prejudice. These historical undercurrents along the lower Rio Grande continue to move through our own time, just like the waters of the river that has shifted, changed its course, and still inevitably found its way to sea level and the open waters of the Gulf of Mexico.

But another gulf—a historical schism and racial divide—commands the landscape where South Texas meets northern Mexico. Contemporary and future generations in both nations must navigate that gulf. The bequests and the burdens that each generation pass down to the next are not unlike the waters of a slow-moving river. From one point on the map to another, the stream keeps moving, but the direction of the waters changes through time. The old sandy channels of the river are still there. Anyone can see where the waters have traveled in the past. But no one can predict with certainty where the crooked river will flow in the future. The forces of nature and the course of a river are as random and unpredictable as the course of human events.

Today the lessons of the crooked river remain more relevant than ever. Perhaps no soldier or statesman of the nineteenth century understood the complexity of the situation better than the legendary General William Tecumseh Sherman. His words should still resonate in our own time. While appearing before the House Military Affairs Committee in November 1877, he offered compelling and convincing testimony, insisting that there was no military solution to the troubles on the Rio Grande. The border remained as porous and unstable as ever, he testified then. Little had changed over the years, despite the army's best efforts. If the present force of four thousand U.S. regulars on the South Texas frontier were doubled, he confessed, the border would still be exposed, unsafe, and open to marauders of the worst types and descriptions. No army, no matter how large, no matter how well trained and equipped, could control such a vast area, he concluded. "I do not believe that it is possible to prevent some kind of disorder on that frontier, any more than it is possible to prevent . . . [violence] in this city of Washington," he opined. After admitting under oath that Texans were also committing depredations south of the border, and that not all lawlessness in South Texas could be blamed on Mexican bandits and Indian raiders, he was asked specifically about the much-demonized Juan Cortina (already living in "exile" near Mexico City). Was Cortina the problem, one congressman inquired? "Cortina is simply a creation," General Sherman answered. "If you kill Cortina, another like creation will take his place." Could anything end the troubles on the border? Only better relations between the two countries and more cooperation between officials on both sides of the river might accomplish that goal, he suggested. Only time would tell, he implied. But he offered no simple solutions, and no promises. He would leave that up to the politicians.[18]

On June 1, 1877, five months before General Sherman's testimony before Congress, Secretary of War George W. McCrary instructed him to issue a general order authorizing General Edward O. C. Ord to dispatch regular troops across the border if such forces were in "hot pursuit" of bandits and thieves. By autumn, however, Sherman's determination to rid the South Texas border of its worst elements already seemed tempered somewhat by the reality of a neighboring Mexico gripped with political turmoil, public corruption, perpetual poverty, and an unsettled population. And fraught by the belief that, to many people on each side of the Rio Grande, the other side of the river represented an opportunity for something better, no matter the boundaries, obstacles, laws, or traditions that might seem to separate them. To those willing to take risks— whether bandits or bankers, rustlers or railroad builders, mining company executives or ambitious filibusters—none of those uncertainties meant any more than a crooked river that could be easily forded.[19]

For years to come U.S. officials cited the Robb Commission findings while asserting the right to intrude upon sovereign Mexican territory as a means of suppressing banditry on the border. Understandably, Mexican leaders denounced any such incursions as serious violations of international law, even long after a formal 1882 agreement between the United States and Mexico recognized the right of each nation's army to cross the international boundary in pursuit of Indian raiders.

At the same time, the people of northern Mexico continued to believe that they had as much right to cattle grazing in South Texas as Captain Richard King or anyone else. After all, they insisted, not that long ago the land below the Nueces had been part of Mexico, and these were *ñañinta*'s (or grandma's) cattle. But the laws of Texas and the United States viewed matters differently.

Regarding the Robb Commission, the tangle of claims and charges submitted to President Grant and the U.S. Congress in 1873 swiftly became hopelessly convoluted in controversy, the conclusions of both the U.S. and Mexican commissions each disputed as wildly exaggerated and biased at best. In the end, the Robb Commission report became little more than political and diplomatic fodder for those in the United States who demanded a military solution to the problems on the border, and to those dreamers and schemers looking to create an American buffer republic of the Sierra Madre south of the Rio Grande. At the same time, the Robb Commission report became hitched to the international political firestorm still raging over the long-running disputes being aired before a joint U.S.-Mexico claims commission, still mired in mediating disputes of citizens in both nations dating back to the war with Mexico.[20]

A Continuing Legacy

After fleeing Brownsville in November 1863, General Hamilton Prioleau Bee commanded a Confederate brigade in the Red River campaign under General Richard Taylor. At the Battle of Pleasant Hill near present-day Pelican, Louisiana, on April 9, 1864, he had two horses shot from under him and suffered a minor wound to the face during a cavalry charge. Soon thereafter, he was assigned briefly to the late Thomas Green's division in General John Wharton's Cavalry Corps. Otherwise, his military service record seemed at best undistinguished, and his accomplishments never lived up to his rank and reputation. Fleeing to Mexico after the surrender in April 1865, he moved his family to Saltillo, Coahuila, then to Cuba and eventually back to Mexico. After a decade of self-imposed exile, he slipped back into Texas when Democrats regained control of the state government. In 1876 he moved to San Antonio, where he lived and practiced law for the rest of his life. He died on October 3, 1897, and is buried in the city's Confederate Veteran's Cemetery.[21]

Following the fall of the Confederacy in the spring of 1865, like scores of others suspected of war crimes, Captain James Duff fled to Mexico. Looking for fortune or just fearing that the hangman's noose awaited him back in Texas, he took up residence in Monterrey. He apparently offered his military "skills" to the French imperial forces of Maximilian, then to the Juaristas. Failing in his attempts to find fortune in Mexico, he probably returned to his native Great Britain. No one knows for sure what later became of him, but a coroner in Surry County, England, issued a death certificate for a James Duff, born in Scotland in 1828, who had died on April 16, 1900, at the age of seventy-two.[22]

In the spring of 1863 Colonel Arthur James Lyon Fremantle continued his tour of the Confederate States as an unofficial observer from Her Majesty's Royal Army. Traveling to San Antonio, then on to Houston and Galveston, he wrote of the Texans he met along the way: "There was much to like in my fellow travelers. They all had a sort of bon-hommie [*sic*] honesty and straightforwardness, a natural courtesy and extreme good nature," all this despite what he termed their "peculiar habits of hanging, shooting, etc." On the train to Galveston he even met the most famous Texan of them all, Sam Houston, whom he described as a "handsome old man, much given to chewing tobacco and blowing his nose with his fingers." He further observed of the Hero of San Jacinto, "Though evidently a remarkable and clever man, he is extremely egotistical and vain."

Over the next three months Colonel Fremantle traveled throughout both the western and eastern theaters of war, becoming acquainted with almost every notable Confederate commander, including Braxton Bragg, Joseph E. Johnston, P. G. T. Beauregard, James Longstreet, Jeb Stuart, and Robert E. Lee. Fremantle witnessed the epic Battle of Gettysburg and Lee's subsequent retreat to Virginia. Ten days later he sailed back to England and soon wrote his recollections, first published under the title *Three Months in the Southern States*. In 1882 he was promoted to major general and assumed field command of a British brigade in the Sudan

Campaign against the charismatic Islamic leader known as the Mahdi, or "chosen one." Ten years later the highly decorated Fremantle received a knighthood from Her Majesty Queen Victoria. He died on September 25, 1901, and is buried in the Woodvale Cemetery, Brighton, East Sussex. Even today, his classic memoir, later reprinted under the title *The Fremantle Diary: Journal of the Confederacy*, remains one of the most vivid, descriptive, and widely read personal accounts penned during the American Civil War.[23]

General Joseph O. Shelby spent two years in Mexico before coming home to his native Missouri. A decade passed before he agreed to a public interview about his experiences south of the border following the war. On a hot afternoon in August 1877, he sat on the front porch of his farmhouse in rural Aullville, Missouri, and spoke with an eager reporter from the *St. Louis Times*, none other than his former adjutant John Newman Edwards. Asked about affairs in Mexico, both past and present, Shelby began by admitting his disappointment that most of his men had chosen to fight for Emperor Maximilian instead of Benito Juárez. He remained somewhat skeptical about Mexico's future, but he spoke favorably of the new president, Porfirio Díaz, both as a military commander and a leader. He declined the opportunity to offer advice to Díaz or the people of Mexico as to how to govern their country. No American was qualified for that, he implied. Then he confirmed that, in that fateful spring of 1865 he had received a letter from his old friend Frank Blair, son of Francis Preston Blair, confidant of the late President Abraham Lincoln. And in that correspondence young Blair had confirmed that his father had assured him that the president had privately indicated that he would smile on any Confederate forces going to Mexico, but only if they collaborated in deposing Emperor Ferdinand Maximilian Joseph. Otherwise, Shelby refused to express any other regrets about the course of events. He apparently had come to accept that direct U.S. intervention in Mexico would have made matters worse and, most likely, would have been doomed to fail. He also avoided any other reference to the late Emperor Maximilian and to the short-lived colony of Carlota that Shelby and his fellow Confederates founded near Vera Cruz.[24]

Shelby continued to enjoy the quiet life of a farmer, and he shunned his celebrity. But in August 1883 he reemerged from private life to testify as a character witness during the trial of renowned outlaw Frank James. In 1893 Shelby accepted an appointment from President Grover Cleveland as U.S. marshal for the Western District of Missouri, a post he held until his death in rural Bates County on February 13, 1897, at the age of sixty-six. He is buried in Forest Hill Cemetery in Kansas City, Missouri.[25]

After fleeing to Mexico in the summer of 1865, General Edmund Kirby Smith spent time in Monterrey. That fall he sailed to Havana before finally returning to the United States in November to take an oath of amnesty under the terms outlined by President Andrew Johnson. For a few years, he served as president of the Atlantic and Pacific Telegraph Company before devoting his life to academic pursuits. In 1870 he accepted an appointment as chancellor of the University of Nashville. Five years later he moved on to the University of the South in Sewanee, Tennessee, where he taught mathematics until his death on March 28, 1893, at the age of sixty-eight. He is buried in the university cemetery on the Sewanee campus.[26]

After escaping the massacre on the Nueces in August 1862, John William Sansom made his way to the Mexican border, then to New Orleans, where he joined other Unionists in exile, including Edmund J. Davis, John L. Haynes, and Andrew Jackson Hamilton. The following year he returned to the Rio Grande as a member of the First Texas Cavalry (Union) and participated in Union raids and skirmishes against Confederate forces for the duration of the war. Afterward, he returned to the Hill Country, farming and raising a family at Hodges Mills in Kendall County. During these years he served as a volunteer Ranger in defending the farms and ranchlands from Indian raiders. In 1883 he moved to Uvalde County to raise cattle and two decades later purchased a home in San Antonio. He lived there at 1102 North Flores Street until his death on June 19, 1920, at the age of eighty-six. He is buried in the city's Mission Burial Park not far from the historic Mission San José.[27]

In the late winter of 1865 General Lewis "Lew" Wallace returned to his post in Baltimore. With no delay, he went on to a distinguished public life that few could have predicted, not even Wallace himself. Following the assassination of President Lincoln, he was appointed to the nine-member military commission that tried and convicted John Wilkes Booth's co-conspirators in the president's death. That autumn Wallace chaired the military tribunal that tried Captain Henry Wirz, commandant of the infamous Camp Sumter at Andersonville, Georgia, where more than thirteen thousand Union prisoners of war died of disease, starvation, and neglect. Wallace's court-martial convicted Wirz of war crimes and sentenced him to hang, thus making Wirz the only person so executed in the aftermath of the Civil War.[28]

A civilian again, Wallace made his way to Mexico in 1867 and served briefly as an adviser to the army of Benito Juárez. Most sources agree that he never received the $200,000 remuneration that allegedly had been promised to him. Regardless, he soon returned to Indiana and made two unsuccessful bids for a seat in Congress. His political career apparently ended, he continued to practice law in his hometown of Crawfordsville. Given to adventure, travels, and new challenges, Wallace accepted President Rutherford B. Hayes's appointment as governor of New Mexico Territory in 1878. During the next three years Governor Wallace worked tirelessly to end the violence and lawlessness unleashed between the Tunstall-McSween and Dolan-Murphy factions during the so-called Lincoln County War. His secret meeting in Santa Fe on March 17, 1879, with the young gunfighter variously called Henry McCarty or Henry Antrim, alias William H. Bonney, but better known to history as Billy the Kid, ended with the fugitive gunman feeling as though he had been betrayed. But that is another story.

In 1881 Wallace received the appointment of U.S. minister to the Ottoman Empire. During his three and a half years in Constantinople (now Istanbul), Wallace became a friend and confidant to Sultan Abdul Hamid II. To some, however, Wallace is best remembered for his literary contributions, especially his 1880 novel set in the first-century Roman Empire. Depicting the odyssey and tribulations of a young Hebrew nobleman, Judah, and his boyhood friend, a Roman patrician named Messala, the novel was titled *Ben-Hur: A Tale of the Christ.* An instant classic, Wallace's work would become the best-selling American novel of the nineteenth century. Soldier, statesman, lawman, and man of letters, seventy-seven-year-old Lew Wallace died at his home on February 15, 1905, and was interred at the nearby Oak Hill Cemetery in Crawfordsville, Indiana.[29]

After his defeat in the controversial 1874 election and his ouster from the office of governor, Edmund Jackson Davis practiced law in Austin and continued to lead the Republican Party in Texas. He conducted an unsuccessful bid for reelection in 1880, then failed in his run for a congressional seat from the Tenth District in 1882. He continued to defend his record during Reconstruction, always rejecting the allegations that he and his so-called Radical Republican administration had brought tyranny to the people of Texas. A native of Florida and a longtime resident of South Texas, he never understood why so many loathed him as a "carpetbagger" from the North. He remained devoted to the Union and Republican political "reforms" and was planning on another run for

Congress when death came on February 7, 1883. He was only fifty-five. One of his political rivals, C. E. McLaughlin, offered a fitting eulogy: "I was always opposed to him politically. As a Republican politician he was ranked political 'pizen.' . . . But personally and socially he was a clever and upright Southern gentleman. . . . The word of Governor Davis was as good as the bond of any Democrat." Davis rests in an honored place in the Texas State Cemetery in Austin. His grave marker towers above those of his Confederate adversaries.[30]

Even in his last years, the colorful old Texas Ranger John Salmon "Rip" Ford lived up to his legend. Elected by the people of Cameron County, he traveled to Austin to serve in the state Constitutional Convention of 1875, where he had a hand in drafting what is to this day the framework of Texas government, the state constitution of 1876. Soon elected to a seat in the Texas state senate, he served the people of his South Texas district with distinction and honor. Ford also used his influence in the legislature to secure continuing funding for McNelly's company to patrol the border, and he even supported a bill extending "extraordinary" powers to the Rangers to arrest outlaws and thieves, without the requirement that the prisoners be promptly turned over to county sheriffs or other local officials.

Although aging and frail, Rip Ford could not abandon his dreams of conquest south of the border. In the autumn of 1877 the old Ranger's words and actions again kindled rumors that an irregular army of Texans was preparing to march into Mexico and establish a buffer state of the Sierra Madre. The *Galveston News* announced that Ford appeared in Corpus Christi on October 4 "on some special and confidential mission," presumably to recruit young adventurers for a "Mexico enterprise." The newspaper also reported that the famed Old Rip even delivered a "spirited" speech to a large crowd at the city market house, the so-called lecture no doubt intended to stir the passions of Texan "patriots" who had had enough of border banditry. But if there ever was such a scheme (secretly supported by Governor Richard Hubbard or not), the purported plan failed to gain popular support. In the words of historian Richard B. McCaslin, perhaps most fellow Texans had just "lost interest in . . . plans to invade Mexico."[31]

At least one member of the U.S. Congress suspected otherwise. When the House Committee on Military Affairs convened in January 1878, Congressman Edward S. Bragg of Wisconsin drew from one witness, Julius Tucker of Brownsville, that Ford was talking "continually" of provoking another conflict with Mexico as a pretext for invasion and conquest. As

Tucker admitted, Ford was the leading spokesman of a faction of South Texas citizens "who have grown old and gray waiting for the time" to return to Mexico and raise the American flag. Bragg went so far as to label Ford a "buccaneer," a freebooter in league with Mexican rustlers and Anglo land pirates and gun smugglers. He even pressed another witness before the committee, John L. Haynes of Brownsville, to admit that Ford still openly promoted the idea that the Sierra Madre Range would serve as a more fitting boundary with Mexico than the Rio Grande. No matter, Bragg's efforts to impugn the integrity of the iconic Texan failed to produce any further controversy, and when Ford arrived in Washington, D.C., later that month to meet with President Rutherford B. Hayes and members of the Texas congressional delegation, he appeared not before Bragg and the Military Affairs Committee but before a friendlier Congressman Schleicher and the Foreign Affairs Committee. No record exists that Old Rip and the short, rotund "badger congressman" appropriately named Bragg ever met face to face.[32]

In his final years, Rip Ford followed quieter pursuits. Stepping back from politics, he held the post of superintendent of the Texas School for the Deaf, an institution still located in Austin. In 1885, owing to failing health, Ford and his wife, Addie, moved to San Antonio to be near their daughter, Mary Louise, and her husband, banker and land broker Joe Maddox. The legendary Ranger captain remained active in the local Masonic lodge and even worked for a few years as tax collector for Bexar County. A local celebrity and popular raconteur who frequented the Menger Hotel and other gathering spots of the city social elite, Ford lived with his wife in their humble residence at 213 Avenue C. During the last decade of his life he wrote his memoirs and devoted his time to preserving the history of the Lone Star State. His memoir, later published as *Rip Ford's Texas*, still ranks as one of the greatest classics in Texas historical literature. After a series of strokes, Old Rip Ford died on November 3, 1897, at his daughter's home at 322 King William Street in San Antonio. His remains rest today in the Confederate Veteran's Cemetery in San Antonio.[33]

After his return from captivity among the Lipan, Francis M. "Frank" Buckelew was hired as a hand on the Jack Ranch in Bandera County. In 1870, at the age of eighteen, he married Nancy Witter in Bandera, and together they raised nine children. For the rest of his days Frank farmed the rocky, timber-covered lands near Medina. Over the years, he also became a well-known storyteller in the Hill Country and a missionary, elder, and lay preacher of the Methodist Church. Battling dementia later in life, he was admitted to the Wichita Falls State Hospital, where he died after five months in residence on December 11, 1930. He is buried in the Oak Rest Cemetery in Medina.[34]

In the weeks following Mackenzie's raid on Remolino, Buckelew's captor, the old Lipan chief Costelietos and his people were marched off to San Antonio and held captive there, literally corralled in open-air downtown stables. But before the army could transport them to Fort Sill, Indian Territory, in late June the aging warrior vanished. Presumably, he escaped his captors and tried to make his way back to Mexico. Lipan tradition maintains that within days Texans "discovered" the old man's body on a roadside south of San Antonio. Whether he was murdered—some claim he was dragged to death or hanged—or he died of natural causes, no one knew for sure. But Colonel Mackenzie remained skeptical of the claims of his death.[35]

The Kickapoo people of the border fared little better. No doubt dispirited and fearful following Mackenzie's raid on Remolino, and knowing their days in Mexico were numbered, more than three hundred impoverished and, in some cases, malnourished men, women, and children at last surrendered to Bureau of Indian Affairs commissioner Henry Atkinson in the autumn of 1873. Accompanied by an army "escort," they followed Atkinson across the Rio Grande and over the remote wilds of the Trans-Pecos. Skirting well west and north of the line of Texas settlements, mostly for the Kickapoo's protection, Atkinson's party marched their captives through the winter cold, beyond the Wichita Mountains to Fort Sill. The following autumn the army relocated them again, further east, this time to Fort Gibson, Indian Territory, where they rejoined many of their kinsmen as "prisoners of war" in November 1874. Their future would be as wards of the U.S. government.[36]

Captain Richard King continued to build and expand his storied ranching empire that sprawled across several South Texas counties. Eventually acquiring over 614,000 acres of rangelands, he revolutionized the cattle industry in South Texas by introducing the scientific breeding of livestock. The popular Santa Gertrudis breed is a direct result of his efforts. During his later years, the enterprising old hacendado also invested in a variety of business interests, including railroad construction and meatpacking. Nearer the end of his life Captain King took up residence in the Menger Hotel in San Antonio, where he died on April 14, 1885, at the age of sixty. His attorney later recalled that the famous South Texas *patrón*, determined to keep his ranch intact, instructed him shortly before his passing "not to let a foot of dear old Santa Gertrudis get away."

King got his wish, even if only for a time. His heirs, the Kleberg family among others, amassed even more rangelands that, altogether, were once larger than the state of Rhode Island. Not until 1925 would King's remains be removed from San Antonio and reinterred in the Chamberlain Cemetery in his namesake town of Kingsville. Perhaps King's former partner, Mifflin Kenedy, left the most poignant and fitting postscript of all, acknowledging that, despite their personal fortunes and successes, "for almost fifty years Captain King and I attempted to Americanize the border, without much success."[37]

After delivering his commission's report to President Grant, Thomas Patten Robb returned to California to enjoy his final years at his rancho estate in Santa Cruz County. There he remained involved in local Republican Party politics and in the affairs of the influential veteran's organization, the Grand Army of the Republic. He died in Santa Cruz on April 18, 1895. Following his service at the Calvary Episcopal Church, conducted by his fellow Grand Army of the Republic members, Robb's son Thomas escorted his father's flag-draped coffin back to Chicago for burial in the city's Park Ridge Cemetery.[38]

After the bandit raid on Nuecestown in April 1875, Thomas John and Martha Noakes never rebuilt their country store, which had served also as a post office. But records indicate that they purchased another store a few miles closer to Corpus Christi. By all accounts Mr. Noakes died soon thereafter, leaving his wife to raise six children on her own. Martha remarried to a man named Hipp in 1879. The date of her death remains unclear.[39]

Following his raid on the Kickapoo and Lipan villages at Remolino, Colonel Ranald Slidell Mackenzie continued to burnish his reputation as an Indian fighter. With the outbreak of the Red River War of 1874 (also known as the "Buffalo War" on the Southern Plains), he commanded a regiment of the Fourth U.S. Cavalry during a campaign to sweep the Comanche from the Llano Estacado of the Texas Panhandle. On September 28, Mackenzie's attack on several hundred Comanche at the Palo Duro Canyon effectively brought Southern Plains Indian resistance to an end. More devastating than the rout of Quanah Parker's band of stragglers was Mackenzie's order to destroy over one thousand Indian ponies.

In March 1875 Colonel Mackenzie assumed command at Fort Sill, Indian Territory, where he oversaw both the Comanche-Kiowa reserve surrounding the Wichita Mountains and the Southern Cheyenne-Arapaho reserve north of the Canadian River. By the late summer of 1876 Colonel Mackenzie accepted reassignment to the Black Hills in Dakota Territory at a time when the Great Sioux Uprising was sweeping the Northern Plains. In the months that followed the vainglorious Lieutenant Colonel George Custer's defeat at Little Bighorn, Mackenzie participated in General George Crook's Winter Campaign against the Northern Cheyenne. On November 25, near the banks of the Powder River, he led elements of the Third, Fourth, and Fifth U.S. Cavalry regiments in an attack on the village of Chief Dull Knife (or Morning Star to the Cheyenne). The Department of War considered the fight on Powder River a decisive victory, yet for some unexplained reason a despondent Mackenzie viewed the result with disappointment and feelings of self-doubt.

Mackenzie's legendary career would soon move full circle back to the Rio Grande border. Following a second tour at Fort Sill, Mackenzie returned to Fort Clark in February 1878. In response to renewed Indian raids into Texas, the following June Colonel Mackenzie commanded a second expedition into Mexico, but this time only after he demanded and received explicit written authorization from General Ord to cross the border. Fording the Rio Grande below Eagle Pass on June 17 and advancing toward the Santa Rosa Mountains with six companies of the Eighth Cavalry, Mackenzie's columns marched more than forty miles before being shadowed by a smaller force of Mexican regulars under Colonel Pedro Valdez. With yet another column of Mexican federal troops commanded by Colonel Jesús Nuncio closing in from the west, Mackenzie reluctantly decided to backtrack to the river and withdraw into Texas without event. In his official report, he refused to use the word "retreat," instead preferring the term "retire."[40]

After service in the Department of New Mexico and on the southern borders of Arizona during the Apache campaigns, Mackenzie returned to Texas in October 1884, this time at the rank of brigadier general commanding the sprawling Department of Texas. He bought a home in San Antonio and weeks later acquired ranch lands near Boerne in neighboring Kendall County.

Then tragedy struck. Mackenzie fell desperately ill with some mysterious disorder. His erratic, demented behavior and deteriorating physical condition led army physicians to diagnose him with "paralysis of the insane," a disorder then often associated with syphilis. Regardless of the cause of his breakdown, he was soon placed aboard a train and escorted to his native New York City for convalescence at Bloomingdale Asylum. By March 1884 the Department of War retired Mackenzie from service, and that summer relatives transported him to his boyhood home of Morristown. In 1886, as his condition worsened, he was again moved, this time to New Brighton, Staten Island. He died there on January 19, 1889, and was laid to rest with full honors at the U.S. Military Academy Post Cemetery at West Point. The legendary general was forty-eight.[41]

Major Zenas Randall Bliss went on to serve his country for another quarter of a century, much of that time on the Texas frontier. With stations at forts Clark, Duncan, Stockton, and Davis, first as a lieutenant colonel with the Nineteenth Infantry then as a colonel in the Twenty-Fourth Infantry, he also commanded the Eighth Military Department of Texas from 1895 to 1897. He retired on May 22, 1897, at the rank of major general. The following year he received the Medal of Honor for his heroism at the Battle of Fredericksburg thirty-six years earlier. He died on January 2, 1900, and is buried in Arlington National Cemetery.[42]

Lieutenant Robert Goldthwaite Carter continued to serve with Colonel Mackenzie during the Red River War (or "Buffalo War") of 1874–75. He participated in both Mackenzie's legendary attack on Comanche villagers at the Palo Duro Canyon on September 28, 1874, and the skirmish six weeks later at Tahoma Lake. The following April, these engagements led to the surrender of the last free band of Comanche, led by Quanah Parker of the Quahadi band. Promoted to first lieutenant in February 1875, Carter was retired from the army with a disability on June 28, 1876. (He had suffered a broken leg five years earlier when a horse fell on him.) During his later life, he taught school and worked for a time in publishing. Not until January 1900 was he awarded the Medal of Honor for his gallantry in action at Blanco Canyon during the Brazos River campaign in October 1871. He died in Washington, D.C., on January 4, 1936, at the age of ninety and is buried at Arlington National Cemetery.[43]

Lieutenant John Lapham Bullis commanded the much-decorated unit of Black Seminole scouts for another nine years. In 1882 he was transferred to Camp Supply, Indian Territory, where he was stationed for six years. Now Captain Bullis returned to his former regiment in Arizona, where he assumed duties as agent to the various Apache bands on the San Carlos Reservation from 1888 to 1893. Moved by the Department of the Army to New Mexico Territory in 1893, he became acting agent for the Jicarilla Apache and the Pueblo. In 1897 Major Bullis returned to Texas, reporting for the position of paymaster at Fort Sam Houston. During the War with Spain in 1898 he saw action in the jungles of Cuba then served in the Philippine Insurrection two years later. In 1904 President Theodore Roosevelt promoted Bullis to brigadier general one day before the old soldier's announced retirement took effect. It was a fitting close to an event-filled forty-two years of military service. During his last years, he lived in a two-story white stone residence at 621 Pierce Street near post. Following a stroke, Bullis died at the Fort Sam Houston Hospital in San Antonio on May 26, 1911, and is buried there on the grounds of the National Cemetery. Camp Bullis in San Antonio, founded in 1917, was named for him.[44]

Sergeant John Kibbits continued to serve the U.S. Army as a Seminole scout for five more years. On September 7, 1878, only six months after his enlistment ended, Old Kibbits died in his sixty-seventh year. Although some sources disagree, he is buried in the Seminole Indian Scout Cemetery in Marathon, Texas, in remote Brewster County. As for the remainder of his company, four would later be awarded the Medal of Honor—privates Pompey Factor, Adam Paine, Isaac Payne, and Sergeant John Ward.[45]

Texas adjutant general William Steele continued to reorganize the state troops and seek increased funding for these Ranger companies from the state legislature until he left the post in January 1879. During his five years in office he oversaw the transition of the Texas Rangers from an irregular body of frontier fighters to a more disciplined and well-organized law enforcement entity under the command of Major John B. Jones. Steele died at his home in San Antonio on January 12, 1885, at the age of sixty-four. He is buried in Austin's Oakwood Cemetery.[46]

Congressman Gustav Schleicher continued his personal crusade to demand increased federal protection on the border with Mexico. He also led Democratic members of the Texas House delegation, including representatives Roger Q. Mills, James Throckmorton, and David Culberson, in breaking party ranks to block a military appropriations bill that would have slashed army funding by 20 percent and no doubt reduced the number of troops stationed on the lower Texas-Mexico border. Following a bruising campaign in the autumn of 1878 he won reelection to a third term in the U.S. House of Representatives from the Sixth District of Texas. The fifty-five-year-old Schleicher died at his home in Washington, D.C., on January 10, 1879. Three days later his colleagues honored him with a state funeral in the U.S. Capitol that was attended by President Rutherford B. Hayes, leaders of Congress, and all justices of the U.S. Supreme Court. After lying in state in the Capitol, his remains were transported to San

Antonio for burial in the Fort Sam Houston National Cemetery. Schleicher County in Southwest Texas, organized in 1887, is named for him.[47]

Lieutenant T. C. Robinson, better known to readers across Texas as "Pidge," wrote his last dispatch to the *Daily State Gazette* on March 16, 1876. From the Ranger camp at Laguna de los Flores he scribbled a rambling letter, admittedly "in haste." Then he wrote this postscript, announcing his abrupt departure from Texas: "I see that some carpet-bagging idiot from Connecticut, who happened to get to the Virginia Legislature, has written a bill taxing all persons who chew tobacco, smoke, drink whiskey, or 'cuss.' I am going home to spend my pay, shall leave on the next steamer. . . . Heaven knows I ought to pay it out for 'cussing.' *Au Revoir.*"

Historian Chuck Parsons records that, only days after Robinson returned to his native Virginia he renewed his involvement in an ongoing blood feud between two families. By all indications, the conflict between Robinson and Jesse E. Mitchell had been building for several years. And the source of the trouble was Robinson's affection for Mitchell's younger sister, Mary Elizabeth, known to family as "Pidgie." Mitchell had apparently disapproved of the courtship and had forbidden Mary Elizabeth from seeing young Robinson. On a peaceful Sunday morning, April 2, near Providence Church along the road to Rustburg, Campbell County, Jesse Mitchell and T. C. Robinson agreed to settle their differences once and for all like "gentlemen." In a shoot-out that resembled both a traditional Southern duel and a Texas gunfight, the participants exchanged pistol fire, each gravely wounding the other. "The difficulty was understood to be on account of a woman," the *Lynchburg Daily News* recorded. Robinson's death the following day was reported in various newspapers, from the *New Orleans Times-Picayune* to the *Galveston Daily News*, even in the *New York Times*. Although severely wounded three times, Mitchell survived.[48]

John Barclay Armstrong had already earned the nickname "McNelly's Bulldog." After his captain was "retired," Armstrong's service to Texas continued. In April 1877 the newly promoted Lieutenant Armstrong assisted in the arrest of John King Fisher—the second time McNelly's men had taken in the infamous horse thief and bandit leader, only to have him go free yet again. Then the following month, Armstrong approached death's door, but no bandit or bad man was behind the danger this time. While staying at the Case Hotel in Goliad, Armstrong suffered a self-inflicted gunshot wound. He was apparently handling his Colt service revolver when he accidentally shot himself through the hip and thigh.

Although the attending physician deemed his injuries life threatening, Armstrong recovered in the coming weeks, yet he walked with a noticeable limp for many months thereafter. Now out of the saddle for a time, and still recuperating from his near-fatal injury, he requested that Adjutant General Steele commission him to track down the notorious man killer John Wesley Hardin, who had reportedly fled to Florida.

Armstrong's dramatic capture of Wes Hardin remains the stuff of Texas legends. On the morning of August 23, 1877, Armstrong and fellow Ranger John Riley Duncan, with the help of Escambia County sheriff William H. Hutchinson, closed in on Texas's most wanted fugitive at the railroad depot in Pensacola, Florida. Hardin sat in the train's plush smoking car, next to a window on the station side, with several members of his gang nearby. Duncan remained outside pacing on the platform alongside the Pullman car while Lieutenant Armstrong entered the front of the coach and Sheriff Hutchinson and Deputy A. J. Perdue walked in through the rear door and approached the twenty-four-year-old Hardin. Realizing that officers of the law had come to arrest him, Hardin grabbed for his revolver, and a struggle ensued. Just then, a limping Armstrong transferred his cane to his left hand while drawing his .45 Colt with his right. Recognizing that the tall lawman sporting a wide-brimmed hat and wielding the long-barreled Colt revolver was a Ranger, Hardin reportedly exclaimed, "Texas, by God!" At that moment one of Hardin's fellow criminals, Jim Mann, rose from his seat and ran toward the door, firing wildly, one bullet passing through Armstrong's hat and grazing his scalp. For several seconds the confines of the railcar filled with flying lead. Amid the roar of gunfire one bullet struck Mann, mortally wounding him as he staggered out the door and onto the station platform, where he collapsed.[49]

Armstrong had narrowly escaped death yet again. But there would be no escape for Wes Hardin. Still pinned to the floor and unable to release his pistol from his suspenders, Hardin allegedly pleaded, "Shoot and be damned. I'd rather die than be arrested." Determined to take him alive, however, Armstrong hit Hardin on the head with the butt of his pistol, striking him so hard that he knocked him unconscious. In no more than a minute, it was all over. Armstrong cuffed his prisoner and dragged him from the train while several other members of Hardin's gang were also taken into custody for extradition back to Texas.[50]

The following year Armstrong moved to Austin, where he met and married young Mary Helena "Mollie" Durst. Some have said that he spent his share of the reward money for capturing Hardin to start up a mercantile business. After a brief stint as a U.S. marshal the former Ranger and Mollie moved to Willacy County in 1882. As much as any contemporary in the storied history of the Texas Rangers, John Barkley Armstrong personifies the transition of the Rangers from a rough-hewn frontier institution to an elite law enforcement and investigative agency renowned the world over. Armstrong died at his ranch house on May 1, 1913, of an apparent heart attack. He is buried in Austin's Oakwood Cemetery.[51]

William Crump Callicott was discharged from the Ranger service on November 30, 1875. He spent most of his life farming the rich bottomlands of Austin County. In 1880 he married Mary Stone, and together they raised five children. In the last decade of his life, despite little education, failing eyesight, and declining health, he did his best to record his memories of McNelly's Rangers. Just months after completing his remembrances for Walter Prescott Webb, the ailing seventy-three-year-old Callicott died of kidney disease in Houston on July 10, 1926. He is buried in the city's Magnolia Cemetery.[52]

After riding with McNelly's Rangers, Jesús Sandoval, "Old Casuse," seems to have disappeared from the historical record, almost as if he had slipped into the brush and vanished in the morning fog along the Rio Grande. Census records and other public documents have failed to reveal what happened to the old ranchero called by some "McNelly's hangman." In the end, his trail runs cold.[53]

In 1878, after an eight-month "hitch" with McNelly's Rangers, Napoleon August Jennings returned home to Philadelphia for a brief time, owing to the death of his father. Feeling "smothered" by the city, however, he again struck off for the West. For the next five years, he tried his hand at a series of jobs, from working and driving cattle to laboring in silver mines. By 1884, again broke, twenty-six-year-old Jennings headed back east to his hometown where he took up a career as a reporter with the *Philadelphia News,* and then with cross-city competitors the *Times* and later the *Tribune.* Not until 1887 did he find a stabler position, landing a job as a staff writer with Charles Dana's *New York Sun.*

Still, the restless writer returned to Texas in 1892 and worked for two years with the *San Antonio Express.* No doubt, during this period he interviewed old Texas Rangers and collected information and documents for his memoir. Between 1894 and 1897 Jennings found employment with Joseph Pulitzer's prestigious *New York Evening World.* In that capacity, he enjoyed targeting New York City police commissioner Theodore Roosevelt in a series of satirical essays, including one sarcastically titled

"Teddy Toddlekins, Boy Detective." Only during the Spanish-American War in 1898, when Jennings lauded the valor and sacrifice of the Rough Riders and their fearless colonel, did his respect for Roosevelt grow into a lifelong admiration for the future president.[54]

That same eventful summer Charles Scribner's Sons of New York published Jennings's dramatic but sometimes fictionalized narrative, *A Texas Ranger*, which George Durham later characterized as "pretty awful." In the coming years "Al" Jennings became a prolific writer, penning articles for periodicals such as the *Saturday Evening Post*, among others. In 1910, when revolution engulfed all of Mexico and forced President Porfirio Díaz into exile, Jennings traveled to Mexico City as a correspondent to report on the events for the *New York Herald*.[55]

When once asked about his account of McNelly's Rangers and, specifically, his tendency to write always in the first person, even about events that he did not actually witness, Jennings reportedly responded, "I am a writing man; I needed money; I had a story to tell; I told it." He died in New York City on December 15, 1919, at the age of sixty-one.[56]

George Preston Durham remembered one of his proudest moments in the service of Texas—the day early in 1877 when badges arrived from Austin and were distributed to the troops of McNelly's company. To Durham and the others, the shiny new Lone Star seal now pinned to their chests represented more than their official recognition as peace officers. It was a rite of passage for each Ranger and for the company, something of a brand of approval, a symbol of state law and authority. Soon after being discharged from the ranging service later that year, Durham returned to the Santa Gertrudis Ranch where Captain Richard King remembered him as one of McNelly's men. Probably with that in mind, King offered him a job as a cowhand for sixty dollars a month, no small sum in those days. A few years later Durham replaced Edward Raymond as foreman of Captain King's El Sauz division. There, on the Alice–Brownsville stage line, he built a home and soon married Richard King's young niece, Caroline Chamberlain. Durham lived and worked there for the rest of his days. "When I go out, I'll go as a McNelly," he later told journalist Clyde Wantland, "He swore me into his outfit, and he never swore me out. . . . I hope I overhaul him one more time when I get over Yonder." Durham died at his home on the El Sauz on May 27, 1940. He is buried in the Raymondville Memorial Cemetery. Durham's colorful account of three years as one of McNelly's Rangers, *Taming the Nueces Strip*, was not published until 1962. The memoir remains a classic in Texas historical literature.[57]

Lieutenant Commander Dewitt Clinton Kells was court-martialed and dishonorably discharged from the U.S. Navy early in 1880, but not because of scheming to provoke war with Mexico. Charged by a board of naval inquiry in New Orleans with "scandalous conduct tending to the destruction of good morals," he was stripped of his commission and relieved from duty for drunkenness, "indebtedness," and "disrespectful" public statements directed at Senator William Kellogg of Louisiana. In sum, his conduct was unbecoming of an officer of the U.S. Navy. After that, the theatrical Commander Kells disappeared from the public record.[58]

As Captain McNelly predicted, John King Fisher met an early and violent end. Although Fisher appeared to cross over to the right side of the law, serving as deputy sheriff of Uvalde County from 1881 to 1883, he never really did "go straight." To the disgust of many, he continued his murdering and thieving ways, even after becoming acting sheriff of Uvalde County when the sheriff was indicted on corruption charges.

Some insisted that Fisher had the makings of a good lawman. But on March 11, 1884, his reckless past and his reputation as a fast gun finally caught up with him. While visiting San Antonio he went with his friend, famed gunman and Austin City marshal Ben Thompson, to the popular Vaudeville Variety Theater. Both Fisher and Thompson were well known among the city's "sporting crowd," Thompson so much so that he was reportedly targeted for some outstanding gambling debts. And the debt to settle involved more than money. Two years earlier Thompson had shot and killed theater proprietor Jack Harris during a confrontation at the poker table. Harris's friends and associates had waited for the moment to even the score.[59]

As it turned out, King Fisher was in the wrong place at the wrong time with the wrong person. While Fisher and Thompson sat in an upstairs theater box, several gunmen seeking to avenge the death of Jack Harris ambushed them. Both Thompson and Fisher died in a blaze of gunfire. Eyewitnesses reported that the "king of South Texas outlaws" was shot at least thirteen times. Friends transported his body back to Uvalde where he was buried on his ranch. His remains were later removed for reinterment in the city's Pioneer Park Cemetery. At the age of thirty, John King Fisher left behind a young wife and three little daughters.[60]

Jesse "Lee" Hall measured up to the expectations of Adjutant General Steele and, more important, the men of Company A, Washington County Volunteers. As acting commander of the special force in the fall and winter of 1876, he moved the company to Cuero, once again, to assist in suppressing the violence of the Sutton-Taylor feud. His apprehension and subsequent prosecution of five of the ringleaders ended the longest and bloodiest feud in Texas history. In February 1877, Hall redeployed his Rangers to the lower Rio Grande and for the next three years focused his operations on keeping the cattle rustlers and border raiders on the run. In March 1877, he successfully directed a "big round up" of dozens of cattle thieves and hide skinners, including a nest of nefarious cow hunters at the village of Dog Town (present-day Tilden) on the Frio River in McMullen County. In sum, his career as a lawman was brief but brilliant. But in some respects, he always remained in McNelly's long shadow.

After his retirement from the ranging service in 1880 Hall served for five years as foreman of the Dull Ranch, headquartered on the rangelands along Cibolo Creek southeast of San Antonio. During that time, he policed the region of robbers and protected his livestock from fence cutters and cattle thieves. After a brief unrewarding tenure as U.S. agent to the Anadarko people in Indian Territory, Hall moved back to San Antonio and entered the mercantile business there. With the outbreak of the Spanish-American War in April 1898, Hall raised and trained two companies of volunteers for service in the First U.S. Volunteer Infantry. Then two years later he reenlisted in the army and served in the Philippines as an officer of the famed Macabebe Scouts (native Filipino) in the campaigns against the Moro insurrectionists. For gallantry at the battles of Aringay and Batangas, Hall was awarded a brevet promotion to the rank of captain.[61]

One fellow Ranger who earlier had served under Hall wrote that he was "the bravest man I ever saw." Maybe that should be his epitaph. As with so many contemporary heroic figures, and many lesser ones, he seemed destined for a tragic end. After a decade of living in obscurity, he died on March 17, 1911, in San Antonio. He was buried in the National Cemetery at Fort Sam Houston. Sadly, some said, his life may have been cut short at sixty-one by his weakness for whiskey and mescal.[62]

Juan Nepomuceno Cortina soon found that his time on the border was fast coming to an end. First a political and diplomatic problem for the increasingly unpopular President Lerdo de Tejada, and then a liability for President Porfirio Díaz, it was only a matter of time until the so-called Red Robber of the Rio Grande became a victim of his own self-made legend. On February 24, 1877, military forces loyal to Porfirio Díaz arrested Cortina in Matamoros and removed him to the comforts of a hacienda in the hills near Mexico City. Cortina passed peacefully into history at Azcapotzalco on October 30, 1894, at the age of seventy-four. Even today mournful *corridos*, or border ballads, speak of his bravado and courage, testimony that people of Mexican heritage remember him as a Robin Hood figure along both banks of the lower Rio Grande. Anglo-Texans remain equally convinced that he was the ruthless bandit chieftain responsible for much if not most of the violence on the lower Texas-Mexico border.[63]

Relieved of command, Leander Harvey McNelly returned home to his farm near Burton. Ashen and gaunt, he remained mostly bedridden in the coming months. To paraphrase novelist Elmer Kelton, death was written in his face. As for Company A, Washington County Volunteers, the unit was effectively disbanded, then reorganized and absorbed into the Frontier Battalion of state troops commanded by Major John B. Jones, who would help transform the state troops from border fighters into a legitimate law enforcement entity.

In some respects, even after all these years McNelly remains more elusive than the bandits and rustlers he hunted. Acknowledging the controversy of McNelly's methods in the field, Walter Prescott Webb lamented, "It was McNelly's misfortune that he was not at the Alamo or Goliad, or at some other place where his courage . . . and audacity could have been exercised in a patriotic cause. Had he performed the remarkable feats there on behalf of freedom that he performed in the Nueces Strip, mainly on behalf of a few stolen King cattle, he would have been a heroic figure in Texas history."[64]

Novelist Larry McMurtry could not have disagreed more. Depicting the legendary Ranger captain as brutal and ruthless, he challenged Webb's dismissal of McNelly's deliberate policy to terrorize his enemies and the contention that "affairs on the border cannot be judged by the standards that hold elsewhere." McMurtry rightly asked, Why not? "Torture is torture, whether inflicted in Germany . . . or along the Nueces Strip. The Rangers, of course, claimed that their ends justified their means," McMurtry concluded. "But people who practice torture always claim that."[65]

On September 14, 1877, Captain McNelly died peacefully, surrounded by family and friends. After his brothers of the local Elks lodge paid their last respects and performed their final rites and rituals, the already-legendary Ranger captain was laid to rest in the Mount Zion Cemetery near the village of Burton. McNelly was only thirty-three years old.[66]

Not long thereafter, an admiring Captain Richard King paid for a modest but impressive obelisk to mark McNelly's gravesite. The inscription on the memorial serves as an appropriate epitaph. The first two lines of the eighteenth-century English poet William Collins's "Ode Written in the Year 1746" read: "How sleep the brave, who sink to rest, / By all their country's wishes blest!"

While not a romantic himself, McNelly still would have approved. He also would have recognized the reverent words of his Lord written on the headstone nearby: "Blessed are the pure of heart, for they shall see God."

It has often been said that legends die hard, and sometimes they never die at all. Leander McNelly, like the young Rangers he commanded and the bandits he hunted, remains a part of the enduring lore of the crooked river that divides Texas from Mexico. Both glorified and vilified, he rides still, somewhere in the mists of history along the border that separates Mexican tradition from Texan myth.

As for the Rio Grande, hardly the river it was a century and a half ago, it rolls on, seeking a path to the Gulf of Mexico. No matter the intervention of dams and reservoirs, droughts and a dozen other factors that have tried to choke it off, the river still finds a crooked course through the hard country of South Texas. Of the people living and working along both banks of the river—they hope only to coexist in peace, without fear and mistrust, sharing the same water, the same land, the same sunshine, and the same future.

Notes

Introduction

1. *Report of the United States Commissioners to Texas,* House Executive Documents, 42nd. Cong., 3rd sess. (serial 1565), H. Misc. Doc. 39, 1–3.

2. *Reports of the Committee of Investigation Sent in 1873 by the Mexican Government to the Frontier of Texas* (New York: Baker, Godwin Printers, 1875), 1 (hereafter cited as *Committee of Investigation*).

3. William Steele, *Report of the Adjutant General of the State of Texas for the Year 1875, Including Mexican Border Troubles,* United States Adjutant General's Office, Letters Received, Main Series, Texas Raids, National Archives Microcopy 666, roll 197 (hereafter cited as Steele, *Report of the Adjutant General,* AGO).

4. Walter Prescott Webb, *The Texas Rangers: A Century of Frontier Defense* (Austin: University of Texas Press, 1964), iv–xvi, 3, 566–67; Chuck Parsons and Marianne E. Hall Little, *Captain L. H. McNelly, Texas Ranger: The Life and Times of a Fighting Man* (Austin: State House Press, 2001), xi–xv.

5. Walter Prescott Webb to Enrique Mendiola, January 29, 1963, Walter Prescott Webb Papers, Dolph Briscoe Center for American History, University of Texas, Austin (hereafter cited as WPWP, DBCAH).

6. Américo Paredes, *A Texas-Mexican Cancionero: Folk Songs of the Lower Rio Grande* (Urbana: University of Illinois Press, 1976), 47–49; James N. Leiker, *Racial Borders: Black Soldiers along the Rio Grande* (College Station: Texas A&M University Press, 2001), 52–53.

7. Ben H. Procter, "The Modern Texas Rangers: A Modern Law Enforcement Dilemma in the Rio Grande Valley," in *Reflections of Western Historians,* ed. John A. Carroll (Tucson: University of Arizona Press, 1969), 215.

8. Walter Prescott Webb, "The Texan's Story," 184–85, WPWP.

9. Ibid.

10. Parsons and Little, *Captain L. H. McNelly,* xi–xv.

11. Walter Prescott Webb, "The Adventures of a Historian," *The Alcalde* (November 1930), 47–50. *The Alcalde* is the alumni publication of the University of Texas at Austin.

12. Ibid.

13. Ibid.

14. Ibid.

15. Ibid.; see also Webb, *Texas Rangers,* 278–79, 550–51.

Prologue

1. Ron Tyler, "Cotton on the Border, 1861–1865," in *Lone Star Blue and Gray: Essays on Texas in the Civil War*, ed. Ralph W. Wooster (Austin: Texas State Historical Association, 1995), 211–16; *The War of the Rebellion: A Compilation of the Official Records of the Union and Confederate Armies*, ser. 1, vol. 4 (Washington, D.C.: Government Printing Office, 1894), 118–19; Stephen A. Townsend, *The Yankee Invasion of Texas* (College Station: Texas A&M University Press, 2006), 3–5; Chauncey Devereux Stillman, *Charles Stillman, 1810–1875* (New York: n.p., 1956), 28–30.

2. John Warren Hunter, "The Fall of Brownsville on the Rio Grande, November, 1863," MSS, DBCAH, 4–6; R. H. Williams, *With the Border Ruffians: Memories of the Far West, 1852–1868*, ed. E. W. Williams (Lincoln: University of Nebraska Press, 1982), 284–85; Jesse Sumpter, *Paso del Aguila: A Chronical of Frontier Days on the Border as Recorded in the Memoirs of Jesse Sumpter*, compiled by Harry Warren (Austin: Encino Press, 1969), 87–88.

3. William Watson, *Adventures of a Blockade Runner* (London: T. Fisher Unwin, 1899), 20–21, 25–27; Williams, *With the Border Ruffians*, 284–85; John C. Rayburn and Virginia Rayburn, eds., *A Century of Conflict, 1821–1913: Incidents in the Lives of William Neale and William A. Neale, Early Settlers in South Texas* (Waco: Texian Press, 1966), 72–80.

4. Rayburn and Rayburn, *A Century of Conflict*, 72–80; James A. Irby, *Backdoor at Bagdad: The Civil War on the Rio Grande* (El Paso: University of Texas at El Paso, 1977), 5–7; Townsend, *Yankee Invasion of Texas*, 5–6.

5. Walter Lord, ed., *The Fremantle Diary: Being the Journal of Lieutenant Colonel Arthur James Lyon Fremantle, Coldstream Guards on His Three Months in the Southern States* (Short Hills, N.J.: Burford Books, 1954), 6; Watson, *Adventures of a Blockade Runner*, 20–21; Emmanuel Domenech, *Missionary Adventures in Texas and Mexico: A Personal Narrative of Six Years' Sojourn in Those Regions* (London: Longman, Brown, Green, Longmans and Roberts, 1858), 217–23, 227–28, 232–40; Nannie M. Tilley, ed., *Federals on the Frontier: The Diary of Benjamin F. McIntyre, 1862–1864* (Austin: University of Texas Press, 1963), 252–54.

6. Irby, *Backdoor at Bagdad*, 7–12.

7. *Committee of Investigation*, 69–70; Pierce to Seward, May 5, 1862, U.S. Department of State, Consular Dispatches, Matamoros, RG 59 (hereafter cited as CDM); Williams, *With the Border Ruffians*, 275; August Santleben, *A Texas Pioneer: Early Staging and Overland Freighting Days on the Frontiers of Texas and Mexico* (New York: Neale, 1910), 52, 71, 168, 183.

8. *War of the Rebellion*, ser. 1, 9:624–25; ibid., ser. 1, 15:1030–32; Thomas T. Smith, Jerry D. Thompson, Robert Wooster, and Ben E. Pingenot, eds., *The Reminiscences of General Zenas R. Bliss, 1854–1876* (Austin: Texas State Historical Association, 2007), 258.

9. *War of the Rebellion*, ser. 1, 15:1015–17, 1030–32; Carl Moneyhon, *Edmund J. Davis of Texas: Civil War General, Republican Leader, Reconstruction Governor* (Fort Worth: TCU Press, 2010), 53–55.

10. Moneyhon, *Edmund J. Davis*, 53–55; Williams, *With the Border Ruffians*, 292–98.

11. Williams, *With the Border Ruffians*, 292–98. Williams changes the names of some participants, referring to Montgomery as "Monson."

12. Vicki Betts, "Private and Amateur Hangings: The Lynching of William W. Montgomery, March 15, 1863," *Southwestern Historical Quarterly* 88 (October 1984): 148–51; Horace Chilton, "Notebook-Diaries," vol. 5, pt. 3, p. 538, Horace Chilton Papers, DBCAH; for background on the enigmatic William Montgomery and his trial for the murder of James Tomerlin of Caldwell County, Texas, in 1852, see Carol Garland, "William Montgomery: Early Caldwell County Settler," *Plum Creek Almanac* 4, no. 1 (Spring, 1986): 4–7.

13. *War of the Rebellion*, ser. 1, 15:1015–17; Pierce to Seward, March 26, 1863, CDM, RG59; Williams, *With the Border Ruffians*, 292–98; J. B. McFarland to C. B. Drake, December 11, 1863, Military Operations in Texas Collection, DBCAH. Hereafter cited as MOTC. See also John L. Haynes to A. J. Hamilton, June 13, 1863, Andrew Jackson Hamilton Papers, DBCAH. Moneyhon, *Edmund J. Davis*, 53–55.

14. *War of the Rebellion*, ser. 1, 15:1126–35.

15. Ibid., 1076, 1130–35.

16. Ibid., ser. 1, vol. 26, pt. 2, 48–51, 67–71; for an understanding of Quintero's complex role in Mexico, see Jorge A. Marban, *Confederate Patriot, Journalist, and Poet: The Multifaceted Life of Jose Augustin Quintero* (Victoria, British Columbia: Friesen Press, 2014).

17. *War of the Rebellion*, ser. 1, 15:1126–35.

18. Lord, *Fremantle Diary*, 6–7.

19. Ibid.

20. Ibid. Historian Carl Moneyhon further documents that Elizabeth "Lizzie" Davis, daughter of prominent Texan Forbes Britton of Corpus Christi, successfully interceded with her father's longtime friend Hamilton Bee to gain the release of her husband (*Edmund J. Davis*, 53–55).

21. Williams, *With the Border Ruffians*, 297.

22. Ibid.; Tilley, *Diary of Benjamin F. McIntyre*, 277–79.

23. Lord, *Fremantle Diary*, 18–19.

24. Ibid.

25. Ibid.; Williams, *With the Border Ruffians*, 246–48, 268–69, 287–98; for John W. Sansom's eyewitness account of the massacre of German Unionists on the Nueces, see Guido E. Ransleben, *A Hundred Years of Comfort in Texas: A Centennial History* (San Antonio: Naylor, 1954), 86–115.

26. Lord, *Fremantle Diary*, 17–21.

27. Ibid.; Williams, *With the Border Ruffians*, 282–85. It should be noted that Williams often refers to these officers as serving under a "General Wasp," an obvious reference to General Hamilton Bee. He also refers to Philip Luckett as "Colonel Lockey." Moreover, "Captain Turner" may have been Captain Richard Taylor, who commanded a company of Duff's partisans.

28. Lord, *Fremantle Diary*, 17–21; see also Thomas North, *Five Years in Texas; or, What You Did Not Hear during the War from January 1861 to January 1865* (Cincinnati: Elm Street, 1870), 104.

29. Stephen Oates, ed., *Rip Ford's Texas* (Austin: University of Texas Press, 1963), 361.

30. Gilbert D. Kingsbury to Mariah McMahon, April 26, 1863, Gilbert D. Kingsbury Papers, DBCAH. Hereafter cited as GKP.

Chapter 1

1. The original manuscript copy of John Sansom's account of the "Battle of the Nueces" and the subsequent massacre of German Unionists may be found at the Dolph Briscoe Center for American History, University of Texas, Austin (DBCAH); it was later published in its entirety in Ransleben, *Hundred Years of Comfort*, 103–15.

2. Ransleben, *Hundred Years of Comfort*, 103–15.

3. Ibid.; Robert Shook, "The Battle of the Nueces, August 10, 1862," *Southwestern Historical Quarterly* 66 (July 1962), 31–42.

4. Shook, "Battle of the Nueces," 31–42; Ransleben, *Hundred Years of Comfort*, 103–15.

5. Williams, *With the Border Ruffians*, 246–48. Williams refers to James Duff as Captain *Dunn*.

6. Ibid.

7. Ransleben, *Hundred Years of Comfort*, 103–15.

8. Ibid.

9. Williams, *With the Border Ruffians*, 248.

10. Ibid.

11. *War of the Rebellion*, ser. 1, 9:615; Williams, *With the Border Ruffians*, 248.

12. Williams, *With the Border Ruffians*, 248.

13. Ibid.

14. Ibid.; *War of the Rebellion*, ser. 1, 9:615.

15. *War of the Rebellion*, ser. 1, 9:615; Sumpter, *Memoirs*, 83–89; William Banta and J. W. Caldwell Jr., *Twenty-Seven Years on the Texas Frontier* (Council Hill, Okla.: L. G. Park, 1933), 185–94.

16. Ransleben, *Hundred Years of Comfort*, 86–95; Williams, *With the Border Ruffians*, 249–56; Lord, *Freemantle Diary*, 18; Lewis Pierce Jr. to William H.

Seward, September 22, 1862, CDM, RG 59; see also Ralph A. Wooster, *Lone Star Regiments in Gray* (Austin: Eakin Press, 2002), 202–4.

17. Ransleben, *Hundred Years of Comfort*, 86–95; Catherine W. McDowell, ed., *Now You Hear My Horn: The Journal of James W. Nichols, 1820–1887* (Austin: University of Texas Press, 1967), 168–77.

18. Jerry Thompson, *Mexican Texans in the Union Army* (El Paso: Texas Western Press, 1986), 10–16.

19. Roy P. Basler, ed., *The Collected Works of Abraham Lincoln* (New Brunswick, New Jersey: Rutgers University Press, 1953), 5:357.

20. Thompson, *Mexican Texans in the Union Army*, 10–16.

21. Edmund J. Davis to Nathaniel P. Banks, August 26, 1863, AGO, RG 94, as quoted in Thompson, *Mexican Texans in the Union Army*, 15; see also A. J. Hamilton to John L. Haynes, November 24, 1862, John L. Haynes Papers, DBCAH.

22. Pierce to Seward, March 1, March 24, April 8, April 26, 1862, CDM, RG59.

23. Pierce to Seward, April 30, 1862, CDM, RG 59.

24. Ibid.

25. Pierce to Seward, August 26, September 21, September 27, 1862, CDM, RG 59; Santleben, *Texas Pioneer*, 32–33.

26. "Journal of James Hampton Kuykendall," December 27–28, 1862, DBCAH; *Committee of Investigation*, 66–68; Thompson, *Mexican Texans in the Union Army*, 8–10; Jerry Thompson, *Vaqueros in Blue and Gray* (Austin: State House Press, 2000), 48–50.

27. *Fort Brown Flag* (Brownsville), January 2, 1863, as quoted in Thompson, *Vaqueros in Blue and Gray*, 49–50.

28. Oates, *Rip Ford's Texas*, 347–48.

29. Ibid.

30. Ibid., 347–48; Tilley, *Diary of Benjamin F. McIntyre*, 254–58.

31. *War of the Rebellion*, ser. 1, 26:447–52; Williams, *With the Border Ruffians*, 290.

32. Williams, *With the Border Ruffians*, 290.

33. *War of the Rebellion*, ser. 1, 26:447–52.

34. Ibid.

35. Ibid.; Chester Barney, *Recollections of Field Service with the Twentieth Iowa Infantry Volunteers; or, What I Saw in the Army* (Davenport, Iowa: privately printed, 1865), 243–45.

36. Barney, *Recollections*, 243–45.

37. *War of the Rebellion*, ser. 1, 26:434–36.

38. Muster rolls of the units organized in Texas may be found in Charles Spurlin, *Texas Volunteers in the Mexican War* (Austin: Eakin Press, 1999); Tyler et al., eds., *The New Handbook of Texas* (Austin: Texas State Historical Association, 1998), 1:458.

39. Williams, *With the Border Ruffians*, 287–89; Tilley, *Diary of Benjamin F. McIntyre*, 254–58; Townsend, *Yankee Invasion of Texas*, 45–67.

40. *War of the Rebellion*, ser. 1, 26:164–65.

41. Ibid.; see also Tom Lea, *The King Ranch* (Boston: Little, Brown and Company, 1957) 1:210–14.

Chapter 2

1. Barney, *Recollections*, 243–45; Tilley, *Diary of Benjamin F. McIntyre*, 246–48.

2. Tilley, *Diary of Benjamin F. McIntyre*, 246–48; Barney, *Recollections*, 243–45; Townsend, *Yankee Invasion of Texas*, 16–17; *War of the Rebellion*, ser. 1, vol. 26, pt. 2, 164–65.

3. *War of the Rebellion*, ser. 1, vol. 26, pt. 2, 164–65.

4. Barney, *Recollections*, 243–46; *War of the Rebellion*, ser. 1, vol. 26, pt. 1, 785, 796–98, 815; Townsend, *Yankee Invasion of Texas*, 18–19.

5. *War of the Rebellion*, ser. 1, vol. 26, pt. 1, 796–98, 815; Jerry Thompson and Lawrence T. Jones III, *Civil War and Revolution on the Rio Grande Frontier: A Narrative and Photographic History* (Austin: Texas State Historical Association, 2004), 54–56.

6. Barney, *Recollections*, 247.

7. Ibid.

8. *War of the Rebellion*, ser. 1, vol. 26, pt. 1, 395–409; Thompson and Jones, *Civil War and Revolution on the Rio Grande*, 60–64.

9. Thompson and Jones, *Civil War and Revolution on the Rio Grande*, 60–64; Tilley, *Diary of Benjamin F. McIntyre*, 256.

10. *War of the Rebellion*, ser. 1, vol. 26, pt. 1, 405; Thompson and Jones, *Civil War and Revolution on the Rio Grande*, 60–62; Napoleon Dana to C. P. Stone, December 11, 1863; Dana to Nathaniel Banks, December 24, 1863, MOTC.

11. Thompson and Jones, *Civil War and Revolution on the Rio Grande*, 60–63.

12. *War of the Rebellion*, ser. 1, vol. 26, pt. 1, 399–400, 843–44, 864–65; ser. 1, vol. 34, pt. 2, 92–93.

13. Ibid.; Thompson and Jones, *Civil War and Revolution on the Rio Grande*, 62–65.

14. *War of the Rebellion*, ser. 1, vol. 26, pt. 1, 399–405; Thompson and Jones, *Civil War and Revolution on the Rio Grande*, 63–64; Tilley, *Diary of Benjamin F. McIntyre*, 288–94.

15. *War of the Rebellion*, ser. 1, vol. 31, pt. 1, 81; Leonard Pierce to Seward, January 16, 1864, CDM, RG, 59; Pierce to Frances Herron, January 15, 1864; Manuel Ruiz to Herron, January 12, 1864; Herron to Ruiz, January 12, 1864, MOTC.

16. *War of the Rebellion*, ser. 1, vol. 34, pt. 1, 84; Thompson and Jones, *Civil War and Revolution on the Rio Grande*, 64.

17. Thompson and Jones, *Civil War and Revolution on the Rio Grande*, 64–65.

18. Oates, *Rip Ford's Texas*, 344–45. Ford's original unedited manuscripts may be found in the Nina Stewart Haley Memorial Library and J. Evetts Haley History Center, Midland, Tex. See John S. Ford, "Memoirs and Reminiscences of Texas History from 1836 to 1888," 8 vols.; *War of the Rebellion*, ser. 1, vol. 34, pt. 2, 979–80; Pryor Lea et al. to Pendleton Murrah, December 15, 1863, Pendleton Murrah Papers, Texas State Library and Archives, Austin (hereafter cited as PMP); Richard B. McCaslin, *Fighting Stock: John S. "Rip" Ford of Texas* (Fort Worth: TCU Press, 2011), 145–54; Townsend, *Yankee Invasion of Texas*, 93–94; *State Gazette* (Austin), December 23, 1863.

19. Richard King to Ford, January 30, 1864, Ford Correspondence, Texas Confederate Military Correspondence, Nita Stewart Haley Memorial Library and J. Evetts Haley History Center, Midland, Texas (hereafter cited as Ford Correspondence, TCMC).

20. W. Jeff Maltby, *Captain Jeff: or Frontier Life in Texas with the Texas Rangers* (Austin: Texian Press, 1967), 123–24.

21. Oates, *Rip Ford's Texas*, 342–45.

22. Ibid., 345–48; *War of the Rebellion*, ser. 1, vol. 34, pt. 3, 739–41; E. B. Nichols to Murrah, September 24, 1864, PMP.

23. Oates, *Rip Ford's Texas*, 348–53; W. J. Hughes, *Rebellious Ranger: Rip Ford and the Old Southwest* (Norman: University of Oklahoma Press, 1964), 216–24.

24. Hughes, *Rebellious Ranger*, 216–24; Wooster, *Lone Star Regiments in Gray*, 210–12.

25. Oates, *Rip Ford's Texas*, 248–53.

26. Ibid., 353–55.

27. Ibid., 355–57.

28. Ibid., 351, 355–57; Benavides's report detailing the Federals' raid on Laredo may be found in *War of the Rebellion*, ser. 1, vol. 34, pt. 1, 647–49; Hughes, *Rebellious Ranger*, 217–18.

29. Ford to J. E. Dwyer, September 3, 1864, Ford Correspondence, TCMC, as quoted in Irby, *Backdoor at Bagdad*, 39. During perusal of the Ford collection, the author was unable to locate the letter cited by Irby above. The index to the collection contained no reference to the letter.

30. Oates, *Rip Ford's Texas*, 262, 377–82.

31. J. F. Tom, July 5, 1864, Absent without Leave Report, July 29, 1864, Ford Correspondence, TCMC; George Lee Robertson to his mother, February 12, 1864, George Lee Robertson Papers, DBCAH (hereafter cited as GLRP); see also Williams, *With the Border Ruffians*, 266–68, 275, 281.

32. Ford to James E. Slaughter, May 16, 1864, Ford Correspondence, TCMC.

33. *War of the Rebellion,* ser. I, vol. 34, pt. 1, 647–48; pt. 2, 1106–7; pt. 3, 176–78, 774–76; Oates, *Rip Ford's Texas,* 359.

34. Oates, *Rip Ford's Texas,* 359–61; Barney, *Recollections,* 272–73; *War of the Rebellion,* ser. 1, vol. 34, pt. 3, 775, 807–8.

35. Williams, *With the Border Ruffians,* 364–65. Consistent with his decision to alter the names of the individuals he criticizes, Williams refers to Ford as "Colonel Franks," yet he identifies him as "Old Rip"; see also Barney, *Recollections,* 282–83.

36. Oates, *Rip Ford's Texas,* 361–62.

37. Ibid., 362–63; *War of the Rebellion,* ser. 1, vol. 34, pt. 1, 1054–56; Frank C. Pierce, *Texas' Last Frontier: A Brief History of the Lower Rio Grande Valley* (Menosha, Wis.: George Banta Publishing, 1917), 48–49.

38. *War of the Rebellion,* ser. 1, vol. 34, pt. 1, 1054–56; Oates, *Rip Ford's Texas,* 361–62.

39. Oates, *Rip Ford's Texas,* 362–63; *War of the Rebellion,* ser. 1, vol. 34, pt. 1, 1054–56; ser. 1, vol. 41, pt. 2, 990.

40. Oates, *Rip Ford' Texas,* 361–66.

41. Williams, *With the Border Ruffians,* 365.

42. *War of the Rebellion,* ser. 1, vol. 34, pt. 3, 786–89; Colonel Ford's military correspondence is filled with references to desertions. See James Duff to Ford, January 21, 1864; Duff to Ford, February 5, 1864; R. H. Williams to Ford, March 1864, Ford Correspondence, TCMC.

43. Unsigned letter received by Governor Pendleton Murrah, January 8, 1864, PMP; Barney, *Recollections,* 273–83.

44. *War of the Rebellion,* ser. 1, vol. 26, pt. 1, 840; Thompson and Jones, *Civil War and Revolution on the Rio Grande,* 67; author Jerry Thompson cites the muster roll of Vidal's company of Union Partisan Rangers from the Texas State Library and Archives. The roll was later reprinted in the *Texas Adjutant General's Report, 1873* (Austin), 111–12.

45. Tilley, *Diary of Benjamin F. McIntyre,* 347; see also Barney, *Recollections,* 279–83.

46. Tilley, *Diary of Benjamin F. McIntyre,* 347–53.

47. Ibid., 353–56.

48. Ibid.

49. Ibid.

50. Ibid.; P. F. Parisot, *The Reminiscences of a Texas Missionary* (San Antonio: St. Mary's Church, 1899), 108.

51. Tilley, *Diary of Benjamin F. McIntyre,* 379–85; see also the series of letters, E. W. Cave to Ford, July 27, 29, and 31, 1864, Ford Correspondence, TCMC; McCaslin, *John S. "Rip" Ford,* 164–69; Townsend, *Yankee Invasion of Texas,* 104–5.

52. E. D. Etchison to William Seward, December 8, 1864, Etchison to W. A. Pike, December 7, 1864, Thomas Mejia to Etchison, January 10, 1865, CDM, RG 59.

53. Ibid., Pierce to Seward, September 1, 1864; Thompson and Jones, *Civil War and Revolution on the Rio Grande*, 86–91; *Texas State Gazette* (Austin), August 10, 1864.

54. Oates, *Rip Ford's Texas*, 371–72.

55. *War of the Rebellion*, ser. 1, vol. 41, pt. 3, 909–912, 973–74.

56. Oates, *Rip Ford's Texas*, 383.

57. *War of the Rebellion*, ser. 1, vol. 41, pt. 3, 973–74; Oates, *Rip Ford's Texas*, 383; Pierce, *Texas' Last Frontier*, 52–53.

58. Williams, *With the Border Ruffians*, 180–81, 198, 225, 275–77.

59. George Lee Robertson to Fanny Robertson, December 13, 1864, GLRP.

Chapter 3

1. Lew Wallace, *Lew Wallace: An Autobiography* (New York: Harper and Brothers, 1906), 2:812–17.

2. Ibid.

3. Ibid.

4. Ibid.; Ulysses S. Grant, *Personal Memoirs of U. S. Grant and Selected Letters, 1839–1865*, ed. Mary McFeely and William S. McFeely (New York: Library Classics of the United States, 1990), 775; Townsend, *Yankee Invasion of Texas*, 117–19.

5. Wallace, *Autobiography*, 820–21.

6. Ibid., 821–22; *War of the Rebellion*, ser. 1, vol. 48, pt. 1, 1276–79; Jeffrey William Hunt, *The Last Battle of the Civil War: Palmetto Ranch* (Austin: University of Texas Press, 2002), 25–30.

7. Wallace, *Autobiography*, 826–32; *War of the Rebellion*, ser. 1, vol. 48, pt. 1, pp. 1280–83.

8. Oates, *Rip Ford's Texas*, 388–89, 396; McCaslin, *John S. "Rip" Ford*, 254.

9. Ibid.; see also Ford's personal notes on the meeting with Wallace, "Interview with General Lew Wallace," TCMC.

10. *War of the Rebellion*, ser. 1, vol. 48, pt. 1, 265–69.

11. *National Tribune*, October 8, 1865, as cited in Hunt, *Last Battle*, 71.

12. George Lee Robertson to Julia, May 8, 1865, GLRP.

13. Oates, *Rip Ford's Texas*, 389; the preferred spelling "Palmito" is used as it is the commonly and historically most favored in South Texas to describe both the ranch and the battle, as opposed to "Palmetto," which refers to the tree that grows wild in the region of the lower Rio Grande.

14. Ibid., 390; John H. Jenkins III, *Recollections of Early Texas: The Memoirs of John Holland Jenkins* (Austin: University of Texas Press, 1987), 232–33.

15. Jenkins, *Recollections of Early Texas*, 232–33; *War of the Rebellion*, ser. 1, vol. 48, pt. 1, 265–69.

16. Oates, *Rip Ford's Texas*, 390.

17. Ibid., 390–91.

18. Ibid. See also *War of the Rebellion*, ser. 1, vol. 48, pt. 1, 265–69; McCaslin, *John S. "Rip" Ford*, 198–201.

19. *War of the Rebellion*, ser. 1, vol. 48, pt. 1, 265–69; Oates, *Rip Ford's Texas*, 392.

20. Oates, *Rip Ford's Texas*, 392; W. H. D. Carrington's account of the Battle of Rancho Palmito may be found in John Henry Brown, *History of Texas from 1685 to 1892* (St. Louis: L. E. Daniell, 1892), 2:435–36; Robertson to his mother, May 17, 1865, GLRP.

21. Philip Sheridan, *Personal Memoirs of P. H. Sheridan: General United States Army* (New York: C. L. Webster, 1888), 2:211–15; Grant, *Personal Memoirs*, 748–53.

22. Thomas Schoonover, ed., *Mexican Lobby: Matías Romero in Washington, 1861–1867* (Lexington: University Press of Kentucky, 1986), 57–58; Thomas Schoonover, trans. and ed., *A Mexican View of America in the 1860s: A Foreign Diplomat Describes the Civil War and Reconstruction* (London: Farleigh Dickinson University Press, 1991), 181–214, 220–29.

23. Schoonover, *Mexican Lobby*, 58–60.

24. Ibid.

25. Ibid.

26. Ibid., 61; Roy Morris Jr., *Sheridan: The Life and Wars of General Philip Sheridan* (New York: Crown, 1992), 264–66.

27. John McAllister Schofield, *Forty-Six Years in the Army* (New York: Century Company, 1897), 379–80.

28. Schoonover, *Mexican Lobby*, 66–68; Sheridan, *Memoirs*, 2: 211–15.

29. John Y. Simon, ed., *The Papers of Ulysses S. Grant*, (Carbondale: Southern Illinois University Press, 1967), 15:156–57, 264–65; *War of the Rebellion*, ser. 1, vol. 47, pt. 3, 649; Paul Bergeron, ed., *The Papers of Andrew Johnson* (Knoxville: University of Tennessee Press, 1989), 8:257–58, 410.

30. Sheridan, *Memoirs*, 2:213–15; Paul Andrew Hutton, *Phil Sheridan and His Army* (Lincoln: University of Nebraska Press, 1985), 20–22; Morris, *Life and Wars of Sheridan*, 265.

31. Ford, "Memoirs," TCM, 1212–13.

32. Ibid.

33. Alexander Watkins Terrell, *From Texas to Mexico and the Court of Maximilian in 1865* (Dallas: Book Club of Texas, 1933), 3–4.

34. Ibid.

35. Terrell, *From Texas to Mexico*, 3–4; John N. Edwards, *Shelby's Expedition to Mexico: An Unwritten Leaf of the War*, ed. Conger Beasley Jr. (Fayetteville: Uni-

versity of Arkansas Press, 2002), 9–10; Anthony Arthur, *General Jo Shelby's March* (New York: Random House, 2010), 58–60.

36. Terrell, *From Texas to Mexico*, 5.

37. Amelia Barr, *All the Days of My Life: An Autobiography* (New York: D. Appleton, 1913), 250; Edwards, *Shelby's Expedition*, 15–16.

38. Barr, *All the Days of My Life*, 250.

39. Edwards, *Shelby's Expedition*, 16; McDowell, *Now You Hear My Horn*, 168–69.

40. Edwards, *Shelby's Expedition*, 16.

41. Ibid., 16–17.

42. Ibid.; Terrell, *From Texas to Mexico*, 6–7.

43. Edwards, *Shelby's Expedition*, 21–26.

44. Ibid., 27.

45. Ibid., 30–31.

46. William Curtis Nunn, *Escape from Reconstruction* (Westport, Conn.: Greenwood Press, 1974), 33.

47. Edwards, *Shelby's Expedition*, 30–31.

48. Ibid.

49. Ibid.; Thomas Westlake, "Memoir of His Civil War Experiences and Post-Civil War Experiences," 131–34, Watson-Westlake Papers, State Historical Society of Missouri, Columbia, Missouri; Thomas Westlake Journal, Western Historical Manuscript Collections, University of Missouri, Columbia, Missouri, as quoted in Arthur, *General Jo Shelby's March*; Al Kinsall, "Timeline of Eagle Pass History," MSS, Eagle Pass Public Library, Eagle Pass, Tex.

50. Terrell, *From Texas to Mexico*, 6–10.

51. Ibid., 11–16.

52. Melinda Rankin, *Twenty Years among the Mexicans: A Narrative of Missionary Labor* (Cincinnati: Central Book Concern, 1881), 122–28.

53. Ibid., 128.

54. Terrell, *From Texas to Mexico*, 16–20.

Chapter 4

1. Thompson and Jones, *Civil War and Revolution on the Rio Grande*, 99–130.

2. Samuel E. Bell and James Smallwood, *The Zona Libre, 1858–1905: A Problem in American Diplomacy* (El Paso: Texas Western Press, 1982), 1–3.

3. Gilbert Kingsbury to the *New York Herald*, March 1, 1864, clipping in Gilbert D. Kingsbury Papers, DBCAH (hereafter cited as GDKP).

4. Ibid.; Kingsbury to General F. J. Herron, n.d., GDKP.

5. Ibid.; Kingsbury to *New York Herald*, March 1, 1864, GDKP.

6. Williams, *With the Border Ruffians*, 284–87.

7. Joe B. Frantz, *Texas: A History* (New York: W. W. Norton, 1984), 86.

8. John A. Loomis, *Texas Ranchman: The Memoirs of John A. Loomis* (Chadron, Neb.: Fur Press, 1982), 27; Robert Robertson, ed., *Her Majesty's Texas: Two English Immigrants in Reconstruction Texas* (College Station: Texas A&M University Press, 1998), 43; Bruce S. Cheeseman, ed., *Maria von Blücher's Corpus Christi: Letters from the South Texas Frontier, 1849–1879* (College: Texas A&M University Press, 2002), 149, 174–78.

9. Samuel L. Maxey, *Maxey's Texas*, ed. David L. Gracy (Austin: Pemberton Press, 1965), 118; Loomis, *Texas Ranchman*, 2; John McAllen to Kingsbury, November 24, 1870, GDKP; Edward King, ed. Robert S. Gray, *Texas: 1874; An Eyewitness Account of Conditions in Post-Reconstruction Texas* (Houston: Cordovan Press, 1974), 87–88, 123–25; R. J. Lauderdale and John M. Doak, *Life on the Range and on the Trail* (San Antonio: Naylor, 1936), 6–7.

10. North, *Five Years in Texas*, 68–74, 161; J. Frank Dobie, *A Vaquero of the Brush Country: John D. Young and J. Frank Dobie* (Austin: University of Texas Press, 1998), 24–25.

11. John Linn, *Reminiscences of Fifty Years in Texas* (Austin: State House Press, 1986), 310.

12. Webb to Mendiola, January 29, 1963, WPWP; Mary Margaret McAllen Amberson, James A. McAllen, and Margaret H. McAllen, *I Would Rather Sleep in Texas: A History of the Lower Rio Grande Valley and the People of the Santa Anita Land Grant* (Austin: Texas State Historical Association, 2003), 313–32; Jane Clements Monday and Frances Brannen Vick, *Petra's Legacy: The South Texas Ranching Empire of Petra Vela and Mifflin Kenedy* (College Station: Texas A&M University Press, 2007), 171–73, 184–88, 228, 232–33; King, *Texas: 1874*, 123–25.

13. Santleben, *Texas Pioneer*, 52.

14. Paul Horgan, *Great River: The Rio Grande in North American History* (New York: Rinehart, 1954), 2:855.

15. Arrell M. Gibson, *The Kickapoos: Lords of the Middle Border* (Norman: University of Oklahoma Press, 1963), 202–19; Thomas A. Britten, *The Lipan Apaches: People of Wind and Lightning* (Albuquerque: University of New Mexico Press, 2009), 220–25.

16. Dorman H. Winfrey and James M. Day, eds., *The Indian Papers of Texas and the Southwest* (Austin: Texas State Historical Association, 1995), 4:127–28.; Webb to Mendiola, January 29, 1963, WPWP; Amberson, McAllen, and McAllen, *I Would Rather Sleep in Texas*, 313–32; Monday and Vick, *Petra's Legacy*, 171–73, 184–88, 228, 232–33.

17. Winfrey and Day, *Indian Papers of Texas and the Southwest*, 4:202, 225–27, 255–59, 261–62, 271–79, 282–87, 307–9, 331–33, 369–73, 402–8, 435, 447.

18. F. M. Buckelew and T. S. Dennis, *Life of F. M. Buckelew: The Indian Captive, as Related by Himself* (Bandera, Tex.: Hunters Printing House, 1925), 11–12,

18–23; A. J. Sowell, *Texas Indian Fighters* (Abilene: State House Press, 1986), 587–88.

19. Buckelew and Dennis, *Life of F. M. Buckelew*, 27–28; Winfrey and Day, *Indian Papers of Texas and the Southwest*, 4:134–36, 229, 258–59.

20. Buckelew and Dennis, *Life of F. M. Buckelew*, 29–32.

21. Ibid.; Sowell, *Texas Indian Fighters*, 587–94.

22. Buckelew and Dennis, *Life of F. M. Buckelew*, 33–34, 40–52.

23. Winfrey and Day, *Indian Papers of Texas and the Southwest*, 4:133–34, 143, 258–59; Sowell, *Texas Indian Fighters*, 588–89.

24. Buckelew and Dennis, *Life of F. M. Buckelew*, 133–34.

25. Ibid.; Winfrey and Day, *Indian Papers of Texas and the Southwest*, 4:258–59.

26. Winfrey and Day, *Indian Papers of Texas and the Southwest*, 4:258–59, 303, 330, 378; Mike Cox, "Two Braids," *TexasEscapes.com*, July 2003.

27. Cox, "Two Braids."

28. For an allegedly firsthand but nevertheless suspicious account of "Two Braids," see Thomas Stringfield, *Captured by the Apaches: Forty Years with This Savage Band of Indians; A True Story by "Two Braids," Tommy Stringfield Who Was Taken Captive in 1870 and Liberated in 1909* (Hamilton, Tex.: Herald Print, 1911).

29. Cox, "Two Braids."

30. Thomas T. Smith et al., eds., *The Reminiscences of Major General Zenas R. Bliss, 1854–1876* (Austin: Texas State Historical Association, 2007), 432–34; *Report of the Commissioner of Indian Affairs to the Secretary of the Interior for the Year 1871* (Washington: Government Printing Office, 1872), 191–96.

31. Felipe A, Latorre and Dolores L. Latorre, *The Mexican Kickapoo Indians* (Austin: University of Texas Press, 1976), 21; *Texas Frontier Troubles: Testimony Taken before the Committee on Foreign Affairs*, 35–40, in *Report and Accompanying Documents of the Committee on Foreign Affairs on the Relations of the United States with Mexico* (Washington: Government Printing Office, 1878; hereafter cited as *Texas Frontier Troubles*).

32. Smith et al., *Bliss Reminiscences*, 430–31.; *Report of the Commissioner of Indian Affairs to the Secretary of the Interior for the Year 1871*, 194–95; *Depredations on the Frontiers of Texas*, Executive Doc. 39, U.S. House of Representatives, 42nd. Cong., 3rd. Sess., 22.

33. Smith et al., *Bliss Reminiscences*, 434–35.

34. Ibid.

35. Ibid.

36. Ibid.; Winfrey and Day, *Indian Papers of Texas and the Southwest*, 4: 331–33.

37. Winfrey and Day, *Indian Papers of Texas and the Southwest*, 4:331–33; Latorre and Latorre, *Mexican Kickapoo Indians*, 87–89, 117–19; Smith et al., *Bliss Reminiscences*, 434–35; King, *Texas: 1874*, 126–29.

38. Ibid.

39. Ibid.

40. *Report of the Commissioner of Indian Affairs to the Secretary of the Interior for the Year 1871*, 194–96; Latorre and Latorre, *Mexican Kickapoo Indians*, 20–21.

41. Loyd M. Uglow, *Standing in the Gap: Army Outposts, Picket Stations, and the Pacification of the Texas Frontier, 1866–1886* (Fort Worth: Texas Christian University Press, 2001), 67–80. Leiker, *Racial Borders*, 48–52.

42. Webb, *Texas Rangers*, 219.

43. John W. Forney, *What I Saw in Texas* (Philadelphia: Ringwald and Brown, 1872), 22.

44. Ibid., 27.

45. Santleben, *Texas Pioneer*, 32–33; Tyler et al., *New Handbook of Texas*, 3:104–5; Arnoldo De León, *They Called Them Greasers: Anglo Attitudes toward Mexicans in Texas, 1821–1900* (Austin: University of Texas Press, 1983), 99.

46. De León, *They Called Them Greasers*, 52–70; Lauderdale and Doak, *Life on the Range*, 6–7.

47. Winfrey and Day, *Indian Papers of Texas and the Southwest*, 4:292–94.

48. Ibid.; one year later, the next Cameron County judge would echo Galvan's complaints. See J. S. Mansur to Davis, February 28, 1870, Edmund J. Davis Papers, Texas State Library and Archives, Austin, Texas (hereafter cited as EJDP).

49. *Texas Frontier Troubles*, 164.

50. Ibid., 166–67.

51. McCaslin, *John S. "Rip" Ford*, 213–14; see also E. Basse to Davis, February 23, 1870, EJDP.

52. McCaslin, *John S. "Rip" Ford*, 214–15; *Daily Ranchero and Republican* (Brownsville), February 19 and 24, 1870.

53. McCaslin, *John S. "Rip" Ford*, 214–215; see also Cruise Carson to Davis, January 12, 1870, EJDP.

54. *Daily Ranchero and Republican* (Brownsville), February 19 and 24, 1870.

55. Ibid.

56. Ibid.

57. McCaslin, *John S. "Rip" Ford*, 216–17.

58. *Daily Ranchero and Republican* (Brownsville), March 26, 1872; see also "Report of the Grand Jury, Cameron County, Texas, August 28, 1871"; William Russell to Davis, April 21, 1872; unidentified news clipping, "District Attorney's Office," December 20, 1871, EJDP.

59. *Daily Ranchero and Republican* (Brownsville), March 26, 1872.

60. *Daily Ranchero and Republican* (Brownsville), February 10, 1872; see also Frank McManus to Davis, December 23, 1871, EJDP.

Chapter 5

1. Thompson and Jones, *Civil War and Revolution on the Rio Grande*, 98.

2. Ibid.

3. Forney, *What I Saw in Texas*, 27.

4. John Austin Stevens, *The Valley of the Rio Grande: Its Topography and Resources* (New York: William C. Bryant, 1864), 21, 32; John Mason Hart, *Empire of Revolution: The Americans in Mexico since the Civil War* (Berkeley: University of California Press, 2002), 1–3; E. Dougherty, *The Rio Grande Valley: A Lecture Delivered before the Lone Star Literary Association of Brownsville, Texas* (Brownsville, Ranchero Book and Job Printing Office, 1867), 29–30.

5. *Daily State Journal* (Austin), July 10–12, 1872; Barry Crouch and Donaly E. Brice, *The Governor's Hounds: The Texas State Police, 1870–1873* (Austin: University of Texas Press, 2011) 123–24; Parsons and Little, *Captain L. H. McNelly*, 108–112.

6. *Daily State Journal* (Austin), July 10–12, 1872.

7. Ibid.; Parsons and Little, *Captain L. H. McNelly*, 108–112; H. W. Graber, *A Terry Texas Ranger: The Life Record of H. W. Graber* (Austin: State House Press, 1987), 333–34.

8. *San Antonio Herald*, July 17, 1872; *Daily State Journal* (Austin), July 10–12, 1872; Parsons and Hall, *Captain L. H. McNelly*, 109–110; Crouch and Brice, *Governor's Hounds*, 131.

9. *The War of the Rebellion*, ser. 1, vol. 26, pt. 1, 215–16; Theophilus Noel, *A Campaign from Santa Fe to the Mississippi: Being a History of the Old Sibley Brigade from the First Organization to the Present Time*, ed. Martin Hardwick Hall and Edwin Adams Davis (Houston: Stagecoach Press, 1961), 67–78, 133–34.

10. Noel, *Campaign from Santa Fe to the Mississippi*, 134–37; Parsons and Little, *Captain L. H. McNelly*, 33–43.

11. Noel, *Campaign from Santa Fe to the Mississippi*, 134–37.

12. John E. Walker to McNelly, May 3, 1865; John G. Walker, Special Order, May 28, 1865, Leander H. McNelly Papers, DBCAH (hereafter cited as LHMP); Parsons and Hall, *Captain L. H. McNelly*, 45–47.

13. C. S. Andum to Headquarters, Cavalry Division, November 25, 1863; E. Kirby Smith, Special Order 221, December 19, 1863; James P. Major to McNelly, May 28, 1865, LHMP; *War of the Rebellion*, ser. 1, 26:597.

14. Crouch and Brice, *Governor's Hounds*, 131.

15. Levi English's testimony may be found in *Depredations on the Frontier of Texas: Message of the President of the United States,* House of Representatives, 43d Cong., 1st. sess., Exec. Doc. 257 (serial 1615), 10–11. Hereafter cited as *Depredations on the Frontier of Texas*.

16. *Daily Ranchero and Republican* (Brownsville), March 26, 1872; see also U.S. Congress, *Congressional Globe*, 42nd Cong., 2nd sess., pt. 5, 3846, 3869, 3888, 4192, 4202, 4318, 4460.

17. Simon, *Papers of Ulysses S. Grant*, 23:23–26.

18. *Report of the United States Commissioners to Texas*, House Executive Documents, 42nd Cong., 3rd sess. (serial 1565) doc. 39, 1–3; Thomas Green to Ulysses S. Grant, n.d., Thomas Green Papers, DBCAH.

19. *Report of the United States Commissioners to Texas*, p. 6–9, 33–36; see also Ernest Wallace, ed., *Ranald S. Mackenzie's Official Correspondence Relating to Texas, 1871–1873* (Lubbock: West Texas Museum Association, 1967), 1:161–68, 171–78, 182–89.

20. *Report of the United States Commissioners to Texas*, 6–9.

21. Ibid.; Bell and Smallwood, *Zona Libre*, 1–3, 21–25, 27–32.

22. Lea, *King Ranch*, 1:273–75.

23. *Committee of Investigation*, 105–7.

24. Jerry Thompson, *Cortina: Defending the Mexican Name in Texas* (College Station: Texas A&M University Press, 2007), 218.

25. Ibid.

26. Lea, *King Ranch*, 1:274–75.

27. *Report of the United States Commissioners to Texas*, 18–19.

28. *New York Times*, October 11, 1872.

29. Ibid., October 5, 1872.

30. *Committee of Investigation*, 423, 441.

31. *Galveston News*, October 27, 1872; *New York Times*, November 2, 1872.

32. *Report of the United States Commissioners to Texas*, pp. 10–19, 21–22, 25–29; see also Thomas Wilson to William Hunter, March 2, 1872, CDM. This letter is typical of Wilson's copious correspondence to be found in his consular dispatches.

33. *Depredations on the Frontiers of Texas*, 2.

34. Ibid., 3.

35. "The Frontier Commission," John S. Ford Papers, TCMC.

36. *Depredations on the Frontier of Texas*, 2–3; "The Frontier Commission," John S. Ford Papers," TCMC, pp. 195–97.

37. *Depredations on the Frontier of Texas*, 3–5, 28–32; *New York Times*, June 30, 1873; "Mexican Border Grievances," *Nation*, August 29, 1878, 125.

38. *Depredations on the Frontiers of Texas*, 4–6, 28–31.

39. Ibid., 32.

40. King and Wells, *Texas: 1874*, 125–29.

41. Ibid., 132–33.

42. *Committee of Investigation*, 60–62, 423.

43. Ibid.

44. Ibid., 440–43; see also a report carried in the *San Antonio Herald* on July 24, 1875, which was reprinted in the *New York Times*, August 2, 1875.

45. *Committee of Investigation*, 83–89, 169–71.

Chapter 6

1. Wallace, *Mackenzie's Official Correspondence*, 1:161–63; Robert G. Carter, *On the Border with Mackenzie; or, Winning West Texas from the Comanches* (New York: Antiquarian Press, 1961), 419–20; Grant, *Personal Memoirs*, 2:541.

2. Ernest Wallace, *Ranald S. Mackenzie on the Texas Frontier* (College Station: Texas A&M University Press, 1993), 96–97; Michael D. Pierce, *The Most Promising Young Officer: A Life of Ranald Slidell Mackenzie* (Norman: University of Oklahoma Press, 1993), 121–23; Charles M. Robinson III, *Bad Hand: A Biography of General Ranald S. Mackenzie* (Austin: State House Press, 1993), 125–30.

3. Wallace, *Mackenzie's Official Correspondence*, 1:161–63.

4. Carter, *On the Border with Mackenzie*, 418–23.

5. Ibid.

6. Carter, *On the Border with Mackenzie*, 416–19.

7. Caleb Pirtle III and Michael F. Cusack, *Fort Clark: The Lonely Sentinel on Texas's Western Frontier* (Austin: Eakin Press, 1985), 57; Alexander Sweet, *Alex Sweet's Texas: The Lighter Side of Lone Star History* (Austin: University of Texas Press, 1986), 88–89.

8. Carter, *On the Border with Mackenzie*, 421–24.

9. Ibid.

10. Ibid.; William H. Leckie, *The Buffalo Soldiers: A Narrative of the Negro Cavalry in the West* (Norman: University of Oklahoma Press, 1967), 101–2; Pirtle and Cusack, *Fort Clark*, 73.

11. Carter, *On the Border with Mackenzie*, 422–24.

12. Ibid.; see also Winfrey and Day, *The Indian Papers of Texas and the Southwest*, 4:273–78, 280–81, 402–7.

13. H. H. McConnell, *Five Years a Cavalryman; or, Sketches of Regular Army Life on the Texas Frontier, 1866–1871* (Norman: University of Oklahoma Press, 1996), 232.

14. Carter, *On the Border with Mackenzie*, 425.

15. Ibid., 419–20; E. B. Beaumont, "Over the Border with Mackenzie," in *Eyewitnesses to the Indian Wars, 1865–1890*, ed. Peter Cozzens (Mechanicsburg, Pa.: Stackpole Books, 2003), 3:437–38; Robert G. Carter, "A Raid into Mexico," in *Eyewitnesses to the Indian Wars, 1865–1890*, ed. Peter Cozzens (Mechanicsburg, PA: Stackpole Books, 2003), 3:444–46.

16. Carter, *On the Border with Mackenzie*, 424–26; Robert G. Carter, *The Old Sergeant's Story: Fighting Indians and Bad Men in Texas from 1870 to 1876*

(Mattituck, N.Y.: John M. Carroll, 1982), 59; Smith et. al., *Bliss Reminiscences,* 439–40.

17. Smith et al., *Bliss Reminiscences,* 424, 437;

18. Ibid.; Wallace, *Mackenzie's Official Correspondence,* 1:165.

19. Carter, *On the Border with Mackenzie,* 428–29.

20. Beaumont, "Over the Border with Mackenzie," 440; Carter, *On the Border with Mackenzie,* 428–29.

21. Beaumont, "Over the Border with Mackenzie," 440; Carter, *On the Border with Mackenzie,* 428–29.

22. Beaumont, "Over the Border with Mackenzie," 440.

23. Carter, *On the Border with Mackenzie,* 431–35.

24. Beaumont, "Over the Border with Mackenzie," 441.

25. Grady McCright, *The Whirlwind: John L. Bullis and His Seminole-Negro Scouts* (Lexington, Ky.: n.p., 2012), 1–3; Pirtle and Cusack, *Fort Clark,* 67–72, 75–76, 81–85.

26. Pirtle and Cusack, *Fort Clark,* 38–44, 50–52; Smith et al., *Bliss Reminiscences,* 429–31.

27. Sherry Robinson, *I Fought the Good Fight: A History of the Lipan Apaches* (Denton: University of North Texas Press, 2013), 291–92.

28. Carter, "A Raid into Mexico," 449–50; Robinson, *I Fought the Good Fight,* 291–92.

29. Carter, *On the Border with Mackenzie,* 442–43.

30. Ibid., 444–45.

31. Ibid.

32. Ibid.

33. Wallace, *Mackenzie's Official Correspondence,* 1:169–70; Carter, *On the Border with Mackenzie,* 447.

34. Ibid., 432, 446–48.

35. Ibid., 446–48; Pierce, *Most Promising Young Officer,* 121–23.

36. Carter, *On the Border with Mackenzie,* 448–51.

37. Ibid.

38. Ibid., 453–57.

39. Ibid.

40. Carter, *On the Border with Mackenzie,* 457–60; Carter, *Old Sergeant's Story,* 18.

41. Carter, *On the Border with Mackenzie,* 457–60.

42. Ibid., 454–55; Robinson, *I Fought the Good Fight,* 292–93.

43. Robinson, *I Fought the Good Fight,* 292–93; Carter, *On the Border with Mackenzie,* 460.

44. Ibid.

45. Carter, *On the Border with Mackenzie,* 460–62.

46. Wallace, *Mackenzie's Official Correspondence*, 1:167–71; Carter, *On the Border with Mackenzie*, 439–42.

47. Wallace, *Mackenzie's Official Correspondence*, 1:171–74.

48. See also Philip Sheridan to C. C. Auger, May 27, 1873, "Private Letter Book of Ranald S. Mackenzie, 1873–1874, 4th Cav.: Troubles with the Indians on the Mexican-Texas Border," MSS, U.S. Army History Institute, Carlisle Barracks, Carlisle, Pennsylvania, 30; Wallace, *Mackenzie's Official Correspondence*, 1:163, 166, 171–72, 178–79, 179–84.

49. Wallace, *Mackenzie's Official Correspondence*, 1:181–84.

50. Mackenzie to Auger, May 29, 1873, "Letter Book of Ranald S. Mackenzie," 30–35.

51. Mackenzie to Auger, June 30, 1873, "Letter Book of Ranald S. Mackenzie," 102–4.

52. Britten, *Lipan Apaches*, 223–26; Gibson, *Kickapoos*, 236–38.

53. Texas, *House Journal*, 15th Legislature, 1st. sess., pp. 47–48; Richard Coke to Gen. E. O. C. Ord, April 24, 1875; Capt. Francis Moore to Post Adjutant, Ringgold Barracks, March 8, 1875; Capt. C. D. Beyer to Post Adj., Ringgold Barracks, March 4, 1875, AGO, roll 196.

Chapter 7

1. *Texas Frontier Troubles*, viii.

2. Ibid.

3. Ibid., xv–xxi.

4. Ibid.; Thaddeus M. Rhodes to W. H. Russell, March 4, 1875; Alexander Leo to Richard Coke, March 4, 1875; William Steele to Coke, March 30, 1875; James A. Ware to Coke, June 1, 1875; Richard Coke Papers, Texas State Library and Archives, Austin (hereafter cited as RCP).

5. *Texas Frontier Troubles*, xv–xxi.; Rayburn and Rayburn, *Century of Conflict*, 116.

6. Rayburn and Rayburn, *Century of Conflict*, 116; Tom Noakes's firsthand account of the raid on Nuecestown is recorded in Leopold Morris, "The Mexican Raid of 1875 on Corpus Christi," *Quarterly of the Texas Historical Association* 4 (October 1900), 128–31; William M. Hager, "The Nuecestown Raid: A Border Incident," *Arizona and the West* 1 (Autumn 1959): 258–70.

7. Morris, "Mexican Raid on Corpus Christi," 132.

8. Ibid., 132–33.

9. Ibid., 133–34.

10. Ibid., 134–36; Hager, "Nuecestown Raid," 267–70.

11. George Durham, *Taming the Nueces Strip: The Story of McNelly's Rangers* (Austin: University of Texas Press, 1962), 18–19; Morris, "Mexican Raid on Corpus Christi," 134–36.

12. Morris, "Mexican Raid on Corpus Christi," 134–36.

13. Ibid.

14. Ibid.

15. Ibid., 136–39.

16. *Corpus Christi Gazette*, March 27, 1875.

17. Morris, "Mexican Raid on Corpus Christi," 136–39.

18. Ibid.

19. *Galveston Weekly News*, April 26, 1875; U.S. Congress, House of Representatives. *Report and Accompanying Documents of the Committee on Foreign Affairs on the Relation of the United States and Mexico* (Washington, D.C.: Government Printing Office, 1878), appendix B, 166; Edward Dougherty to Coke, April 28, 1875, RCP; De León, *They Called Them Greasers*, 99.

20. *Texas House Journal*, 15th Legislature, 1st. sess., 47–48; Richard Coke to E. O. C. Ord, April 24, 1875; Capt. Francis Moore to Post Adj., Ringgold Barracks, March 8, 1875; Capt. C. D. Beyer to Post Adj., Ringgold Barracks, March 4, 1875, AGO, roll 196; Steele to Coke, March 30, 1875; Ord to Coke, May 15, 1875, RCP.

21. *Texas House Journal*, 15th Legislature, 1st. sess., 47–48; Steele, *Report of the Adjutant General*; William Steele to Coke, March 30, 1875, Steele to Coke, May 30, 1875, RCP.

22. Ibid.

23. Frederick Wilkins, *The Law Comes to Texas: The Texas Rangers, 1870–1901* (Austin: State House Press, 1999), 25–29; Mike Cox, *The Texas Rangers: Wearing the Cinco Peso, 1821–1900* (New York: Forge, 2008), 211–19; to combat the growing wave of violence, a company of Tejano Rangers was also raised in Webb County and led by Captain Refugio Benavides. Tyler et al., *New Handbook of Texas*, 1:484–85.

24. Durham, *Taming the Nueces Strip*, 46; Napoleon A. Jennings, *A Texas Ranger* (Norman: University of Oklahoma Press, 1997), 59; William Callicott, "Memoirs," 26, DBCAH.

25. Durham, *Taming the Nueces Strip*, 72

26. Ibid., 5, 24, 97.

27. Parsons and Little, *Captain L. H. McNelly*, 173–74.

28. Durham, *Taming the Nueces Strip*, 12–13, 16; Jennings, *A Texas Ranger*, 63–64.

29. Durham, *Taming the Nueces Strip*, 2–9; William Callicott, "Reminiscences," 1–2, DBCAH; Parsons and Little, *Captain L. H. McNelly*, 174

30. Durham, *Taming the Nueces Strip*, 13–17, 37–38, 42–43; Jennings, *A Texas Ranger*, 49–51, 60.

31. Chuck Parsons, *"Pidge": Texas Ranger* (College Station: Texas A&M University Press, 2013), 5–10; Chuck Parsons, *"Pidge," A Texas Ranger from Virginia:*

The Life and Letters of Lieutenant T. C. Robinson, Washington County Volunteer Militia Company "A" (Wolfe City, Tex.: Henington, 1985), 1–4, 6–8.

32. Parsons and Little, *Captain L. H. McNelly*, 196–200.

33. Jennings, *A Texas Ranger*, 63; Chuck Parsons, *John B. Armstrong: Texas Ranger and Pioneer Ranchman* (College Station: Texas A&M University Press, 2007), 1–7.

34. John McClane to William Steele, April 18, 1875, Adjutant General's Papers, Texas State Library and Archives, Austin (hereafter cited as TAGP); Webb, *Texas Rangers*, 238.

35. Callicott, "Reminiscences," 1–2; Durham, *Taming the Nueces Strip*, 40.

36. McNelly's order was reprinted in the *Galveston Daily News*, May 4, 1875.

37. Ibid.; Parsons, *Life and Letters of Lieutenant Robinson*, 72; *San Antonio Daily Express*, May 3, 1875.

38. *Texas Adjutant General Report*, pp. 8–10, AGO, roll 196; Leander H. McNelly to William Steele, May 14, 1875, TAGP.

39. Durham, *Taming the Nueces Strip*, 17–19.

40. Ibid., 19–20.

41. Ibid., 20–21

42. Ibid.

43. Ibid.

44. Ibid.; Parsons, *Life and Letters of Lieutenant Robinson*, 72.

45. Durham, *Taming the Nueces Strip*, 21–23; Webb, *Texas Rangers*, 238–39.

46. Durham, *Taming the Nueces Strip*, 24.

47. Ibid., 24–26.

48. Ibid., 24–27, 39.

49. Don Graham, *Kings of Texas: The 150-Year Saga of an American Ranching Empire* (Hoboken, N.J.: John Wiley and Sons, 2003), 137–38; Durham, *Taming the Nueces Strip*, 28–33; in his classic account of Richard King's empire and legacy, Tom Lea fails to mention McNelly's company of Rangers stopping at the Santa Gertrudis. See Lea, *King Ranch*.

50. Durham, *Taming the Nueces Strip*, 28–33.

51. Ibid.; Graham, *Kings of Texas*, 138–39.

52. Ibid.; Durham, *Taming the Nueces Strip*, 32–33.

53. Ibid.

54. Durham, *Taming the Nueces Strip*, 33.

55. Webb, *Texas Rangers*, 238–41.

56. Ibid.; Durham, *Taming the Nueces Strip*, 41–42.

57. Jennings, *A Texas Ranger*, 120–22.

58. Durham, *Taming the Nueces Strip*, 40, 44, 53–55, 85–86; Jennings, *A Texas Ranger*, 74–75, 78–79; 134–37, 139–41.

59. Callicott, "Memoirs," 9–11; Callicott, "Reminiscences," 3–6.

60. Callicott, "Reminiscences," 3–6.

61. J. Frank Dobie, "Foreword," in Jennings, *A Texas Ranger*, viii.

62. Callicott, *Memoirs*, 9–11.

63. Jennings, *A Texas Ranger*, 74–75, 78.

64. Parsons, *Life and Letters of Lieutenant Robinson*, 82–83.

65. *Voz del pueblo* (Matamoros), news clipping, n.d., CDM.

66. Durham, *Taming the Nueces Strip*, 55.

67. Rev. 6:7–8 (ESV); The author learned of the legend of the "she-preacher" from residents of Brownsville and Matamoros on February 11–12, 1994; see Michael Collins, "The Texas Devils: McNelly's Rangers and the Palo Alto Fight," in *Papers of the Second Palo Alto Conference* (Brownsville, Tex.: National Park Service, United States Department of Interior, Palo Alto National Historic Site, 1997), 128–34.

68. William Steele to Coke, May 31, 1875, RCP.

Chapter 8

1. Jerry Thompson, *A Wild and Vivid Land: An Illustrated History of the South Texas Border* (Austin: Texas State Historical Association, 1997), 1–2; Jane Clements Monday and Betty Bailey Colley, *Voices from the Wild Horse Desert: The Vaquero Families of the King and Kenedy Ranches* (Austin: University of Texas Press, 1997), xix–xxv, 38; Amberson, McAllen, and McAllen, *I Would Rather Sleep in Texas*, x–xii, 18; Brian Robertson, *Wild Horse Desert: The Heritage of South Texas* (Edinburg, Tex.: Santander Press, 1985), 1–4.

2. Durham, *Taming the Nueces Strip*, 3–7; Parsons and Hall, *Captain L. H. McNelly*, 159–66.

3. Durham, *Taming the Nueces Strip*, 42–44.

4. Ibid.

5. Ibid.; Rayburn and Rayburn, *Century of Conflict*, 120; *Texas Frontier Troubles*, 143–47.

6. *Texas Frontier Troubles*, 14–15; Durham, *Taming the Nueces Strip*, 47; Steele, *Report of the Adjutant General*, 32–33; Parsons and Little, *Captain L. H. McNelly*, 122, 211–12

7. McCaslin, *John S. "Rip" Ford*, 213, 224–26; Hughes, *Rebellious Ranger*, 248–49.

8. Rayburn and Rayburn, *Century of Conflict*, 119–21.

9. U.S. Congress, House of Representatives. *Report and Accompanying Documents of the Committee on Foreign Affairs on the Relation of the United States and Mexico*. Washington, D.C.: Government Printing Office, 1878), 188–97 (hereafter cited as *Report of the Committee on Foreign Affairs*).

10. *Texas Frontier Troubles*, 39–43; Parsons and Hall, *Captain L. H. McNelly*,

193–94; Callicott, "Reminiscences," 3–4; Parsons, *Life and Letters of Lieutenant Robinson*, 74.

11. Rayburn and Rayburn, *Century of Conflict*, 120–22.

12. Parsons, *Life and Letters of Lieutenant Robinson*, 75–77; Jennings, *A Texas Ranger*, 122–24.

13. Durham, *Taming the Nueces Strip*, 55–59; Jennings, *A Texas Ranger*, 122–24; Callicott, "Reminscences," 8–10.

14. Callicott, "Reminiscences," 11–12.

15. Ibid.; Durham, *Taming the Nueces Strip*, 62; Jennings, *A Texas Ranger*, 123–25.

16. Rayburn and Rayburn, Century of *Conflict*, 121–22.

17. Callicott, "Reminiscences," 12.

18. Ibid., 20.

19. Rayburn and Rayburn, *Century of Conflict*, 120–22; Durham, *Taming the Nueces Strip*, 63–66; *Galveston Daily News*, June 13, 1875. Revealing the racist sentiments of the times, the headline of the news read "They Give the Greasers a Taste of Old Times."

20. Joseph P. O'Shaughnessy to Steele, June 14, 1875; Albert Wood to Steele, June 16, 1875, TAGP.

21. Steele, *Report of the Adjutant General*, AGO, roll 197.

22. Thompson, *Cortina*, 226; *Report of the Committee on Foreign Affairs*, appendix B, 182; Parsons and Little, *Captain L. H. McNelly*, 194–98, 274; Jennings, *A Texas Ranger*, 69; Rayburn and Rayburn, *Century of Conflict*, 122.

23. Durham, *Taming the Nueces Strip*, 63–64; *Galveston Daily News*, June 13, 1875.

24. Durham, *Taming the Nueces Strip*, 66–67.

25. McNelly to Steele, June 14, 1875, TAGP; Jennings, *A Texas Ranger*, 128–30.

26. Callicott, "Reminiscences," 20; Durham, *Taming the Nueces Strip*, 69.

27. Jennings, *A Texas Ranger*, 71–72.

28. McNelly to Steele, June 14, July 6, July 7, 1875, TAGP; Durham, *Taming the Nueces Strip*, 70–78.

29. Coke to McNelly, July 9, 1875, RCP; a copy of the same letter may also be found in the Leander McNelly Papers, Albert and Ethel Herzstein Library, San Jacinto Museum of History, San Jacinto Battlefield State Historic Site. Hereafter cited as LMPSJ.

30. Durham, *Taming the Nueces Strip*, 85–86.

31. *Texas Frontier Troubles*, 83–84.

32. Durham, *Taming the Nueces Strip*, 91–95.

33. McNelly to Steele, November 12, 1875, TAGP.

34. Michael G. Webster, "Intrigue on the Rio Grande: The *Rio Bravo* Affair," *Southwestern Historical Quarterly* 74 (October 1970): 149.

35. Coke to Ulysses S. Grant, May 29, 1875, RCP.

36. *Corpus Christi Gazette*, April 24, June 5, 1875.

37. Ord to Colonel R. C. Drum, AGO, roll 197.

38. Webster, "Intrigue on the Rio Grande," 155.

39. Thompson, *Cortina*, 228–29.

40. Thomas Wilson to Hamilton Fish, October 14, 1875, CDM.

41. Ibid.

42. Ibid.; Wilson to Fish, October 26, 1875, October 27, 1875; Wilson to D. C. Kells, October 26, 1875, CDM.

43. Wilson to Fish, November 8, 1875, CDM.

44. Webster, "Intrigue on the Rio Grande," 159.

45. McNelly to Steele, November 9, 1875, TAGP.

46. Webster, "Intrigue on the Rio Grande," 159.

47. Webb, *Texas Rangers*, 256; Webster, "Intrigue on the Rio Grande," 164; Parsons and Little, *Captain L. H. McNelly*, 213–18.

Chapter 9

1. Parsons, *Life and Letters of Lieutenant Robinson*, 95; Jennings, *A Texas Ranger*, 51.

2. Joshua 3:1–3 NASB 1977.

3. Ord to Steele, November 19, 1875, TAGP; Robert Potter to Steele, November 20, 1875; Potter to D. R. Clendenin, November 18, 1875; James Randlett to Potter, November 8, 1875, AGO, roll 198.

4. Durham, *Taming the Nueces Strip*, 103–5; Jennings, *A Texas Ranger*, 8–83;

5. McNelly to Steele, November 12, 1875; McNelly to Steele, November 18, 1875, TAGP.

6. Randlett to Potter, November 8, 1875, AGO; Potter to Randlett, November 16, 1875, roll 198; Parsons and Hall, *Captain L. H. McNelly*, 221–23.

7. Parsons and Hall, *Captain L. H. McNelly*, 221–23; Potter to Helanus Dodt and Randlett, November 16, 1875, AGO, roll 198.

8. Randlett to Dodt, December 1, 1875, AGO, roll 198.

9. Ibid.

10. Randlett to Dodt, December 1, 1875; "The Alcalde," November 17, 1875, AGO, roll 198; McNelly to Steele, November 12, 1875, TAGP.

11. Randlett to Dodt, December 1, 1875, AGO, roll 198; Parsons and Hall, *Captain L. H. McNelly*, 221–23.

12. Randlett to Dodt, December 1, 1875; Garcia to John Williamson, November 19, 1875; Potter to Clendenin, November 18, 1875, AGO, roll 198.

13. Randlett to Dodt, December 1, 1875; Alexander to Dodt, November 29, 1875, AGO, roll 198.

14. Parsons, *Life and Letters of Lieutenant Robinson*, 87–89.

15. Callicott, "Memoirs," 2–3.

16. Parsons, *Life and Letters of Lieutenant Robinson*, 87–89; McNelly to Steele, November 19, 1875, TAGP.

17. Durham, *Taming the Nueces Strip*, 104; Callicott, "Memoirs," 5.

18. Callicott, "Memoirs," 5–6; Durham, *Taming the Nueces Strip*, 104.

19. McNelly to Steele, November 19, 1875, TAGP; Callicott, "Memoirs," 3–4.

20. Parsons, *Life and Letters of Lieutenant Robinson*, 87–89; McNelly to Steele, November 19, 1875, TAGP; Callicott, "Memoirs," 3–4; Durham, *Taming the Nueces Strip*, 104.

21. Parsons, *Life and Letters of Lieutenant Robinson*, 87–89.

22. Callicott, "Memoirs," 6; Ord to Steele, November 19, 1875, TAGP.

23. Callicott, "Memoirs," 7.

24. Parsons, *Life and Letters of Lieutenant Robinson*, 87–89; Callicott, "Memoirs," 7–8.

25. McNelly to Steele, November 20, 1875; McNelly to Steele, November 22, 1875, TAGP; Callicott, "Memoirs," 8–9; Parsons, *Life and Letters of Lieutenant Robinson*, 87–89.

26. Callicott, "Memoirs," 8–9; Ord to Steele, November 20, 1875, TAGP.

27. McNelly to Steele, November 20, 1875, TAGP; Callicott, "Memoirs," 9–11.

28. Ord to Steele, November 19, 1875, TAGP.

29. McNelly to Steele, November 20, 1875; McNelly to Steele, November 22, 1875, TAGP.

30. Wilson to Steele, November 20, 1875; A. J. Alexander to Dodt, November 29, 1875, TAGP.

31. Potter to Alexander, November 20, 1875, TAGP; Durham, *Taming the Nueces Strip*, 115–16.

32. McNelly to Potter, November 20, 1875, as quoted in Durham, *Taming the Nueces Strip*, 119, and in Jennings, *A Texas Ranger*, 92; the referenced telegram apparently has long since disappeared from the Adjutant General's Papers in the Texas State Library and Archives.

33. Callicott, "Memoirs,"16–17; Durham, *Taming the Nueces Strip*, 116–18.

34. Jennings, *A Texas Ranger*, 94.

35. Callicott, "Memoirs," 16–17; Jennings, *A Texas Ranger*, 94–96; Durham, *Taming the Nueces Strip*, 116–18.

36. Durham, *Taming the Nueces Strip*, 116–18; Jennings, *A Texas Ranger*, 94–96.

37. Parsons, *Life and Letters of Lieutenant Robinson*, 89.

38. McNelly to Steele, November 21, 1875; Alexander to Dodt, November 29, 1875, TAGP; *Denison Daily Cresset*, November 23, 1875. Like other newspaper

accounts, the report depicted McNelly's command as "doomed," predicting "another Alamo"; see also the *Dallas Daily Herald*, November 23, 1875.

39. McNelly to Garcia, November 21, 1875, TAGP; transcription and translation of three separate letters, all dated the same, Garcia to McNelly, November 21, 1875, TAGP.

40. Durham, *Taming the Nueces Strip*, 124–25; Parsons, *Life and Letters of Lieutenant Robinson*, 90.

41. Durham, *Taming the Nueces* Strip, 124–25; Callicott, "Memoirs," 25; see also McNelly to Steele, November 22, 1875, TAGP.

42. McNelly to Steele, November 27, 1875, TAGP.

43. Wilson to Fish, November 19, 1875, CDM.

44. Ibid.

45. *San Antonio Daily Express*, December 2, 1875; Parsons and Little, *Captain L. H. McNelly*, 252.

46. *San Antonio Daily Express*, December 1, 1875.

47. Ibid., December 2, 1875.

48. Jennings, *A Texas Ranger*, 99–100.

49. Ibid.

50. Ibid., 100–101.

51. *San Antonio Daily Express*, December 10, 1875.

52. Ibid.

53. Durham, *Taming the Nueces Strip*, 131–32.

54. Ibid., 133.

55. Ibid., 130–33.

Chapter 10

1. Jennings, *A Texas Ranger*, 102.

2. Durham, *Taming the Nueces Strip*, 134–35, 148–49.

3. Parsons, *Life and Letters of Lieutenant Robinson*, 87–91.

4. *Biographical Encyclopedia of Texas* (New York: Southern Pub. Co., 1880); Christine Schott, "Gustavus Schleicher: A Representative of the Early German Emigrants in Texas," *West Texas Historical Association Year Book* (1952): 28; Tyler et al., *New Handbook of Texas*, 5:918–19; *Memorial Addresses on the Life and Character of Gustave Schleicher, Delivered in the House of Representatives and in the Senate, Forty-Fifth Congress, Third Session* (Washington, D.C.: Government Printing Office, 1880).

5. Tyler et al., *New Handbook of Texas*, 5:918–19.

6. Ibid.; *New York Times*, February 24, 1878.

7. *New York Times*, February 24, 1878.; Tyler et al., *New Handbook of Texas*, 5:918–19.

8. Tyler et al., *New Handbook of Texas*, 5:918–19.

9. *Report of the Committee on Foreign Affairs*, 167.

10. Ibid.; L. H. McNelly's name was mistakenly recorded as "S. H. McNally."

11. *Report of the Committee on Foreign Affairs*, 167–68.

12. Ibid.; Parsons and Little, *Captain L. H. McNelly*, 254–56.

13. *Report of the Committee on Foreign Affairs*, 167–68.

14. Ibid., 168

15. Ibid.

16. Ibid., 168–69.

17. Ibid.

18. Ibid., 169.

19. Ibid., 169–70.

20. Ibid., 170–71.

21. Ibid., 171–72.

22. Ibid., 172.

23. Ibid.

24. Ibid.

25. Ibid.

26. Ibid.

27. Ibid., 173–77.

28. Ibid., 184–88.

29. Ibid.

30. Ibid., 188–96.

31. Ibid., 197.

32. Jennings, *A Texas Ranger*, 44–45.

33. Ibid.

34. Ibid.

35. Ibid.

36. Ibid.

37. Ibid.

38. Ibid., 109–110; Durham, *Taming the Nueces Strip*, 137.

39. Jennings, *A Texas Ranger*, 108–9.

40. Ibid.

41. Ibid.; Parsons and Little, *Captain L. H. McNelly*, 93.

42. Ibid.

43. Charles M. Robinson III, *The Men Who Wear the Star: The Story of the Texas Rangers* (New York: Random House, 2000), 215–17.

44. Ibid.; Ovie C. Fisher, *King Fisher: His Life and Times* (Norman: University of Oklahoma Press, 1966), 76.

45. Durham, *Taming the Nueces Strip*, 134–36.

46. Ibid., 130.

47. Jennings, *A Texas Ranger*, 105–7.

48. Durham, *Taming the Nueces Strip*, 139–40.

49. Jennings, *A Texas Ranger*, 111.

50. Durham, *Taming the Nueces Strip*, 139–40.

51. Ibid., 140–41.

52. Ibid., 141–43; Jennings, *A Texas Ranger*, 110–15; Parsons and Little, *Captain L. H. McNelly*, 264–66.

53. Jennings, *A Texas Ranger*, 113–14.

54. Durham, *Taming the Nueces Strip*, 141; Jennings, *A Texas Ranger*, 112–13.

55. Ibid.

56. Durham, *Taming the Nueces Strip*, 144–45.

57. Ibid., 146–47.

58. Ibid.; Fisher, *King Fisher*, 78.

59. Durham, *Taming the Nueces Strip*, 147–48.

60. Ibid., 148–55.

61. Ibid., 132–35.

62. Parsons and Little, *Captain L. H. McNelly*, 289–94; McNelly to Ford, June 8, 1876, TCMC.

63. McNelly to Ford, June 8, 1876, TCMC.; Durham, *Taming the Nueces Strip*, 154–57.

64. *San Antonio Daily Express*, June 17, 1876.

65. Durham, *Taming the Nueces Strip*, 155–56.

66. Ibid., 157.

Postscripts from Purgatory

1. Dora Neill Raymond, *Captain Lee Hall of Texas* (Norman: University of Oklahoma Press, 1940), 3–11.; Frederick Remington, "How the Law Got into the Chaparral," *Harper's New Monthly Magazine* 94 (December 1896), 60–69.

2. Raymond, *Captain Lee Hall*, 11–19, 29–30, 35–39.

3. Durham, *Taming the Nueces Strip*, 158; Jennings, *A Texas Ranger*, 117–18.

4. Raymond, *Captain Lee Hall*, 43–48; Parsons and Little, *Captain L. H. McNelly*, 274–75, 284; Durham, *Taming the Nueces Strip*, 158.

5. Durham, *Taming the Nueces Strip*, 158–59; Jennings, *A Texas Ranger*, 122–23; Parsons, *John B. Armstrong*, 27–29.

6. Jennings, *A Texas Ranger*, 122.

7. Durham, *Taming the Nueces Strip*, 158–59; Jennings, *A Texas Ranger*, 123

8. Durham, *Taming the Nueces Strip*, 158–59.

9. Jennings, *A Texas Ranger*, 122–24; Durham, *Taming the Nueces Strip*, 158–60.

10. Ibid.; Jennings, *A Texas Ranger*, 124–25; Parsons, *John B. Armstrong*, 27–29.

11. Durham, *Taming the Nueces Strip*, 159–60; Jennings, *A Texas Ranger*, 124.

12. Ibid.

13. Thomas N. Devine to Steele, September 4, 1877; Dan Mullen to Steele, September 3, 1877, TAGP; Jennings, *A Texas Ranger*, 125.

14. Angelina Key to William Steele, February 1877, AGP.

15. Ibid.; see also *Daily Democratic Statesman*, October 14, 1876.

16. Parsons and Little, *Captain L. H. McNelly*, 279; *Galveston Daily News*, September 6, 1876.

17. Durham, *Taming the Nueces Strip*, 159–61.

18. *Texas Border Troubles*, Miscellaneous Documents of the House of Representatives, 45th Cong., 2nd. sess., vol. 6, no. 64 (serial 1820), 17–29, 33–41; *Galveston Daily News*, January 6, 1877. The headline announced, "Cattle Stealing Resumed" on the lower border with Mexico.

19. *Report and Accompanying Documents of the Committee on Foreign Affairs*, xvi.

20. *Claims on the Part of Citizens of the United States and Mexico under the Convention of July 4, 1868 between the United States and Mexico*, 44th Cong., 2nd. sess., Senate Exec. Doc. 31, 1–4. The report documents that claims awarded to citizens of Mexico against the United States totaled a mere $150,498.41, while the awards to U.S. citizens against Mexico grew to $3,975,123.79, a disparity of twenty-six to one.

21. Tyler et al., *New Handbook of Texas*, 1:458.

22. Ibid., 2:718.

23. Lord, *Fremantle Diary*, v–ix, 47, 53–54.

24. Arthur, *General Jo Shelby's March*, 195–97.

25. Ibid., 218–24.

26. Tyler et al., *New Handbook of Texas*, 5:1093–94.

27. Ibid., 879–80; John W. Sansom to James W. Throckmorton, November 17, 1866, James W. Throckmorton Papers, Texas State Library and Archives, Austin; Sansom to Davis, April 30, 1870, EJDP.

28. See the Indiana Historical Society's synopsis online, "Lew Wallace," *Notable Hoosiers*, www.indianahistory.org/our-collections/reference/notable-hoosiers/lew-wallace.

29. Ibid.; Robert M. Utley, *Billy the Kid: A Short and Violent Life* (Lincoln: University of Nebraska Press, 1989), 139–40, 147, 174–75, 185–88.

30. Kenneth Hendrickson Jr., *The Chief Executives of Texas: From Stephen F. Austin to John B. Connally, Jr.* (College Station: Texas A&M University Press, 1995), 90–95; Moneyhon, *Edmund J. Davis*, 219–23, 270–74.

31. *Galveston News*, October 8, 15, 1877; Leander H. McNelly to Ford, June 8, 1876, Ford Correspondence, TCMC; McCaslin, *John S. "Rip" Ford*, 232–33; "The Mexican Border Grievances," *Nation*, (April 1878): 125–26. The report claimed

that South Texas still boasted of "would-be officers and volunteers . . . Confederate military men who would gladly march [into Mexico] under the old flag."

32. U.S. House of Representatives, Miscellaneous Documents, 54th Cong., 2nd. sess., vol. 6, no. 64, ser. 1820; "Texas Border Troubles," 224–40, 250–81; McCaslin, *John S. "Rip" Ford*, 232–33; for Ford's testimony, see "Texas Frontier Troubles," 66–71.

33. John S. Ford Biographical File, Texana Collection, San Antonio Public Library, San Antonio; McCaslin, *John S. "Rip" Ford*, 247–75.

34. J. Marvin Hunter, *Pioneer History of Bandera County: Seventy-Five Years of Intrepid History* (Bandera: Hunter's Printing House, 1922); Irene Van Winkle, "Moffett Tale Hearkens Back to Texas Ranger, Boy Captive," *West Kerr Current*, http://wkcurrent.com/moffett-tale-hearkens-back-to-texas-ranger-boy-captive-p1666-71.htm.

35. Robinson, *I Fought the Good Fight*, 293.

36. Gibson, *Kickapoos*, 253–56.

37. Tyler et al., *New Handbook of Texas*, 3:1107.

38. Robert L. Nelson, "Robb, Thomas Patten (1819–1895)," Santa Cruz Public Libraries, www.santacruzpl.org/history/articles/1104/.

39. Tyler et al., *New Handbook of Texas*, 4:1059.

40. Pierce, *Most Promising Young Officer*, 197–201.

41. Ibid., 218–33.

42. Smith et al., *Bliss Reminiscences*, xv–xx.

43. Tyler et al., *New Handbook of Texas*, 1:1001; Charles M. Neal Jr., *Valor across the Lone Star State: The Congressional Medal of Honor in Frontier Texas* (Austin: Texas State Historical Association, 2002), 85–100.

44. Tyler et al., *New Handbook of* Texas, 1:823–24; McCright, *Whirlwind*, 83–95; John L. Bullis Biographical File, Texana Collection, San Antonio Public Library, San Antonio, Texas.

45. Tyler et al., *New Handbook of Texas*, 1:1001; Neal, *Valor across the Lone Star State*, 276–77, 305–7, 325–28.

46. Tyler et al., *New Handbook of Texas*, 6:79.

47. *Life and Character of Gustav Schleicher Delivered in the House and Senate, Forty-Fifth Congress, Third Session* (Washington, D.C.: Government Printing Office, 1880); see also Robert Wooster, *The American Military Frontiers: The United States Army in the West, 1783–1900* (Albuquerque: University of New Mexico Press, 2009), 240–42.

48. Parsons, *Life and Letters of Lieutenant Robinson*, 96–119.

49. Parsons, *John B. Armstrong*, 47–61.

50. Ibid.; John Wesley Hardin, *The Life of John Wesley Hardin: As Written by Himself* (Norman: University of Oklahoma Press, 1961), 117–21.

51. Parsons, *John B. Armstrong*, 74–79, 86–103.

52. Webb, *Texas Rangers*, 241; Chuck Parsons, ed., "Bill Callicott, Reminiscences," Texas Ranger Hall of Fame and Museum, 1–5, www.texasranger.org/E-Books/Callicott,%20William%20-%20Reminiscences.pdf.

53. Historical traces of Jesús Sandoval vanish soon after he disappears from the records of Texas State troops; He may be the same "Jesús Sandobal" indicted for murder in March 1873 in Starr County. See James B. Gillett, *Fugitives from Justice: The Notebook of Texas Ranger Sergeant James B. Gillett* (Austin: State House Press, 1997), 98; Chuck Parsons, "Jesús Sandoval: McNelly's Enforcer," *The Texas Ranger Dispatch* 32 (2011), www.texasranger.org/dispatch/Backissues/Dispatch_Issue_32.pdf.

54. Ben H. Procter, prologue to *A Texas Ranger*, by Napoleon A. Jennings (Chicago: Lakewood Press, R. R. Donnelly and Sons, 1992), xlvii–lxvii.

55. Ibid.; Durham, *Taming the Nueces Strip*, 136.

56. Procter, prologue to *A Texas Ranger*, xvi–xvii.

57. Durham, *Taming the Nueces Strip*, 177–78.

58. U.S. House. *Investigation by the Committee on Naval Affairs: Testimony Taken.* 44th Cong., 1st. sess., Misc. Doc. 170, pt. 5, 122–25.

59. Fisher, *King Fisher*, 134–43.

60. Ibid.

61. Raymond, *Captain Lee Hall*, 82–85; Tyler et al., *New Handbook of Texas*, 3:414.

62. Tyler et al., *New Handbook of Texas*, 3:414.

63. Ibid., 2:343.

64. Durham, *Taming the Nueces Strip*, x; Elmer Kelton, *Captain's Rangers* (New York: Tom Doherty Associates, 1968), 211.

65. Webb, *Texas Rangers*, 242–46; Larry McMurtry, *In a Narrow Grave* (Encino, Calif.: Encino Press, 1968), 41.

66. Parsons and Hall, *Captain L. H. McNelly*, 297–99.

Bibliography

Manuscripts and Archival Collections

Adjutant General's Papers. Texas State Library and Archives, Austin.

Bee, Hamilton P., Papers. Dolph Briscoe Center for American History, University of Texas, Austin.

Callicott, William. "Memoirs." Dolph Briscoe Center for American History, University of Texas, Austin.

———. "Reminiscences." Dolph Briscoe Center for American History, University of Texas, Austin.

Coke, Richard, Papers. Texas State Library and Archives, Austin.

Davis, E. J., Papers. Texas State Library and Archives, Austin.

Ford, John S., Papers. Texas Confederate Museum Collection. Nita Stewart Haley Memorial Library and J. Evetts Haley History Center, Midland, Tex.

Ford, John S. "Memoirs and Reminiscences of Texas History from 1836 to 1888." MSS. 8 vols. Nita Stewart Haley Memorial Library and J. Evetts Haley History Center, Midland, Texas.

Green, Thomas, Papers. Dolph Briscoe Center for American History, University of Texas, Austin.

Hamilton, Andrew Jackson, Papers. Texas State Library and Archives, Austin.

Haynes, John L., Papers. Dolph Briscoe Center for American History, University of Texas, Austin.

Kingsbury, Gilbert, Papers. Dolph Briscoe Center for American History, University of Texas, Austin.

Kinsall, Al. "Timeline of Eagle Pass History." MSS. Eagle Pass Public Library, Eagle Pass, Tex.

Kuykendall, James Hampton. "Journal of James Hampton Kuykendall." Dolph Briscoe Center for American History, University of Texas, Austin.

Hunter, John Warren. "The Fall of Brownsville on the Rio Grande, November, 1863." Dolph Briscoe Center of American History.

Mackenzie, Ranald S. "Private Letter Book of Ranald S. Mackenzie, 1873–1874. 4th Cavalry." U.S. Army History Institute, Carlisle Barracks, Carlisle, Pa.

McNelly, Leander, Papers. Albert and Ethel Herzstein Library, San Jacinto Museum of History, San Jacinto Battlefield State Historic Site.

McNelly, Leander H., Papers. Dolph Briscoe Center for American History, University of Texas, Austin.

Military Operations in Texas Correspondence. Dolph Briscoe Center for American History, University of Texas, Austin.

Murrah, Pendleton, Papers. Texas State Library and Archives, Austin.

Ranger Correspondence. Texas State Library and Archives, Austin.

Ranger Muster Rolls. Texas State Library and Archives, Austin.

Throckmorton, James W., Papers. Texas State Library and Archives, Austin.

Webb, Walter Prescott, Papers. Dolph Briscoe Center for American History, University of Texas, Austin.

Westlake, Thomas. "Memoir of His Civil War Experiences and Post-Civil War Experiences." Watson-Westlake Papers. State Historical Society of Missouri, Columbia, Missouri.

Government Documents

Memorial Addresses on the Life and Character of Gustav Schleicher, Delivered in the House of Representatives and in the Senate, Forty-Fifth Congress, Third Session. Washington, D.C.: Government Printing Office, 1880.

Report of the Adjutant General of the State of Texas for the Year 1875, Including Mexican Border Troubles, United States Adjutant General's Office (Houston: n.p., 1875). *Letters Received, Main Series, Texas Raids,* National Archives Microcopy 666, roll 197.

Report of the Commissioner of Indian Affairs to the Secretary of the Interior for the Year 1871. Washington: Government Printing Office, 1872.

Reports of the Committee of Investigation Sent in 1873 by the Mexican Government to the Frontier of Texas. New York: Baker Goodwin Printers, 1875.

Texas House Journal. 15th Legislature, 1st. sess.

U.S. Congress. *Congressional Globe.* 42nd Cong., 2nd sess., pt. 5.

———. House. *Depredations on the Frontiers of Texas.* Exec. Doc. 39. 42nd Cong., 3rd. sess.

———. House. *Depredations on the Frontiers of Texas.* Exec. Doc. 257. 43rd. Cong., 1st. sess.

———. House. *Investigation by the Committee on Naval Affairs: Testimony Taken.* 44th Cong., 1st. sess., Misc. Doc. 170, pt. 5.

———. House. *Report and Accompanying Documents of the Committee on Foreign Affairs on the Relation of the United States and Mexico.* Washington, D.C.: Government Printing Office, 1878.

———. House. *Report of the United States Commissioners to Texas.* Exec. Doc. 39. 42nd. Cong., 3rd. sess.

———. House. *Texas Border Troubles.* 44th Cong., 1st. sess., Misc. Doc. 343.

———. House. *Texas Border Troubles.* 45th Cong., 2nd. Sess., Misc. Doc. 64.

———. House. *Texas Frontier Troubles: Testimony Taken before the Committee on Foreign Affairs.*

————. Senate. *Claims on the Part of Citizens of the United States and Mexico under the Convention of July 4, 1868 between the United States and Mexico.* 44th Cong., 2nd. sess. Exec. Doc. 39.

U.S. Department of the Army. Letters Received. Main Series. Texas Raids. Adjutant General's Office. 1780s to 1917. RG 94. National Archives. Washington, D.C. Microfilm edition, 666.

U.S. Department of State. Consular Dispatches, Matamoros, Mexico, 1826–1906. RG 59. Records of the U.S. Department of State, Washington, D.C. Microfilm edition.

The War of the Rebellion: A Compilation of the Official Records of the Union and Confederate Armies. 128 vols. Washington, D.C.: U.S. Government Printing Office, 1880–1901.

Newspapers

Daily Democratic Statesman (Austin)
Daily Ranchero and Republican (Brownsville)
Daily State Journal (Austin)
Dallas Daily Herald
Denison Daily Cresset
Fort Brown Flag (Brownsville)
Galveston Daily News
Galveston Weekly News
New York Times
Rio Grande Sentinel (Brownsville)
San Antonio Daily Express
San Antonio Herald
Texas State Gazette (Austin)
Voz del pueblo (Matamoros)

Books

Alonzo, Armando C. *Tejano Legacy: Rancheros and Settlers in South Texas, 1734–1900.* Albuquerque: University of New Mexico Press, 1998.

Amberson, Mary Margaret McAllen, James A. McAllen, and Margaret H. McAllen. *I Would Rather Sleep in Texas: A History of the Lower Rio Grande Valley and the People of the Santa Anita Land Grant.* Austin: Texas State Historical Association, 2003.

Anderson, Gary Clayton. *The Conquest of Texas: Ethnic Cleansing in the Promised Land, 1820–1875.* Norman: University of Oklahoma Press, 2005.

Arthur, Anthony. *General Jo Shelby's March.* New York: Random House, 2010.

Banta, William, and J. W. Caldwell Jr. *Twenty-Seven Years on the Texas Frontier.* Council Hill, Okla.: L. G. Park, 1933.

Barney, Chester. *Recollections of Field Service with the Twentieth Iowa Infantry Volunteers; or, What I Saw in the Army.* Davenport, Iowa: privately printed, 1865.

Barr, Amelia. *All the Days of My Life: An Autobiography.* New York: D. Appleton, 1913.

Basler, Roy P., ed. *The Collected Works of Abraham Lincoln.* 8 vols. New Brunswick, N.J.: Rutgers University Press, 1953.

Bell, Samuel E., and James Smallwood. *The Zona Libre, 1858–1905: A Problem in American Diplomacy.* El Paso: Texas Western Press, 1982.

Bergeron, Paul, ed. *The Papers of Andrew Johnson.* 16 vols. Knoxville: University of Tennessee Press, 1989.

Biographical Encyclopedia of Texas. New York: Southern Pub. Co., 1880.

Boomhower, Ray E. *The Sword and the Pen: A Life of Lew Wallace.* Indianapolis: Indiana Historical Society Press, 2005.

Britten, Thomas. *The Lipan Apaches: People of Wind and Lightning.* Albuquerque: University of New Mexico Press, 2009.

Brown, John Henry. *History of Texas from 1685 to 1892.* 2 vols. St. Louis: L. E. Daniell, 1892.

Buckelew, F. M, and T. S. Dennis. *Life of F. M. Buckelew: The Indian Captive, as Related by Himself.* Bandera, Tex.: Hunter's Printing House, 1925.

Carter, Robert G. *The Old Sergeant's Story: Fighting Indians and Bad Men in Texas from 1870 to 1876.* Mattituck, N.Y.: John M. Carroll, 1982.

———. *On the Border with Mackenzie: Or Winning West Texas From the Comanches.* New York: Antiquarian Press, 1961.

Chatfield, W. H. *Twin Cities of the Border and the Country of the Rio Grande.* New Orleans: E. P. Brandao, 1893.

Cheeseman, Bruce, ed. *Maria von Blücher's Corpus Christi: Letters from the South Texas Frontier, 1849–1879.* College Station: Texas A&M University Press, 2002.

Cox, Mike. *The Texas Rangers: Wearing the Cinco Peso, 1821–1900.* New York: Forge, 2008.

Crouch, Barry, and Donaly E. Brice. *The Governor's Hounds: the Texas State Police, 1870–1873.* Austin: University of Texas Press, 2011.

De León, Arnoldo. *The Tejano Community, 1836–1900.* Dallas: Southern Methodist University Press, 1982.

———. *They Called Them Greasers: Anglo Attitudes toward Mexicans in Texas, 1821–1900.* Austin: University of Texas Press, 1983.

Dobie, J. Frank. *A Vaquero of the Brush Country: John D. Young and J. Frank Dobie.* Austin: University of Texas Press, 1998.

Domenech, Emmanuel. *Missionary Adventures in Texas and Mexico: A Personal Narrative of Six Years' Sojourn in Those Regions.* London: Longman, Brown, Green, Longmans and Roberts, 1858.

Dougherty, E. *The Rio Grande Valley: A Lecture Delivered before the Lone Star Literary Association of Brownsville, Texas.* Brownsville, Texas: Ranchero Book and Job Printing Office, 1867.

Durham, George. *Taming the Nueces Strip: The Story of McNelly's Rangers.* Austin: University of Texas Press, 1962.

Edwards, John N. *Shelby's Expedition to Mexico: An Unwritten Leaf of the War.* Edited by Conger Beasley Jr. Fayetteville: University of Arkansas Press, 2002.

Fisher, Ovie C. *King Fisher: His Life and Times* (Norman: University of Oklahoma Press, 1966.

Forney, John W. *What I Saw in Texas.* Philadelphia: Ringwald and Brown, 1872.

Frantz, Joe B. *Texas: A History.* New York: W. W. Norton, 1984.

Gammel, H. P. N. *Laws of Texas, 1822–1897.* 32 vols. Austin: Gammel Books, 1898.

Gibson, Arrell M., *The Kickapoos: Lords of the Middle Border.* Norman: University of Oklahoma Press, 1963.

Gillett, James B. *Fugitives from Justice: The Notebook of Texas Ranger Sergeant James B. Gillett.* Austin: State House Press, 1997.

Graber, H. W. *A Terry Texas Ranger: The Life Record of H. W. Graber.* Austin: State House Press, 1987.

Graham, Don. *Kings of Texas: The 150-Year Saga of An American Ranching Empire.* Hoboken, N.J.: John Wiley and Sons, 2003.

Grant, Ulysses S. *Personal Memoirs of U. S. Grant and Selected Letters, 1839–1865.* Edited by Mary McFeely and William S. McFeely. New York: Library Classics of the United States, 1990.

Hardin, John Wesley. *The Life of John Wesley Hardin: As Written by Himself.* Norman: University of Oklahoma Press, 1961.

Hart, John Mason. *Empire of Revolution: The Americans in Mexico since the Civil War.* Berkeley: University of California Press, 2002.

Hendrickson, Kenneth E., Jr. *The Chief Executives of Texas: From Stephen F. Austin to John B. Connally, Jr.* College Station: Texas A&M University Press, 1995.

Horgan, Paul. *Great River: The Rio Grande in North American History.* 2 vols. New York: Rinehart, 1954.

Hughes, W. J. *Rebellious Ranger: Rip Ford and the Old Southwest* (Norman: University of Oklahoma Press, 1964.

Hunt, Jeffrey William. *The Last Battle of the Civil War: Palmetto Ranch.* Austin: University of Texas Press, 2002.

Hunter, J. Marvin. *Pioneer History of Bandera County: Seventy-Five Years of Intrepid History* (Bandera: Hunter's Printing House, 1922.

Hutton, Paul Andrew. *Phil Sheridan and His Army.* Lincoln: University of Nebraska Press, 1985.

Irby, James. *Backdoor at Bagdad: The Civil War on the Rio Grande.* El Paso: University of Texas at El Paso, 1977.

Jenkins, John H, III. *Recollections of Early Texas: The Memoirs of John Holland Jenkins.* Austin: University of Texas Press, 1987.

Jennings, Napoleon A. *A Texas Ranger.* Norman: University of Oklahoma Press, 1997.

Kelton, Elmer. *Captain's Rangers.* New York: Tom Doherty Associates, 1968.

King, Edward. *Texas: 1874; An Eyewitness Account of Conditions in Post-Reconstruction Texas.* Edited by Robert S. Gray. Houston: Cordovan Press, 1974.

Latorre, Felipe A, and Dolores L. Latorre. *The Mexican Kickapoo Indians.* Austin: University of Texas Press, 1976.

Lauderdale, R. J., and John M. Doak. *Life on the Range and On the Trail.* San Antonio: Naylor, 1936.

Lea, Tom. *The King Ranch.* 2 vols. Boston: Little, Brown and Company, 1957.

Leckie, William H. *The Buffalo Soldiers: A Narrative of the Negro Cavalry in the West.* Norman: University of Oklahoma Press, 1967.

Leiker, James N. *Racial Borders: Black Soldiers Along the Rio Grande.* College Station: Texas A&M University Press, 2002.

Linn, John. *Reminiscences of Fifty Years in Texas.* Austin: State House Press, 1986.

Loomis, John A. *Texas Ranchman: The Memoirs of John A. Loomis.* Chadron, Nebr.: Fur Press, 1982.

Lord, Walter, ed. *The Fremantle Diary: Being the Journal of Lieutenant Colonel Arthur James Lyon Fremantle, Coldstream Guards on His Three Months in the Southern States.* Short Hills, N.J.: Burford Books, 1954.

Lubbock, Francis R. *Six Decades in Texas; or, Memoirs of Francis Richard Lubbock, Governor of Texas in Wartime, 1861–1863: A Personal Experience in Business, War, and Politics.* Edited by C. W. Rains. Austin: Ben C. Jones and Co., 1900.

Maltby, W. Jeff. *Captain Jeff: Or Frontier Life in Texas with the Texas Rangers.* Austin: Texian Press, 1967.

Marban, Jorge A. *Confederate, Patriot, Journalist, and Poet: The Multifaceted Life of Jose Augustin Quintero* (Victoria: British Columbia: Friesen Press, 2014.

Maxey, Samuel L. *Maxey's Texas.* Edited by David L. Gracy. Austin: Pemberton Press, 1965.

McCaslin, Richard B. *Fighting Stock: John S. "Rip" Ford of Texas.* Fort Worth: TCU Press, 2011.

McConnell, H. H. *Five Years a Cavalryman; or, Sketches of Regular Army Life on the Texas Frontier, 1866–1871.* Norman: University of Oklahoma Press, 1996.

McCright, Grady. *The Whirlwind: John L. Bullis and His Seminole-Negro Scouts.* Lexington, Ky.: n.p., 2012.

McMurtry, Larry. *In a Narrow Grave.* Encino, Calif.: Encino Press, 1968.

Monday, Jane Clements, and Betty Bailey Colley. *Voices from the Wild Horse Desert: The Vaquero Families of the King and Kenedy Ranches.* Austin: University of Texas Press, 1997.

Monday, Jane Clements, and Frances Brannen Vick. *Petra's Legacy: The South Texas Ranching Empire of Petra Vela and Mifflin Kenedy*. College Station: Texas A&M University Press, 2007.

Moneyhon, Carl. *Edmund J. Davis of Texas: Civil War General, Republican Leader, Reconstruction Governor*. Fort Worth: TCU Press, 2010.

Montejano, David. *Anglos and Mexicans in the Making of Texas, 1836–1986*. Austin: University of Texas Press, 1987.

Morris, Roy, Jr. *Sheridan: The Life and Wars of General Philip Sheridan*. New York: Crown, 1992.

Mulroy, Kevin. *Freedom on the Border: The Seminole Maroons in Florida, the Indian Territory, Coahuila, and Texas*. Lubbock: Texas Tech University Press, 1993.

Neal, Charles M., Jr. *Valor across the Lone Star State: The Congressional Medal of Honor in Frontier Texas*. Austin: Texas State Historical Association, 2002.

Nichols, James W. *Now You Hear My Horn: The Journal of James W. Nichols, 1820–1888*. Edited by Catherine W. McDowell. Austin: University of Texas Press, 1967.

Noel, Theophilus. *A Campaign from Santa Fe to the Mississippi: Being a History of the Old Sibley Brigade from the First Organization to the Present Time*. Edited by Martin Hardwick Hall and Edwin Adams Davis. Houston: Stagecoach Press, 1961.

North, Thomas. *Five Years in Texas; or, What You Did Not Hear during the War from January 1861 to January 1865*. Cincinnati: Elm Street, 1870.

Nunn, William Curtis. *Escape from Reconstruction*. Westport, Conn.: Greenwood Press, 1974.

Oates, Stephen, ed. *Rip Ford's Texas*. By John Salmon Ford. Austin: University of Texas Press, 1963.

O'Neal, Bill. *Encyclopedia of Western Gunfighters*. Norman: University of Oklahoma Press, 1979.

Paredes, Américo. *Folklore and Culture on the Texas-Mexican Border*. Austin: University of Texas Press, 1993.

———. *A Texas-Mexican Cancionero: Folk Songs of the Lower Rio Grande*. Urbana: University of Illinois Press, 1976.

Parisot, P. F. *The Reminiscences of a Texas Missionary*. San Antonio: St. Mary's Church, 1899.

Parsons, Chuck. *John B. Armstrong: Texas Ranger and Pioneer Ranchman*. College Station: Texas A&M University Press, 2007.

———. *"Pidge": Texas Ranger*. College Station: Texas A&M University Press, 2013.

———. *"Pidge," A Texas Ranger from Virginia: The Life and Letters of Lieutenant T. C. Robinson, Washington County Volunteer Militia Company "A"*. Wolfe City, Tex.: Henington, 1985.

Parsons, Chuck, and Marianne E. Hall Little. *Captain L. H. McNelly: Texas Ranger*. Austin: State House Press, 2001.

Pierce, Frank C. *Texas' Last Frontier: A Brief History of the Lower Rio Grande Valley*. Menosha, Wis.: George Banta Publishing, 1917.

Pierce, Michael D. *The Most Promising Young Officer: A Life of Ranald Slidell Mackenzie*. Norman: University of Oklahoma Press, 1993.

Pirtle, Caleb, III, and Michael F. Cusack. *Fort Clark: The Lonely Sentinel on Texas's Western Frontier*. Austin: Eakin Press, 1985.

Rankin, Melinda. *Twenty Years among the Mexicans: A Narrative of Missionary Labor*. Cincinnati: Central Book Concern, 1881.

Ransleben, Guido E. *A Hundred Years of Comfort in Texas: A Centennial History*. San Antonio: Naylor, 1954.

Rayburn, John C., and Virginia Rayburn, eds. *A Century of Conflict, 1821–1913: Incidents in the Lives of William Neale and William A. Neale, Early Settlers in South Texas*. Waco: Texian Press, 1966.

Raymond, Dora Neill. *Captain Lee Hall of Texas*. Norman: University of Oklahoma Press, 1940.

Reid, Jan, ed. *Rio Grande*. Austin: University of Texas Press, 2004.

Rippey, J. Fred. *The United States and Mexico*. New York: Alfred A. Knopf, 1926.

Robertson, Brian. *Wild Horse Desert: The Heritage of South Texas*. Edinburg, Tex.: New Santander Press, 1985.

Robertson, Robert, ed. *Her Majesty's Texas: Two English Immigrants in Reconstruction Texas*. College Station: Texas A&M University Press, 1998.

Robinson, Charles M., III. *Bad Hand: A Biography of General Ranald S. Mackenzie*. Austin: State House Press, 1993.

———. *The Men Who Wear the Star: The Story of the Texas Rangers*. New York: Random House, 2000.

Robinson, Sherry. *I Fought the Good Fight: A History of the Lipan Apaches*. Denton: University of North Texas Press, 2013.

Santleben, August. *A Texas Pioneer: Early Staging and Overland Freighting Days on the Frontiers of Texas and Mexico*. New York: Neale, 1910.

Schofield, John McAllister. *Forty-Six Years in the Army*. New York: Century Company, 1897.

Schoonover, Thomas, ed. *Mexican Lobby: Matias Romero in Washington, 1861–1867*. Lexington: University Press of Kentucky, 1986.

———, ed. *A Mexican View of America in the 1860s: A Foreign Diplomat Describes the Civil War and Reconstruction*. London: Farleigh Dickinson University Press, 1991.

Sheridan, Philip. *Personal Memoirs of P. H. Sheridan: General United States Army*. New York: C. L. Webster, 1888.

Simon, John Y., ed. *The Papers of Ulysses S. Grant*. 30 vols. Carbondale: Southern Illinois University Press, 1967–1971.

Smith, Thomas T. *The Old Army in Texas: A Research Guide to the U.S. Army in Nineteenth-Century Texas*. Austin: Texas State Historical Association, 2000.

Smith, Thomas T., Jerry Thompson, Robert Wooster, and Ben Pingenot, eds. *The Reminiscences of Major General Zenas R. Bliss, 1854–1876*. Austin: Texas State Historical Association, 2007.

Sowell, A. J. *Texas Indian Fighters*. Abilene: State House Press, 1986.

Spurlin, Charles. *Texas Volunteers in the Mexican War*. Austin: Eaken Press, 1998.

Stevens, John Austin. *The Valley of the Rio Grande: Its Topography and Resources*. New York: William C. Bryant, 1864.

Stillman, Chauncey Devereux. *Charles Stillman*. New York: Chauncey Devereux Stillman, 1956.

Stringfield, Thomas. *Captured by the Apaches: Forty Years with This Savage Band of Indians; A True Story by "Two Braids," Tommy Stringfield, Who Was Taken Captive in 1870 and Liberated in 1909*. Hamilton, Tex.: Herald Print, 1911.

Sumpter, Jesse. *Paso del Aguila: A Chronicle of Frontier Days on the Texas Border as Recorded in the Memoirs of Jesse Sumpter*. Compiled by Henry Warren. Austin: Encino Press, 1969.

Sweet, Alexander. *Alex Sweet's Texas: The Lighter Side of Lone Star History*. Austin: University of Texas Press, 1986.

Terrell, Alexander Watkins. *From Texas to Mexico and the Court of Maximilian in 1865*. Dallas: Book Club of Texas, 1933.

Thompson, Jerry. *Cortina: Defending the Mexican Name in Texas*. College Station: Texas A&M University Press, 2007.

———. *Mexican Texans in the Union Army*. El Paso: Texas Western Press, 1986.

———. *Vaqueros in Blue and Gray*. Austin: State House Press, 2000.

———. *A Wild and Vivid Land: An Illustrated History of the South Texas Border*. Austin: Texas State Historical Association, 1997.

Thompson, Jerry, and Lawrence T. Jones III. *Civil War and Revolution on the Rio Grande Frontier: A Narrative and Photographic History*. Austin: Texas State Historical Association, 2004.

Thrapp, Dan. *Encyclopedia of Frontier Biography*. 3 vols. Glendale, Calif.: Arthur H. Clark Company, 1988.

Tilley, Nannie M., ed. *Federals on the Frontier: The Diary of Benjamin F. McIntyre, 1862–1864*. Austin: University of Texas Press, 1963.

Townsend, Stephen A. *The Yankee Invasion of Texas*. College Station: Texas A&M University Press, 2006.

Tyler, Ron, Douglas E. Barnett, Roy R. Barkley, Penelope C. Anderson, and Mark F. Odintz, eds. *The New Handbook of Texas*. 6 vols. Austin: Texas State Historical Association, 1996.

Uglow, Loyd M. *Standing in the Gap: Army Outposts, Picket Stations, and the Pacification of the Texas Frontier, 1866–1886*. Fort Worth: Texas Christian University Press, 2001.

Utley, Robert. *Billy the Kid: A Short and Violent Life*. Lincoln: University of Nebraska Press, 1989.

————. *Frontier Regulars: The United States Army and the Indian, 1866–1890*. New York: Macmillan, 1973.

————. *Lone Star Justice: The First Century of the Texas Rangers*. Oxford: Oxford University Press, 2002.

Valerio-Jiménez, Omar S. *River of Hope: Forging Identity and Nation in the Rio Grande Borderlands*. Durham: Duke University Press, 2013.

Wallace, Ernest, ed. *Ranald Mackenzie's Official Correspondence Relating to Texas, 1871–1873*. 2 vols. Lubbock: West Texas Museum Association, 1967.

————. *Ranald S. Mackenzie on the Texas Frontier*. College Station: Texas A&M University Press, 1993.

Wallace, Lew. *An Autobiography*. 2 vols. New York: Harper and Brothers, 1906.

Watson, William. *The Civil War Adventures of a Blockade Runner*. London: T. Fisher Unwin, 1899.

Webb, Walter Prescott. *The Texas Rangers: A Century of Frontier Defense*. Austin: University of Texas Press, 1973.

Wilkins, Frederick. *The Law Comes to Texas: The Texas Rangers, 1870–1901*. Austin: State House Press, 1999.

Williams, R. H. *With the Border Ruffians: Memories of the Far West, 1852–1868*. Edited by E. W. Williams. Lincoln: University of Nebraska Press, 1982.

Winfrey, Dorman, and James M. Day, eds. *The Indian Papers of Texas and the Southwest*. 4 vols. Austin: Texas State Historical Association, 1995.

Wooster, Ralph. *Lone Star Regiments in Gray*. Austin: Eakin Press, 2002.

Wooster, Robert. *The American Military Frontiers: The United States Army in the West, 1783–1900*. Albuquerque: University of New Mexico, 2009.

Articles and Book Chapters

Beaumont, E. B. "Over the Border with Mackenzie." In *Eyewitnesses to the Indian Wars, 1865–1890*, vol. 3, edited by Peter Cozzens, 437–43. Mechanicsburg, Pa.: Stackpole Books, 2003.

Carter, Robert G. "A Raid into Mexico." In *Eyewitnesses to the Indian Wars, 1865–1890*, vol. 3, edited by Peter Cozzens, 444–54. Mechanicsburg, Pa.: Stackpole Books, 2003.

Cheeseman, Bruce S. "'Let Us Have 500 Good Determined Texans': Richard King's Account of the Union Invasion of South Texas, November 12, 1863, to January 20, 1864." *Southwestern Historical Quarterly* 101 (July 1997): 77–95.

Collins, Michael. "The Texas Devils: McNelly's Rangers and the Palo Alto Fight." In *Papers of the Second Palo Alto Conference*, 128–33. Brownsville, Tex.: National Park Service, United States Department of Interior, Palo Alto National Historic Site, 1997.

Delaney, Robert. "Matamoros: Port for Texas during the Civil War." *Southwestern Historical Quarterly* 58 (April 1955): 470–80.

Frantz, Joe B. "Leander H. McNelly." In *Rangers of Texas*, edited by Roger N. Conger. Waco: Texian Press, 1969.

Garland, Carol. "William Montgomery: Early Caldwell County Settler." *Plum Creek Almanac* 4, no. 1 (Spring 1986): 4–7.

Hager, William M. "The Nuecestown Raid: A Border Incident." *Arizona and the West* 1 (Autumn 1959): 258–70.

"The Mexican Border Grievances." *Nation*. 26 (August 29, 1878): 125–26.

Morris, Leopold. "The Mexican Raid of 1875 on Corpus Christi." *Quarterly of the Texas State Historical Association* 4 (October 1900): 128–39.

Nackman, Mark. "The Making of the Texan Citizen Soldier." *Southwestern Historical Quarterly* 78 (January 1975): 231–53.

Oates, Stephen A. "John S. 'Rip' Ford: Prudent Cavalryman, CSA." In *Lone Star Blue and Gray: Essays on Texas in the Civil War*, edited by Ralph W. Wooster, 313–36. Austin: Texas State Historical Association, 1995.

Procter, Ben H. "The Modern Texas Rangers: A Modern Law Enforcement Dilemma in the Rio Grande Valley." In *Reflections of Western Historians*, edited by John A. Carroll. Tucson: University of Arizona Press, 1969.

———. Prologue to *A Texas Ranger*, by Napoleon A. Jennings. Chicago: Lakeside Press; R. R. Donnelley & Sons, 1992.

Remington, Frederic. "How the Law Got into the Chaparral." *Harper's New Monthly Magazine* 94 (December 1896): 60–69.

Schott, Christine. "Gustavus Schleicher: A Representative of Early German Emigrants in Texas." *West Texas Historical Association Year Book* (1952): 28–35.

Shook, Robert. "Battle of the Nueces, August 10, 1862." *Southwestern Historical Quarterly* 66 (July 1962): 31–42.

Smith, David. "Conscription and Conflict on the Texas Frontier, 1863–1865." In *Lone Star Blue and Gray: Essays on Texas in the Civil War*, 275–88. Austin: Texas State Historical Association, 1995.

Tyler, Ron. "Cotton on the Border, 1861–1865." In *Lone Star Blue and Gray: Essays on Texas in the Civil War*, edited by Ralph W. Wooster, 211–34. Austin: Texas State Historical Association, 1995.

Van Winkle, Irene. "Moffett Tale Hearkens Back to Texas Ranger, Boy Captive." *West Kerr Current*. http://wkcurrent.com/moffett-tale-hearkens-back-to-texas -ranger-boy-captive-p1666–71.htm.

Webb, Walter Prescott. "The Adventures of a Historian." *Alcalde* (November 1930): 47–50.

Webster, Michael G. "Intrigue on the Rio Grande: The *Rio Bravo* Affair." *Southwestern Historical Quarterly* 74 (October 1970): 147–59.

Miscellaneous

Bullis, John L. Biographical File. Texana Collection. San Antonio Public Library. San Antonio.

Cox, Mike. "Two Braids." *TexasEscapes.com*. July 2003.

Ford, John S. Biographical File. Texana Collection. San Antonio Public Library. San Antonio.

Nelson, Robert L. "Robb, Thomas Patten (1819–1895)," Santa Cruz Public Libraries. www.snatacruzpl.org/history/articles/1104.

Parsons, Chuck, ed. "Bill Callicott Reminiscences." Texas Ranger Hall of Fame and Museum, 1–5. www.texasranger.org/E Books/Callicott,%20William%20 Reminiscences.pdf.

———. "Jesús Sandoval: McNelly's Enforcer." *The Texas Ranger Dispatch* 32 (2011). www.texasranger.org/dispatch/Backissues/Dispatch_Issue_32.

"Lew Wallace." *Notable Hoosiers*. Indiana Historical Society. www.indianahistory .org/our-collections/reference/notable-hoosiers/lew-wallace.

Webster, Michael G. "Texan Manifest Destiny and the Mexican Border Conflict, 1865–1880." PhD dissertation. Indiana University, 1972.

Index